9597

0597

The Catholic Tradition:
The Savior, Vol. 2

The Catholic Tradition

REV. CHARLES J. DOLLEN
DR. JAMES K. McGOWAN
DR. JAMES J. MEGIVERN
EDITORS

The Catholic Tradition

The Saviour
Volume 2

A Consortium Book

Library of Congress Card Catalog Number: 79-1977
ISBN: 0-8434-0733-6
ISBN: 0-8434-0725-5 series

The publisher gratefully acknowledges permission to quote from the following copyrighted sources. In cases where those properties contain scholarly apparatus such as footnotes, such footnotes have been omitted in the interest of the general reader.

ANDREWS AND McMEEL, INC.
    Chapter 1 from *Christ the Sacrament of the Encounter with God* by Edward Schillebeeckx, O.P. Copyright © 1963 by Sheed and Ward, Inc. Reprinted by permission of Andrews and McMeel, Inc.

DODD, MEAD & COMPANY, INC.
    Selection from *The Everlasting Man* by G. K. Chesterton reprinted by permission of Dodd, Mead & Company, Inc. and the Estate of the late G. K. Chesterton. Copyright 1925 by Dodd, Mead & Company, Inc., copyright renewed 1953 by Oliver Chesterton.

GATEWAY EDITIONS, LTD.
    Selections from *The Lord* by Romano Guardini. Copyright 1954 by Henry Regnery Company. Reprinted with permission from Gateway Editions, Ltd., South Bend, Indiana.

B. HERDER BOOK CO.
    Chapters 12 and 15 from *The Mysteries of Christianity* by Matthias Joseph Scheeben, translated by Cyril Vollert, S.J., copyright 1946.

MACMILLAN PUBLISHING CO., INC.
    Chapter 1 from *Jesus, God and Man* by Rev. Raymond E. Brown, S.S. Copyright © 1967 by Raymond E. Brown, S.S. Reprinted by permission of Macmillan Publishing Co., Inc.

GABRIEL MORAN
    Selection from *Theology of Revelation* by Gabriel Moran. Herder & Herder, copyright © 1966. Reprinted by permission of Gabriel Moran.

Table of Contents

VOLUME 2

MATTHIAS JOSEPH SCHEEBEN   1
   The Mysteries of Christianity   3

GILBERT KEITH CHESTERTON   49
   The Everlasting Man   51

FRANCIS XAVIER DURRWELL   89
   The Resurrection   91

ROMANO GUARDINI   117
   The Lord   119

KARL ADAM   163
   The Christ of Faith   165

WALTER JOHN BURGHARDT   197
   The Mystery of the Woman   199

BERNARD J. F. LONERGAN   219
   Collection   221

EDWARD SCHILLEBEECKX   249
   Christ the Sacrament of the Encounter with God 251

THE CATHOLIC TRADITION: The Saviour

KARL RAHNER   283
   Theological Investigations   285

ALOYS GRILLMEIER   325
   Christ in Christian Tradition   327

RAYMOND EDWARD BROWN   347
   Jesus, God and Man   349

GABRIEL MORAN   375
   Theology of Revelation   377

DAVID TRACY   393
   Blessed Rage for Order   395

Matthias Joseph Scheeben

1835-1888

Matthias Scheeben, in his thirty years as professor of theology at the seminary in Cologne, made many contributions to the Church of his day, but none proved so lasting and broad as his book on The Mysteries of Christianity. The reason for its great influence and popularity was not readily available to English-speaking Christians until 1946, when the revised edition was finally rendered into an English translation that did it justice by the American Jesuit theologian, Cyril Vollert.

Scheeben's unique approach organized the Christian faith according to its nine key mysteries: Trinity, Creation, Sin, Incarnation, Eucharist, Church, Justification, Glorification, and Predestination. While any such method has its drawbacks, especially the danger of distorting perspective, there is no denying the beauty and power of his achievement. Catechism truths that had become all too dry and meaningless through passive repetition suddenly sparkled with new life when set in this dynamic framework.

Part Four, on the Incarnation, is made up of five chapters, from which the following selection has drawn two (chapter 12 on the God-Man and chapter 15 on His role as Mediator). They more than adequately demonstrate Scheeben's approach, the power of his style and language, and the way in which his teaching is rooted entirely in the Chalcedonian tradition.

Among the theologians represented in this collection on the Savior, Scheeben stands as something of a transitional figure. When he is read today, it is clear that something is afoot. He knows the controversies of the past, the issues of the Scholastics, the distinctions of the Fathers, but his manner of dealing with them reveals that these questions no longer hold the position which they formerly did. Scheeben can be viewed as the last of the old and the first of the new. He stands with one foot in each era. Writing well over a century ago, he knew that much of what had gone before him had changed, but the real revolutions were only beginning to occur. When he wrote this work, Pius IX was pope; when he revised it more than twenty years later, Leo XIII had assumed that position. Even greater changes were to come, and the Biblical revival especially would have an impact on Christology.

Meantime, however, the future is partially anticipated in the way that Scheeben combines his speculative abilities with his knowledge of the Fathers and Scholastics, drawing out in systematic form the fuller implications he finds in each. And as he does so, he continues to insist on his basic conviction of the unity of the mysteries in the Mystery: "Thus the mystery of the God-Man, when grasped in its mysterious sublimity, diffuses the clearest rays of light over all the other mysteries, since they are all related to it."

THE MYSTERIES
OF CHRISTIANITY

CHAPTER XII

50. NATURE AND CONSTITUTION OF THE GOD-MAN

Thus far we have examined three mysteries: the mystery of God, or the Trinity of divine persons; the mystery of man in his supernatural union with God and sanctification by God; and the mystery of man's separation from God in the dissolution of his supernatural fellowship with God through sin. The mystery of the God-man stands in closest and most sublime relationship with all three. In Him we find the most perfect prolongation and revelation of the interior productions of the Godhead, the restoration and reestablishment of man's supernatural union with God, and finally full compensation for the extirpation and obliteration of sin.

The mysterious character of the Incarnation is more commonly acknowledged than that of any other mystery. And indeed, where should we look for the mystery of Christianity if Christ, its foundation, its crown, and its center, were not a mystery? Besides, the general recognition of this fact is easily accounted for. The Trinity, although a still more exalted truth than the Incarnation, is nevertheless a necessary truth, which some have thought they could, if not conceive, at any rate demonstrate, on account of its objective necessity. With regard to the other truths, which refer to justice and injustice, beatitude and wretchedness, and generally to the good and evil states of man, one may easily come to look upon them as quite intelligible, if care is not exercised to distinguish sharply between natural and supernatural states. The Incarnation, on the contrary, appears to be a supernatural, extraordinary work of God under all circumstances, at least in some respect. But the full grandeur and sublimity of this work, both as regards its nature and particularly as regards its function and significance, have often been grossly misunderstood, or at least have not been sufficiently appreciated. In their endeavor to gauge its value and significance by the norm of natural reason, some have pulled it down from its supernatural eminence and have thereby jeopardized its object, if they have not altogether destroyed it.

This we shall see in due course. To rectify this abuse at the very outset, so as not to be led astray concerning its nature by a preconceived, one-sided, or erroneous notion of the import or necessity of the Incarnation, we wish first of all to fix our attention on its nature as faith proposes it to us. After that we shall examine its function and significance in the order of things, and determine the sense in which necessity may be predicated of this mystery.

The God-man is the new, heavenly Adam, of whom the first, earthly Adam was only the figure, or rather the reverse image. Sacred Scripture itself presents Him to us in this guise, and we believe that the mystery of His nature and His meaning cannot be set forth in a better, more adequate, and more profound way than by this comparison. The sequel must show whether we err in this conviction.

Even the first Adam was no ordinary man. He was elevated to a superhuman dignity, indeed to a dignity that simply surpassed the capabilities of all creatures, and was adorned with supernatural gifts and qualities. He was an adopted child of God, and therefore had a share in the divine nature. He was united to God in an ineffable manner, and God Himself dwelt in him, not as He does in mere creatures, but as in His own special sanctuary, through His own Spirit, whom He poured forth into him. The first Adam, although earthly and a creature by nature, was made heavenly, nay divine, by a wonderful grace of God.

As a result of God's grace, Adam himself was an incomparably greater and more sublime mystery than that which the rationalists have fashioned for themselves in their notion of the God-man. The very men who have no true concept of the one person in Christ, and who imagine two persons joined together in Christ, likewise fall short of ascribing a real participation in the divine nature to the human person in Adam or in Christ. They would have it that Christ occupied a unique position in God's favor and was intimately associated with Him, that He acted as God's envoy and worked in special harmony with Him, that He kept His human will exquisitely attuned to the will of God. But these are all merely moral and purely external relationships, such as can be procured even among men by adoption. By themselves they do not establish any real communication and unity between man and God. They do not even suffice for the idea of true divine adoption, in which the creature not only receives definite rights from God, but by the communication of the divine nature participates in the divine life and the divine holiness, and becomes a supernatural likeness of God.

Conversely, he who cannot rise to the notion of the deification and the supernatural sanctification and glorification of the first man, or at any rate fails to grasp this idea in its full purity and precision, blocks the way, so far as in him lies, to a correct conception and appreciation of the still higher mystery of the Incarnation. If with upright faith he accepts the doctrine taught by the Church, he can indeed still grasp and hold fast to the idea of the God-man. But he can do so only by making a leap; with a sudden spring he vaults straightway from a low level to the very highest, without traversing the intermediate stages. Through faith he undoubtedly arrives at the summit; but if he does not pass through the intervening steps he will not be able so accurately to gauge the immeasurable distance between the summit and the base. It is for this reason that we have premised the idea of the first man's supernatural dignity and nobility, so that it may serve as the starting point and the point of intersection leading to the idea of the God-man. Great was the mystery of the first Adam; all the greater and more sublime must the mystery of the second Adam appear when compared and contrasted with it.

The union and conformity with God involved in the mystery of the first Adam are so inconceivably and inexpressibly great and unprecedented that, even with the aid of the many concepts and comparisons at our command, we can gain only a faint inkling of the truth. The holy Fathers vie with one another in proposing the boldest expressions and metaphors, so as in some degree to illustrate it and make it intelligible. We are not surprised that, when subsequently they seek to describe the unity of the God-man, they can scarcely find any new expressions and figures to characterize it in its contradistinction to the union of Adam with God.

Even when discoursing on grace they state that God thereby dwells in man as the soul dwells in the body to which it communicates its own life, or that the creature is engulfed and consumed, permeated and transfigured, by God as iron is by fire, as a drop of water by a great quantity of wine. They are unable to find stronger, more striking illustrations for the Incarnation. But this circumstance, far from betraying us into confusing the hypostatic union of the God-man with the union which grace effects between man and God, must rather induce us to regard the former as a superlatively great and doubly sublime mystery. For the fact that we are obliged to employ the same images to illustrate the most diverse supernatural objects, is to be ascribed only to the deficiency of our intellects and the baseness of the natural things from which we derive our concepts and figures.

Is, then, all perception of the difference between the hypostatic union and the union effected by grace to be withheld from us? By no means. As under the guidance of revelation we are able to form an analogous concept of man's grace and sanctity from ideas and images of natural things, so under the guidance of the same revelation, by employing another analogy, a comparison of natural things according to another point of view, we can form a distinct, although ever analogous and hence imperfect and dim notion of the Incarnation. Let us endeavor to do so.

By grace the first man was deified, but he was not made God or turned into God, if we may so speak. It is only in a figurative sense that the Fathers refer to the deified man as God, that is, as a different God by similarity, not by identity, but only in the sense in which we are accustomed to speak of the so-called parhelion or mock sun as the sun. When man, the original bearer and possessor of a purely human nature, became also the possessor and bearer of a share in the divine nature through grace, he did not become another, but remained the same person. He did not lose himself; he continued to belong to himself. By participation in the divine nature he only acquired a new possession, a new, higher, supernatural character, by

6

which he was transformed into God's image, was made like to God in a supernatural manner, and in consequence of this resemblance necessarily entered into a most intimate union and unity with his divine Exemplar. Accordingly God dwells in him as the soul in the body, but only so far as the soul communicates of its life to the body, not so far as it really constitutes one essence with the body. Hence man is immersed in God as iron in fire, as a drop of water in wine, but only to the extent that the fire by its penetrating propinquity communicates of its flame, its brightness, and its heat to the iron, and the wine communicates of its color, its aroma, and its taste to the drop of water, not to the extent that the flame-emitting body actually merges with the fire-shot metal, or the wine actually merges with the water to form a single whole. All this is extraordinarily marvelous, supernatural, and mysterious; but, that a God-man may come into being, a marvel of a wholly different order is required.

For in this case it is not sufficient that a human nature merely lay aside its natural imperfections and be endowed with a likeness of the divine nature. The nature must cease to possess itself, to be its own, to belong to itself; it must be inserted and, as it were, incorporated in a divine person, a subject that is by nature a bearer and possessor of the divine nature, so that the bearer and possessor of the divine nature becomes likewise bearer and possessor of a human nature. Only in this case do we have a subject that is at once possessor of a divine and a human nature, and hence can be called both God and man; a subject that makes its appearance not only as deified man, but as God become man, as God-man. God must clothe Himself with human nature, must put it on, as in the deification of man the man must put on the form and character of God. In this event humanity is engrafted in a divine person, as in the other case a shoot of divinity is, so to speak, engrafted in man.

Both cases are utterly astounding, supernatural, and mysterious: that a human person share in the divine nature, and that a divine person assume a human nature. St. Peter Chrysologus, in a flight of ecstatic wonderment at God's ineffable love for us men, even fancies that the first is more marvelous than the second. This is perhaps true so far as in the first case an elevation

7

of man to a dizzying height, whereas in the second a descent, a climbing-down of God, is the first thing to strike our attention. But if we consider the elevation of the human nature in both cases, this is beyond comparison more amazing and sublime in the case in which the human nature ceases to belong to itself, in which it is not merely clothed with divine splendor but becomes literally a nature of God, a nature belonging to God, and in the person to whom it belongs constitutes one being with the divine nature and essence, in which consequently the divinity not only gives of its life to the human nature, but combines with it to form one substantial whole, as the soul does with the body, or the wine with the drop of water.

This union is absolutely miraculous and supernatural and hence mysterious if only for the reason that two extremes which are separated by so immeasurable a distance as the finite and the infinite combine to form one whole, and that the lowest joins with the highest in the closest fashion conceivable. But it is unprecedented and supernatural also because of the particular way it unites the two substances. For it unites them in one personal, hypostatic whole, without at the same time merging or fusing them into one nature. Body and soul in man are joined not only in unity of person, but also in unity of nature; or better, they constitute one person only so far as they also constitute one nature. Among natural things, which are accessible to our reason, we nowhere find a personal or hypostatic union part from union in nature. Only when two substances constitute a single complete nature, can both belong to a personal or hypostatic whole and be possessed by it. Obviously, however, the divine nature cannot descend so low as to merge with a created nature to form a third nature; this contradicts the absolute simplicity, immutability, and independence of the divine nature. Consequently, if the divine nature unites itself with a created nature to form one whole, the resulting union must be a purely personal, purely hypostatic union, which neither presupposes nor involves a union in nature. It can only be a union by which the divine nature, without losing its independence, draws the created nature to itself and makes the latter its own, and by which, accordingly, it forms a whole with this created nature without itself becoming merged in the

8

whole; rather, the divine nature manifests its own absolute independence in its possession and domination of the assumed nature.

Such a purely personal or purely hypostatic union is without parallel or comparison in created nature, for the simple reason that no created substance is so independent or is so much the master of its independence that it can completely draw another substance to itself and make it its own without reciprocally being drawn to it and becoming merged with it. If a union of this sort is possible at all, it is possible only with God and by God's power. But since what is possible only with God and by God's power is positively known only from what actually takes place among creatures, this union must be viewed by us as being so sublime and transcendent that our reason of itself cannot so much as suspect its possibility, let alone demonstrate it positively.

Hence the God-man is an absolutely supernatural mystery for two reasons: first, because the human nature in Him is not joined to another created essence, but is elevated above all the boundaries of the created world and united to the divine substance far more closely than it could be through grace; and secondly, because this kind of union is not a union in nature, nor is it a union such as could be found in the sphere of created nature at all, but is an absolutely unique, supereminent union.

Therefore whoever would define and appraise this mystery according to the natural concepts of his reason must inevitably distort it. He does one of two things. He comes to an abrupt halt before the infinite chasm separating the finite from the infinite, and also sees his speculations brought up short when confronted with the natural autonomy and personality which rational nature implies; and then he will be able to think of no union of the finite, human nature with God that would bridge that chasm and raise the human nature to be a nature of God. Or, with the aid of faith, he apprehends the incredible intimacy of the union, but perceives it under the concept of a union in nature, in which case he lowers the divine nature as much as he raises the human nature. Neither of the two, neither the Nestorian nor the Eutychian, rises to a true concept of the

9

supernatural, towering elevation of the human nature without debasing the divine nature. The former rejects the elevation of the lower nature, whereas the latter, in elevating the lower nature, cannot retain the sublimity of the higher nature; but this must endure undiminished in the very union.

To attain to a notion of the mystery we must, therefore, suffer ourselves to be led by revelation and soar above the circle of rational concepts, and thus discern in human nature a potency for union with God and perfectibility through the agency of God which our reason cannot in the remotest degree uncover or even surmise. We must then represent this union and perfectibility through the agency of God which our reason cannot in the remotest degree uncover or even surmise. We must then represent this union and perfectibility not according to the norm of that hypostatic union which is implicated in or based upon a union in nature, but as an eminent and purely hypostatic union purged of all the imperfections that accompany a union in nature.

Since the concept of Christ's supernatural union is formed only by analogy, by purifying and transforming natural concepts of a hypostatic union, and besides is asserted in a sphere in which the autonomy and immeasurable distance of the extremes to be united seem to preclude every union other than that of mutual converse, it must remain obscure, vastly more obscure than the idea of natural union from which it is derived.

For the latter, too, is obscure and mysterious in its own way. Indeed the correct notion of the union between soul and body is one of the most profound and difficult problems of all philosophy. Whoever has reflected upon this problem even slightly, or has cast but a glance at the muddle of views on it, will easily be convinced of this. Those who have attempted to clear up every last bit of obscurity in it have destroyed the true union of nature and hypostasis, by assuming only a certain mutual interchange, a mutual operation, and a reciprocal harmony between soul and body, as between two autonomous substances. Hence we cannot take it amiss if these philosophers, in explaining the hypostatic union of the Logos with human nature on the analogy of the union between soul and body, have in this case hoped to find the matter wholly comprehensible. But if the soul as the substantial form of the body constitutes one nature and hence also one hypostasis with it, we have before us a marvelous reality that is couched in severely accurate language, but is for all that unfathomable in its essence; and so we have to regard the higher union in Christ as a still more unfathomable mystery.

But as the notion of the hypostatic union in Christ necessarily shares in the obscurity of the notion of the union between soul and body in man, an obscurity that must increase in proportion to the former's elevation over the latter, so on the other hand the former must receive more light the more sharply we mark it off from the latter's limitations and the more decisively we divest it of all the latter's imperfections. The concept of the purely hypostatic union stands here in the same relationships as the concept of the purely hypostatic distinction in the Trinity. If we assert it, all the contradictions that reason with its natural concepts would discern in the dogma vanish automatically; they vanish so completely that the foundations on which they might rest contribute to their extinction. For example, the infinite gap between the finite and the infinite is so far from standing in the way of the hypostatic union, that the latter essentially presupposes an infinite preponderance of the one element over the other, since otherwise it could not make that other completely its own.

The natural totality of a rational nature, which makes every substantial union with a superior nature impossible, is not absolute, and hence admits of a domination, even an unconditional domination and appropriation by Him on whom it is in any case wholly dependent together with all that it is. This is all the more readily perceived inasmuch as this nature not only loses nothing by being thus assumed, but rather is incalculably enriched. On God's part, finally, purely hypostatic union with a created nature, far from entailing any imperfection, nowhere more splendidly manifests His infinite perfection than here. For God can draw a created nature so powerfully to Himself, permeate it so deeply, and clasp it to Himself with so unalterably firm an embrace that He can call it His own without in any way being subjected to it, only because He is the absolutely independent, the absolutely simple, and the absolutely immutable being.

11

To be sure, it might appear that the Son of God, even when considered as the suppositum or bearer of the human nature, would be debased and composite. But when we say that He sustains the human nature and makes Himself the bearer of it, we do not mean to imply that He takes it to Himself as something higher or complementary. Rather we mean that He, as the nobler and as infinitely perfect, begins to possess in a uniquely perfect way and to rule with absolute authority that which is lower and which originates from Him with all the perfection it has. The assumption of the lower to the higher, or rather the absolute dominion of the lower by the higher, whereby the former becomes the exclusive property of the latter: such is the notion of the purely hypostatic union. Far from losing any of its nobility, the superior hypostasis can exercise such dominion only because of its sublime dignity and divine personality.

Thus in the case of the Incarnation, no less than in that of the Trinity, if only we accommodate our ideas to their sublime objects and have regard for the supernaturalness of the latter, or better, if we view the object from the right distance, we can succeed in forming a notion which, although faint and imperfect, dispels all the clouds that could disfigure or distort its object. Here again it will be true that a conscious awareness of the darkness that surrounds our eye will cause the object of its contemplation to stand forth the more clearly and distinctly.

51. THE ATTRIBUTES OF THE GOD-MAN

The elevation of a human nature to the status of a nature of God, the engrafting of it on a divine hypostasis, the organic incorporation of it in a divine person whose living flesh it becomes: that is the heart of the supernatural mystery of the Incarnation. But besides this infinitely august dignity and nobility which the human nature receives in Christ, or rather in very consequence thereof, the mystery hidden in Christ's humanity shelters still further supernatural, mysterious things within it.

In the first place, the hypostatic union between the human nature and the Godhead immeasurably transcends the union of a human person with God by grace, and essentially excludes a fusion of the divinity with the humanity to form one nature, which is the natural function and result of a hypostatic union. But we should fail to have a full appreciation of its force and significance were we to overlook the fact that by virtue of and because of the hypostatic union between the humanity and the divinity, the humanity participates in the nature of the divinity.

The perfection with which God can equip and adorn the nature of a mere man by grace when He adopts him as His child, cannot be wanting in the human nature of Him who is His natural Son. The humanity of God's Son not only can, but must possess the endowment and perfection which God presents to the children of His grace, precisely because it is to become or has become the nature of God's Son. The humanity hypostatically united in the highest conceivable union with the divinity in the person of the Son must, if any nature, and in a measure equalled by no other, participate in the nature of God, must be pervaded, shot through, transfigured by it, vitalized by it, must be made conformable and like to it, must be fashioned in its image; in a word, the divine humanity, the humanity which belongs to God, must be deified to the full capacity of its own condition. Is it conceivable that God, whereas He raised to His own level the first Adam who stood so remote from Him, in order to communicate to him of His own life through His Spirit, would not do the same for the humanity which is embodied in His Son and is united in the closest way to the source of divine life as the body is united to the soul? Is it thinkable that God, who set a mere man on fire with the flame of His own nature, clothed him with His own glory, and filled him with the aroma of His own sweetness, would not do all this for that humanity which in the most intimate of all unions is plunged into the fire of the divine sun, and is absorbed like a drop of water in a river of wine?

Surely not. That union and glory which could and did become the portion of a mere creature's nature, could not be wanting to the humanity of Christ which was joined to God in a special and unique manner, and in the highest possible manner. The hypostatic union does not exclude the perfection which is become the portion of the nature of a mere man. On the contrary, it implies the presence of that perfection in itself, it requires and demands it, calls it forth. Therefore the difference between the supernatural condition of the first Adam and that of the second Adam consists precisely in this, that the first Adam possessed it not of himself, not by reason of the power and right of his person, but out of sheer grace, whereas the second Adam possesses it of Himself, that is, by the power and right of His person, and hence by nature. The splendor of the divine nature was for the first Adam only the raiment of an adoptive child of God, freely granted from without as a grace. But in the case of Christ's humanity it bursts forth from the divine person, who thereby manifests even in His humanity the dignity and power dwelling in Him by nature. The divine life flowed to the humanity of the first Adam from a source widely separated from it, situated outside it. The humanity of Christ receives that divine life from a source interiorly united to it, just as life is conveyed to the members of the body from the head, or to the branches from the vine to which they are joined.

In itself the humanity of Christ, according to its substance and nature, was like that of the first Adam. To this extent there were included in it no greater privileges than in the nature of the first Adam. All the privileges transcending Adam's nature also transcend Christ's humanity, and are supernatural with respect to it. The humanity of Christ was not holy, or free from inordinate concupiscence, suffering, and death by virtue of its nature; all the prerogatives of sanctity and integrity were gifts added to it by God. But because it was united to God in so extraordinary a manner, the right to these privileges and the source from which they sprang were embodied in it by virtue of this union. The God-man had essentially in Himself the right and the power to endow His humanity with all the wealth of sanctity and integrity that it was in any way capable of. Indeed, since His dignity is the highest possible, and since on the other hand His humanity also must posssess an endowment in keeping with this supreme dignity, this endowment must differ in compass and wealth from the endowment of all mere creatures as heaven differs from earth. And since, further, the humanity of Christ draws its wealth immediately from the divine source abiding in it, that wealth must be so abundant that it surpasses beyond comparison the supernatural riches of all creatures combined, as a mighty torrent surpasses the tiny rivulet that drains off from it. And so, although this wealth is not absolutely infinite, it cannot be gauged by the amount apportioned to mere creatures. Hence, as contrasted with the latter, it appears infinite. In a word, it is so abundant that it is the very fullness of grace and of all supernatural gifts.

Accordingly, though Christ is certainly a true man, we may not think of His person, as bearer of the humanity, and of this humanity itself, in too human a fashion. All the wonders and mysteries that are discerned in Christ's humanity are nothing in comparison with the hypostatic union, and follow as a matter of course once this is supposed. Even in the case of the first man, we may not gauge the greatness of his privileges according to the norm of his nature, because the love of God was more generous toward him than his nature was. Much less in the case of Christ should we be hesitant in expecting great and incomprehensible things for His humanity from the infinite dignity and power of His person.

As has been stated, the first Adam possessed all his prerogatives of sanctity and integrity only by virtue of the extraordinary love and liberality of God. Since he was called to the sonship of God by grace alone, as we also are, God gave to him, as He does to us, only the dignity of His sonship in the first instance, together with the power to work in the state of this dignity for the attainment of his inheritance. He was united to God in a supernatural manner, but was not from the outset admitted to the glory of the children of God and to the face-to-face vision of God. Called as he was by grace, he was for a time to remain in an intermediate stage, at a transition point between the rank of God's servants and that of His fully reborn children.

With the God-man such a period of separation is inconceivable. He was the Son of God by nature. As God, He possessed the divine nature wholly and essentially, and therefore had from the beginning the right and power, even as man and in His humanity, to enjoy the full sonship of God, to heap up all its goods in His humanity; hence not only those which we receive in the state of sanctifying grace, but also those which we await in the state of glory. Therefore His soul's participation in the

15

divine nature meant not merely holiness and grace; it meant fully achieved glory and beatitude from the very first instant. Not only could this be so, it had to be so, unconditionally. It is unthinkable that the Son of God would not from the beginning have stood in closest and highest union with His Father even in His human nature, and that He would have strengthened and perfected this union only by degrees. But such would be the case if He had not from the first instant looked upon His Father face to face, if He had had to stand afar off like a stranger, and if, as a result, He had not been able to embrace His Father with that love in which the blessed in heaven are consumed. As there is no closer union with God than hypostatic, personal union, there can be no kind of union with God by knowledge and love that did not exist from the beginning in consequence of the hypostatic union of Christ's humanity with the Son of God. Owing to the hypostatic union, that humanity from the moment of its conception was present in God's bosom, to which creatures are raised only gradually and imperfectly; and in God's bosom it had also to gaze upon God's countenance, and to embrace God not with a love of longing and striving, but with a love of possession and fruition. Hence, as far as union with God is concerned, there was no *status viae* for Christ's humanity, as there is for us. From the very beginning Christ stood at the end of the road, at the summit of the mountain, which we must strive to gain by degrees, and to which we have to be raised by the grace of God. Christ is a *comprehensor,* as the theologians say. He is not only holy, but also in possession of divine glory and happiness; He is transfigured and beatified.

With this there is connected another, equally sublime privilege of Christ and His humanity. The first Adam, and the same is true of every creature, does not by virtue of his natural origin stand in indissoluble union with God: even grace, by itself, does not raise creatures to such a union. Grace is sanctifying, grace is divine holiness, and repels grave sin to the extent that it cannot coexist with grave sin in one and the same subject. But so long as it is not yet joined to the immediate vision of God, so long as it is not yet transformed into the light of glory, it does not take possession of the human will and prevail upon it to the extent that the will cannot withdraw from its influence, it does not fetter man so firmly to God that man cannot tear himself loose from God. It is only heavenly glory that perfects sanctity; and so Adam, so any creature in the state of grace, could sin in spite of his sanctity.

But Christ was in the state of glory from the beginning, and hence in the state of perfected holiness. Accordingly sin was utterly impossible in Him. And it had to be impossible; for if Christ's humanity had sinned, the sinful act would have had to be ascribed to the divine person to whom the humanity belongs. Since all the actions of Christ's human nature were under the control of the divine person, the impeccability of that nature is founded upon and postulated by the hypostatic union alone, and is also in some degree explained and conceived in terms of it. But that impeccability is perfectly clarified and understood only when we perceive that not only must the divine person ward off all sin from the humanity assumed by Him, but also that in consequence of the hypostatic union the humanity itself is the recipient of a condition and transferred to a state that necessarily excludes all thought of the possibility of sin, and does away entirely with the need of an immediate inter- ference on the part of the divine person for the prevention of sin. For if Christ's humanity enjoys the vision of God, it is thereby placed beyond the possibility of sinning; sin simply cannot arise, and so does not have to be prevented by any higher, positive influence.

Thus the humanity of Christ, owing to the hypostatic union, was joined to God by a union which in manner and degree was supremely perfect from the beginning, and so could be neither strengthened nor dissolved; or, what comes to the same, Christ's soul, so far as it was orientated toward God, was in the state of the most perfect supernatural sanctity, glory, and beatitude. In highest measure and richest fullness it participated in the divine nature with all the latter's own sanctity, glory, and beatitude, and thereby proved itself to be a humanity belonging to the Son of God and worthy of Him.

But what was the situation with Christ's humanity regarded according to its lower side, in relation to the body and the lower faculties of the soul, and also in respect to the higher faculties in their dealings with creatures; briefly, in the sphere in which the gift of integrity operated in the case of the first man?

Without doubt the right to all the goods of the gift of integrity and the power to realize them dwelt interiorly in the God-man, in the humanity united to the Son of God. This fact by itself alone gave to the God-man an incalculable advantage over the first Adam, who possessed these goods not by right, but by grace, not by his own power, but by influx from without. But there is much more to be said. The God-man had in Himself the right and the power to adorn His humanity with the most perfect integrity from the very outset, and also to glorify and beatify it from every point of view, that is, to diffuse throughout His whole nature the supernatural immortality, glory, and beatitude which transfiguration by divine fire shed over the higher reaches of His soul. Consequently from the first moment, at His very entrance into the world, He had the right and the power to appear in the same splendor and glory into which He actually entered only after His resurrection.

The gift of integrity and the glory of the body stand in a relation to each other like that between grace and the glory of the soul. During this life the soul is placed in supernatural harmony with God by grace, and is thereby made ready to be filled with God's glory by transfiguration. In the same way the first man's body was placed in fullest harmony with the soul by the gift of integrity, in order one day to be wholly pervaded and completely spiritualized by the power and glory of the soul. These two stages came to the first Adam successively, because both were supernatural with regard to him, and hence God at His good pleasure could separate the inchoate from the consummate grace. But in the case of the second Adam, who is not earthly but heavenly by nature, the two stages could coincide.

In the same way that Christ did not attain to glory of the soul through the gift of sanctity alone, He did not necessarily require the gift of integrity as an intermediate stage leading to glory of the body. Indeed, the glory of the soul of Christ, if it were left to exercise its connatural influence, would have had to pervade and transfigure His entire nature, and hence establish

His body in the state of glory from the first moment of its existence. If this did not occur, if Christ restrained the divine fire into which His soul was plunged so that it did not lay hold of His entire nature and transfigure it, that very fact is a miracle of the most exalted kind and a new, great mystery whose import we shall consider later. It is a self-renunciation by which Christ withheld from Himself a glory which He could lay claim to and effect in Himself, which He did not lack for the reason that He was as yet unable to have it, but which rather He voluntarily denied Himself; a self-renunciation which accordingly bore witness to His power over the glory of His body even more than the actual possession of it would.

In reality, however, Christ not only did not glorify His whole nature from the beginning; He did not, in fact, even confer upon it all the gifts of integrity that had been imparted to the first Adam. Hence His humanity, though immensely superior to that of the first Adam in holiness, was far inferior to Adam's humanity as regards integrity. But this lesser perfection of the second Adam's humanity as compared with that of the first is only apparent. The essence of integrity, its innermost substance, was just as perfect in Christ as in Adam, or even more so. For in what does the essence of integrity consist? Does it consist in this, that the nature cannot suffer at all, that it cannot be disintegrated? By no means. In spite of integrity, Adam could still suffer, and he could also die. The incapacity to suffer and die belongs to the state of the glorified body, as incapacity to sin belongs to the state of the glorified soul. Adam's integrity rather consisted in the fact that by a special divine ordinance his lower faculties could not be stimulated apart from and contrary to his will, and consequently, as matters stood, that suffering and particularly death could not effect an entrance against his will. But is this not the case with Christ in a far higher degree? Not only by a special grace and ordinance of God, but in His own right and by His own power Christ was able to impede any modification of His nature that did not accord with His will, and so He was also able to keep all suffering and death at a distance from Himself. He suffered and died not because He had to, or because He could not prevent it, but because He willed to. He could have warded off suffering and

19

death even if all the external causes which are of a nature to produce suffering and death had rushed upon Him; according to the more probable opinion of theologians, Adam could not have done this. Therefore He really possessed integrity in its essence, that is, the inviolability and invulnerability of nature. He had it by right and in His power; and having it by His own right and with an inborn power to procure it, He possessed it more perfectly than Adam did. But He made no use of it, as far as suffering and death are concerned, because He could will and love suffering and death as a most excellent good, because He could manifest Himself and willed to manifest Himself as true Son of God in suffering and death as well as in impassibility and immortality.

But from another angle He had of necessity to assert uncompromisingly His absolute dominion over His nature. Whereas He could forgo immunity to suffering and death, He could in no way permit propensities and appetites to rise in Him which would contradict the absolute holiness and the dignity of His person and His human nature. He could not allow inordinate cravings for sinful objects to agitate Him, or let concupiscence of the senses in any way strive against the judgment of His intellect or even anticipate it. In this we observe again an incomparable superiority of the integrity of the second Adam over that of the first Adam. To be sure, Adam, too, had perfect dominion of will over all his proclivities and appetites, a dominion which he should not give up, but which he actually could give up, inasmuch as it did not pertain to him necessarily, but was dependent on the continuing uprightness of his will. But Christ possesses such dominion necessarily, because of His personal dignity and power. Besides, His will is unalterably holy; so holy that it cannot even admit the presence of an opposing inclination, even though it would be able to suppress it or hold it in check. Therefore in this respect Christ is incomparably more inviolate and invulnerable than Adam, and possesses an incomparably more perfect integrity, both virtually and formally.

Still more impressively, if we may speak thus, do the dignity and power of the divinity residing in Christ's humanity manifest themselves in another way. Not only does this humanity experience the operations of the divine person's dignity and power dwelling in it, but by virtue of the hypostatic union it is called to share in the divine power and activity of the person. In its own actions the humanity becomes the *instrumentum coniunctum* of this divine person, and these actions themselves thereby receive an infinite dignity and efficacy, in a word, an infinite value.

By his participation in the divine nature even the first Adam received a power which, in a certain sense, was infinite, because it immensely surpassed all natural power, and further because it rendered him capable of knowing and loving the infinite God, and of meriting the possession of God. But the infinity of this power was purely relative, and was restricted to his own personal development. This power did not enable him to perform external works like those of God, nor did it enable him to merit all of God's goods simply, but only for himself, and according to the measure of grace apportioned to him.

But the humanity of the God-man operates on the basis of the fullness of the divinity residing in it, not merely on the basis of a participation in the divine nature. Therefore its activity, although finite in itself, is of infinite dignity and value, because it is backed up by the dignity of an infinite person. Consequently God can be infinitely honored by this activity, and an adequate satisfaction can be offered to God's offended majesty. Further, all the good of God and the possession of God Himself can be purchased and merited by it, not only for the God-man in His own person, but universally, for all other persons.

Because of this same plenitude of the divinity and its power, the humanity of Christ is able to operate in a supernatural manner within itself, and also to perform acts which are of supernatural benefit to all creatures and to achieve much that in itself can be effected only by the infinite power of God. Thus the humanity of Christ can communicate to others the supernatural life which it possesses itself.

In brief, the hypostatic union enables the humanity of Christ to acquire for others without numerical restriction, and to produce in them its own supernatural prerogatives. The grace conferred upon it for its own endowment is an overflowing, fruitful, self-communicating grace, which was not the case with

Adam. Adam could serve only as a point of departure from which the Holy Spirit transferred to others the grace bestowed on him. The God-man, on the contrary, in His very humanity is a profuse source of grace in the proper sense of the word.

Thus in Christ's humanity we distinguish a threefold supernatural mystery, a threefold elevation above its natural condition, a threefold reception of the divine nature, a threefold deification and sanctification. The first of these mysteries is the foundation of the other two. The initial mystery is the hypostatic union with the person of the Logos, whereby the humanity is deified as a nature belonging to God. Secondly, springing from this union and rooted in it, come the transfiguration of the humanity and its assimilation to God by grace and glory, wherein it participates in the nature of the divinity. Finally, there arises the relation of the humanity to the Logos in virtue of which it becomes the latter's instrument in His supernatural activity. All this immensely transcends our ideas of the capacity of human nature, and indeed the entire range of our natural powers of comprehension.

All three mysteries may be synthesized under the notion of the anointing by which the man in the God-man becomes Christ, that is, the Anointed. The fact that the humanity is anointed is no mystery for us; it is something natural. But the ointment which is poured over it and into it is a mystery far greater than the mysteries wherein the angels and saints are anointed by the grace of the Holy Spirit.

For the anointing of Christ is nothing less than the fullness of the divinity of the Logos, which is substantially joined to the humanity and dwells in it incarnate, which so permeates and perfumes it with its fragrance and life-giving force that through the humanity it can extend its influence to others and imbue them also with its power and its fragrance. When the Fathers say that Christ is anointed with the Holy Spirit, they mean that the Holy Spirit has descended into the humanity of Christ in the Logos from whom He proceeds, and that He anoints and perfumes the humanity as the distillation and fragrance of the ointment which is the Logos Himself. Properly, however, only God the Father can be regarded as the source of the ointment poured out upon Christ, because He alone communicates to the

22

Son the divine dignity and nature with which the humanity that is assumed to the Son's person is formally anointed. As this ointment imbues the humanity with the fullness of the divinity, it raises the humanity to the highest conceivable dignity and sets it upon God's own throne where, borne by a divine person, it becomes worthy of the same adoration as that paid to God Himself.

This is the divine ointment which, flowing down from the wellspring of the Godhead into the creature and submerging the creature in God, constitutes not merely a deified man, but the true God-man. This is the mystery of Christ par excellence. He is anointed not merely by divine deputation for the discharge of an office, nor even merely by the outpouring of the Holy Spirit in His deifying grace, but by personal union with the principle of the Holy Spirit. Hence the divine ointment is contained in the very make-up of Christ's being, and constitutes Him a divine-human being.

Accordingly "Christ" and the "God-man" mean one and the same thing. Both names, the one figurative, the other without any figure, express in different forms the august and incomprehensible mystery residing in the person of Jesus. The name "Jesus" directly signifies the person according to the function which He was to exercise in behalf of men here upon earth, but not according to His inner being and constitution: it signifies the latter only indirectly, so far as the function of the Redeemer presupposes the divine-human constitution of the person to whom it is committed. The mysterious make-up of the person Himself is indicated directly by the name "Christ," which thereupon enables us to apprehend in their mysterious character the significance and the range of the function which Christ as Jesus is called to exercise. And thus the Apostle speaks of the "mystery of Christ" into which he had been initiated, and of "the unsearchable riches of Christ" which he proclaims to the nations, riches that have an inestimable greatness decreed in the wonderful anointing of Christ, riches that are poured forth upon Christ along with the fullness of the divinity, and are thence spread over all those who by their union with Christ become Christs themselves and are one Christ with Him. Later we shall return to the significance which the idea expressed by

23

the name "Christ" has for the position and the influence of the person of Christ with regard to the universe.

CHAPTER XV

62. THE MEDIATORY FUNCTION OF THE GOD-MAN

To acquire a deeper and more adequate understanding of the God-man's sublime and universal plan, we must contemplate Him from another angle, which is essentially connected with the view of Him hitherto gained, but affords us many a new insight into His functions.

Thus far we have been regarding the God-man chiefly in His relation to man and the universe, as their head. But at the same time He necessarily occupies a middle position between God and creatures. Or better, He is mediator between God and creatures in His capacity as the supernatural head of the universe in general, and of the human race in particular. The notion of this mediatorship, when viewed in its inmost nature and its vast compass, serves excellently to place the whole supernatural significance of the Incarnation in its proper perspective.

When Christ's mediatorship is mentioned, we at once think of His conciliatory function, the intermediacy of reconciliation between sinful mankind and God. But this function is only a single subordinate factor in the idea of the God-man's mediatorship. The mediation in question is essentially the negotiation of an ineffably noble and surpassingly intimate union and intercourse of God with the creature and of the creature with God, although it includes the reconciliation of the creature with God, and indeed a reconciliation unparalleled in its kind. Such is the notion we gain from a simple analysis of the nature of the Incarnation and its relation to God and man.

The God-man is the product of the personal, hypostatic union of divinity with humanity; He is in truth God and man. As man He is at one with the whole human race, indeed, with the created world, for He is its head. As God He is united in the most real and intimate fashion possible with His Father, from whom He proceeds, and with the Holy Spirit, whom He breathes forth. Though in the world and at one with the world, He reaches into the innermost recesses of the Godhead, is God

24

Himself, and is one with the Father and the Holy Spirit. Consequently in His person He raises the world up to the closest proximity, the most intimate union, with the eternal Father; on the other hand, the union which He has with the Father, He extends outside of God, and conveys to the entire world. He links God and God's creature together in so close a union and mutual relationship that all separation of the creature from God caused by the creature's defection, and also the infinite distance which nature itself sets up between the creature and God, even abstracting from the creature's fall, are surmounted and abolished.

Thus through the sublime miracle of His personal union, Christ is the substantial and supremely real bond which marvelously associates the most widely separated opposites. The immediate effect of this bond is a union of the creature with God, a union that is willed for its own sake and is substantial, a union by which the substantial unity between the Father and the Son is to be communicated to the creature and glorified in such communication. The inspiring words of the Savior: "that they may be one, as We also are one: I in them, and Thou in Me; that they may be made perfect in one" [John 17:22 f.], are here perfectly fulfilled.

St. Hilary explains these words in the sense of a substantial union whereby the oneness of nature between the Son and the Father is to be transmitted to us, when in referring to Christ's union with us he brings in the Eucharist: "If the Word is truly made flesh and we truly partake of the Word made flesh in the bread of the Lord, must we not conclude that He abides in us by nature, since He, born as man, has inseparably taken to Himself the nature of our flesh, and has joined the nature of His flesh to the nature of eternity [i. e., the divinity] under the sacrament of His flesh which is to be distributed to us? For all of us are thus one, since the Father is in Christ and Christ is in us . . . . Therefore He is in us by His flesh and we are in Him, for what we are is with Him in God." "And so," continues St. Hilary later, "we are taught that a perfect unity is established through the mediator. For, while we abide in Him, He abides in the Father; and while abiding in the Father, He abides in us. This is the way we mount up to unity with the Father." "The divine Logos," says St. Cyril of Alexandria in like vein, "wishing to confer a great grace, nay, in some sense an infinite grace, upon the human family, draws all together into a certain oneness with Himself. By assuming a human body He has taken up His dwelling in us; but He has the Father in Himself, being His Word and reflection."

By the union with the Father which Christ achieves in His person, "we are lifted up to oneness with the majesty of the Father," we are made substantially akin to Him as a truly divine race; we share in the manner of the Son's union with the Father, and also in its power.

For such a union of man with God the Father is unthinkable unless we were meant to participate in the prerogatives and the life of the divine nature, just as the Son participates in the majesty and life of the Father by His substantial oneness with the Father. This living union, the root of which is substantial union, can be nothing else than participation in the divine nature by the grace of sonship. How could the Father take us, in His Son, to His bosom, if He desired merely to enter into a simple relation of peace with us, but not into the intimate friendship and fellowship of life? This substantial union can be necessary or appropriate only if another union, measuring up to it, a supernatural oneness of life, of glory, and of beatitude, is to be established and sealed by it.

St. Athanasius was aware of this when he explained the necessity of a mediator who would be truly human and divine: "Man would not have experienced deification by union with a mere creature, unless the Son of God were truly God; nor would man have been brought nigh to the Father, if it had not been the true, substantial Word of the Father who assumed flesh. And as we should have been freed neither from sin nor from damnation if the flesh assumed by the Word were not really and essentially human flesh—for with a thing foreign to us we have nothing in common—so man would not have been deified if it had not been the Word substantially proceeding from the Father, the Father's own true Word, that took our flesh. For this union was contrived that the true and, so to say, substantial divinity might bind the true and natural man to itself, and that the welfare and deification of man might be made to endure."

From the standpoint of its activity, the substantial mediatorship of Christ may be conceived in a twofold way: first, in a more physical sense, as a bridge or channel that establishes contact between God and creature, and so we have been regarding it thus far; secondly, as a certain reciprocal and real pledging of God and the creature, by which the most intimate, noble, and changeless friendship and love are inaugurated and made secure on both sides. Thus Irenaeus stated that the Logos has brought God to man through the Father's Spirit (whom the Apostle calls the pledge of our inheritance), and conversely has inserted man in God by the assumption of human nature, and thus has truly and lastingly conferred incorruptibility on us. In another passage he remarks that the Son of God, by making Himself like to us and us like to Him, has brought it about that man became dear to the Father (and was thus assured of the Father's love). Tertullian designates the mediatorship as the function of a depositary, a guarantor of pledges. "He [Jesus], called the depositary of God and of man because of the deposits of both parties entrusted to Him, guards the deposit of the flesh in Himself as the pledge of the whole sum. For as He has left us the pledge of the Spirit, so He has accepted from us the pledge of the flesh, and has taken it up to heaven as the earnest of the whole sum that is one day to follow after. Rest assured, flesh and blood: you have taken possession of heaven and the kingdom of God in Christ."

We need no longer call attention to the fact that the mutual friendship, love, and kindness which rest upon so excellent a pledging cannot be purely natural, or a mere restoration. This pledging is of such a sort that in it God bestows on us and makes our own His most precious and His dearest possession, the Spirit of His heart in His Son, and that He must love the assumed flesh as His own, and consequently must love us, too, as belonging to Himself. With right, therefore, the Fathers agree with the Apostle in basing upon the pledge of the Holy Spirit the hope for the inheritance of the children of God, and upon the possession which God takes of our nature the confidence that He, treating it as His own, will lavish His ever-lasting love upon it.

The meaning of Christ's substantial mediatorship is not exhausted by the supernatural union of the creature with God which it formally establishes and seals. At the same time it makes Christ a born mediator in His activity; it is the foundation for His active mediatorship. We may no more concentrate on the former without the latter than we may on the latter without the former. However, it is manifest that the latter as well as the former, to be appreciated in its full import, must be conceived as an instrument effecting an absolutely supernatural unity and union of the creature with God.

In His active mediatorship Christ negotiates a certain interchange between God and the creature: God's activity with regard to the creature, and the creature's activity with regard to God.

In the concrete: Christ first appears as God's emissary to creatures. Proceeding from the Father while nevertheless remaining with Him, and bearing the fullness of the divinity in Himself, He comes to the creature not as a mere authorized agent with delegated authority, but as the personal representative of God, anointed by the unguent of the divine nature and essence as one endowed with divine activity.

It is clear that the divine activity, to the exercise of which this legate is appointed, must be most extraordinary. For He proceeds from the interior of the Godhead, is equipped with unheard-of power, and in Him God approaches so very near to the creature. In drawing so near to us, in descending so far to us, in sending the Son of His bosom to us, God must unlock the depths of the Godhead and deliver over to creatures the fullness of its riches in the person of His own Son who comes to us. The Son of God made man must transmit to creatures the divine light, the divine truth, of which He is the incarnate Word, and by which creatures are raised to a participation in divine knowledge. As the only-begotten of the Father, as "the Son of His love," He must transmit the grace of the children of God, by giving to all who believe in Him the power to be made the sons of God. He must deliver to creatures a new, higher kingdom of divine dominion, by taking special possession of them in the name of God, and by bringing it about through the power proceeding from Him that God may live and hold sway in them and make them reflect His splendor as the body reflects the soul united to it. In short, anointed with the ointment of His divinity, He is destined by His procession from the Father to be prophet as the mediator of supernatural enlightenment, to be priest as the mediator of supernatural graces, and to be king as the mediator of the supernatural divine kingdom.

But He is also mediator of men, and of creatures in general, at the court of God. By bringing God so close to creatures that God, as it were, pours Himself into creatures and lives in them, He brings creatures so close to God that in their offices to God they attain to God's infinity, otherwise unapproachable for them. He acts in creatures as their head, and they conduct themselves toward God in His name. Thus, as mediator of creatures to God, He can and should offer to God the hymn of an acknowledgment and praise proportionate to His majesty. Thus He can and should bring it about that in Him and with Him creatures pay to God a tribute of adoration and satisfaction which is worthy of God's infinite eminence, and which counterbalances the affront done to Him by sin. Thus, finally, He can and should subject creatures so completely to God's dominion that in Him and with Him creatures serve their Lord with a kingly service, and their homage is no longer that of slaves but of royal personages summoned to joint rule. As He represents God among men in the capacity of prophet, priest, and king, so He represents men at the court of God as a prophet who in their stead sings God's praises as they are unable to do, as a priest who in their behalf gives to God the supreme tribute which they are wholly incapable of supplying, and lastly as a king who in place of them and through them renders to God the noble, free service of a Son.

The functions of the God-man's mediatorship are manifestly summed up in His priesthood. When He brings God's grace down to us, it is clear that at the same time He is acting as prophet to convey to us the light of truth which is implied in this grace, and in which this grace and its author are known; and that He is a king who founds and rules the kingdom of God, for this is nothing other than the kingdom of grace. And on the other hand, if He alone is able in the creature's name to pay worthy tribute to God, then He, and He alone, will be in a position to render to God the praise and obedience which His infinite majesty demands.

Indeed, the entire mediatorship of Christ is at bottom nothing but a priesthood, just as His priesthood is nothing but a mediatorship between God and man. But Christ's priesthood is a unique, superhuman, heavenly priesthood, which brings God down to creatures and raises creatures up to God in a supernatural, mysterious intercommunion, for it is the organ of a supernatural activity of God in man's behalf, and of a supernatural worship which man pays to God. However, we shall arrive at a complete notion of Christ's priesthood and mediatorship only when we come to consider the effects and inner relationship of the two functions that thus meet in the God-man.

Owing to the fact that in the God-man God draws so amazingly near to us with the power of His grace and works His influence upon us, there is abolished the immeasurable chasm that separated the creature from God, whether on account of the creature's natural lowliness or on account of his guilt: and in the grace of divine sonship, together with the extinction of the guilt, a supernatural union of the creature with God is inaugurated. But God's plan is not that the God-man should simply bring this oneness with God down with Him from heaven; rather He is literally to purchase it, earn it by His religious subjection, and so draw it down from heaven. For its firmer foundation and strengthening this oneness is to be achieved in a way that obliges God on His part to establish and effect it. But God can be thus obligated only if the creature offers Him an infinitely valuable price through the cult instituted by the God-man.

Consequently the sacerdotal mediatorship of the God-man must culminate in the fact that, by the worship He offers to God in the name of creatures, He purchases and merits the union with God which He is appointed to accomplish as God's instrument.

Even as substantial mediator the God-man sets up between God and the creature a bond that can and must result from the union of both in grace, seeing that God draws near to the creature with the power of His grace, and that the creature becomes worthy of union with God by grace, because of his relation to the God-man as his head. But this bond is strengthened and sealed only by the active or moral mediatorship exercised by Christ in His priesthood, since it is only in such mediatorship that an interchange of counterbalancing offices takes place.

If man is brought into union with God through the mediation of the God-man, then the God-man, who is the mediator in the acquisition of grace, becomes also the mediator in the gratitude owed for this gift. Surely gratitude for a gift, if it is to be adequate, must be as great as the price for which the gift was bought. By himself the creature can no more return due thanks for his supernatural union with God than he can merit it by himself. Only the God-man, and the homage He renders, is sufficiently worthy and valuable for this end; by His oblation He must crown and perfect the union of the creature with God, a union which He had founded.

How Christ actually realizes the worship which He offers to God, and the bond which He draws between God and man, and in particular how His moral mediatorship thereby becomes a thoroughly real and substantial mediatorship, so that He not only performs works in God's honor but also presents to God a substantial gift of infinite value, we will show later when we treat of the sacrifice of Christ.

Such, in outline, is the idea of the exalted mediatorship of the God-man. Clearly it is not reducible simply to the satisfying of some need grounded in nature, but evinces an exceedingly lofty, supernatural character, and has as its essential effect not only the restoration of a natural unity that had been sundered, but also the foundation and perfecting of an absolutely supernatural, mysterious union between the creature and God. Consequently it must be an august mystery in itself.

In the concrete, of course, Christ is mediator for the restoration of a unity that had been severed, and therefore His mediatory activity has necessarily the character of atonement. This atonement, however, is intended not only to extinguish sin, but to set up an ineffably close and tenacious bond between

31

the parties to be reconciled, such as prior to sin could be neither claimed nor surmised, at least not by natural man.

Christ's mediatory office with regard to material creatures and to the angels might be explained in a similar manner. But we should merely have to repeat in other words what we have already stated about the significance of Christ as head of the entire universe.

Accordingly we conclude this section with the reflection that the significance of the God-man as mediator is no less sublime and mysterious than His significance as head. The mysterious character of the Incarnation is not at all destroyed by this significance, or by the appropriateness and necessity of the Incarnation which it implies. On the contrary, such considerations accentuate the mystery.

63. SUBJECTIVE SIGNIFICANCE, FOR GOD AND MAN, OF THE INCARNATION AND ITS ECONOMY

The purposes that we have listed as determining and dominating the idea of the Incarnation in God's sight are entirely objective in character: they are found in an order of things which was established by the Incarnation and is to be crowned by the Incarnation, in the continuation of the Trinitarian communication and self-glorification of God to the whole outside universe, and in the foundation and perfecting of a most sublime, supernatural union of the creature with God.

All the other aims and effects of the mystery are of a more subjective nature, as regards both God and creatures: as regards God, who in carrying out the project and achieving its objective, intrinsic ends (the *finis operis*) intends to assert and reveal those of His attributes that cooperate in its execution; as regards creatures, who receive great spiritual profit from their knowledge of the origin, nature, and effects of the mystery.

Thus in carrying out the Incarnation, God displays His power by the production of so noble and arduous a work; His wisdom, by the temperate yet effective disposition of means leading to the highest goal; His goodness, by wishing to communicate Himself to creatures in so unparalleled a fashion that He incorporates them in His only-begotten Son, and gives Him to them as the pledge and purchase price for their liberation from guilt and acquisition of grace; His sanctity and justice, by willing to extend outside of Himself, the glorification which He receives within the Godhead, and to remit sin only after condign satisfaction. The manifestation of these attributes we call God's subjective aims (*finis operantis*), because they do not determine the intrinsic character of the object will, but presuppose it as determined according to its idea, and follow more from the relationship of the effect to its cause than from the nature of the effect as such. Therefore these aims may always be mentioned when explaining the origin of the Incarnation, but they do not disclose the proper, intrinsic motive of the effect as it is in itself, and do not lead to an understanding of the idea of it; rather, in order to be fully understood, these aims presuppose the understanding of the idea.

Whoever would be satisfied with these aims would be like the art critic who, in accounting for the existence of a painting and its beauty, would say no more than that the artist wished to reveal the whole of his genius and skill in this creation. The art critic would satisfy us only if he explained the inner motive which inspired the artist and guided him in executing the painting, and by the understanding of which alone we can appreciate how the picture is really so beautiful, and how, consequently, it could have inspired the artist and shows forth his art. In the same way theological science does not give a full account of the tremendous work which the Incarnation is, unless it discloses the great idea that underlies it, and consequently shows how God was able and willed to reveal His power, His wisdom, His goodness and holiness, in carrying it out. The inner motive here is the wonderful extension of the Trinitarian productions to the whole outside universe, as well as the surpassing union of creatures with God that is thereby brought about.

In like manner the subjective meaning which the Incarnation has for the man who contemplates it lies outside its proper idea, although it automatically follows therefrom, and in any case was comprised in God's plan. To the objective idea of the Incarnation belongs the fact that man is raised to the status of a member of Christ and to the sonship of God, in order through Christ to glorify God in a supernatural manner and to be happy in God. Whence it follows automatically, and God also intends this, that man is roused to the practice of good and the avoidance of evil by his knowledge of the Incarnation, that in Christ he beholds the model he is to imitate, that this intimate union of God with him strengthens his confidence, makes an awareness of God easy for him, and enkindles and inflames his love. But all these subjective effects of the Incarnation are conceivable only on the basis of the objective effects. That is, they presuppose that we are called to be members and brethren of Christ by the objective power and significance of the Incarnation. This bearing which the Incarnation has on the guidance and stimulation of our life, so as to make it pleasing to God, enables us to give an account of the Incarnation only because it has called us to so high an estate.

Such an account would be quite impossible if by a life pleasing to God we should understand no more than the development of our nature—as we have previously seen—although the fact that the Incarnation is of supreme importance for the ravages and needs of nature is not excluded. It has a closer connection with the unfolding of man's supernatural life.

We desire here to call attention to some profound but seldom applied thoughts of St. Thomas, which enable us to see this relation in its proper perspective.

In the *Summa contra Gentiles* (lib. IV, c. 54), St. Thomas shows how admirably the Incarnation is adapted to the purpose of rendering easy for man the pursuit of his supernatural end, that is, the vision of God.

In the first place, he points out, man might doubt his ability to attain to so marvelous a union of his intellect with the divine essence as is necessary for the beatific vision, because of the immeasurable disparity between the two natures. But the still higher, hypostatic union of a divine person with human nature shows us that the lesser union must be possible, and hence strengthens our hope for its consummation. Moreover, it strengthens our hope all the more since it brings the excellence of our nature home to our consciousness, and shows us that we, elevated as we are above all creatures, can and ought to achieve perfect happiness in closest union with God.

Matthias Joseph Scheeben

If man is destined to the immediate vision of God, and hence to a participation in the knowledge proper to God, with regard to the road leading to this goal he can have no other teacher than God Himself. That this instruction which man receives from God may take place in a manner befitting man's nature, it appears suitable that God Himself should come to him in visible form, that God's own Word should personally communicate such participation in the divine cognition, and that the Son of God should usher us into the bosom of His Father. Thus the Incarnation of the Logos is admirably adapted to the formation of supernatural faith in us.

Further, the intimate love for God, by which we are to tend to supernatural union with Him, cannot be better roused and inflamed than by the love which God Himself displays most perfectly by assuming our nature and wishing to become our brother. The closer God draws to us and the more He comes down to our level, the more tender and trusting will be our love for Him, and the more ardently our love must long to be united with Him also in His divinity.

It is apparent that these reasons which St. Thomas advances are not derived from the corruptness of our nature or the sinfulness clinging to it, but from the elevation of nature above itself. We are so insistent in stressing this point because of the general tendency to explain the appearance of the Son of God in the flesh exclusively on the basis of our nature's inclination to sensuality. Certainly the Incarnation is, and must be, a means whereby man lifts himself out of the servitude of sense to all that is spiritual. But more important is the visible appearance of God in the flesh as a pledge that He will one day reveal Himself to us in His essence. The visible appearance of God can be recognized as a suitable means for raising us up out of sensuality only in view of our destination to the immediate vision of the divine essence. If we were not thus raised, but were merely to be freed from servitude to sensuality, this means would be disproportionate.

64. JUSTIFICATION AND FURTHER DEVELOPMENT OF THE DOCTRINE ABOUT THE MEANING AND MOTIVATION OF THE INCARNATION. THE GOD-MAN IN EVERY RESPECT THE FOCAL POINT AND CENTER OF GRAVITY OF THE WORLD

In explaining, as we have done, the meaning and motivation of the Incarnation and its relation with its end, have we not come into conflict with the view which, if not dogmatically established, is commonly held in the Church? Does not the Church teach us that the Son of God became man on account of us men (*propter nos homines*), and indeed to save us from sin? Is not the doctrine of the Fathers fairly constant, that it was precisely the need and the wretched estate of the human race that prevailed upon Him, who otherwise would have had no reason for doing so, to come down from heaven? Is it not the common opinion that the Incarnation is in itself an abasement unworthy of God, so that the Son of God not only would not have become man, but could not have done so, if sin had not made it necessary? Accordingly does it not seem that the motivation of the Incarnation is to be sought not so much in the lofty regions where we have located them, as in man's dire need resulting from sin?

Well and good. But have we denied that the Son of God became man for the sake of us men, and to save us from sin? Not at all. We have expressly taught that the Incarnation is pre-eminently for the benefit of us men, and hence that God willed it out of indescribable love and benevolence toward us. Indeed, this love shows itself greatest of all by not merely releasing man in the most complete manner from sin and its consequences, but by willing further to raise him to an astounding sublimity and glory that surpasses all understanding.

Again, have we denied that the Incarnation is designed precisely to free fallen man from his sin, and that consequently God's love, which is the motive of the Incarnation, is a merciful love? We deny only that the wealth of this love is limited to the claims of compassion, and that the principle and motive of the Incarnation can be found in such limitation. This motive can be no other than the boundless love which God displays after man's sin, contrary to all expectation and beyond all our

notions. And further, we deny that the elevation of fallen man
was the only end or at any rate the highest end, and that love
for man was the only motive or the highest motive of the Incarnation. The glory of Christ and of God Himself is the highest
aim, and the love of God for Himself and for Christ is the
highest motive of the Incarnation. Often as the holy Fathers
assign the necessary restoration of fallen man as the end of the
Incarnation, and God's mercy as its motive, no less often do
they insist that God in His overflowing love has decreed to give
us incalculably more, and to elevate us incomparably higher
after the Incarnation than He had done before. "Since the
fullness of life enjoyed by the human race," says St. Leo,
"had collapsed in our first parents, God in His mercy willed,
through His only-begotten Son Jesus Christ, to come to the
assistance of the creature made to His likeness, in such wise
that the repairing of nature should not come from outside that
nature, and that its second state should advance beyond the
dignity of its own origin. Happy the nature, if it had not fallen
from that state which God had ordained; happier, if it remains
in that state which God has restored. It was a great thing to
have received its form from Christ, but it is a greater thing to
have its substance in Christ."

If, then, the Fathers make it a rule to stress the forgiveness and extinction of sin as the end of the Incarnation, this is
explained quite simply from other reasons, without assuming
that this aim is objectively the ultimate purpose of the Incarnation. They usually portray that side of the Incarnation which
appears to the human race from the standpoint of the actual
plight in which it finds itself; they emphasize that effect which
is most indispensable to us and which is at the same time the
preliminary condition for all the higher effects. They behold in
it especially the means of banishing the evil which burdens the
race, without thereby denying or even losing sight of the
incalculable goods which it is meant to convey to us. Otherwise
why should they call Adam's sin happy, for the reason that it
has brought us such and so great a Redeemer, if they thought
that Christ was merely to do away with sin, without conferring
any higher good than existed before the Fall?

Hence the effacement of sin must be regarded as a subordinate objective, and the sin itself as an occasion which God awaited in order to manifest His love to men in so astounding a manner, and to give the God-man an opportunity to display His inexhaustible power on all sides, in the conquest of evil as well as in the inauguration of good.

Thus when we profess in the Creed that the Son of God became man *propter nos homines,* we do not thereby signify that love for us men was the first and highest motive of the Incarnation. Love for creatures is never the highest motive for God's external works. The phrase, "God acts out of pure love for creatures," means, wherever employed, that God's external operations are not motivated by personal need or performed for His own utility. Manifestly God loves creatures only in Himself, and hence wills to glorify Himself in them. In the present case God could not will the God-man out of sheer love for creatures, seeing that the God-man Himself is worth infinitely more than all mere creatures. Consequently creatures exist for Him and are loved for His sake even more than He exists for them and is loved and willed on their account. Hence God's love for Himself, by which He wills the external manifestation of His Trinitarian glory, and His love for the God-man, to whom He wills to communicate Himself in an infinite way, as He does to no creature, is the motive for the Incarnation even more than is the redemption and elevation of creatures. We by no means exclude this, but rather suppose it as self-understood, when with grateful hearts we so often proclaim that the Son of God has become man for the sake of us men.

So, too, the angels, in the hymn by which they announced to men the birth of Emmanuel and sang of its joyous fruits, placed the glory of God ahead of the peace which was thereby to come to men. True, we are accustomed to look upon ourselves as the goal and the motive of the Incarnation, and accordingly we lay stress on God's love for us. But we do so in order to impress on ourselves the truth that God was not compelled to the Incarnation by any sort of necessity, least of all by any need on His part, and that the whole benefit arising from it can accrue only to us. We do so in order to excite our wonder at the purity and disinterestedness of the love which gave us

Christ, and thus to discharge the first and highest duty which so great a benefit lays on us, the duty of gratitude. We might add that as a rule we emphasize that aspect of a thing which is of prime importance and interest to ourselves.

These reasons likewise explain why Sacred Scripture itself almost always depicts the Incarnation as ordained to our salvation and benefit. Furthermore, just as God's love for us, whereby He loves us in Himself and for Himself, appears infinitely purer, holier, and greater than if He loved us merely for our own sake, so the love with which God gives us Christ out of love for Him is more precious and valuable for us than if He had given us Christ only for our own sake, loving us on account of ourselves.

However rightly we may raise the question, whether Christ would have become man in case Adam had not sinned, at any rate this much must be held, that even then the main ends of the Incarnation could have motivated its realization. The relations of the Incarnation to the founding and perfecting of the order of grace, to the perfecting of the universe in general, and to the infinite glorification of God, would have been pertinent in that case also. Thus, for example, St. Thomas, who answers the question in the negative, or rather declines to treat it, in other passages suggests many reasons for the Incarnation which are entirely independent of sin and the Fall, and have to do exclusively with the institution of the supernatural order. To have any meaning, the question must seemingly inquire whether some of the aims actually intended by God are sufficient to motivate the Incarnation, if sin is left aside. In reality and in the concrete the Incarnation is envisaged together with the Fall, but without doubt in such wise that God has associated the permission of the Fall itself with the decree of the Incarnation.

Hence we must categorically reject as untenable the opinion that the Incarnation would have been unworthy of God apart from the anguish of mankind that resulted from the Fall, and that God could not have been induced to effect it unless He had been, as it were, forced thereto by man's distress.

In proceeding with a refutation of this view, we shall be preparing the way for a vindication of the idea of the absolutely supernatural character of the Incarnation at the precise juncture where the God-man most completely humbles Himself.

In the first place, is there any need on man's part which God could not alleviate in any other way than by the abasement of Himself? Nearly all the Fathers and theologians declare themselves decisively against such a view, and contend that many other means were at the disposal of God's wisdom and omnipotence, not only to free man from his sin, but even to restore him to his supernatural union with God.

But even supposing that the Incarnation were the only means: would God have been able to abase Himself to please man, to make a sacrifice of Himself for man? Does God exist for men's sake, or man for God's sake? And although God embraces man with an infinite love, this love is infinite only because God loves man in Himself and loves Himself in man. If, then, the Incarnation really involves an abasement of God, this could not be justified by any need on man's part.

However, does any such abasement of God really take place? God stoops down to man's level by becoming man, without however quitting His exalted position; this condescension is precisely the truest and most perfect proof of His greatness. God descends to the lowliness of humanity; but He thereby raises humanity, which He assumes, to His own level, to His own majesty. When the Son of God becomes man, the Father prolongs the eternal generation into the outside world, utters His infinite Word from the interior of the Godhead to the exterior, and by this very utterance gains the greatest glory which He can attain in His external works. And so the Incarnation could have taken place without man's sin; there is no reason why it could not have occurred on this supposition, since its very highest goal, the infinite glory of God, could have been attained.

The Apostle's words, "He emptied Himself," cannot be applied to the Incarnation as such. Otherwise the Son of God even now in heaven would have to be in a state of self-divestment, self-emptying—which has never been maintained by anyone.

The Son of God has divested, emptied ($\dot{\epsilon}\kappa\acute{\epsilon}\nu\omega\sigma\epsilon\nu$) Himself not by the very fact of assuming human nature, but by assuming human nature in its condition of lowliness, imperfection, and passibility, just as it is possessed by mere men, and by not pervading and filling it with His divine glory and happiness from the beginning, and particularly by allowing Himself, like any other man, to appear in its lower and more external aspect ("in habit found as a man," that is, mere man), and not as the God-man. In short, He divested and emptied Himself in the sense that as man He waived claim to the glory and happiness which were His due as Son of God, and did not transfigure and glorify the "form of a servant" in the way in which per se it should have been transfigured and glorified as belonging to the "form" of the Son of God, and in the way in which it actually was transfigured and glorified after His resurrection.

But at any rate was not this state, so far short of the dignity of the God-man, an abasement which He could take upon Himself only on account of man's need? If the God-man could not have taken this self-emptying upon Himself for other reasons than the crushing distress of man, for which on our hypothesis no other relief was at hand, He could not have done so for this purpose either, at least He could not have done so purely for man's sake. Man's plight is explained only by the demands of God's offended honor; and just as God could have forgone an adequate satisfaction if He had so willed, so He would actually have had to forgo it if the self-emptying of the God-man had been something intrinsically unworthy of Him.

But suffering and death are not in themselves ignominious; they are such only when they freight the subject with a compelling necessity, in consequence of nature or of sin, and against his will. When voluntarily assumed or accepted they are, according to circumstances, the highest honor and ornament. No one, to be sure, as long as there is question only of his own well-being, will prefer suffering to impassibility, death to life, mortality to immortality. We take suffering upon ourselves only to gain a greater good. But a person suffers for others not only to relieve a need or to acquire a good for them, but also for the sole reason that he shows his love and esteem better by suffering than by all the deeds he performs for their benefit or by all the goods he gives them. Suffering thus undertaken is

41

obviously an act of the purest self-sacrifice and the most sublime virtue, and hence is more honorable and lovable than impassibility.

If we apply these considerations to Christ, we perceive that He could have taken suffering and death upon Himself out of love for man, to redeem him, but still more out of love for God, to restore to Him the honor of which He had been robbed and the exactions of which gave rise to man's need of redemption. This material abasement involved no moral abasement, since suffering and death, arising from Christ's free will and undertaken for the noblest motives, were most honorable for Him, much more honorable than immunity to suffering.

Upon looking more closely into the matter, we see that what makes suffering honorable is not the distress or the need of him for whom one suffers; rather it is the freedom and the noble motive of the sufferer. Consequently suffering is the more honorable the greater the freedom of the person concerned, and the less he is limited in his love to the bare need of the beloved. Hence we should be disparaging Christ's honor if we were to hold that He had allowed Himself to be subjected to suffering merely because, in consequence of sin, God had some need of the restitution of His honor, or the sinner had need of redemption. Christ appears most majestic in His suffering, if from boundless love for God and man He suffers more than the need strictly requires, and at the same time suffers not only to relieve the need, but by His suffering to give to God the highest possible glory, and to creatures the proof of a love which is worth incalculably more than the aid He accords them in their wretchedness, more even than all the benefits which He can confer on them.

This is demonstrable particularly with reference to God's glory, which is the highest and worthiest objective both of the Incarnation as a whole and of the suffering experienced in the assumed humanity.

God is in general honored by the fact that the creature subjects himself to Him in acknowledgment of His supreme majesty, and makes an oblation of himself to God. This oblation does not necessarily require that the creature suffer and annihilate himself for God's sake; only propitiatory sacrifice in reparation of violated honor is essentially bound up with suffering and renunciation. But it would be a grievous error to think that God could demand a sacrifice of renunciation, and the creature offer such, only in atonement for sin. Nothing is more opposed to the spirit of Christianity. It is precisely by renunciation and self-abdication that we offer God the greatest honor, and attest our unreserved adoration and boundless love for Him in the most noble and excellent manner. Otherwise why do the saints love suffering so much, and nothing more than suffering? Because they thereby satisfy for their own or others' sins? No, but because they place their supreme happiness and honor in magnifying and glorifying God by the abasement of themselves. They love suffering and death because they thereby become like the God-man, who had in fullest measure glorified His Father and Himself in this very way. As the adoration and love of the God-man are of infinite value on account of the dignity of His person, they had to be proven and carried through in the most perfect manner by His endurance of the greatest sufferings, such as no mere creature has ever undergone. This overflow of suffering was not needed to satisfy for man's sins; a single drop of Christ's blood, even a single tear, would have fully sufficed. Only because Christ was to glorify God so perfectly that no higher degree is conceivable, did the measure of His suffering have to be in keeping with the infinite dignity of the offerer, and the infinite value of the sacrificial Lamb.

Regarded from this standpoint, the voluntary abasement and self-renunciation of the God-man constitute the greatest triumph, indeed an infinite triumph, of God's honor and glory. But Christ also celebrated His supreme triumph therein; for He is greatest when He most glorifies God. Hence His abasement is not an abasement unworthy of Him. By divesting Himself of the glory that is His as the Son of God, He proves most magnificently that He is God's true Son, who wishes to glorify His Father in every possible way, and in the absolutely highest way. In His suffering and death He appears even greater and nobler than He does in His glorified, impassible body after His resurrection. Even in His glorified body the marks of His voluntary suffering are the most beautiful pearls that adorn

Him, and make Him far more attractive than the brilliant light that encompasses Him.

This glorification of God, procured through the most extreme self-annihilation, such as was impossible in a purely spiritual nature, was the worthiest objective the Son of God had in assuming a created nature, a human nature capable of suffering. The infinite love which the Son bore for His Father and which in His divinity He could manifest only by the co-possession and co-fruition of the Father's glory, impelled Him to glorify His Father by the perfect surrender and divestment of Himself in a nature subject to pain. This love also impelled Him to associate the members of His mystical body in the same project and for the same end. Are these conclusions an exaggeration? May we not make bold to add that this self-annihilation, so far as it was achieved in the name of creation and for the benefit of creation, was intended to make it possible for creatures to offer God the most sublime homage, and that thus it was destined to acquire and assure the highest favor and grace for them from God's side? Are we out of joint with the sense of Christianity, or do we not rather express its very soul, if we assert that not only was the world's sickness to be cured, but the world itself was to be raised to the summit of honor and glory, by no other means than Christ's suffering?

No, the death of God's Son on the cross does not have to be justified by the necessity of the Cross. We believe rather that God has connected the restoration of the world with the cross of His Son in order to glorify the Cross. Therefore, if the abasement of the God-man would not have taken place except in consequence of sin, sin was not merely a ground for its necessity, but was also and to a greater extent an occasion, distinct from the dishonor to God and the ingratitude of men contained in it, for showing forth the glory of God and His love for Himself and for men in so imposing a way. Indeed, the revelation of God's glory and love reaches its peak in the employment of sin as an instrument, so to speak, for the attainment of its ends. By the very fact that Christ satisfies for sin, God's honor is not merely saved, but is further glorified according to a new aspect. This is all the more true if He compels sin in the midst of its supreme triumph to take part in the conquest of itself. Sin celebrated its triumph when it strove and actually contrived to slay God's Anointed. But at the very moment that Christ seemed to succumb to it, He performed the supreme act of adoration and glorification of God. That act did more than merely compensate for sin. It drew the most precious honey from the poison of its sting, forced sin to achieve an effect opposite to its intention, and deeply humiliated sin in a way that not even the everlasting punishments of hell could equal, thereby securing for God a triumph that would not have been possible without sin.

Although not motivated by sin alone, Christ's suffering, as the Incarnation in general, remains in fact connected with sin as with its occasion and a reason for its necessity. The predominant concern of Sacred Scripture and the Fathers in presenting Christ's Passion under this sole aspect is explained by their desire to depict the greatness of the benefits it has brought to us.

Accordingly we have no reason for thinking that the Incarnation, or even the abasement of the God-man unto the death of the cross, is justified only as a means motivated by the purpose of exterminating sin or compensating for sin. Indeed, we demean the God-man if we regard the humiliation implied in His incarnation and death merely as a means for the attainment of ends which are far below Him, such as the salvation of men, or are incidental to the order of the world, such as the compensation for sin which had been rendered necessary.

The infinite dignity of the God-man makes it impossible for Him to play a subordinate, secondary role in God's plan. All that He is and does cannot exist exclusively for the sake of man or on account of sin. In everything He is willed essentially for His own sake and for God's sake. If He is given to men and delivered up for men, men at the same time belong to Him more than He belongs to them; and as His surrender conduces to their advantage, so it redounds to His own honor and to the glorification of His Father. As He and His activity are ordained to the salvation of men and of the whole world, so men and the whole world are ordained to Him as their head and king who, in freeing them from the servitude of evil, makes of them His kingdom, and along with Himself lays them at the feet of His heavenly Father, that God may be all in all.

THE CATHOLIC TRADITION: The Saviour

In the divine plan, with the Incarnation as an organic part, the Incarnation itself is the first and most essential member. Around this everything else revolves, to this everything else is joined and subordinated, through this everything else receives its definite position and meaning.

St. Anselm's question (*Cur Deus homo?*) has an immediately practical aspect: Why did we stand in need of the God-man and His suffering? But we may also grasp the question scientifically according to its entire range: What, in God's eyes, was the end proportionately adequate to this infinite project? If we consider this latter aspect, we must seek the answer in the mysterious regions of an order that is wholly supernatural, in the design of a most extraordinary communication and glorification of God. This is an order in which every other world order is taken up as in a higher and more universal order. The answer to the question *Cur Deus homo?* is then also an answer to the question *Cur mundus?* or *Ad quid mundus?* What direction is given to the world by the Incarnation? This question, although ordinarily too little noted in theological science, is as much in place as the first question.

God alone can give us the answer to both questions. He can do so either explicitly or implicitly, that is, by revealing to us the mystery of the Incarnation, and then leaving it to our reflection to infer the end to which He has destined this work, and the end to which He has destined the world with reference to it. But the second question admits of solution only in terms of the first, not vice versa, since in the last analysis the world is not the ultimate end, but Christ is the ultimate end of the world. This second way of proceeding is as fruitful and illuminating as the first is fruitless and one-sided.

Pursuing this second method, we understand at the outset that Christ is both the end and the beginning of the way mapped out by the Lord at His creation of the world. We perceive why, from the outset, God had diffused a supernatural splendor over the whole of creation, and particularly why He communicated grace to the human family as a solidary body, in the person of its progenitor. All this pointed to the king whose realm the whole world was to become, and whose body the human race was to become. We gain an insight into the origin and the frightful malice of the sin of the angels, and perceive it in its entire mysterious profundity. We apprehend the basic reason why God could allow the angels to fall, and why He could permit all mankind to fall through their instigation: because He not only knew that the havoc thus wrought would be repaired, but wished to utilize it for the supreme revelation of His goodness and glory.

Thus the mystery of the God-man, when grasped in its mysterious sublimity, diffuses the clearest rays of light over all the other mysteries, since they are all related to it. It sheds light not only over those mysteries which flow from it after its realization in the fullness of time, but also over those which God had previously summoned forth or permitted in view of it. As it is the central point of the entire supernatural order of the world and its history, so too, despite its obscurity, it is the beam of light which, under the guidance of faith, enables us to penetrate that order down to its deepest abysses.

Like the sun in the midst of the planets, Christ stands in the midst of creatures as the heart of creation, from whom light, life, and movement stream forth to all its members and toward whom all gravitate, so as in Him and through Him to find their rest in God. According to outward appearances and in practical life, the sun is regarded by us only as an abundant source of aid designed for the well-being of the earth. In the same way we are accustomed to think of Christ as the helper and liberator sent to us by God, as our Jesus from whom we have everything to hope for. But just as science in the course of time has demonstrated that it is not the earth which attracts the sun, but the sun which attracts the earth, so scientific theology, if it is to apprehend Christ in all His meaning, must forge ahead to the point where it will consider Him as the center of gravity of the entire world order, and hence grasp the full sense of the words: "I will draw all things to Myself." It must learn to know Him as the Christ, the Anointed par excellence, in whom are concentrated the supreme union and the most intimate friendship between God and the creature. And this realization will become eminently practical, especially if we do not regard the priesthood of Christ merely as an office which He discharges at the court of God in our behalf. We should rather perceive that we must attach ourselves to this High Priest, so as in Him and through Him to render to God the honor which He expects from His creation. We will presently come back to this point.

Gilbert Keith Chesterton
1874-1936

Chesterton was born of a middle-class family in London and with his brother Cecil was immersed in literature from his earliest years. His career can be divided into four periods: 1) before 1900: first at St. Paul's School (where he led the debating club and edited its journal), then at the Slade School of Art, and later at University College, he had not yet found himself and later destroyed much of what he wrote in this early period. 2) 1900-1908: he became "a Fleet Street legend" due to his witty essays, poems, and fantasies and began his weekly column in the Daily News. *3) 1908-1921: his career as a Christian apologist, beginning with his famous* Orthodoxy, *and marked by his debating with Hilaire Belloc, H. G. Wells, And G. B. Shaw. 4) 1922-1936: his years as a Catholic, dating from his reception into the Church until his death. This was his most prolific period; sometimes he would write as many as 10,000 words a week, and he also began weekly broadcasts on the BBC. In the final year of his life Pope Pius XI bestowed on him the title of Defender of the Catholic Faith.*

"G.K.C." was a legend in his own time. A man of multiple talents, he was highly critical of all manner of developments in modern society, but never let this turn him sour. He invested great confidence in the ultimate rationality of the Common Man, and was probably unsurpassed among English writers in

his mastery of the paradox. It was this ability to see two sides and to hold them in dialectical tension that marked him as principally a man of balance. He loved to point out how every half-truth was also half-false.

It should be obvious from the above that Chesterton is not included here as an original theologian. He would have been the first to scoff at such an idea. But he was one of the most effective communicators of simple Christian truths that the English language has yet seen. His biographies of Francis of Assisi (1923) and Thomas Aquinas (1933) are classics of that genre.

The Everlasting Man (1925) shows us Chesterton at his best, developing, as he describes it, the thesis "that those who say that Christ stands side by side with similar myths . . . are only repeating a very stale formula contradicted by a very striking fact." The book was written, as Christopher Hollis has observed, "to correct the childishly simple story of a regular progress of history which H. G. Wells had popularised in his Outline of History. *Its contentions were in essence two. Man was not . . . an animal who merely differed in degree from other animals. . . . And likewise Christ was not . . . a man who merely differed in degree from other men."*

The two parts of the book are thus: 1) On the Creature Called Man, and 2) On the Man Called Christ. The latter consists of six chapters, of which the first two are given in the following selection, along with the conclusion which summarizes the whole book. There are undoubtedly points in Chesterton's arguments that are questionable as well as points that are passé, but seldom has Christian orthodoxy found so articulate a defender. His manner of discourse is consistent and cogent but never abstruse. His particular vision is perhaps best summarized in his statement in the final paragraph of the conclusion: "It was the soul of Christendom that came forth from the incredible Christ; and the soul of it was common sense."

THE EVERLASTING MAN

PART TWO

ON THE MAN CALLED CHRIST

I: THE GOD IN THE CAVE

This sketch of the human story began in a cave; the cave which popular science associates with the cave-man and in which practical discovery has really found archaic drawings of animals. The second half of human history, which was like a new creation of the world, also begins in a cave. There is even a shadow of such a fancy in the fact that animals were again present, for it was a cave used as a stable by the mountaineers of the uplands about Bethlehem; who still drive their cattle into such holes and caverns at night. It was here that a homeless couple had crept underground with the cattle when the doors of the crowded caravanserai had been shut in their faces; and it was here beneath the very feet of the passers-by, in a cellar under the very floor of the world, that Jesus Christ was born. But in that second creation there was indeed something symbolical in the roots of the primeval rock or the horns of the prehistoric herd. God also was a Cave-Man, and had also traced strange shapes of creatures, curiously coloured, upon the wall of the world; but the pictures that he made had come to life.

A mass of legend and literature, which increases and will never end, has repeated and rung the changes on that single paradox; that the hands that had made the sun and stars were too small to reach the huge heads of the cattle. Upon this paradox, we might almost say upon this jest, all the literature of our faith is founded. It is at least like a jest in this; that it is something which the scientific critic cannot see. He laboriously explains the difficulty which we have always defiantly and almost derisively exaggerated; and mildly condemns as improbable something that we have almost madly exalted as incredible; as something that would be much too good to be true, except that it is true. When that contrast between the cosmic creation and the little local infancy has been repeated, reiterated, underlined, emphasised, exulted in, sung, shouted, roared, not to say howled, in a hundred thousand hymns, carols, rhymes, rituals, pictures, poems, and popular sermons, it may be suggested that we hardly need a higher critic to draw our attention to something a little odd about it; especially one of the sort that seems to take a long time to see a joke, even his own joke. But about this contrast and combination of ideas one thing may be said here, because it is relevant to the whole thesis of this book. The sort of modern critic of whom I speak is generally much impressed with the importance of education in life and the importance of psychology in education. That sort of man is never tired of telling us that first impressions fix character by the law of causation; and he will become quite nervous if a child's visual sense is poisoned by the wrong colours on a golliwog or his nervous system prematurely shaken by a cacophonous rattle. Yet he will think us very narrow-minded, if we say that this is exactly why there really is a difference between being brought up as a Christian and being brought up as a Jew or a Moslem or an atheist. The difference is that every Catholic child has learned from pictures, and even every Protestant child from stories, this incredible combination of contrasted ideas as one of the very first impressions on his mind. It is not merely a theological difference. It is a psychological difference which can outlast any theologies. It really is, as that sort of scientist loves to say about anything, incurable. Any agnostic or atheist whose childhood has known a real Christmas has ever afterwards, whether he likes it or not, an association in his mind between two ideas that most of mankind must regard as remote from each other; the idea of a baby and the idea of unknown strength that sustains the stars. His instincts and imagination can still connect them, when his reason can no longer see the need of the connection; for him there will always be some savour of religion about the mere picture of a mother and a baby; some hint of mercy and softening about the mere mention of the dreadful name of God. But the two ideas are not naturally or necessarily combined. They would not be necessarily combined for an ancient Greek or a Chinaman, even

52

for Aristotle or Confucius. It is no more inevitable to connect God with an infant than to connect gravitation with a kitten. It has been created in our minds by Christmas because we are Christians; because we are psychological Christians even when we are not theological ones. In other words, this combination of ideas has emphatically, in the much disputed phrase, altered human nature. There is really a difference between the man who knows it and the man who does not. It may not be a difference of moral worth, for the Moslem or the Jew might be worthier according to his lights; but it is a plain fact about the crossing of two particular lights, the conjunction of two stars in our particular horoscope. Omnipotence and impotence, or divinity and infancy, do definitely make a sort of epigram which a million repetitions cannot turn into a platitude. It is not unreasonable to call it unique. Bethlehem is emphatically a place where extremes meet.

Here begins, it is needless to say, another mighty influence for the humanisation of Christendom. If the world wanted what is called a non-controversial aspect of Christianity, it would probably select Christmas. Yet it is obviously bound up with what is supposed to be a controversial aspect (I could never at any stage of my opinions imagine why); the respect paid to the Blessed Virgin. When I was a boy a more Puritan generation objected to a statue upon my parish church representing the Virgin and Child. After much controversy, they compromised by taking away the Child. One would think that this was even more corrupted with Mariolatry, unless the mother was counted less dangerous when deprived of a sort of weapon. But the practical difficulty is also a parable. You cannot chip away the statue of a mother from all round that of a new-born child. You cannot suspend the new-born child in mid-air; indeed you cannot really have a statue of a new-born child at all. Similarly, you cannot suspend the idea of a new-born child in the void or think of him without thinking of his mother. You cannot visit the child without visiting the mother; you cannot in common human life approach the child except through the mother. If we are to think of Christ in this aspect at all, the other idea follows as it is followed in history. We must either leave Christ out of Christmas, or Christmas out of Christ, or we must admit, if only as we

53

admit it in an old picture, that those holy heads are too near together for the haloes not to mingle and cross.

It might be suggested, in a somewhat violent image, that nothing had happened in that fold or crack in the great grey hills except that the whole universe had been turned inside out. I mean that all the eyes of wonder and worship which had been turned outwards to the largest thing were not turned inward to the smallest. The very image will suggest all that multitudinous marvel of converging eyes that makes so much of the coloured Catholic imagery like a peacock's tail. But it is true in a sense that God who had been only a circumference was seen as a centre; and a centre is infinitely small. It is true that the spiritual henceforward works inwards instead of outwards, and in that sense is centripetal and not centrifugal. The faith becomes, in more ways than one, a religion of little things. But its traditions in art and literature and popular fable have quite sufficiently attested, as has been said, this particular paradox of the divine being in the cradle. Perhaps they have not so clearly emphasised the significance of the divine being in the cave. Curiously enough, indeed, tradition has not very clearly emphasised the cave. It is a familiar fact that the Bethlehem scene has been represented in every possible setting of time and country, of landscape and architecture; and it is a wholly happy and admirable fact that men have conceived it as quite different according to their different individual traditions and tastes. But while all have realised that it was a stable, not so many have realised that it was a cave. Some critics have even been so silly as to suppose that there was some contradiction between the stable and the cave; in which case they cannot know much about caves or stables in Palestine. As they see differences that are not there, it is needless to add that they do not see differences that are there. When a well-known critic says, for instance, that Christ being born in a rocky cavern is like Mithras having sprung alive out of a rock, it sounds like a parody upon comparative religion. There is such a thing as the point of a story, even if it is a story in the sense of a lie. And the notion of a hero appearing, like Pallas from the brain of Zeus, mature and without a mother, is obviously the very opposite of the idea of a god being born like an ordinary baby and entirely dependent on a mother. Whichever ideal we might

54

prefer, we should surely see that they are contrary ideals. It is as stupid to connect them because they both contain a substance called stone as to identify the punishment of the Deluge with the baptism in the Jordan because they both contain a substance called water. Whether as a myth or a mystery, Christ was obviously conceived as born in a hole in the rocks primarily because it marked the position of one outcast and homeless. Nevertheless it is true, as I have said, that the cave has not been so commonly or so clearly used as a symbol as the other realities that surrounded the first Christmas.

And the reason for this also refers to the very nature of that new world. It was in a sense the difficulty of a new dimension. Christ was not only born on the level of the world, but even lower than the world. The first act of the divine drama was enacted, not only on no stage set up above the sight-seer, but on a dark and curtained stage sunken out of sight; and that is an idea very difficult to express in most modes of artistic expression. It is the idea of simultaneous happenings on different levels of life. Something like it might have been attempted in the more archaic and decorative medieval art. But the more artists learned of realism and perspective, the less they could depict at once the angels in the heavens and the shepherds on the hills, and the glory in the darkness that was under the hills. Perhaps it could have been best conveyed by the characteristic expedient of some of the medieval guilds, when they wheeled about the streets a theatre with three stages one above the other, with heaven above the earth and hell under the earth. But in the riddle of Bethlehem it was heaven that was under the earth.

There is in that alone the touch of a revolution, as of the world turned upside down. It would be vain to attempt to say anything adequate, or anything new, about the change which this conception of a deity born like an outcast or even an outlaw had upon the whole conception of law and its duties to the poor and outcast. It is profoundly true to say that after that moment there could be no slaves. There could be and were people bearing that legal title, until the Church was strong enough to weed them out, but there could be no more of the pagan repose in the mere advantage to the state of keeping it a servile state. Individuals became important, in a sense in which no instruments can be important. A man could not be a means to an end, at any rate to any other man's end. All this popular and fraternal element in the story has been rightly attached by tradition to the episode of the Shepherds; the hinds who found themselves talking face to face with the princes of heaven. But there is another aspect of the popular element as represented by the shepherds which has not perhaps been so fully developed; and which is more directly relevant here.

Men of the people, like the shepherds, men of the popular tradition, had everywhere been the makers of the mythologies. It was they who had felt most directly, with least check or chill from philosophy or the corrupt cults of civilisation, the need we have already considered; the images that were adventures of the imagination; the mythology that was a sort of search; the tempting and tantalising hints of something half-human in nature; the dumb significance of seasons and special places. They had best understood that the soul of a landscape is a story and the soul of a story is a personality. But rationalism had already begun to rot away these really irrational though imaginative treasures of the peasant; even as systematic slavery had eaten the peasant out of house and home. Upon all such peasantries everywhere there was descending a dusk and twilight of disappointment, in the hour when these few men discovered what they sought. Everywhere else Arcadia was fading from the forest. Pan was dead and the shepherds were scattered like sheep. And though no man knew it, the hour was near which was to end and to fulfil all things; and though no man heard it, there was one far-off cry in an unknown tongue upon the heaving wilderness of the mountains. The shepherds had found their Shepherd.

And the thing they found was of a kind with the things they sought. The populace had been wrong in many things; but they had not been wrong in believing that holy things could have a habitation and that divinity need not disdain the limits of time and space. And the barbarian who conceived the crudest fancy about the sun being stolen and hidden in a box, or the wildest myth about the god being rescued and his enemy deceived with a stone, was nearer to the secret of the cave and knew more about the crisis of the world, than all those in the circle of cities round the Mediterranean who had become content with cold abstractions or cosmopolitan generalisations; than all those who were spinning thinner and thinner threads of thought out of the transcendentalism of Plato or the orientalism of Pythagoras. The place that the shepherds found was not an academy or an abstract republic; it was not a place of myths allegorised or dissected or explained or explained away. It was a place of dreams come true. Since that hour no mythologies have been made in the world. Mythology is a search.

We all know that the popular presentation of this popular story, in so many miracle plays and carols, has given to the shepherds the costume, the language, and the landscape of the separate English and European countrysides. We all know that one shepherd will talk in a Somerset dialect or another talk of driving his sheep from Conway towards the Clyde. Most of us know by this time how true is that error, how wise, how artistic, how intensely Christian and Catholic is that anachronism. But some who have seen it in these scenes of medieval rusticity have perhaps not seen it in another sort of poetry, which it is sometimes the fashion to call artificial rather than artistic. I fear that many modern critics will see only a faded classicism in the fact that men like Crashaw and Herrick conceived the shepherds of Bethlehem under the form of the shepherds of Virgil. Yet they were profoundly right; and in turning their Bethlehem play into a Latin Eclogue they took up one of the most important links in human history. Virgil, as we have already seen, does stand for all that saner heathenism that had overthrown the insane heathenism of human sacrifice; but the very fact that even the Virgilian virtues and the sane heathenism were in incurable decay is the whole problem to which the revelation to the shepherds is the solution. If the world had ever had the chance to grow weary of being demoniac, it might have been healed merely by becoming sane. But if it had grown weary even of being sane, what was to happen, except what did happen? Nor is it false to conceive the Arcadian shepherd of the Eclogues as rejoicing in what did happen. One of the Eclogues has even been claimed as a prophecy of what did happen. But it is quite as much in the tone and incidental diction of the great poet that we feel the potential sympathy with the great event; and even in their own human phrases the voices of the Virgilian shepherds might more than once have broken upon more than the tenderness of Italy. . . . . *Incipe, parve puer, risu cognoscere matrem.* . . . . They might have found in that strange place all that was best in the last traditions of the Latins; and something better than a wooden idol standing up forever for the pillar of the human family; a household god. But they and all the other mythologists would be justified in rejoicing that the event had fulfilled not merely the mysticism but the materialism of mythology. Mythology had many sins; but it had not been wrong in being as carnal as the Incarnation. With something of the ancient voice that was supposed to have rung through the groves, it could cry again: 'We have seen, he hath seen us, a visible god.' So the ancient shepherds might have danced, and their feet have been beautiful upon the mountains, rejoicing over the philosophers. But the philosophers had also heard.

It is still a strange story, though an old one, how they came out of orient lands, crowned with the majesty of kings and clothed with something of the mystery of magicians. That truth that is tradition has wisely remembered them almost as unknown quantities, as mysterious as their mysterious and melodious names; Melchior, Caspar, Balthazar. But there came with them all that world of wisdom that had watched the stars in Chaldea and the sun in Persia; and we shall not be wrong if we see in them the same curiosity that moves all the sages. They would stand for the same human ideal if their names had really been Confucius or Pythagoras or Plato. They were those who sought not tales but the truth of things; and since their thirst for truth was itself a thirst for God, they also have had their reward. But even in order to understand that reward, we must understand that for philosophy as much as mythology, that reward was the completion of the incomplete.

Such learned men would doubtless have come, as these learned men did come, to find themselves confirmed in much that was true in their own traditions and right in their own reasoning. Confucius would have found a new foundation for the family in the very reversal of the Holy Family; Buddha would have looked upon a new renunciation, of stars rather than jewels and divinity than royalty. These learned men would still have the right to say, or rather a new right to say, that there was truth in their old teaching. But after all these learned men would have come to learn. They would have come to complete their conceptions with something they had not yet conceived; even to balance their imperfect universe with something they might once have contradicted. Buddha would have come from his impersonal paradise to worship a person. Confucius would have come from his temples of ancestor-worship to worship a child.

We must grasp from the first this character in the new cosmos; that it was larger than the old cosmos. In that sense Christendom is larger than creation; as creation had been before Christ. It included things that had not been there; it also included the things that had been there. The point happens to be well illustrated in this example of Chinese piety, but it would be true of other pagan virtues or pagan beliefs. Nobody can doubt that a reasonable respect for parents is part of a gospel in which God himself was subject in childhood to earthly parents. But the other sense in which the parents were subject to him does introduce an idea that is not Confucian. The infant Christ is not like the infant Confucius; our mysticism conceives him in an immortal infancy. I do not know what Confucius would have done with the Bambino, had it come to life in his arms as it did in the arms of St. Francis. But this is true in relation to all the other religions and philosophies; it is the challenge of the Church. The Church contains what the world does not contain. Life itself does not provide as she does for all sides of life. That every other single system is narrow and insufficient compared to this one; that is not a rhetorical boast; it is a real fact and a real dilemma. Where is the Holy Child amid the Stoics and the ancestor-worshippers? Where is Our Lady of the Moslems, a woman made for no man and set above all angels? Where is St. Michael of the monks of Buddha, rider and master of the trumpets, guarding for every soldier the honour of the sword? What could St. Thomas Aquinas do with the mythology of Brahminism, he who set forth all the science and rationality and even rationalism of Christianity? Yet even if we compare Aquinas with Aristotle, at the other extreme of reason, we shall find the same sense of something added. Aquinas could understand the most logical parts of Aristotle; it is doubtful if Aristotle could have understood the most mystical parts of Aquinas. Even where we can

59

hardly call the Christian greater, we are forced to call him larger. But it is so to whatever philosophy or heresy or modern movement we may turn. How would Francis the Troubadour have fared among the Calvinists, or for that matter among the Utilitarians of the Manchester School? Yet men like Bossuet and Pascal could be as stern and logical as any Calvinist or Utilitarian. How would St. Joan of Arc, a woman waving on men to war with the sword, have fared among the Quakers or the Doukhabors or the Tolstoyan sect of pacifists? Yet any number of Catholic saints have spent their lives in preaching peace and preventing wars. It is the same with all the modern attempts at Syncretism. They are never able to make something larger than the Creed without leaving something out. I do not mean leaving out something divine but something human; the flag or the inn or the boy's tale of battle or the hedge at the end of the field. The Theosophists build a pantheon; but it is only a pantheon for pantheists. They call a Parliament of Religions as a reunion of all the peoples; but it is only a reunion of all the prigs. Yet exactly such a pantheon had been set up two thousand years before by the shores of the Mediterranean; and Christians were invited to set up the image of Jesus side by side with the image of Jupiter, of Mithras, of Osiris, of Atys, or of Ammon. It was the refusal of the Christians that was the turning-point of history. If the Christians had accepted, they and the whole world would have certainly, in a grotesque but exact metaphor, gone to pot. They would all have been boiled down to one lukewarm liquid in that great pot of cosmopolitan corruption in which all the other myths and mysteries were already melting. It was an awful and an appalling escape. Nobody understands the nature of the Church, or the rising note of the creed descending from antiquity, who does not realise that the whole world once very nearly died of broadmindedness and the brotherhood of all religions.

Here it is the important point that the Magi, who stand for mysticism and philosophy, are truly conceived as seeking something new and even as finding something unexpected. That tense sense of crisis which still tingles in the Christmas story and even in every Christmas celebration, accentuates the idea of a search and a discovery. The discovery is, in this case, truly a scientific discovery. For the other mystical figures in the miracle play; for

the angel and the mother, the shepherds and the soldiers of
Herod, there may be aspects both simpler and more supernatural,
more elemental or more emotional. But the Wise Men must be
seeking wisdom; and for them there must be a light also in the
intellect. And this is the light; that the Catholic creed is catholic
and that nothing else is catholic. The philosophy of the Church
is universal. The philosophy of the philosophers was not universal. Had Plato and Pythagoras and Aristotle stood for an instant
in the light that came out of that little cave, they would have
known that their own light was not universal. It is far from certain, indeed, that they did not know it already. Philosophy also,
like mythology, had very much the air of a search. It is the
realisation of this truth that gives its traditional majesty and
mystery to the figures of the Three Kings; the discovery that
religion is broader than philosophy and that this is the broadest
of religions, contained within this narrow space. The Magicians
were gazing at the strange pentacle with the human triangle
reversed; and they have never come to the end of their calculations about it. For it is the paradox of that group in the cave,
that while our emotions about it are of childish simplicity, our
thoughts about it can branch with a never-ending complexity.
And we can never reach the end even of our own ideas about
the child who was a father and the mother who was a child.

We might well be content to say that mythology had come
with the shepherds and philosophy with the philosophers; and
that it only remained for them to combine in the recognisation
of religion. But there was a third element that must not be ignored
and one which that religion forever refuses to ignore, in any
revel or reconciliation. There was present in the primary scenes
of the drama that Enemy that had rotted the legends with lust
and frozen the theories into atheism, but which answered the
direct challenge with something of that more direct method
which we have seen in the conscious cult of the demons. In the
description of that demon-worship, of the devouring detestation
of innocence shown in the works of its witchcraft and the most
inhuman of its human sacrifice, I have said less of its indirect
and secret penetration of the saner paganism; the soaking of
mythological imagination with sex; the rise of imperial pride into
insanity. But both the indirect and the direct influence make

61

themselves felt in the drama of Bethlehem. A ruler under the Roman suzerainty, probably equipped and surrounded with the Roman ornament and order though himself of eastern blood, seems in that hour to have felt stirring within him the spirit of strange things. We all know the story of how Herod, alarmed at some rumour of a mysterious rival, remembered the wild gesture of the capricious despots of Asia and ordered a massacre of suspects of the new generation of the populace. Everyone knows the story; but not everyone has perhaps noted its place in the story of the strange religions of men. Not everybody has seen the significance even of its very contrast with the Corinthian columns and Roman pavement of that conquered and superficially civilised world. Only, as the purpose in his dark spirit began to show and shine in the eyes of the Idumean, a seer might perhaps have seen something like a great grey ghost that looked over his shoulder; have seen behind him filling the dome of night and hovering for the last time over history, that vast and fearful face that was Moloch of the Carthaginians; awaiting his last tribute from a ruler of the races of Shem. The demons also, in that first festival of Christmas, feasted after their own fashion.

Unless we understand the presence of that enemy, we shall not only miss the point of Christianity, but even miss the point of Christmas. Christmas for us in Christendom has become one thing, and in one sense even a simple thing. But like all the truths of that tradition, it is in another sense a very complex thing. Its unique note is the simultaneous striking of many notes; of humility, of gaiety, of gratitude, of mystical fear, but also of vigilance and of drama. It is not only an occasion for the peace-makers any more than for the merry-makers; it is not only a Hindu peace conference any more than it is only a Scandinavian winter feast. There is something defiant in it also; something that makes the abrupt bells at midnight sound like the great guns of a battle that has just been won. All this indescribable thing that we call the Christmas atmosphere only hangs in the air as something like a lingering fragrance or fading vapour from the exultant explosion of that one hour in the Judean hills nearly two thousand years ago. But the savour is still unmistakable, and it is something too subtle or too solitary to be covered by our use of the word peace. By the very nature of the story the rejoicings in the cavern were rejoicings in a fortress or an out-law's den; properly understood it is not unduly flippant to say they were rejoicings in a dug-out. It is not only true that such a subterranean chamber was a hiding-place from enemies; and that the enemies were already scouring the stony plain that lay above it like a sky. It is not only that the very horse-hoofs of Herod might in that sense have passed like thunder over the sunken head of Christ. It is also that there is in that image a true idea of an outpost, of a piercing through the rock and an entrance into an enemy territory. There is in this buried divinity an idea of *undermining* the world; of shaking the towers and palaces from below; even as Herod the great king felt that earthquake under him and swayed with his swaying palace.

That is perhaps the mightiest of the mysteries of the cave. It is already apparent that though men are said to have looked for hell under the earth, in this case it is rather heaven that is under the earth. And there follows in this strange story the idea of an upheaval of heaven. That is the paradox of the whole position; that henceforth the highest thing can only work from below. Royalty can only return to its own by a sort of rebellion. Indeed the Church from its beginnings, and perhaps especially in its beginnings, was not so much a principality as a revolution against the prince of the world. This sense that the world had been conquered by the great usurper, and was in his possession, has been deplored or derided by those optimists who identify enlightenment with ease. But it was responsible for all that thrill of defiance and a beautiful danger that made the good news seem to be really both good and new. It was in truth against a huge unconscious usurpation that it raised a revolt, and originally so obscure a revolt. Olympus still occupied the sky like a motionless cloud moulded into many mighty forms; philosophy still sat in the high places and even on the thrones of the kings, when Christ was born in the cave and Christianity in the catacombs.

In both cases we may remark the same paradox of revolu-tion; the sense of something despised and of something feared. The cave in one aspect is only a hole or corner into which the outcasts are swept like rubbish; yet in the other aspect it is a hiding-place of something valuable which the tyrants are seeking like treasure. In one sense they are there because the inn-keeper would not even remember them, and in another because the king can never forget them. We have already noted that this paradox appeared also in the treatment of the early Church. It was important while it was still insignificant, and certainly while it was still impotent. It was important solely because it was intolerable; and in that sense it is true to say that it was intolerable because it was intolerant. It was resented, because, in its own still and almost secret way, it had declared war. It had risen out of the ground to wreck the heaven and earth of heathenism. It did not try to destroy all that creation of gold and marble; but it contemplated a world without it. It dared to look right through it as though the gold and marble had been glass. Those who charged the Christians with burning down Rome with firebrands were slanderers; but they were at least far nearer to the nature of Christianity than those among the moderns who tell us that the Christians were a sort of ethical society, being martyred in a languid fashion for telling men they had a duty to their neighbours, and only disliked because they were meek and mild.

Herod had his place, therefore, in the miracle play of Bethlehem because he is the menace to the Church Militant and shows it from the first as under persecution and fighting for its life. For those who think this is a discord, it is a discord that sounds simultaneously with the Christmas bells. For those who think the idea of the Crusade is one that spoils the idea of the Cross, we can only say that for them the idea of the Cross is spoiled; the idea of the Cross is spoiled quite literally in the cradle. It is not here to the purpose to argue with them on the abstract ethics of fighting; the purpose in this place is merely to sum up the combination of ideas that make up the Christian and Catholic idea, and to note that all of them are already crystallised in the first Christmas story. They are three distinct and commonly contrasted things which are nevertheless one thing; but this is the only thing which can make them one. The first is the human instinct for a heaven that shall be as literal and almost as local as a home. It is the idea pursued by all poets and pagans making myths; that a particular place must be the shrine of the god or the abode of the blest; that fairyland is a land; or that the return of the ghost must be the resurrection of the body. I do not here reason about the refusal of rationalism to satisfy this need. I only say that if the rationalists refuse to satisfy it, the pagans will not be satisfied. This is present in the story of Bethlehem and Jerusalem as it is present in the story of Delos and Delphi; and as it is *not* present in the whole universe of Lucretius or the whole universe of Herbert Spencer. The second element is a philosophy *larger* than other philosophies; larger than that of Lucretius and infinitely larger than that of Herbert Spencer. It looks at the world through a hundred windows where the ancient stoic or the modern agnostic only looks through one. It sees life with thousands of eyes belonging to thousands of different sorts of people, where the other is only the individual standpoint of a stoic or an agnostic. It has something for all moods of man, it finds work for all kinds of men, it understands secrets of psychology, it is aware of depths of evil, it is able to distinguish between real and unreal marvels and miraculous exceptions, it trains itself in tact about hard cases, all with a multiplicity and subtlety and imagination about the varieties of life which is far beyond the bald or breezy platitudes of most ancient or modern moral philosophy. In a word, there is more in it; it finds more in existence to think about; it gets more out of life. Masses of this material about our many-sided life have been added since the time of St. Thomas Aquinas. But St. Thomas Aquinas alone would have found himself limited in the world of Confucius or Comte. And the third point is this; that while it is local enough for poetry and larger than any other philosophy, it is also a challenge and a fight. While it is deliberately broadened to embrace every aspect of truth, it is still stiffly embattled against every mode of error. It gets every kind of man to fight for it, it gets every kind of weapon to fight with, it widens its knowledge of the things that are fought for and against with every art of curiosity or sympathy; but it never forgets that it is fighting. It proclaims peace on earth and never forgets why there was war in heaven.

This is the trinity of truths symbolised here by the three types in the old Christmas story; the shepherds and the kings and that other king who warred upon the children. It is simply not true to say that other religions and philosophies are in this respect its rivals. It is not true to say that any one of them combines these characters; it is not true to say that any one of them pretends to combine them. Buddhism may profess to be equally mystical; it does not even profess to be equally military. Islam may profess to be equally military; it does not even profess to be equally metaphysical and subtle. Confucianism may profess to satisfy the need of the philosophers for order and reason; it does not even profess to satisfy the need of the mystics for miracle and sacrament and the consecration of concrete things. There are many evidences of this presence of a spirit at once universal and unique. One will serve here which is the symbol of the subject of this chapter; that no other story, no pagan legend or philosophical anecdote or historical event, does in fact affect any of us with that peculiar and even poignant impression produced on us by the word Bethlehem. No other birth of a god or childhood of a sage seems to us to be Christmas or anything like Christmas. It is either too cold or too frivolous, or too formal and classical, or too simple and savage, or too occult and complicated. Not one of us, whatever his opinions, would ever go to such a scene with the sense that he was going home. He might admire it because it was poetical, or because it was philosophical, or any number of other things in separation; but not because it was itself. The truth is that there is a quite peculiar and individual character about the hold of this story on human nature; it is not in its psychological substance at all like a mere legend or the life of a great man. It does not exactly in the ordinary sense turn our minds to greatness; to those extensions and exaggerations of humanity which are turned into gods and heroes, even by the healthiest sort of hero-worship. It does not exactly work outwards, adventurously, to the wonders to be found at the ends of the earth. It is rather something that surprises us from behind, from the hidden and personal part of our being; like that which can sometimes take us off our guard in the pathos of small objects or the blind pieties of the poor. It is rather as if a man had found an inner room in the very heart of his own house, which he had never suspected; and seen a light from within. It is as if he found something at the back of his own heart that betrayed him into good. It is not made of what the world would call strong materials; or rather it is made of materials whose strength is in that winged levity with which they brush us and pass. It is all that is in us but a brief tenderness that is there made eternal; all that means no more than a momentary softening that is in some strange fashion become a strengthening and a repose; it is the broken speech and the lost word that are made positive and suspended unbroken; as the strange kings fade into a far country and the mountains resound no more with the feet of the shepherds; and only the night and the cavern lie in fold upon fold over something more human than humanity.

II: THE RIDDLES OF THE GOSPEL

To understand the nature of this chapter, it is necessary to recur to the nature of this book. The argument which is meant to be the backbone of the book is of the kind called the *reductio ad absurdum*. It suggests that the results of assuming the rationalist thesis are more irrational than ours; but to prove it we must assume that thesis. Thus in the first section I often treated man as merely an animal, to show that the effect was more impossible than if he were treated as an angel. In the sense in which it was necessary to treat man merely as an animal, it is necessary to treat Christ merely as a man. I have to suspend my own beliefs, which are much more positive; and assume this limitation even in order to remove it. I must try to imagine what would happen to a man who did really read the story of Christ as the story of a man; and even of a man of whom he had never heard before. And I wish to point out that a really impartial reading of that kind would lead, if not immediately to belief, at least to a bewilderment of which there is really no solution except in belief. In this chapter, for this reason, I shall bring in nothing of the spirit of my own creed; I shall exclude the very style of diction, and even of lettering, which I should think fitting in speaking in my own person. I am speaking as an imaginary heathen human being, honestly, staring at the Gospel story for the first time.

Now it is not at all easy to regard the New Testament as a New Testament. It is not at all easy to realise the good news as new. Both for good and evil familiarity fills us with assumptions and associations; and no man of our civilisation, whatever he thinks of our religion, can really read the thing as if he had never heard of it before. Of course it is in any case utterly unhistorical to talk as if the New Testament were a neatly bound book that had fallen from heaven. It is simply the selection made by the authority of the Church from a mass of early Christian literature. But apart from any such question, there is a psychological difficulty in feeling the New Testament as new. There is a psychological difficulty in seeing those well-known words simply as they stand and without going beyond what they intrinsically stand for. And this difficulty must indeed be very great; for the result of it is very curious. The result of it is that most modern critics and most current criticism, even popular criticism, makes a comment that is the exact reverse of the truth. It is so completely the reverse of the truth that one could almost suspect that they had never read the New Testament at all.

We have all heard people say a hundred times over, for they seem never to tire of saying it, that the Jesus of the New Testament is indeed a most merciful and humane lover of humanity, but that the Church has hidden this human character in repellent dogmas and stiffened it with ecclesiastical terrors till it has taken on an inhuman character. This is, I venture to repeat, very nearly the reverse of the truth. The truth is that it is the image of Christ in the Churches that is almost entirely mild and merciful. It is the image of Christ in the Gospels that is a good many other things as well. The figure in the Gospels does indeed utter in words of almost heartbreaking beauty his pity for our broken hearts. But they are very far from being the only sort of words that he utters. Nevertheless they are almost the only kind of words that the Church in its popular imagery ever represents him as uttering. That popular imagery is inspired by a perfectly sound popular instinct. The mass of the poor are broken, and the mass of the people are poor, and for the mass of mankind the main thing is to carry the conviction of the incredible compassion of God. But nobody with his eyes open can doubt that it is chiefly this idea of compassion that the popular machinery of the Church does seek to carry. The popular imagery carries a great deal to excess the sentiment of 'Gentle Jesus, meek and mild.' It is the first thing that the outsider feels and criticises in a Pieta or a shrine of the Sacred Heart. As I say, while the art may be insufficient, I am not sure that the instinct is unsound. In any case there is something appalling, something that makes the blood run cold, in the idea of having a statue of Christ in wrath. There is something insupportable even to the imagination in the idea of turning the corner of a street or coming out into the spaces of a market-place, to meet the petrifying petrifaction of *that* figure as it turned upon a generation of vipers, or that face as it looked at the face of a hypocrite. The Church can reasonably be justified therefore if she turns the most merciful face or aspect towards men; but it is certainly the most merciful aspect that she does turn. And the point is here that it is very much more specially and exclusively merciful than any impression that could be formed by a man merely reading the New Testament for the first time. A man simply taking the words of the story as they stand would form quite another impression; an impression full of mystery and possibly of inconsistency; but certainly not merely an impression of mildness. It would be intensely interesting; but part of the interest would consist in its leaving a good deal to be guessed at or explained. It is full of sudden gestures evidently significant except that we hardly know what they signify; of enigmatic silences; of ironical replies. The outbreaks of wrath, like storms above our atmosphere, do not seem to break out exactly where we should expect them, but to follow some higher weather-chart of their own. The Peter whom popular Church teaching presents is very rightly the Peter to whom Christ said in forgiveness, 'Feed my lambs.' He is not the Peter upon whom Christ turned as if he were the devil, crying in that obscure wrath, 'Get thee behind me, Satan.' Christ lamented with nothing but love and pity over Jerusalem which was to murder him. We do not know what strange spiritual atmosphere or spiritual insight led him to sink Bethsaida lower in the pit than Sodom. I am putting aside for the moment all questions of doctrinal inferences or expositions, orthodox or otherwise; I am simply imagining the effect on a man's mind if he did really do what these critics are always talking about doing; if he did really read the New Testament without reference to orthodoxy and even without reference to doctrine. He would find a number of things which fit in far less with the current unorthodoxy than they do with the current orthodoxy. He would find, for instance, that if there are any descriptions that deserved to be called realistic, they are precisely the descriptions of the supernatural. If there is one aspect of the New Testament Jesus in which he may

69

be said to present himself eminently as a practical person, it is in the aspect of an exorcist. There is nothing meek and mild, there is nothing even in the ordinary sense mystical, about the tone of the voice that says 'Hold thy peace and come out of him.' It is much more like the tone of a very businesslike lion-tamer or a strong-minded doctor dealing with a homicidal maniac. But this is only a side issue for the sake of illustration; I am not now raising these controversies; but considering the case of the imaginary man from the moon to whom the New Testament is new.

Now the first thing to note is that if we take it merely as a human story, it is in some ways a very strange story. I do not refer here to its tremendous and tragic culmination or to any implications involving triumph in that tragedy. I do not refer to what is commonly called the miraculous element; for on that point philosophies vary and modern philosophies very decidedly waver. Indeed the educated Englishman of to-day may be said to have passed from an old fashion, in which he would not believe in any miracles unless they were ancient, and adopted a new fashion in which he will not believe in any miracles unless they are modern. He used to hold that miraculous cures stopped with the first Christians and is now inclined to suspect that they began with the first Christian Scientists. But I refer here rather specially to unmiraculous and even to unnoticed and inconspicuous parts of the story. There are a great many things about it which nobody would have invented, for they are things that nobody has ever made any particular use of; things which if they were remarked at all have remained rather as puzzles. For instance, there is that long stretch of silence in the life of Christ up to the age of thirty. It is of all silences the most immense and imaginatively impressive. But it is not the sort of thing that anybody is particularly likely to invent in order to prove something; and nobody so far as I know has ever tried to prove anything in particular from it. It is impressive, but it is only impressive as a fact; there is nothing particularly popular or obvious about it as a fable. The ordinary trend of hero-worship and myth-making is much more likely to say the precise opposite. It is much more likely to say (as I believe some of the gospels rejected by the Church do say) that Jesus displayed a divine precocity and began his mission at a miraculously early age. And there is indeed something strange in the thought that he who of all humanity needed least preparation seems to have had most. Whether it was some mode of the divine humility, or some truth of which we see the shadow in the longer domestic tutelage of the higher creatures of the earth, I do not propose to speculate; I mention it simply as an example of the sort of thing that does in any case give rise to speculations, quite apart from recognised religious speculations. Now the whole story is full of these things. It is not by any means, as badly presented in print, a story that it is easy to get to the bottom of. It is anything but what these people talk of as a simple Gospel. Relatively speaking, it is the Gospel that has the mysticism and the Church that has the rationalism. As I should put it, of course, it is the Gospel that is the riddle and the Church that is the answer. But whatever be the answer, the Gospel as it stands is almost a book of riddles.

First, a man reading the Gospel sayings would not find platitudes. If he had read even in the most respectful spirit the majority of ancient philosophers and of modern moralists, he would appreciate the unique importance of saying that he did not find platitudes. It is more than can be said even of Plato. It is much more than can be said of Epictetus or Seneca or Marcus Aurelius or Apollonius of Tyana. And it is immeasurable more than can be said of most of the agnostic moralists and the preachers of the ethical societies; with their songs of service and their religion of brotherhood. The morality of most moralists, ancient and modern, has been one solid and polished cataract of platitudes flowing forever and ever. That would certainly not be the impression of the imaginary independent outsider studying the New Testament. He would be conscious of nothing so commonplace and in a sense of nothing so continuous as that stream. He would find a number of strange claims that might sound like the claim to be the brother of the sun and moon; a number of very startling pieces of advice; a number of stunning rebukes; a number of strangely beautiful stories. He would see some very gigantesque figures of speech about the impossibility of threading a needle with a camel or the possibility of throwing a mountain into the sea. He would see a number of very daring simplifications of the difficulties of life; like the advice to shine upon everybody indifferently as does the sunshine or not to worry about the future any more than the birds. He would find on the other hand some passages of almost impenetrable darkness, so far as he is concerned, such as the moral of the parable of the Unjust Steward. Some of these things might strike him as fables and some as truths; but none as truisms. For instance, he would not find the ordinary platitudes in favour of peace. He would find several paradoxes in favour of peace. He would find several ideals of non-resistance, which taken as they stand would be rather too pacific for any pacifist. He would be told in one passage to treat a robber *not* with passive resistance, but rather with positive and enthusiastic encouragement, if the terms be taken literally; heaping up gifts upon the man who had stolen goods. But he would not find a word of all that obvious rhetoric against war which has filled countless books and odes and orations; not a word about the wickedness of war, the wastefulness of war, the appalling scale of the slaughter in war and all the rest of the familiar frenzy; indeed not a word about war at all. There is nothing that throws any particular light on Christ's attitude towards organised warfare, except that he seems to have been rather fond of Roman soldiers. Indeed it is another perplexity, speaking from the same external and human standpoint, that he seems to have got on much better with Romans than he did with Jews. But the question here is a certain tone to be appreciated by merely reading a certain text; and we might give any number of instances of it.

The statement that the meek shall inherit the earth is very far from being a meek statement. I mean it is not meek in the ordinary sense of mild and moderate and inoffensive. To justify it, it would be necessary to go very deep into history and anticipate things undreamed of then and by many unrealised even now; such as the way in which the mystical monks reclaimed the lands which the practical kings had lost. If it was a truth at all, it was because it was a prophecy. But certainly it was not a truth in the sense of a truism. The blessing upon the meek would seem to be a very violent statement; in the sense of doing violence to reason and probability. And with this we come to another important stage in the speculation. As a prophecy it really was fulfilled; but it was only fulfilled long afterwards. The monasteries were the most practical and prosperous estates and experiments in reconstruction after the barbaric deluge; the meek did really inherit the earth. But nobody could have known anything of the sort at the time—unless indeed there was one who knew. Something of the same thing may be said about the incident of Martha and Mary; which has been interpreted in retrospect and from the inside by the mystics of the Christian contemplative life. But it was not at all an obvious view of it; and most moralists, ancient and modern, could be trusted to make a rush for the obvious. What torrents of effortless eloquence would have flowed from them to swell any slight superiority on the part of Martha; what splendid sermons about the Joy of Service and the Gospel of Work and the World Left Better Than We Found It, and generally all the ten thousand platitudes that can be uttered in favour of taking trouble—by people who need take no trouble to utter them. If in Mary the mystic and child of love Christ was guarding the seed of something more subtle, who was likely to understand it at the time? Nobody else could have seen Clare and Catherine and Teresa shining above the little roof at Bethany. It is so in another way with that magnificent menace about bringing into the world a sword to sunder and divide. Nobody could have guessed then either how it could be fulfilled or how it could be justified. Indeed some freethinkers are still so simple as to fall into the trap and be shocked at a phrase so deliberately defiant. They actually complain of the paradox for not being a platitude.

But the point here is that if we *could* read the Gospel reports as things as new as newspaper reports, they would puzzle us and perhaps terrify us much *more* than the same things as developed by historical Christianity. For instance: Christ, after a clear allusion to the eunuchs of eastern courts, said there would be eunuchs of the kingdom of heaven. If this does not mean the voluntary enthusiasm of virginity, it could only be made to mean something much more unnatural or uncouth. It is the historical religion that humanises it for us by experience of Franciscans or Sisters of Mercy. The mere statement standing by itself might very well suggest a rather dehumanised atmosphere; the sinister and inhuman silence of the Asiatic harem and divan. This is but one instance out of scores; but the moral is that the Christ of the Gospel might actually seem more strange and terrible than the Christ of the Church.

I am dwelling on the dark or dazzling or defiant or mysterious side of the Gospel words, not because they had not obviously a more obvious and popular side, but because this is the answer to a common criticism on a vital point. The freethinker frequently says that Jesus of Nazareth was a man of his time, even if he was in advance of his time; and that we cannot accept his ethics as final for humanity. The freethinker then goes on to criticise his ethics, saying plausibly enough that men cannot turn the other cheek, or that they must take thought for the morrow, or that the self-denial is too ascetic or the monogamy too severe. But the Zealots and the Legionaries did not turn the other cheek any more than we do, if so much. The Jewish traders and Roman tax-gatherers took thought for the morrow as much as we, if not more. We cannot pretend to be abandoning the morality of the past for one more suited to the present. It is certainly not the morality of another age, but it might be of another world.

In short, we can say that these ideals are impossible in themselves. Exactly what we cannot say is that they are impossible for us. They are rather notably marked by a mysticism which, if it be a sort of madness, would always have struck the same sort of people as mad. Take, for instance, the case of marriage and the relations of the sexes. It might very well have been true that a Galilean teacher taught things natural to a Galilean environment; but it is not. It might rationally be expected that a man in the time of Tiberius would have advanced a view conditioned by the time of Tiberius; but he did not. What he advanced was something quite different; something very difficult; but something no more difficult now than it was then. When, for instance, Mahomet made his polygamous compromise we may reasonably say that it was conditioned by a polygamous society. When he allowed a man four wives he was really doing something suited to the circumstances, which might have been less suited to other circumstances. Nobody will pretend that the four wives were like the four winds, something seemingly a part of the order of nature; nobody will say that the figure four was written forever in stars upon the sky. But neither will anyone say that the figure four is an inconceivable ideal; that it is beyond

74

the power of the mind of man to count up to four; or to count the number of his wives and see whether it amounts to four. It is a practical compromise carrying with it the character of a particular society. If Mahomet had been born in Acton in the nineteenth century, we may well doubt whether he would instantly have filled that suburb with harems of four wives apiece. As he was born in Arabia in the sixth century, he did in his conjugal arrangements suggest the conditions of Arabia in the sixth century. But Christ in his view of marriage does not in the least suggest the conditions of Palestine in the first century. He does not suggest anything at all, except the sacramental view of marriage as developed long afterwards by the Catholic Church. It was quite as difficult for people then as for people now. It was much more puzzling to people then than to people now. Jews and Romans and Greeks did not believe, and did not even understand enough to disbelieve, the mystical idea that the man and the woman had become one sacramental substance. We may think it an incredible or impossible ideal; but we cannot think it any more incredible or impossible than they would have thought it. In other words, whatever else is true, it is not true that the controversy has been altered by time. Whatever else is true, it is emphatically not true that the ideas of Jesus of Nazareth were suitable to his time, but are no longer suitable to our time. Exactly how suitable they were to his time is perhaps suggested in the end of his story.

The same truth might be stated in another way by saying that if the story be regarded as merely human and historical, it is extraordinary how very little there is in the recorded words of Christ that ties him at all to his own time. I do not mean the details of a period, which even a man of the period knows to be passing. I mean the fundmentals which even the wisest man often vaguely assumes to be eternal. For instance, Aristotle was perhaps the wisest and most wide-minded man who ever lived. He founded himself entirely upon fundamentals, which have been generally found to remain rational and solid through all social and historical changes. Still, he lived in a world in which it was thought as natural to have slaves as to have children. And therefore he did permit himself a serious recognition of a difference between slaves and free men. Christ as much as Aristotle lived in a world that took slavery for granted. He did not particularly denounce slavery. He started a movement that could exist in a world with slavery. But he started a movement that could exist in a world without slavery. He never used a phrase that made his philosophy depend even upon the very existence of the social order in which he lived. He spoke as one conscious that everything was ephemeral, including the things that Aristotle thought eternal. By that time the Roman Empire had come to be merely the *orbis terrarum*, another name for the world. But he never made his morality dependent on the existence of the Roman Empire or even on the existence of the world. 'Heaven and earth shall pass away; but my words shall not pass away.'

The truth is that, when critics have spoken of the local limitations of the Galilean, it has always been a case of the local limitations of the critics. He did undoubtedly believe in certain things that one particular modern sect of materialists do not believe. But they were not things particularly peculiar to his time. It would be nearer the truth to say that the denial of them is quite peculiar to our time. Doubtless it would be nearer still to the truth to say merely that a certain solemn social importance, in the minority disbelieving them, is peculiar to our time. He believed, for instance, in evil spirits or in the psychic healing of bodily ills; but not because he was a Galilean born under Augustus. It is absurd to say that a man believed things because he was a Galilean under Augustus when he might have believed the same things if he had been an Egyptian under Tutankhamen or an Indian under Gengis Khan. But with this general question of the philosophy of diabolism or of divine miracles I deal elsewhere. It is enough to say that the materialists have to prove the impossibility of miracles against the testimony of all mankind, not against the prejudices of provincials in North Palestine under the first Roman Emperors. What they have to prove, for the present argument, is the presence in the Gospels of those particular prejudices of those particular provincials. And, humanly speaking, it is astonishing how little they can produce even to make a beginning of proving it.

So it is in this case of the sacramental marriage. We may not believe in sacraments, as we may not believe in spirits, but it is quite clear that Christ believed in this sacrament in his own way and not in any current or contemporary way. He certainly did not get his argument against divorce from the Mosaic law or the Roman law or the habits of the Palestinian people. It would appear to his critics then exactly what it appears to his critics now; an arbitrary and transcendental dogma coming from nowhere save in the sense that it came from him. I am not at all concerned here to defend that dogma; the point here is that it is just as easy to defend it now as it was to defend it then. It is an ideal altogether outside time; difficult at any period; impossible at no period. In other words, if anyone says it is what might be expected of a man walking about in that place at that period, we can quite fairly answer that it is much *more* like what might be the mysterious utterance of a being beyond man, if he walked alive among men.

I maintain therefore that a man reading the New Testament frankly and freshly would *not* get the impression of what is now often meant by a human Christ. The merely human Christ is a made-up figure, a piece of artificial selection, like the merely evolutionary man. Moreover there have been too many of these human Christs found in the same story, just as there have been too many keys to mythology found in the same stories. Three or four separate schools of rationalism have worked over the ground and produced three or four equally rational explanations of his life. The first rational explanation of his life was that he never lived. And this in turn gave an opportunity for three or four different explanations; as that he was a sun-myth or a corn-myth, or any other kind of myth that is also a monomania. Then the idea that he was a divine being who did not exist gave place to the idea that he was a human being who did exist. In my youth it was the fashion to say that he was merely an ethical teacher in the manner of the Essenes, who had apparently nothing very much to say that Hillel or a hundred other Jews might not have said; as that it is a kindly thing to be kind and an assistance to purification to be pure. Then somebody said he was a madman with a Messianic delusion. Then others said he was indeed an original teacher because he cared about nothing but Socialism; or (as others said) about nothing but Pacifism. Then a more grimly scientific character appeared who said that Jesus would never have been heard of at all except for his prophecies of the end of the world. He was important merely as a Millennarian like Dr. Cumming; and created a provincial scare by announcing the exact date of the crack of doom. Among other variants on the same theme was the theory that he was a spiritual healer and nothing else; a view implied by Christian Science, which has really to expound a Christianity without the Crucifixion in order to explain the curing of Peter's wife's mother or the daughter of a centurion. There is another theory that concentrates entirely on the business of diabolism and what it would call the contemporary superstition about demoniacs; as if Christ, like a young deacon taking his first orders, had got as far as exorcism and never got any further. Now each of these explanations in itself seems to me singularly inadequate; but taken together they do suggest something of the very mystery which they miss. There must surely have been something not only mysterious but many-sided about Christ if so many smaller Christs can be carved out of him. If the Christian Scientist is satisfied with him as a spiritual healer and the Christian Socialist is satisfied with him as a social reformer, so satisfied that they do not even expect him to be anything else, it looks as if he really covered rather more ground than they could be expected to expect. And it does seem to suggest that there might be more than they fancy in these other mysterious attributes of casting out devils or prophesying doom.

Above all, would not such a new reader of the New Testament stumble over something that would startle him much more than it startles us? I have here more than once attempted the rather impossible task of reversing time and the historic method; and in fancy looking forward to the facts, instead of backward through the memories. So I have imagined the monster that man might have seemed at first to the mere nature around him. We should have a worse shock if we really imagined the nature of Christ named for the first time. What should we feel at the first whisper of a certain suggestion about a certain man? Certainly it is not for us to blame anybody who should find that first wild whisper merely impious and insane. On the contrary, stumbling on that rock of scandal is the first step. Stark staring incredulity is a far more loyal tribute to that truth than a modernist metaphysic that would make it out merely a matter of degree. It were better to rend our robes with a great cry against blasphemy, like Caiaphas in the judgment, or to lay hold of the man as a maniac possessed of devils like the kinsmen and the crowd, rather than to stand stupidly debating fine shades of pantheism in the presence of so catastrophic a claim. There is more of the wisdom that is one with surprise in any simple person, full of the sensitiveness of simplicity, who should expect the grass to wither and the birds to drop dead out of the air, when a strolling carpenter's apprentice said calmly and almost carelessly, like one looking over his shoulder: 'Before Abraham was, I am.'

CONCLUSION: THE SUMMARY OF THIS BOOK

I have taken the liberty once or twice of borrowing the excellent phrase about an Outline of History; though this study of a special truth and a special error can of course claim no sort of comparison with the rich and many-sided encyclopedia of history, for which that name was chosen. And yet there is a certain reason in the reference; and a sense in which the one thing touches and even cuts across the other. For the story of the world as told by Mr. Wells could here only be criticised as an outline. And, strangely enough, it seems to me that it is only wrong as an outline. It is admirable as an accumulation of history; it is splendid as a storehouse or treasury of history; it is a fascinating disquisition on history; it is most attractive as an amplification of history; but it is quite false as an outline of history. The one thing that seems to me quite wrong about it is the outline; the sort of outline that can really be a single line, like that which makes all the difference between a caricature of the profile of Mr. Winston Churchill and of Sir Alfred Mond. In simple and homely language, I mean the things that stick out; the things that make the simplicity of a silhouette. I think the proportions are wrong; the proportions of what is certain as compared with what is uncertain, of what played a great part as compared with what played a smaller part, of what is ordinary and what is extraordinary, of what really lies level with an average and what stands out as an exception.

I do not say it as a small criticism of a great writer, and I have no reason to do so; for in my own much smaller task I feel I have failed in very much the same way. I am very doubtful whether I have conveyed to the reader the main point I meant about the proportions of history, and why I have dwelt so much more on some things than others. I doubt whether I have clearly fulfilled the plan that I set out in the introductory chapter; and for that reason I add these lines as a sort of summary in a concluding chapter. I do believe that the things on which I have insisted are more essential to an outline of history than the things which I have subordinated or dismissed. I do not believe that the past is most truly pictured as a thing in which humanity merely fades away into nature, or civilisation merely fades away into barbarism, or religion fades away into mythology, or our own religion fades away into the religions of the world. In short I do not believe that the best way to produce an outline of history is to rub out the lines. I believe that, of the two, it would be far nearer the truth to tell the tale very simply, like a primitive myth about a man who made the sun and stars or a god who entered the body of a sacred monkey. I will therefore sum up all that has gone before in what seems to me a realistic and reasonably proportioned statement; the short story of mankind.

In the land lit by that neighbouring star, whose blaze is the broad daylight, there are many and very various things, motionless and moving. There moves among them a race that is in its relation to others a race of gods. The fact is not lessened but emphasised because it can behave like a race of demons. Its distinction is not an individual illusion, like one bird pluming itself on its own plumes; it is a solid and a many-sided thing. It is demonstrated in the very speculations that have led to its being denied. That men, the gods of this lower world, are linked with it in various ways is true; but it is another aspect of the same truth. That they grow as the grass grows and walk as the beasts walk is a secondary necessity that sharpens the primary distinction. It is like saying that a magician must after all have the appearance of a man; or that even the fairies could not dance without feet. It has lately been the fashion to focus the mind entirely on these mild and subordinate resemblances and to forget the main fact altogether. It is customary to insist that man resembles the other creatures. Yes; and that very resemblance he alone can see. The fish does not trace the fish-bone pattern in the fowls of the air; or the elephant and the emu compare skeletons. Even in the sense in which man is at one with the universe it is an utterly lonely universality. The very sense that he is united with all things is enough to sunder him from all.

Looking around him by this unique light, as lonely as the literal flame that he alone has kindled, this demigod or demon of the visible world makes that world visible. He sees around him a world of a certain style or type. It seems to proceed by certain rules or at least repetitions. He sees a green architecture that builds itself without visible hands; but which builds itself into a very exact plan or pattern, like a design already drawn in the air by an invisible finger. It is not, as is now vaguely suggested, a vague thing. It is not a growth or a groping of blind life. Each seeks an end; a glorious and radiant end, even for every daisy or dandelion we see in looking across the level of a common field. In the very shape of things there is more than green growth; there is the finality of the flower. It is a world of crowns. This impression, whether or not it be an illusion, has so profoundly influenced this race of thinkers and masters of the material world, that the vast majority have been moved to take a certain view of that world. They have concluded, rightly or wrongly, that the world had a plan as the tree seemed to have a plan; and an end and crown like the flower. But so long as the race of thinkers was able to think, it was obvious that the admission of this idea of a plan brought with it another thought more thrilling and even terrible. There was someone else, some strange and unseen being, who had designed these things, if indeed they were designed. There was a stranger who was also a friend; a mysterious benefactor who had been before them and built up the woods and hills for their coming, and had kindled the sunrise against their rising, as a servant kindles a fire. Now this idea of a mind that gives a meaning to the universe has received more and more confirmation within the minds of men, by meditations and experiences much more subtle and searching than any such argument about the external plan of the world. But I am concerned here with keeping the story in its most simple and even concrete terms; and it is enough to say here that most men, including the wisest men, have come to the conclusion that the world has such a final purpose and therefore such a first cause. But most men in some sense separated themselves from the wisest men, when it came to the treatment of that idea. There came into existence two ways of treating that idea; which between them make up most of the religious history of the world.

The majority, like the minority, had this strong sense of a second meaning in things; of a strange master who knew the secret of the world. But the majority, the mob or mass of men, naturally tended to treat it rather in the spirit of gossip. The gossip, like all gossip, contained a great deal of truth and falsehood. The world began to tell itself tales about the unknown being or his sons or servants or messengers. Some of the tales may truly be called old wives' tales; as professing only to be very remote memories of the morning of the world; myths about the baby moon or the half-baked mountains. Some of them might more truly be called travellers' tales; as being curious but contemporary tales brought from certain borderlands of experience; such as miraculous cures or those that bring whispers of what has happened to the dead. Many of them are probably true tales; enough of them are probably true to keep a person of real common sense more or less conscious that there really is something rather marvellous behind the cosmic curtain. But in a sense it is only going by appearances; even if the appearances are called apparitions. It is a matter of appearances—and disappearances. At the most these gods are ghosts; that is, they are glimpses. And for the rest, the whole world is full of rumours, most of which are almost avowedly romances. The great majority of the tales about gods and ghosts and the invisible king are told, if not for the sake of the tale, at least for the sake of the topic. They are evidence of the eternal interest of the theme; they are not evidence of anything else, and they are not meant to be. They are mythology or the poetry that is not bound in books— or bound in any other way.

Meanwhile the minority, the sages or thinkers, had withdrawn apart and had taken up an equally congenial trade. They were drawing up plans of the world; of the world which all believed to have a plan. They were trying to set forth the plan seriously and to scale. They were setting their minds directly to the mind that had made the mysterious world; considering what sort of a mind it might be and what its ultimate purpose might be. Some of them made that mind much more impersonal than mankind has generally made it; some simplified it almost to a blank; a few, a very few, doubted it altogether. One or two of the more morbid fancied that it might be evil and an enemy; just one or two of the more degraded in the other class worshipped demons instead of gods. But most of these theorists were theists: and they not only saw a moral plan in nature, but they generally laid down a moral plan for humanity. Most of them were good men who did good work: and they were remembered and reverenced in various ways. They were scribes; and their scriptures became more or less holy scriptures. They were law-givers; and their tradition became not only legal but ceremonial. We may say that they received divine honours, in the sense in which kings and great captains in certain countries often received divine honours. In a word, wherever the other popular spirit, the spirit of legend and gossip, could come into play, it surrounded them with the more mystical atmosphere of the myths. Popular poetry turned the sages into saints. But that was all it did. They remained themselves; men never really forgot that they were men, only made into gods in the sense that they were made into heroes. Divine Plato, like Divus Caesar, was a title and not a dogma. In Asia, where the atmosphere was more mythological, the man was made to look more like a myth, but he remained a man. He remained a man of a certain special class or school of men, receiving and deserving great honour from mankind. It is the order or school of the philosophers; the men who have set themselves seriously to trace the order across any apparent chaos in the vision of life. Instead of living on imaginative rumours and remote traditions and the tail-end of exceptional experiences about the mind and meaning behind the world, they have tried in a sense to project the primary purpose of that mind *a priori*. They have tried to put on paper a possible plan of the world; almost as if the world were not yet made.

Right in the middle of all these things stands up an enormous exception. It is quite unlike anything else. It is a thing final like the trump of doom, though it is also a piece of good news; or news that seems too good to be true. It is nothing less than the loud assertion that this mysterious maker of the world has visited his world in person. It declares that really and even recently, or right in the middle of historic times, there did walk into the world this original invisible being; about whom the thinkers made theories and the mythologists hand down myths; the Man Who Made the World. That such a higher personality exists behind all things had indeed always been implied by all the best thinkers, as well as by all the most beautiful legends. But nothing of this sort had ever been implied in any of them. It is simply false to say that the other sages and heroes had claimed to be that mysterious master and maker, of whom the world had dreamed and disputed. Not one of them had ever claimed to be anything of the sort. Not one of their sects or schools had ever claimed that they had claimed to be anything of the sort. The most that any religious prophet had said was that he was the true servant of such a being. The most that any visionary had ever said was that men might catch glimpses of the glory of that spiritual being; or much more often of lesser spiritual beings. The most that any primitive myth had ever suggested was that the Creator was present at the Creation. But that the Creator was present at scenes a little subsequent to the supper-parties of Horace, and talked with tax-collectors and government officials in the detailed daily life of the Roman Empire, and that this fact continued to be firmly asserted by the whole of that great civilisation for more than a thousand years—that is something utterly unlike anything else in nature. It is the one great startling statement that man has made since he spoke his first articulate word, instead of barking like a dog. Its unique character can be used as an argument against it as well as for it. It would be easy to concentrate on it as a case of isolated insanity; but it makes nothing but dust and nonsense of comparative religion.

It came on the world with a wind and rush of running messengers proclaiming that apocalyptic portent; and it is not unduly fanciful to say that they are running still. What puzzles the world, and its wise philosophers and fanciful pagan poets, about the priests and people of the Catholic Church is that they still behave as if they were messengers. A messenger does not dream about what his message might be, or argue about what it probably would be; he delivers it as it is. It is not a theory or a fancy but a fact. It is not relevant to this intentionally rudimentary outline to prove in detail that it is a fact; but merely to point out that these messengers do deal with it as men deal with a fact. All that is condemned in Catholic tradition, authority, and dogmatism and the refusal to retract and modify, are but the natural human attributes of a man with a message relating to a fact. I desire to avoid in this last summary all the controversial complexities that may once more cloud the simple lines of that strange story; which I have already called, in words that are much too weak, the strangest story in the world. I desire merely to mark those main lines and specially to mark where the great line is really to be drawn. The religion of the world, in its right proportions, is not divided into fine shades of mysticism or more or less rational forms of mythology. It is divided by the line between the men who are bringing that message and the men who have not yet heard it, or cannot yet believe it.

But when we translate the terms of that strange tale back into the more concrete and complicated terminology of our time, we find it covered by names and memories of which the very familiarity is a falsification. For instance, when we say that a country contains so many Moslems, we really mean that it contains so many monotheists; and we really mean, by that, that it contains so many men; men with the old average assumption of men—that the invisible ruler remains invisible. They hold it along with the customs of a certain culture and under the simpler laws of a certain law-giver; but so they would if their law-giver were Lycurgus or Solon. They testify to something which is a necessary and noble truth; but was never a new truth. Their creed is not a new colour; it is the neutral and normal tint that is the background of the many-coloured life of man. Mahomet did not, like the Magi, find a new star; he saw through his own particular window a glimpse of the great grey field of the ancient star-light. So when we say that the country contains so many Confucians or Buddhists, we mean it contains so many pagans whose prophets have given them another and rather vaguer version of the invisible power; making it not only invisible but almost impersonal. When we say that they also have temples and idols and priests and periodical festivals, we simply mean that this sort of heathen is enough of a human being to admit the popular element of pomp and pictures and feasts and fairy-tales. We only mean that Pagans have more sense than Puritans. But what the gods are supposed to *be*, what the priests are commissioned to *say*, is not a sensational secret like what those running messengers of the Gospel had to say. Nobody else except those messengers has any Gospel; nobody else has any good news; for the simple reason that nobody else has any news.

Those runners gather impetus as they run. Ages afterwards they still speak as if something had just happened. They have not lost the speed and momentum of messengers; they have hardly lost, as it were, the wild eyes of witnesses. In the Catholic Church, which is the cohort of the message, there are still those headlong acts of holiness that speak of something rapid and recent; a self-sacrifice that startles the world like a suicide. But it is not a suicide; it is not pessimistic; it is still as optimistic as St. Francis of the flowers and birds. It is newer in spirit than the newest schools of thought; and it is almost certainly on the eve of new triumphs. For these men serve a mother who seems to grow more beautiful as new generations rise up and call her blessed. We might sometimes fancy that the Church grows younger as the world grows old.

For this is the last proof of the miracle; that something so supernatural should have become so natural. I mean that anything so unique when seen from the outside should only seem universal when seen from the inside. I have not minimised the scale of the miracle, as some of our milder theologians think it wise to do. Rather I have deliberately dwelt on that incredible interruption, as a blow that broke the very backbone of history. I have great sympathy with the monotheists, the Moslems, or the Jews, to whom it seems a blasphemy; a blasphemy that might shake the world. But it did not shake the world; it steadied the world. That fact, the more we consider it, will seem more solid and more strange. I think it a piece of plain justice to all the unbelievers to insist upon the audacity of the act of faith that is demanded of them. I willingly and warmly agree that it is, in itself, a suggestion at which we might expect even the brain of the believer to reel, when he realised his own belief. But the brain of the believer does not reel; it is the brains of the unbelievers that reel. We can see their brains reeling on every side and into every extravagance of ethics and psychology; into pessimism and the denial of life; into pragmatism and the denial of logic; seeking their omens in nightmares and their canons in contradictions; shrieking for fear at the far-off sight of things beyond good and evil, or whispering of strange stars where two and two make five. Meanwhile this solitary thing that seems at first so outrageous in outline remains solid and sane in substance. It remains the moderator of all these manias; rescuing reason from the Pragmatists exactly as it rescued laughter from the Puritans. I repeat that I have deliberately emphasised its intrinsically defiant and dogmatic character. The mystery is how anything so startling should have remained defiant and dogmatic and yet become perfectly normal and natural. I have admitted freely that, considering the incident in itself, a man who says he is God may be classed with a man who says he is glass. But the man who says he is glass is not a glazier making windows for all the world. He does not remain for after ages as a shining and crystalline figure, in whose light everything is as clear as crystal.

But this madness has remained sane. The madness has remained sane when everything else went mad. The madhouse has been a house to which, age after age, men are continually coming back as to a home. That is the riddle that remains; that anything so abrupt and abnormal should still be found a habitable and hospitable thing. I care not if the sceptic says it is a tall story; I cannot see how so toppling a tower could stand so long without foundation. Still less can I see how it could become, as it has become, the home of man. Had it merely appeared and disappeared; it might possibly have been remembered or explained as the last leap of the rage of illusion, the ultimate myth of the ultimate mood, in which the mind struck the sky and broke. But the mind did not break. It is the one mind that remains unbroken in the break-up of the world. If it were an error, it seems as if the error could hardly have lasted a day. If it were a mere ecstasy, it would seem that such an ecstasy could not endure for an hour. It has endured for nearly two thousand years; and the world within it has been more lucid, more level-headed, more reasonable in its hopes, more healthy in its instincts, more humourous and cheerful in the face of fate and death, than all the world outside. For it was the soul of Christendom that came forth from the incredible Christ; and the soul of it was common sense. Though we dared not look on His face we could look on His fruits; and by His fruits we should know Him. The fruits are solid and the fruitfulness is much more than a metaphor; and nowhere in this sad world are boys happier in apple-trees, or men in more equal chorus singing as they tread the vine, than under the fixed flash of this instant and intolerant enlightenment; the lightening made eternal as the light.

Francis Xavier Durrwell
1912-

Francis X. Durrwell was born in Alsace, France, in 1912. He joined the Redemptorists, was ordained a priest, and took a degree at the Biblical Institute in Rome, after which he taught for twelve years in the seminary of his order.

When The Resurrection *was first published in France in 1950, it was an immediate success. In retrospect those were not very happy days for the Catholic theological renewal. Pius XII's* Humani Generis *had had a depressing effect and several of the promising French thinkers were under a shadow. So Durrwell's book was something of a harbinger of better days. By 1960, when it was translated into English by Rosemary Sheed, it had gone into its fifth French edition, and Pope John XXIII had announced plans for Vatican II.*

The power of the book lies in its constant proximity to the New Testament texts. It is obviously the fruit of long reflection, the kind of work that only matures gradually. Its popular reception can only be interpreted as proof that it set forth an idea whose time had come. As the author says in his Foreword, "Not so long ago theologians used to study the Redemption without mentioning the Resurrection at all. The fact of Easter was made to yield its utmost value as a piece of apologetics; but no one thought of examining it in itself as one of the inexhaustible mysteries of our salvation."

It was not only the content but also the timing of Durrwell's book that accounts for its impact. The renewal of the theology of the Resurrection obviously goes hand in hand with the renewal of the Liturgy, especially that of Easter and Holy Week. So the work can be seen as part of the coalition of movements building up the call for reform that found expression in Vatican II.

But the book's greatest significance is in its method. Subtitled "A Biblical Study," it arrived on the theological scene as something quite unprecedented in recent Catholic theology. The author stated that he was not writing for specialists in biblical theology but rather that he wanted to offer a doctrinal synthesis for the use of speculative theologians and pastors. But Durrwell was overly modest in this regard. There was not a biblical theologian in sight who had demonstrated either the interest or the ability in achieving the masterly synthesis he had attempted.

The book is organized into nine chapters which focus so closely on the New Testament texts from different angles that there is bound to be some overlap and repetition. The style is sometimes dense, and subsequent studies have understood some passages in other ways, so that in these respects Durrwell's work shows some signs of age. But that cannot detract from the role it played in its early days, introducing many to a richer, more biblical theological style, preparing the way for integrating doctrine and liturgy, and in general deepening appreciation for the role of the Risen Christ.

The selection that follows is from chapter four, "The Effects of the Resurrection in Christ," the first two parts, exploring the rich meaning of two of the great New Testament titles of Christ: first, "Lord," and then "Son of God."

THE RESURRECTION

CHAPTER IV

THE EFFECTS OF THE RESURRECTION IN CHRIST

When our Lord died, the centurion bore witness that "indeed this man was a son of God." (Matt. xxvii. 54; Mark xv. 39.) Throughout the day he had heard the Son of God talked of; the expression seemed to him well fitted to express his admiration, but it did not hold for him the depths of meaning it came to have later. St. Luke suggests the sort of meaning the legionary must have intended, when he attributes to him the comment: "Indeed this was a just man." (xxiii. 47.) When Thomas the Apostle saw Christ again after his resurrection, he fell upon his knees: "My Lord and my God!" (John xx. 28.) These were two characteristic reactions to Christ, the one before the Resurrection, the other after it. A change had taken place in Christ which called for a deepening of the evaluation made of him before.

Henceforth two titles were to stand out in the minds of those who believed in Christ, "Lord" (*Kyrios*), and "True Son of God". The Epistle to the Hebrews drew from its study of the resurrection a third title to add to these: "Eternal Priest".

I. CHRIST THE LORD

The word *kyrios* ("lord") and its Semitic equivalents, *mar* and *adon*, indicate legitimate domination and power, and originally meant, "Master", or, more strongly, "Sovereign".

The Septuagint uses it for God in place of the ineffable name Iahweh, for Iahweh is the legitimate master, lord and absolute sovereign of Israel and of the universe. The title thus gains a sense of transcendence, though its application is never restricted to the Divinity as such, for it continues primarily to express power and domination.

In the ancient East, the Semitic term had long had two possible evocations. On the one hand, it had become the formal title for kings, and on the other, it was used for sovereign gods. The late Hellenistic period inherited this, and bestowed the title of "lord" upon its kings and some of its gods. Thus the commonly accepted meaning of the word was not unlike that given it by the Septuagint, but lacked its solemn majesty.

As a royal title, the name was fitting for the Messiah, the supreme king; and in him it also rose to its religious significance, because of the transcendence prophesied for the hero of Israel.

The Septuagint gave him this title, speaking of "the Lord, [Iahweh] Father of my Lord [the Messiah]". (Ecclus. li. 14.) In so doing, it took its inspiration from Psalm cx. 1: "The Lord said to my Lord: Sit thou at my right hand." Our Lord was later to give this same interpretation of the psalm, and the fact that his enemies did not contradict him suggests that this was the accepted exegesis, and that the Palestinian Jew also called the Messiah his "lord".

For Christians Christ was this divine King-Messiah. The earliest Palestinian communities called him "Maran" (our Lord") and the Greek communities proclaimed him "Kyrios".

In the first public profession of faith in Christ we read: "Let all the house of Israel know most certainly that God hath made both Lord and Christ this same Jesus whom you have crucified." (Acts ii. 36.) In St. Peter's mind the two terms are even more closely joined: God has made Jesus the Lord-Messiah.

Following what must have been a recognized proceeding among the Hellenic communities, St. Paul applies to our Lord those texts of the Old Testament in which "Kyrios" takes the place of the name of Iahweh. This title is not equivalent to the name of God here any more than it is in the Septuagint; it only indicates lordship, but in this case it is the lordship of God.

The words "Christ" and "Lord" suggest each other. The lordly title affirms his transcendence, his equality with Iahweh, but in the sense of a messianic transcendence; it conjures up the royal exercise of divine lieutenancy in the world.

i. Christ the Lord in the Synoptics and the Acts

If this is the case, the royal and sacred title must have been applied to our Lord from the first moment when his disciples recognized the messianism of their rabbi. The evidence for this was slow to win their minds and was at first sporadic and without great display. Peter's messianic profession (Matt. xvi. 16) was the result of a special enlightenment of his own. To many people the claim to messiahship appeared ridiculous. "Prophesy unto us, O Christ!" (Matt. xxvi. 68); "Hail king!" (Matt. xxvii. 29.) Christ did not claim the title of Lord and those around him only used it in a weakened sense, rather the same as "Rabbi" or "Master".

However, Christ did give himself this title on one occasion, claiming also the glory of lordship and sovereignty over all things. He told two of the disciples to go and get him a mount: "And if any man shall say to you, What are you doing? say ye that the Lord hath need of him." (Mark xi. 3.) He entered into the Holy City, the city of King David, amid messianic acclamation: "Hosanna, blessed is he that cometh in the name of the Lord!" It was a day when all things bowed to the will of God, and if men were silent the very stones would cry out. (Luke xix. 40.) It was a Sunday, and God was anticipating by exactly a week the glory of Christ's coming.

From Easter onwards, "Kyrios" became the characteristic title of Christ. His glorification revealed the sovereign lordship of this man—a revelation which, true to God's way of doing things, came not so much by verbal affirmation as by realization. "This statement that Christ is Lord because of the Resurrection is a thread running throughout the New Testament." The preaching of the Apostles, from the beginning, consistently linked the exercise of lordly power with the exaltation of the Saviour. "For the Apostle [St. Paul] as for the first community of Christians, it is invariably the Resurrection that has established Christ in his power as Kyrios."

Christ had himself announced that his kingdom would be inaugurated that day. Welding his death and forthcoming glorification into a single moment, he had said to his judges: "Hereafter you shall see the Son of Man sitting on the right hand of the

Power and coming upon the clouds of heaven." (Matt. xxvi. 64.) Caiaphas had asked: "Art thou the Messiah, Son of God?" and our Lord replied that he was, and that henceforward they themselves should see he was. For from then on the Son of Man was to be seated at the right hand of the Power, invested with God's lieutenancy; he was to come into the world in the majesty of heavenly kingship.

After the Resurrection, our Lord declared: "All power is given to me in heaven and on earth." (Matt. xxviii. 18.)

When St. Peter was expounding Christ's messiahship to the multitude gathered outside the upper room (Acts ii. 22-36), he began by reminding them of the miracles which were, as it were, Christ's credentials during his life on earth. Death was able to vanquish him, for such was God's plan; now God had raised him up again. David seemed only to be prophesying of himself when he said: "Thou wilt not leave my soul in Sheol, nor suffer thy Holy One to see corruption." (Ps. xv. 10.) But in fact he was foretelling the Messiah: "He was a prophet, and knew that God had sworn an oath, that of his seed one should sit upon his throne. Foreseeing this, he spoke of the resurrection of Christ." (ii. 30-1.) As early as this the Apostles' argument was already permeated by the conviction that the assurance given to David would be fulfilled in the glorification of Christ: the Resurrection reminds the Apostle of the throne of David. The Ascension and sending of the Spirit completed the exposition: Christ mounted once again the throne that had long been empty, but which stood thenceforth in heaven. (ii. 33-5.) And he concludes, "Therefore let all the House of Israel know most certainly, God hath made both Lord and Christ this same Jesus whom you have crucified." (ii. 36.)

The Sanhedrin forbade the Apostle "to speak in this name." But he disobeyed and declared before the council: "The God of our fathers hath raised up Jesus, whom you put to death, hanging him upon a gibbet. Him hath God exalted with his right hand, to be Head and Saviour, to give repentance to Israel and remission of sins." (v. 30-1.)

What does he mean by this? Has Peter forgotten that even before the Passion he had confessed to his Master: "Thou art the Christ"? No indeed, but now the lordship of Jesus of Nazareth is revealed; the era of the Messiah is begun: Christ is endowed with messianic powers and placed officially at the head of God's people to lead them to the source of repentance and forgiveness. Rejected in the Passion, the stone has become the head of the corner and from henceforth there is no salvation in any other name. (iv. 11-12.)

In the synagogue of Antioch in Pisidia, St. Paul develops his argument for Christ's messiahship along similar lines. (Acts xiii. 23-39.) He unfolds the history of Israel, recalls the promise of a Saviour given to David, and preaches Christ, to whom the Baptist bore witness, and whom the inhabitants of Jerusalem failed to recognize. This Christ, God raised from the dead, that is the most important fact, the final point in the history of Israel, and the conclusion of the exposition of Christ's messiahship. (xiii. 23-39.)

The Resurrection is not a proof; it is the fulfilment of the messianic promise: "And we declare unto you [the realization of] that promise which was made to our fathers. God hath fulfilled it to us, their children, by raising up Jesus, as in the second psalm also is written, 'Thou art my son; this day have I begotten thee.'" In Psalm II,: the Messiah-King publishes amid the nations that are in revolt the decree constituting him King: "The Lord hath said to me: Thou art my son, this day have I begotten thee." The kings of the ancient East claimed to be sons of their national gods, and based their authority on that origin. Christ's kingship dates from the "this day" of his divine generation, and that day blazed out in the Resurrection. For the Jews of Antioch, St. Paul does not unfold all the meaning of this filiation; he simply declares the enthronement of the Messiah and leaves it at that.

He does, however, bring a further prophetic text to the support of his statement (xiii. 34): "And to show that he raised him up from the dead, not to return now any more to corruption, he said thus: I will give you the holy things [promised to] David, the assured things." (The text is from Isa. lv. 3.) It is in the resurrection of David's son that the messianic benefits promised to David the father are given, and in the incorruptibility of his life they are assured forever.

Later, when he is defending himself to King Agrippa, he says again that the hope of the Twelve Tribes has been fulfilled

in the resurrection of Christ. (Acts xxvi. 6-8.) Through this Son
of David's entry into the majesty of incorruptible life, Israel's
triumph has begun, and the good things of the "latter days" are
theirs.

ii. Christ the Lord in Paul's Epistles

In proportion as the preaching of the Apostles moved away
from the Jewish centre of interest, the formal title of the risen
Christ lost its primitive complexion. "Christos" ("Messiah") became a proper name to be used without any article, suggesting the
Redemption but not recalling the Hebrew messianism. "Kyrios"
came more explicitly than before to indicate the divine being
revealed in the Resurrection and the universality of his dominion.
But the bond between Christ's enthronement as Lord and his
resurrection remained firm: "If thou confess with thy mouth
that Jesus is Lord, and believe in thy heart that God hath raised
him up from the dead, thou shalt be saved." (Rom. x. 9.)

During his first captivities, the Apostle had time to consider
the scope of Christ's exaltation, and follow its repercussions
throughout the whole cosmos.

(a) Universal Dominion

The Epistle to the Philippians, which gives the best account
of the humiliations of the Son of God in the flesh, gives a parallel account of their repercussions in glory: "He emptied himself
. . . he humbled himself unto death . . . For which cause God
also hath exalted him, and hath given him a name which is above
all names: that in the name of Jesus every knee should bow, of
those that are in heaven, on earth, and under the earth: and that
every tongue should confess that Jesus Christ is Lord in the glory
of God the Father." (ii. 7-11.) God has exalted Christ, giving
him a name above all others, the only sovereign name, the name
proper to Iahweh himself, the "Lord-God". From the beginning
Christ possessed "the condition of God": the giving of the name
is no mere title of honour: for the Semites, the name and the
being described by the name are one. This name, superior to all
others, which compels the adoration of all creatures, can indicate
none other than the sovereign majesty of God and his dominion
over all things. The divine power is conferred upon this Jesus

who once hung on a gibbet, and forces from us the acclaim, "Lord Jesus Christ!"

Every creature on the "three levels" of the world bends the knee at this name, paying to it the homage given only to God, in heaven, on earth, and in the depths below the earth. (ii. 10.) Who are these vassals? The angels, certainly, men, and since all must be included, the demons, for these are the three categories of being who inhabit these dwellings. So say most interpreters. It may be pointed out that evil spirits also dwell in the air and the high places (Eph. ii. 2; vi. 12), and that those who dwell under the earth seem more properly identified with the dead in Sheol, as Paul says: "To this end Christ died and rose again, that he might be Lord both of the dead and of the living." (Rom. xiv. 9.) But did he intend any such literal interpretation? Surely we must believe that he "meant by this triple designation to affirm the submission to Christ of all beings, animate and inanimate, in short, of the whole universe." The man who accepted humiliation of his own free will, is established at the very summit of creation, in the power and glory of God.

(b) Lord of the World to Come

The Epistles to the Ephesians and the Colossians are concerned with defending Christ's absolute primacy in the world and with defining its nature; for them Christ constitutes the actual principle of the cosmos: "Who is the image of the invisible God, the first-born of every creature: for in him were all things created in heaven and on earth, visible and invisible . . . All things were created by him and for him; and he is before all, and by him all things subsist." (Col. i. 15-17.)

This Christ as principle of the cosmos is not the pre-existing Word—this would fit neither Paul's perspective nor that of John's prologue—but Christ "in whom we have redemption" (i. 14), the visible image of God (i. 15), head of the Church. (i. 18.) But he is a Christ who has passed beyond the weakness of his earthly existence: he holds the primacy over all things, "the first-born from the dead . . . in whom it hath well pleased God that all fullness should dwell". (i. 18-19.)

Christ is "the first-born of every creature". (i. 15.) He holds priority both of cause and of duration over the rest of creation.

The reason given by the Apostle—"for in him were all things created"—presupposes both priorities. St. Paul insists on that of duration: "He is [exists] before all." (i. 17.) This is, of course, a prerogative of divinity, but then the Christ of the Resurrection is wholly divine. Lifted up into the life of God, in the fullness of time (which, in the mind of St. Paul is the fullness of reality), Christ is set before all things. While on earth, his age was measured as the world measures age, but henceforward he is wholly seen in God, at the summit and origin of creation.

The title "first-born of every creature", while placing Christ above the rest of creation, does not separate him wholly from it; he becomes its principle, because of the fullness of being God has implanted in him: "He is indeed principle of them all . . . because in him it hath well pleased the Father that all fullness should dwell." (Col. i. 19.) The *pleroma* ("fullness") which, in biblical thought and the philosophy of the time, meant "the universe filled by the creative presence of God", is primarily present, in all its being and power, in him.

It is "in him" that God calls everything into being ($\dot{\epsilon}\kappa\tau\acute{\iota}\sigma\theta\eta$) and maintains it ($\ddot{\epsilon}\kappa\tau\iota\sigma\tau\alpha\iota$) (i. 16). The world is based on him as "upon its focal point, where all the threads, all the generating lines of the universe are knotted together and co-ordinated".

As principle, Christ is the centre of cohesion and harmony; everything starts from him and returns to him (i. 16-18). The world, as it were, pulls itself together in him and becomes a cosmos, an ordered universe. "In him all things stand and stand fast [$\sigma\upsilon\nu\acute{\epsilon}\sigma\iota\eta\kappa\epsilon\nu$]." They are centred upon him, and depend on him for their existence, for in him dwells the whole power of God. "If anyone could have an instantaneous vision of the whole universe, past, present and future, he would see all things ontologically depending from Christ, and wholly intelligible only through him."

Though he had always been Son of God, Christ did not become the centre and universal bond of the cosmos until after he had saved and reunited the shattered world in his sacrifice: "It pleased the Father . . . through him to reconcile all things [by directing them] to himself, making peace through the blood of his cross, through him (I say) both the things that are on earth, and the things that are in heaven." (i. 20.) In Christ God does not reconcile the universe with himself, but re-establishes the harmony among things, making them all converge towards Christ. All the powers of heaven and all the creatures of earth have their culmination in him and are reunited at this pinnacle of the world's architecture, for once risen he holds the fullness of all things.

There was a time during our Lord's human existence when the various planes and lines of the universe had not yet come to culminate in him. The world remained broken apart, with a crack across the universe at the point where the upper and lower creations joined in man, until the sin that caused the crack was wiped out by the blood of the Cross. Standing in this centre of the universe, because of his carnal being, Christ bore that fissure in himself during his life on earth. But by his death and resurrection he wiped out the contrasts and, lifted to the pinnacle of all things, joined the shattered pieces together again in himself. Henceforth he was to be a magnet drawing all creation, and reuniting it in himself. "He that descended is the same also that ascended above all the heavens, that he might fill all things." (Eph. iv. 10.)

Clearly, these declarations are something of an anticipation. The world we live in is still torn apart, the submission of the angels is not yet complete, the rule of death has not been abolished. The world of harmony and peace, centred wholly upon Christ, belongs to the end of time. In the Epistles of the Captivity, the Apostle is bringing the eye of prophecy to bear on the world; he is judging it by a principle, by the death and resurrection of Jesus, by that cosmic revolution which took place in its entirety in Christ, but whose effects have not yet spread out over the world. The great epistles, more conscious of the delays of history, only look forward to the submission of all things to Christ and universal peace at the end. (1 Cor. xv. 24-8.)

The lordship of the universe is an eschatological attribute of Christ's, but it is a reality from the Resurrection onwards. The Lord of the next world is none other than the Christ of Easter; in his glory he is the end and fullness in which all things subsist and are consummated: "It hath well pleased the Father that all fullness should dwell in him." (Col. i. 19.)

Because he is the end and pinnacle of all things, the action of Christ in glory goes back to the beginnings of the world; he is the first because he is the last, the goal, the *pleroma* containing all reality. One day the world will receive its perfect form from him, and will live only by him and his redemption. But the beginning is also dependent upon this goal; the whole world and the whole of time is suspended from him. "All things were created by him and for him." (Col. i. 16.)

That is why carnal realities herald the spiritual ones which must of necessity follow, for they depend upon them. "If there is a psychic body, there is also a spiritual body . . . that which is psychic first, then that which is spiritual." (1 Cor. xv. 44, 46.) The Old Testament heralded the coming of the later era as a shadow falls in front of a body: "All was a shadow of things to come, but the body [that this shadow outlined] is of Christ." (Col. ii. 17.) The dead letter was the notification of the heavenly and complete reality, of the Lord who is life-giving Spirit (cf. 2 Cor. iii.) The Christ of glory is the prince of the past and of all lower realities, because he is lord of the world to come, possessor of all fullness, having primacy over all things by God's will. (Col. i. 18-19.)

(c) Lord of the Angels

There can therefore have been little understanding of the Christian mystery in those Judaizers who lessened the absolute lordship of Christ by setting angels (Col. ii. 18), thrones, dominations and principalities (i. 16; ii. 10, 15) between God and men.

Certainly, when the world was left to itself, those creatures who were the most powerful must have ruled it. Christ himself became lower than they (Heb. ii. 7); an evil spirit several times confronted him (Luke iv. 2-13; xxii. 31; John xiv. 30), and a good angel came to strengthen him (Luke xxii. 43.)

But by his resurrection, Christ "was made better than the angels" (Heb. i. 4); "the almighty power wrought in his resurrection" lifted him "above all principality and power, and virtue, and dominion, and every name that is named". (Eph. i, 19, 21.) Their dominion over the world was snatched from them. The whole angelic host was drawn into the Saviour's exaltation and fastened to his triumphal chariot: "And [God] despoiling the principalities and powers, he hath exposed them confidently in open show, dragging them in triumph in Christ." (Col. ii. 15.)

Who are these angels? Good angels or bad? St. Paul does distinguish between the two (2 Cor. xi. 14; 1 Tim. v. 21), but he is not concerned with the distinction here.

The angels made subject to Christ by the Father are heavenly beings appointed to govern the world, who direct the stars, who preside over the fates of nations by means of the civil authority (1 Cor. ii, 8; and perhaps Rom. xiii. 1), who were mediators between God and Israel, and promulgated the Law. The Apostle shares this conception with the whole of Jewish apocalyptic writing.

Before Christ took the reins of the world, these powers held dominion over the universe; men were subject to them (Gal. iv. 3) and paid homage to them by obeying the laws promulgated by them. The Galatians and Colossians still thought they were subject to them, as also to Mosaic practices. "The Colossians had been told that the Law had been given by angels, because they had lent their aid to promulgating it, and did not look with indifference upon disrespect to the Torah." But in Christ's death "the certificate of debt" for which we were responsible and which placed us at the mercy of the powers' vengeance was wiped out by God; he stripped them of all hostile power by binding them to Christ's triumph. (Col. ii. 14-15.)

The Apostle is not concerned here with the goodness or badness of these angels, but with their function. His tone of hostility towards them was due to the attempts of innovators to continue to allot to them the part they had played. They were the rulers of a world which did not move in the orbit of Christ, principles of a way of life belonging to the past. They are contrasted with Christ in the same way as the Law, and the whole carnal order. Just as the flesh contradicted the spiritual economy by its weakness and often by its wickedness, so also did these powers, because they were of the order of "weak elements of the world", and because there were malevolent beings among their number. The latter, stripped of the autonomy of their power, represent disarmed adversaries in the triumph of Christ.

Christ's supremacy over the angelic powers is not, in the Apostle's mind, any mere marginal effect of the exaltation of the risen Christ; it is of its essence. Christ is the only Mediator and even the Church, since she works amid the world, can profess faith in Christ alone only if the powers that rule the world are also subject to this same head. Later in life the Apostle was to find it necessary to cleanse the atmosphere of the Asiatic communities from pre-gnostic influences, and to insist that "there is one Mediator between God and men, the man Christ Jesus". (1 Tim. ii. 5.) There are now no intermediaries acting between God and man save Christ, or in Christ.

Christ's relationships with inanimate creation and with the angelic world do not follow the same pattern as his relationship with his Church. Some writers, carried away by their passion for synthesis, have thought that the whole of creation could be comprehended in the one concept of the Church with Christ at its head. "The body of Christ" would then take on fantastic dimensions, "becoming cosmic, and embracing spiritual and material creation in a vast whole". The universe of the angels, mankind rising up from the pedestal of the material creation, the whole cosmos, would thus constitute the multiform body over which Christ, as head, presides.

Several texts seem to place the angels, the Church and the world alongside each other in the same subordination to Christ. God re-establishes the whole universe under the one head (Eph. i. 10); Christ is the head of the powers (Col. ii. 10), as of the Church (Col. i. 18); he fills all things (Eph. iv. 10), as well as the Church. (Col. ii. 10.)

The recapitulation of all things is certainly not limited to the establishment of the Church, but embraces the whole cosmos. But loftier than Christ's cosmic role is his role as "head of the body": "He raised him up from the dead, and set him on his right hand in the heavenly places, above all principality . . . He hath subjected all things under his feet, and above all hath made him head over the Church, which is his body." (Eph. i. 20-23.) To be head is a function of lordship; but in Christ's sphere of influence, one area is marked off from the rest—the Church. This role lifts him a degree above mere sovereignty over the angels; it is the highest rung in Christ's elevation. The Apostle surveys the honours of the risen Saviour (Eph. i. 19-23); his seat at the right hand of God, his being lifted above the spirits, the subjection of all creatures beneath his feet—all these are, as it were, a staircase leading up to his function as head. Lordship of the cosmos is directed towards the dignity of being head of the Church.

The power of head of the faithful and the dominion over the angels derive from the same fullness of power, and the former rests upon the latter: "In him dwelleth all the fullness of the Godhead corporeally, and in him you are filled [function of the head of the Church], who is the head of all principality and power." (Col. ii. 9-10.) But the two titles, though most closely related, are not the same. The title of head, given to Christ, master of the powers, expresses supreme dignity and dominion; but the Church alone is the body to which Christ communicates his personality and his life.

Because the Church is identified with the Saviour's physical body (cf. chapters v and vi), the relationship between it and its head are unique and cannot extend to the world of the angels. The point of identification between Christ and the Church lies in bodily human nature. In it the Saviour carried out his work of salvation, having accepted it in its carnal state that he might be numbered among a sinful race, and then having drawn it into the life of God. We are in turn made part of it and gain for our bodily being death to the flesh and divine life. Everything in St. Paul goes to show that salvation in Christ is prepared only for human nature, and fitted to it alone. The purely spiritual creature may bathe in the influence of Christ, but cannot penetrate into the focal point where the divine transformation takes place, Christ's bodily humanity.

Dominion over the powers and power over the faithful are thus on quite different levels, and this inequality is expressed in the way each is stated. "The powers are subjected, put down by force, and are placed under Christ's feet by his victory. On the other hand, the Church is one with him, even if she is subjected to him." All proclaim that "Jesus Christ is Lord" (Phil. ii, 11), but the faithful call him familiarly and lovingly "our Lord"; they belong to him in a special sense, for he belongs to them.

iii. Christ the Lord in the Apocalypse

Christ's lordship, as set out in the Apocalypse, would need a long study.

In his glorification, Christ underwent a profound transformation. We know how the Semites attached the importance of the reality to the name. "To him that overcometh I will give the hidden manna, and I will give him a white stone, and in the stone a new name written, which no man knoweth but he that receiveth it." (Apoc. ii. 17.) The image of the stone suggests the analogy of several uses: the precious stone in a ring with a name carved on it, or the *tessera*, the entrance fee to the theatres. The important thing is that it is white, the colour of those who possess the life of Christ (cf. iii. 5), and that it bears the new name which indicates a renewal of nature such as can be understood only by those who have experienced it.

And to the Church of Philadelphia Christ declares: "He that shall overcome, I will make him a pillar in the house of my God; and he shall go out no more; and I will write upon the name of my God, and the name of the city of my God, the new Jerusalem, which cometh down out of heaven from my God, and my new name." (iii. 12).

The believer has three names inscribed upon him, which express his new being and where he belongs: he is the Church's, he is Christ's, he is God's. Christ has inscribed his new name upon the believer. The Apocalypse, being "the gospel of the risen Christ" does not know the old one. The new is known only to him who bears it: "His eyes were as a flame of fire, and on his head were many diadems, and he had a name written which no man knoweth but himself. He was clothed with a garment saturated with blood; and his name is called, The Word of God." (xix. 12-13.)

The new name to replace the old means a transformation similar to that which occurs in the believer, and defines the new mode of existence of the glorified Christ: the existence of the Word of God.

Although the Apocalypse lacks the Pauline notion of all things being reconciled and recapitulated in the risen Lord, it does bring one new element to enrich Christ's Lordship: the Resurrection places the reins of history in the hands of the Savior. Providence becomes Christian; events are presided over by Christ, Saviour of all who believe.

Francis Xavier Durrwell

To Christians who had already been persecuted and were to be persecuted more and more violently, St. John unfolds the synthesis of the supernatural history of the Church. The drama takes place on two stages at once, heaven and earth; Christ in heaven is the producer. The leitmotiv is given in the introductory vision. (i. 9-20.) In the midst of the seven golden candlesticks, the Apostle perceives the features of Christ in the glory of his divinized humanity: "I was dead, and behold I am living forever and ever." The light of divinity, at once bright and soft, illuminates his face; his look pierces like a fire, his voice has the majesty of great waters. The bronze feet suggest stability of power; the sword coming from his mouth the power of his words. In his right hand he holds seven stars. The golden candlesticks represent seven Churches, the whole Christian Church. The stars are the angels, their mysterious representatives; Christ holds them in his mighty but gentle right hand. The whole book sets out to affirm that the risen Christ is present among the golden candlesticks, and to record the history of the stars in his hand.

In Chapter IV the curtain rises on the scene of heaven. Seated on his throne, God holds in his hand a scroll sealed with seven seals and containing the fate of the world. The whole court waits for him who is to carry out this decree, when Christ appears, risen from the dead. He is the Lamb and the Lion, both victim and the victorious hero; he has seven horns and seven eyes "which are the seven spirits of God", for fullness of the Spirit's vision and might. God gives him the plan for the new history of the world and charges him to carry it out. And immediately the whole universe offers homage to Christ and also to God, "every creature, which is in heaven, and on the earth, and under the earth and in the sea". (v. 13.)

This exalting of the Lamb brings the salvation of God into the world ruled by the Dragon, and brings about that crisis in the universe whose development forms the new history. With solemn deliberation, he breaks the seven seals and unfolds the designs whereby God will bring the crisis to its solution. Isaiah foretold of the Servant that after his death "the will of the Lord shall be prosperous in his hand". (liii. 10.) His will that the faithful be saved governs all that happens so that even the victories of the infernal dragon are turned to their good. Presided over by the Lamb, history steadily directs some towards "the pool of fire and brimstone" (xx. 9), and others towards the heavenly Jerusalem.

2. MIGHTY SON OF GOD

Related to the title of Christ the Lord is the name "Son of God".

It even seems as though at the time of our Lord the two titles were one. "Thou art the Son of God, thou art the King of Israel!" cried Nathaniel (John i. 49): "Thou art the Christ, the Son of the living God!" declared St. Peter (Matt. xvi. 16): "Art thou the Christ, the Son of God?" asked Caiaphas. (Matt. xxvi. 63.)

Scripture attributed to the Son of David this title and the prerogative of God's paternal love: "I will be to him a father, and he will be to me a son." (2 Kings vii. 14; cf. Ps. lxxxviii. 28.) The mysterious seventh verse of Ps. II, "Thou art my son; this day have I begotten thee", was given a simple messianic interpretation which St. Paul was content to adopt in talking to the Jews of Antioch. (Acts xiii. 33.) Various Jewish apocryphas used the terms "Messiah" and "Son of God" synonymously. (Enoch cv. 2; 4 Est. vii. 28 (probable text); xiii. 32, 52.)

The Jews had no idea of a Messiah who would really be God's Son. Caiaphas' question must be interpreted as a messianic one, similar to the first disciples' professions of faith. (John i. 49; Matt. xiv. 33.) In the first part of the Angel Gabriel's message, the context does not demand any more literal interpretation for the phrase "Son of the Most High". Mark, and, even more, Luke, realized that in the mouth of his contemporaries the title "Son of God" was primarily messianic, for they make it interchangeable with that of Christ. Luke iv. 41 is a typical example: "Devils went out from many, crying out and saying: Thou art the Son of God. And rebuking them he suffered them not to speak, for they knew that he was the Christ.

Certainly the title takes on a profound religious significance when the Father inspires its use (Matt. xvi. 16); and the Apostles clearly felt God's presence in Christ (Matt. xiv. 33; Luke v. 8); but not until after the Resurrection was their faith formulated in an invocation reserved to Iahweh himself: "My Lord and my God!" (John xx. 28.)

i. Birth as Son

If their eyes were wholly opened to the mystery of Christ from then on, it was because the mystery had broken through the cover that concealed it. Before, Christ had been born Son of David in the weakness of the flesh, but in the Resurrection he was established Son of God in the glory of power, according to the spirit of holiness. (Rom. i. 4.)

It was not that Christ underwent any substantial transformation. St. Paul writes that he has been set apart for the Gospel of God . . . concerning his Son, of the race of David according to the flesh and constituted Son of God in power by the Resurrection. Christ, therefore, is Son quite beyond and before any event of history. The humiliations of his time on earth covered his dignity as Son but did not efface it. They did, however, make it suffer a real eclipse, for the weakness of the flesh was a servile livery, a disguise put on over the sonship which made him appear as simply a son of David. The Resurrection was not simply a declaration like the one that guaranteed Jesus of Nazareth to the Jews after his baptism; it produced a complete change in his existence. Christ reaped the benefits of the sonship in his bodily humanity. In short, he was established Son of God; he was so already, but now he was established "Son of God in the glory of power", established in the existence proper to the Son of God.

The Resurrection was not merely a coming back to life, but a birth into a new life which Christ did not have in his bodily humanity. Before the Christian can have a regeneration, Christ must have one. Born of the Virgin into the life of a son of man, on Easter day he was reborn into the life of the Son of God. St. Paul is not afraid of the notion of Christ's having a second birth. At Easter he interprets the Father as making that solemn statement, "Thou art my Son; this day have I begotten thee." (Acts xiii. 33.) "This day" starts at the first instant of Christ' existence (Rom. i. 3; Phil. ii. 6), but its high noon is at Easter. Following his birth into the world in Bethlehem, comes a new Christmas in a blaze of light.

The prophecy of the Old Testament had linked the titles "Messiah" and "Son of God" (2 Sam. vii. 14; Ps. ii. 7), though with no idea how close to God that sonship would be. The union of the two remained constant in the person of Christ and in the mind of his disciples (Matt. xvi. 16 and Mark viii. 29; Matt. xvi. 20; Acts ix. 20, 22) and the effects of both were parallel in their unfolding. Our Lord was the Christ who "is to come" because he was the Son of David yet begotten by God. To St. John the coming was synonymous with divine generation. The sonship was stated with reserve at first, and the Messiahship was certainly not thrust forward; but at Easter both appeared in their full power.

ii. Birth in the Spirit

The new life in the believer is the effect of the Spirit (I Cor. vi. 11), as is the sonship. (Rom. viii. 14-17.) One can only be a son in the Spirit of the Son. (Gal. iv. 6.) One must be born again of the Spirit, declares the fourth gospel (iii. 5), and St. Paul speaks of "the regeneration and renovation of the Holy Ghost". (Tit. iii. 5.) Christ's new birth springs from the same principle, as St. Paul tells us implicitly; according to him, the Father raises Christ by the Spirit (Rom. viii. 11), and the Spirit forms the life-principle in the glorified Christ (I Cor. xv. 45), Christ in his existence as Son.

The Apostle stands in the same doctrinal line as the gospel of his disciple St. Luke. The angel had said: "The Holy Ghost shall come upon thee and the power of the Most High shall overshadow thee, and therefore also he who shall be born of thee shall be called holy, the Son of God." (Luke i. 35.) The angel does not attribute the divine effect to the virginal conception as such, but to the intervention of the Holy Ghost. In the Old Testament every child born miraculously is marked by holiness—as with Isaac, born according to the Spirit (Gal. iv. 29), and Samson the Nazarite and Samuel. Born of a unique intervention of the Spirit, who is the holiness and power of the Most High, the Child of the Virgin Mary was to be holy with a unique holiness, the Son of God. This was not because of the Virgin Birth as such, but because of the working of the Spirit which, in effecting that virgin birth, consecrated a human being to holiness and to divine sonship.

iii. Image of the Father

According to St. Luke, the Spirit had divinized the man Christ from the beginning, and now, according to St. Paul, he was bringing that divinization to its conclusion. By the action of the outpouring of the Spirit that raised him, the Father begets Christ more completely like himself; our Lord is changed into a perfect image of the Father. When St. Paul speaks of Christ as "the image of the invisible God" (Col. i. 15; 2 Cor. iv. 4), he is not thinking of the Word in his pre-existence, but of Christ whom he sees in the light of that Resurrection. He recognizes the Father in the features of that shining face, in "the glory of Christ who is the image of God". (2 Cor. iv. 4.) The Apostle is quite aware that the Saviour was divine when he was on earth; but here he only sees Christ come into that life of glory which alone corresponds to the full reality of his being; "in him dwelleth all the fullness of the Godhead corporeally"—in other words, his corporeal being is filled with the divine plenitude. In his resurrection Christ showed himself in his true condition, revealing the divine traits that had been blurred by the humiliation he had chosen to undergo. (Phil. ii. 5-9.)

For St. John too, Christ is the image of the Father, his revelation in the world. His mission is to make known the name of the Father (John xvii. 11, Greek text); to spread the knowledge of that name. He gave it to the world by his preaching, but even more by his own being as Son, which revealed the most intimate and most essential thing about God, his quality of being Jesus' Father.

Even during his life on earth Christ declared, "Who seeth me seeth my Father" (John xiv. 9; xii. 45); this was a partial anticipation of the future, for it was to be "in that day [of the glorification] you shall know, that I am in my Father." (xiv. 20.) If the Father was to be known in the Son, the Son had to be revealed in his sonship, in the glory that he possessed with the Father and with which he was again to be wholly filled in his exaltation. (xvii. 5.) Thus he asks for his glorification in order that both the Father and he whom he has sent may be known. (xvii. 1-4.)

John's thought, though very different from Paul's in its expression, remains parallel with it in substance: in the Resurrection Christ's sonship is affirmed and the image of the Father is revealed. "We might say that in the Incarnation the Son of God was born Son of Man, and that in the Resurrection the Son of Man was born Son of God." The birth is a unique one: Christ is born into the life of the Son by entering the bosom of the Father.

In order that the features of his Father's beauty may be seen, the Spirit must wipe out "the likeness of sinful flesh". (Rom. viii. 3.) The flesh, as such, stands in contrast to God; it indicates being, but only being that is not affected by the holiness of God, that remains in the isolation of a creature. To speak of a life of the flesh is to recall the framework of death that surrounds it. Christ was Son even in his carnal state, but only because he was not to remain in it.

No part of his flesh resisted the action of the Spirit. Christ became spirit even in his body, and it is in the life of the Spirit that the essential feature of likeness to God resides, for "God is Spirit"—that is why the heavenly spirits are called the sons of God (cf. Luke xx. 36)—and the Holy Spirit, like the glory which belongs to him, is an expression of the divine nature.

Before the Resurrection the mystery of Christ had been hidden by his body; now it was expressed by it. Being a Man-Spirit Christ now declared himself Man-God.

iv. A Life Forever New

The coming of the Spirit has swept away the ruin left by Adam (Rom. vii. 6); it renovates (Tit. iii. 5) and creates not merely a renewed being, but a *new being* ($\kappa\alpha\iota\nu\dot{\eta}$ $\kappa\tau\dot{\iota}\sigma\iota\varsigma$). It has not simply introduced a new sort of man to the world, but places man at the starting-point of this whole new life, at birth (Tit. iii. 5); and all that the power of the sacrament has not yet succeeded in re-creating will gradually yield to this baptismal youthfulness. (2 Cor. iv. 16; Col. iii. 10.) The Spirit is youth, for he is life (Rom. viii. 11; I Cor. xv. 45; 2 Cor. iii. 6); a life that will never fail, for it is the life of God.

110

Francis Xavier Durrwell

Since the believer finds his newness of life by conforming himself to the risen Christ, and this newness is constantly renewed as he conforms to him more closely (Col. iii. 10), we must take it that Christ will never grow any older than he was at the Resurrection, that his life remains new, that his body, new-born in the Spirit, never grows beyond the moment of his Easter birth and therefore that the Father's action in raising Christ continues eternally in its single moment.

It is true that, using as we must the past tense of the verbs by which we express it, the raising action of the Father is part of past history as far as we are concerned. But though it belongs to our time, to one precise moment of it, yet it has an eternal actuality. When the believer meets Christ's resurrection, it is as the astonishing and new thing it first was. Every man who shares in the new life in Christ, no matter when in history he does so, is said by St. Paul to rise with him, to be taken up in the very act of the Saviour's resurrection.

Earlier on, when he attributed the phrase: "Thou art my son, this day have I begotten thee" to the Father in raising Christ (Acts xiii. 33), he made no attempt to unfold its theological depths to the Jews. But saying it again—"He was constituted Son of God . . . by the Resurrection" (Rom. i. 4)—he explains further. The Resurrection brought Christ wholly to birth in the life of the Son, extending to his whole being the glory of his eternal generation. And in that birth there is no "tomorrow". Alongside our ancestor Adam, the old man, who continues to decay within us (2 Cor. iv. 16), here is the young Adam, the new man, Son of God, in the everlasting newness of his sonship.

We thus have a number of elements to fit together. The Resurrection is a divine birth; the life of the glorified Christ never grows older than the date of his birth; believers at any time in history can profit in Christ from the same raising action which profits their Saviour. We might conclude that the Resurrection remains forever in act, thus giving Paul's thought a philosophical expression foreign to it. But we should be mutilating that thought if we retained only those statements that place the Resurrection in the past and ignored those which presuppose that God's act of raising is a permanent lasting reality. We must accept ideas

111

which seem mutually exclusive, and see the Resurrection as both an event preceded and followed by others and a divine action outside history.

The eschatological nature of the Resurrection gives a biblical formula for this philosophical concept of a permanent actuality in the Resurrection. Christ has left "this present time", he has come to the end of time. The Epistle to the Hebrews was to explain that the immolation took him through the antechamber of heaven, the Holies, image of changing and imperfect things, and brought him into the full reality, the Holy of Holies. He has come to fulfilment, to his goal and perfection. The history of the world is virtually accomplished, for death and resurrection, in Christ, have brought the final fullness of time which, in Scripture, is not merely the norm, but the reality of history. The Church is moving towards that fullness which he will one day attain, when she has come to "the stature of Christ" in glory, but Christ already possesses it himself alone and fully. Thus he has advanced no further than the first moment of his glorification, for that is his fullness and his goal.

v. Established in Power

Rom. i. 4 sets the power alongside the dignity of the Son: "He was established Son of God in power." Christ is established in power; power is a mark of the new life. The Apostle contrasts the two phases of Christ's existence: that of Son of David in the weakness of the flesh (i. 3), and that of Son of God, which, to stand in antithesis to the first, calls for a mention of the power of God. To be fully elevated as Son of God, Christ must be enthroned in the power of God.

Power was the attribute the Jews were most constant in giving God. The phrase "the power of Iahweh" indicated God himself, and so did simply "the Power". The angel announced that the Child would be the Son of God because his conception was to be the result of "the power of the Most High" (Luke i. 35), and Christ foretold his coming in power as the manifestation of his divine sonship: "Hereafter you shall see the Son of Man sitting at the right hand of the Power" (Matt. xxvi. 64), associated with God in his most essential quality. Christ's enthronement in the dignity of the Son called for a communication and demonstration of infinite power.

And indeed, after the Resurrection Christ was to say to his Apostles, "All power is given to me." (Matt. xxviii. 18.)

The bestowal of power was implied in the very action whereby God raised him up. The Resurrection inspires boundless wonder in St. Paul, and he exhausts his entire vocabulary in attempting to describe the infinite might of God (Eph. i. 19ff.) Any return from death to life is to him a revelation of God's power (Rom. iv. 17), but does not astound him. At Troas he performed that very miracle with no special *éclat*. (Acts. xx. 10.) His marvelling at the "operation of the might of God" in Christ was because it was a manifestation of the whole of God's power. The Pauline theology of justification yields this general law: the nature of the cause is carried on in the effect. God raises up the Saviour and those that believe in him by the Spirit, and therefore Christ and they that are his become spirit (I Cor. xv. 44ff.); he raises them by his glory (Rom. vi. 4) and they live in glory. (I (I Cor. xv. 43; 2 Cor. iii. 18; Phil. iii. 21.) He gives life by his power (2 Cor. xiii. 4), by an extraordinary working of power, and Christ rises up clothed in infinite power, and our bodies once "sown in weakness, shall rise in power". (I Cor. xv. 43.) That power is none other than the working of the Spirit; and the power of the risen Christ is infinite, because there is no limit to the interpenetration of Christ by the Spirit.

vi. The Father's Heir

If he is Son, then he is heir, heir of God (Gal. iv. 7; Rom. viii. 17). Christ on earth, in his saving humanity, had not yet received the inheritance. The glory, power, and universal dominion stood, as it were, empty, awaiting Christ's coming of age. St. Paul suggests this in the Epistle to the Galatians. (iv. 1-8.) Though men were heirs in virtue of the promise, they had not yet come into the enjoyment of the goods brought by the Messiah, for the time was not yet ripe. Meanwhile, they were living as children, under the tutelage of the Law and "the elements of the world". Christ, born in the flesh, lived among them subject to the same regime of childhood and servitude, that he might bring them in him to the sonship and its inheritance. In his glorification, our Lord has inherited the whole Divinity, the life of God, in so far as bodily humanity can live that life, his attributes of power and holiness, and all that belongs to the Father, Creator of the world. Redeemed mankind, coming into this inheritance, are co-heirs with Christ.

vii. Fully Free

Constituted in the fullest dignity of his sonship, Christ has done with servitude. The flesh, that mark of slavery imprinted upon Christ on earth which made it possible for his divine liberty to be fettered, has been destroyed.

For the Spirit has established his sway over him unchecked, "and where the Spirit of the Lord is, there is liberty." (2 Cor. iii. 17.) The Spirit of God knows no coercion; his activity and his charismatic manifestations scorn the laws of nature and even of reason (I Cor. xiv.) He comes and goes in mystery, baffling all our calculations (cf. John iii. 8); he is God's spontaneity breaking out into the world. Henceforth all the restrictions inherent in Christ's carnal nature are done away with: gone is all subjection to any law other than that which belongs to his own new life—the Law of Moses has no more hold over him—gone all limitations of time and space. He came out of the tomb before the angel rolled away the stone, he stood amid the Apostles when they were behind shuttered doors. Did he pass through solid stone, through the walls of the upper room? Where did he stay before his ascension when he was not appearing to anyone? He stayed with the Father in the Holy Spirit, which makes these questions meaningless, for the laws of our space no longer bound him.

viii. The Universal Man

In laying aside the flesh whereby he belonged to the Jewish nation, Christ set himself above all the national differences of men. St. Paul makes an antithesis, as type and antitype, of circumcision on the one hand, and on the other, of the death and resurrection of Christ. He distinguishes the circumcision of the Jews from the immaterial circumcision of Christ, which we receive in our union with the Saviour's burial and new life. (Col. ii.

11-12.) Although when he was eight days old he was marked as belonging to one nation, the circumcision of his death and resurrection, which is "a despoiling of the body of the flesh" (Col. ii. 11), has unfastened him from the Jewish structure, and this universal Man can now become the foundation for the worldwide Church, whose members will henceforth be neither Greeks nor Jews nor barbarians.

The unfettered liberty Christ enjoys, the entry into his inheritance, the universality, the exaltation in power, and the sonship which sums them all up—all this, we must remember, is the work of the Holy Spirit.

The Old Testament has already made us familiar with the ways of God's Spirit; though his working in Christ goes far beyond anything he has done before, it still continues along a line we recognize. By him God opens out upon the world, and in him man opens upon the infinity of God. The Spirit as it were breaks into limited beings, opens them wide and unfolds them. Thanks to him Israel, breaking off from the rest of mankind, had made an approach to the holiness of God, had become a miracle in the history of the ancient world; its prophets had broken the bonds of time and space. Thanks also to him, Christ received a communication of the Godhead in his human nature, and was in contact with the infinity of God's attributes; he overcame the laws of his material nature and all the restrictions they laid upon him, and as we shall see, his very individuality in some sense opened out to embrace all believers within itself.

Romano Guardini
1885-1968

Born in Verona, Italy, raised in Mainz, Germany, educated at the universities of Tübingen, Berlin, and Freiburg, Romano Guardini brought the Christian faith to life for innumerable contemporaries. From Berlin before World War II and from Munich after it, his voice was constantly one that brought enlightenment and encouragement as he stimulated those around him to new thought.

Among his memorable products, The Lord *holds a special place. He says in the preface, "This book is no scientific documentation of history or theology. Its chapters are the spiritual commentaries of some four years of Sunday services undertaken with the sole purpose of obeying as well as possible the Lord's command to proclaim him, his message and works. The author wishes to point out that he offers nothing "new": neither a new understanding of Christ nor a better Christological theory." It is thus Guardini the preacher rather than the technical theologian at work.*

But that disclaimer ought to mislead no one. For in his rich theological vision, these roles were not that far apart: good theology by definition must be pastoral, good preaching must be theological. The book serves to illustrate what made up the substance of Guardini's sermons that were so popular in Munich in the post-war years. It contains 84 of what he referred to above as "spiritual commentaries," divided into seven parts. We have selected four from part two and three from part four to give something of the flavor of this unusual work.

Polarity was Guardini's trademark. He managed to hold in creative tension the objective and the subjective, the ontological and the psychological, the static and the dynamic, always acknowledging the specific value of each and the loss that occurred if one or the other were forgotten. It is the way in which he brings the contemporary into dialogue with the traditional that gives his thought a fuller dimension.

In a different context Guardini once said: "It is time to realize that all divisions have only a methodological value and that what really exists is the world and man in the world, as called by God and judged and redeemed." In this perspective he saw the need for a broader Christology than that which was formulated before the rise of modern psychology and associated sciences. Merely to repeat the past when an entirely new context has arisen is necessarily to distort. Fidelity to a living tradition requires the constant effort to adapt to new circumstances and to penetrate to new insight.

Part of the appeal of Guardini's approach, the reason for the enthusiastic response that he often elicited from people who were otherwise alienated from traditional religion, was the thoroughness with which he let Christian convictions permeate his outlook. If the Gospel were indeed "good news," it could not be a message that the world and everything in it was simply sin and evil. If Christ is Savior in any meaningful sense, then His Church must be wide open to the world, which is admittedly "in sin" but not beyond Redemption. A message that climaxes in Resurrection ought not to lose that joyous perspective at any point, no matter how real the problems confronting it.

THE LORD

T he meditations on Part One dealt with the origin of the Lord and that season of his life which is often referred to as the spring of his public activity. It was then that the power of his personality and the vital truth of his gospel gripped all who saw him. Everywhere hearts unfolded; miracle flowered on miracle, and it seemed as though now surely the approaching kingdom of God must appear in all its unconcealed abundance.

The records of this period are climaxed by the Sermon on the Mount. At the end of Part One we treated the first half of the Sermon, beginning with the powerful and disquieting Beatitudes. It has been claimed that the Sermon on the Mount promulgated Jesus' ethics, in which he clearly revealed the new relationship of man to himself, to others, to the world, and to God: in short, Christian ethics as differentiated from those of the Old Testament and from all other existent ethical codes. But this interpretation is not exact. Once we restrict the word ethics to its modern, specific sense of moral principles it no longer adequately covers the Sermon on the Mount. What Jesus revealed there on the mountainside was no mere ethical code, but a whole new existence—admittedly, one in which an *ethos* is also immediately evident.

Consciousness of this new existence breaks through forcefully in the Beatitudes. Startling words define as "blessed" those whom we naturally consider far from blessed, whereas those we naturally count blessed, the Beatitudes insist are threatened with woe! (Luke 6:24-26). We have tried to interpret this as a transvaluation from 'above' so great and revolutionary that it can be expressed only by the complete reversal of our natural sense of values. How does the resultant new life with all it includes compare with the traditional norms of the Old Testament?

Jesus himself gives the answer: "Do not think that I have come to destroy the Law or the Prophets. I have come not to destroy, but to fulfill" (Matt. 5:17). His message is new, but it does not destroy what was; it challenges it to develop its highest potentialities.

Now follows a row of sketches in which these potentialities are illuminated: Matthew 5:21-30; 33-42; 45-48; and Luke 6: 34-35. They all have the same pattern. First: "You have heard that it was said to the ancients . . ." then: "But I say to you . . ." followed by the clarification of the seeming contradiction. Four of these precepts are concerned with man's attitude to his neighbor, three treat the relationship of justice and love, the fourth the relationship to the opposite sex. In between come instructions on man's attitude to God: "Again, you have heard that it was said to the ancients, 'Thou shalt not swear falsely, but fulfill thy oaths to the Lord.' But I say to you not to swear at all: neither by heaven, for it is the throne of God; nor by the earth, for it is his footstool; nor by Jerusalem, for it is the city of the great King. Neither do thou swear by thy head, for thou canst not make one hair white or black. But let your speech be, 'Yes, yes'; 'No, no'; and whatever is beyond these comes from the evil one" (Matt. 5:33-37).

The old Law demanded that when you said something under oath, it be absolutely true; that when you made a vow to God, you keep it. The Lord says: You should not swear at all. Why not? Because everything you could possibly swear by belongs to God, the Majesty above all things, unapproachable, untouchable, holy.

What does the act of swearing under oath actually mean? That what I say is true, so true that I make God my witness. It is as true as God's existence, as his truth. He who swears thus brings God into his statement. He couples his truth with that of God and demands that God vouch for it. Jesus says: How dare you? All the majesty of the Hebraic conception of God (which to avoid all danger of personification forbade even the creation of his likeness) revolts here. Jesus goes straight to the heart of the problem; he no longer draws the line between right and wrong, true oath and false, but much sooner: between divine truth and human truth. How can man, who is full of untruth, place himself with his testimony beside God, the Holy One? He should not swear at all; divine majesty should loom so huge in his heart that his simplest 'yes' or 'no' is as reliable as an oath. Thus the commandment forbidding perjury is supplanted by a far profounder general love of truth, which does not swear at all because it knows and loves God's holiness too well to associate it with any personal testimony. An added dimension of truth permeates and guarantees everything that is said with an entirely new conscientiousness. Then come the words: "You have heard that it was said, 'An eye for an eye,' and 'A tooth for a tooth.' But I say to you not to resist the evildoer; on the contrary, if someone strike thee on the right cheek, turn to him the other also; and if anyone would go to law with thee and take thy tunic, let him take thy cloak as well; and whoever forces thee to go for one mile, go with him two. To him who asks of thee, give; and from him who would borrow of thee, do not turn away" (Matt. 5:21-24).

The old commandment, fifth of the Ten from Sinai, runs: Thou shalt not kill. Jesus seizes upon the wickedness that is expressed by murder and traces it back to its origin in the murderer's heart. What breaks out in violence is already present in the evil word or intent, or rather, everything that follows is the result of that intent. The intent then, not the deed that expresses it, is decisive. Notice that Jesus does not even mention downright hatred; a brother's irritation or having "anything against thee" is enough to sow the dragon-seed of evil. From irritation grows anger; from anger the word; from the word the deed.

"You have heard that it was said to the ancients, 'Thou shalt not kill'; and that whoever shall kill shall be liable to judgment. But I say to you that everyone who is angry with his brother shall be liable to judgment; and whoever says to his brother, 'Raca,' shall be liable to the Sanhedrin; and whoever says, 'Thou fool!', shall be liable to the fire of Gehenna. Therefore, if thou art offering thy gift at the altar, leave thy gift before the altar and go first to be reconciled to thy brother, and then come and offer thy gift" (Matt. 5:21-24).

The Old Law used justice as its norm of human behavior. As others treat you, so shall you treat them. Violence may be returned for violence, evil for evil. The justice of the day consisted in not returning more evil than the amount received, and naturally one was allowed to protect oneself from anything that seemed threatening. Christ says: That is not enough. As long as you cling to "justice" you will never be guiltless of injustice. As long as you are entangled in wrong and revenge, blow and counterblow, aggression and defense, you will be constantly drawn into fresh wrong. Passion, by its very definition, surpasses measure—quite aside from the fact that the claim to vengeance in itself is wrong because it lies outside our given rôle of creature. He who takes it upon himself to avenge trampled justice never restores justice. The moment discussion of wrong begins, wrong stirs in one's own heart, and the result is new injustice.

If you really want to get anywhere, you must extricate yourself from the whole embroilment and seek a position far removed from all pro's and con's. You must introduce a new force, not that of self-assertion, but of selflessness; not so-called justice, but creative freedom. Man is really just only when he seeks more than mere justice. More not merely quantitatively, but qualitatively. He must find a power capable of breaking the ban of injustice, something strong enough and big enough to intercept aggression and disarm it: love.

"You have heard that it was said, 'Thou shalt love thy neighbor, and shalt hate thy enemy.' But I say to you, love your enemies, do good to those who hate you, and pray for those who persecute and calumniate you, so that you may be children of your Father in heaven, who makes his sun to rise on the good and evil, and sends rain on the just and the unjust. For if you love those that love you, what reward shall you have? Do not even the publicans do that? And if you salute your brethren only, what are you doing more than others? Do not even Gentiles do that? You therefore are to be perfect, even as your heavenly Father is perfect."

The thought is underlined again, deepened in the words: "And if you lend to those from whom you hope to receive in return, what merit have you? For even sinners lend to sinners that they may get back as much in return" (Luke 6:34). The Old Law had taught man to render love for love, hate for hate. It was a question of feeling, a so-called justice of the heart. Precisely for this reason its "love" was unfree. It was a partial reaction, counterpart to equally legitimate hate. Such love lived from the love it received. It was still a piece of immediate human existence, mixture of attraction and repulsion. And now the Lord says:

Your "justice of the heart" is, in itself, an impossibility. 'Justifiable' hatred will always be greater than the hatred to which it responds; it will only create fresh injustice and with it the 'justification' for fresh hatred. As for love that is dependent on the love of another, it will always be trammelled, unsure of itself and uncreative. It is not yet genuine love, for that is so all-inclusive, that there is no room for any other sentiment beside it.

True justice then is possible only when exalted by a bearing justified not by the emotions, but by the free creative power of the heart. There lies the starting-point of all true love. Independent of the attitude of the other, it is free to fulfill its intrinsic possibilities. It stands much higher than justice. It is capable of loving also when it apparently has all grounds for hate. Thus it gains the power to unseat that hate and to overcome it. By this process true justice of the heart is established, that justice which enables a man to look into the heart of his adversary. There he perhaps learns that the 'wrong' inflicted was not really a wrong at all, but the result of inheritance, destiny, necessity; now, as a brother in their joint human guilt, he can concede even his natural enemy his rights before God.

"You have heard that it was said to the ancients, 'Thou shalt not commit adultery.' But I say to you that anyone who so much as looks with lust at a woman has already committed adultery with her in his heart.

"So if thy right eye is an occasion of sin to thee, pluck it out and cast it from thee; for it is better for thee that one of thy members should perish than that thy whole body should be thrown into hell" (Matt. 5:27-30).

The sixth is the commandment that protects the honor and order of family life. But Jesus teaches that its meaning goes much deeper. It demands not only respect for those of the opposite sex, who are also children of the same Heavenly Father, but also respect for one's own purity, which is not private property, but part of the mystery of love between the redeemed individual and his God.

From the disposition comes the deed; thus a glance, an unspoken thought can profane a marriage. As long as you judge behavior solely by the presence or absence of the actual evil deed, you will be unable to avoid that deed. You cannot cope successfully with the evil act until you tackle it as the root of all action: the attitude of the heart as expressed in glance and word. What is really demanded is not superficial order, but intrinsic purity and respect. These in their turn require spiritual self-control and careful guarding of the natural reactions.

A little reflection on Jesus' interpretation of the Commandments will make us realize what he wants for us: the awakening of the whole human being as God meant him to be. In other words, through the Commandments given Moses, God's holy will reveals itself. It must be obeyed; by obeying, man best attains his own perfection. Unfortunately, appalled by the greatness of the demands, he 'protects' himself from them by limiting their sense. This he does primarily by artificially distinguishing between interior and exterior conduct, judging only the visible, tangible misdeed as really evil. What does not come to the surface is not very important.

But the Lord says: Man is an entity in which there are no compartments. His every act has its degrees of being, first of which is inevitably the attitude of the heart as reflected in word, gesture, bearing. If you draw the line only at the actual deed, you are bound to overstep it. If you tolerate the evil word, the subsequent deed is already half accomplished. If you establish evil in your thoughts, you have sown the seed for the subsequent act. The man, not only his hand, must be good inside and outside. Indeed, essentially the heart is more important than the hand, though the hand is apparently responsible for the greater effects. Once a thought has become deed, it is already a piece of world continuity and no longer contains itself. When yet dependent on the liberating act for expression, its intrinsic virtue or malice is more apparent. It is the first yes or no to passion that decides. Thus Jesus elevates the current conception of mere physical prohibition to a positive command, and substitutes for the mere omission of sin, active virtue.

The other protective covering that man has constructed between himself and God is rationality. It says: Certainly man should be good, but everything within reason. He should be philanthropic—with moderation. He should consider the welfare of others—but of course with an eye to their deservingness and strictly within the boundaries of his own interests. The Lord replies:

You won't get far with that! Man is incapable of justice as long as he aims solely at justice. True justice can be obtained only from above, from a vantage point higher than itself. Man invariably metes out injustice when he tries to distribute a certain measured amount of justice. Justice is only for those who act in the strength of love, which does not measure but gives and creates. You will not even be capable of rendering good for good before you gain a higher level of being than that of mere goodness: that of love. Not until your goodness is protected by love, will it be pure.

To desire no more than justice, "Do not even the Gentiles do that?" That is ethics. You, though, have been summoned by the living God. With ethics alone you will neither satisfy God nor fulfill your intrinsic possibilities. God is the Holy One. Goodness is one of the names of him whose essence is inexpressible. And he desires not only obedience to the commands of an "abstract good," but also your personal affection. More, he wants you to risk *love* and the new existence which springs from it. Only in love is genuine fulfillment of the ethical possible. Love is the New Testament!

Admittedly, this is beyond human power. To purify the heart so completely that from the very start respect for the dignity of the other controls the natural passions; to disarm hatred, surrounding it and overcoming its would-be violence in the perfect freedom of love; to return good for evil, benefit for enmity, all this surpasses human strength, and one should not treat such demands lightly. It is better to struggle against them, or to remain in fear and hope on the threshold of grace than to speak of them glibly as principles of that higher code of ethics generally accepted since Jesus Christ. Actually, they are no less than a vocation to a new life.

We are invited to participate in the sanctity of him whose omnipotence and holiness are contained in the pure freedom of love; hence, of one who stands above good and evil, just and unjust. Truly, this is no longer a question of mere ethics—ethics which made such demands would be immoral—but of faith, of self-surrender to a command that is simultaneously a promise, promise of grace, without which all hope of fulfillment would be futile.

In the measure that man attains that which is higher than ethics, does he awaken the new *ethos* in which the Old Testament is simultaneously fulfilled and transcended.

CHAPTER II

SINCERITY IN VIRTUE

The Sermon on the Mount then demands that the Christian regulate his conduct not according to "justice," but according to *Caritas,* for only through love is true justice (and goodness) possible. But how can we be sure that out love is sincere? Human nature is all too prone to self-deception.

Jesus says: "Be merciful, therefore, even as your Father is merciful. Do not judge, and you shall not be judged; do not condemn, and you shall not be condemned. Forgive, and you shall be forgiven. . . ." And again: "For if you forgive men their offences, your heavenly Father will also forgive you your offences" (Luke 6:36-37; Matt. 6:14-15). "For with what measure, it shall be measured to you" (Luke 6:38).

Pity is a troublesome sensation; it saddles one with a sense of obligation. Man's egoism is therefore eager to protect him from it by isolating him from his neighbor: He is he, not I. He is there, not here. I recognize, honor and regret his need; however, it is not really my concern. . . . As long as we think thus, our so-called justice cannot possibly be taken seriously, and our "love" is illusory. To this attitude Jesus says: Your

love will become genuine only when you lower the barrier between yourself and the other, when you put yourself in his
place with the question, If I were he, what would I wish in the
way of help? The measure of your response to that wish, is the
measure of your love. (See Matt. 7:12.)

The thought is clear enough; but what demands it makes!
If we go into them deeply enough we begin to feel the fundamental safety of our personal existence dangerously questioned.
How can anyone meet such requirement? How can I, when
others do not? Naturally, if everyone acted accordingly, if
human life were so ordered—but Jesus mentions no such if's
and and's! He simply commands us to follow his instructions.
Only from the depths of a great faith is it possible to obey.
One must be utterly convinced that such obedience evokes a
divine reaction in our relationship to God, that when we act
according to his will we participate in divine creation, in the
forming of a new world, for it is creative conduct that is demanded here.

When man so acts, he not only becomes good in himself
and before God, but the divine goodness dormant in him
becomes active power. This is what the Lord means when he
speaks of "salt" that has not lost its flavor; "light" which
lights the whole house.

"You are the light of the world. A city set on a mountain
cannot be hidden. Neither do men light a lamp and put it under
the measure, but upon the lamp-stand, so as to give light to all
in the house. Even so let your light shine before men, in order
that they may see your good works and give glory to your
Father in heaven" (Matt. 5:14-16).

Divine goodness is incarnated in the person who opens
his heart to it; it radiates from him. The will that advances in
virtue, the soul that progresses in sanctity is a dynamic force
that stirs also the recipient of good, disarms and encourages
him. Through the God-reflecting act of a fellow creature, God
and his holy will become apparent, and the receiver of good in
his turn recalls his own potentialities for good, feels himself
summoned by God. But isn't it dangerous to execute God's
will with the desire to resemble "the salt of the earth," the
"city set on a mountain," "the light of the world"? Precisely;

hence the warning: "Do not give to dogs what is holy, neither throw your pearls before swine, or they will trample them under their feet and turn and rend you" (Matt. 7:6). "What is holy" is the flesh from the sacrificial altar. When the sacred rites are over, beware of flinging the remains to dogs! Neither should he who has "pearls" cast them before swine, those half wild herds like the ones we encounter in the incident at Gerasa, who (enraged to discover that they are not edible) only trample upon them and furiously turn on him who has flung them.

These parables clearly warn against indiscriminately presenting the mystery of divine life to the crowd. One must never allow it to be profaned, must avoid goading the general sense of earthliness until it becomes a hungry, disappointed beast that turns upon one in fury. A warning to be prudent, for men are as they are; the Lord is no idealist. But the admonition goes deeper. This more perfect justice must, above all, be selfless. The Lord warns us also to guard against ourselves, against the deeply rooted human traits of vanity, complacency and egoism.

"Therefore when thou givest alms, do not sound a trumpet before thee, as the hypocrites do . . . that they may be honored by men. Amen I say to you, they have received their reward. But when thou givest alms, do not let thy left hand know what thy right hand is doing, so that thy alms may be given in secret. . ." (Matt. 6:2-4).

Give unperceived. He who gives in order to be seen and praised already has his reward. Then his works are not displayed that people might praise God as revealed in him, but that they praise his own personal excellence. Indeed, it is not enough that no third person witness one's generosity, the giver's own right hand should not see what the left does! Not even before oneself should an act of charity be paraded or revelled in. Send that inner, applauding spectator away, and let the act, observed only by God, stand on its own. It is a question here of virtue's intrinsic modesty, of that delicacy essential to the purity from which alone God can radiate.

We have it again in the words: "And when you fast, do not look gloomy like the hypocrites, who disfigure their faces in order to appear to men as fasting. Amen I say to you, they have received their reward. But thou, when thou dost fast, anoint thy head and wash thy face, so that thou mayest not be seen fasting by men, but by thy Father, who is in secret; and thy Father, who sees in secret, will reward thee" (Matt. 6:16-18).

Here is a suggestion superior to any commandment, though mentioned in none; one that gives all we do its ultimate value: when you fast—in other words, when you inflict heavy penance on yourself for your sins—perfume your head and wash your face bright. Let all you do seem effortless, self-understood. More: disguise it under an air of festiveness from others and from yourself to protect it from the least cloud of self-approbation or ambiguity. Then the purity of the act will truly radiate God. Christ stresses this doing of good before God alone a second and a third time:

"Again, when you pray, you shall not be like the hypocrites, who love to pray standing in the synagogues and at the street corners . . . go into thy room, and closing thy door, pray to thy Father in secret; and thy Father, who sees in secret, will reward thee" (Matt. 6:5-6).

Again the warning. Naturally "thy room" does not mean domestic privacy in preference to temple or church, but underlines the private, rather than public spirit of the act, for it is possible to be private in church, and 'behind closed doors' on the market-place. When you pray, do not be wordy. Do not suppose for one moment that God can be influenced by the number or choice of your words. Remember, you are conversing with him who knows everything. Actually, your words are superfluous, yet he does want them. They too should be modest. When you pray remind yourself that he sees better than you what you need, though he wants you to ask for it. When you speak to God, he 'hears' you before the words are uttered, for everything in you stands open before him—even your innermost thoughts. When you really know this, not only with the brain but with the heart, your praying will be as Jesus wants it.

In these teachings of Christ one often repeated word gives us pause: reward. Contemporary ethics have declared: The motive of recompense belongs to a lower moral plane than that to which we have progressed. The superior modern has no use for it.

Obviously, the claim is not void of truth. If I perform an act in order to reach some particular goal, I am necessarily somehow bound to the connecting link between its means and its end. If though, I do it simply because it is right, I am not even conscious of means or end, but only of its ethical sense, the fulfillment of duty. In the first instance I am bound by practical necessity; in the second I am also bound, but differently, in conscience, freedom. I can attain the end without freedom, but the sense never. There is something rich, magnanimous, kingly in freedom of this kind which considers itself degraded by the mere thought of 'payment.' The purely moral value has majesty. When I do something good, that good bears its own sense within it; it needs no further justification. Indeed, any additional motive would only lessen its intrinsic worth. The purity of the act is threatened by thought of "reward." I do not *want* to do a thing for reward; I prefer to do it for its own sake, which for me is sufficient. We cannot but agree. Yet Jesus speaks of reward—repeatedly and at decisive moments.

At this point we realize how much depends upon our own personal acceptance of Holy Scripture as the word of God. If I see in the Bible only a profound religious text, I most likely resort to my own discernment and interpret it myself. In so doing I am almost bound to conclude that the idea of virtue for the sake of reward is a remnant of the old, still unpurified morality, and that on this point Jesus' ethics have since been surpassed.

If, however, I accept *a priori* every word of the New Testament as the word of God, then, seeing how much emphasis Jesus places on reward, particularly here where he is proclaiming the very essence of Christian behavior, I conclude that the idea of reward must be profounder than most moderns suspect, and that underlying these teachings' ethical intent there must be a subtler motivation that completely escapes the attention. And there is. As we understand it, what the New Testament says is this: At the root of your "pure ethics" lurks the possibility of a monstrous pride that is particularly difficult to unmask. To desire good for its own intrinsic dignity, and so purely that the pleasure of goodness is the sole and entirely satisfying

130

motive behind our virtue—this is something of which God alone is capable. Only God can perform good in the pure freedom of self-expression; only he finds fulfillment rather than self-denial in majestic magnanimity. Yet modern man has assumed this prerogative for himself. He places the moral attitude and the divine attitude on a par. He has so determined the moral attitude that the ego behind it can only be God, tacitly taking it for granted that human ego, indeed all ego, actually is God. Here lies the moral pride of the age, at once as terrible as it is tenacious.

Jesus' idea of reward is a warning-call to humility. He says: You man—with all your possibilities of perceiving and desiring good—you are nevertheless creature! With all your possibilities of free choice, you remain creature! Anselm of Canterbury wrote of this moral danger. The almost illimitable possibilities of free choice tempt man to omnipotence without God, to feel himself God's equal. It can be overcome by reminding ourselves that even in the practice of virtue we are subject to God's judgment. The fruit of the good deed (of the moral decision and the effort spent on performing it) does not follow autonomously, but is God-given as "reward."

But we must go still deeper.

The idea of reward can be undignified, but only when coupled with a false conception of God. The God of whom Jesus speaks is he who urges me to love him by enabling me to love with his divine power. It is from him that I receive both the love necessary for my act and its "reward": his esteem, itself love. As genuine love grows it begins to say: I love God because he is God. I love him because he is worthy to be who he is. I wish my act to affirm him to whom the multitudes of the angels cry: "Worthy is the Lamb who was slain to receive power and divinity and wisdom and strength and honor and glory and blessing" (Apoc. 5:12).

And suddenly all thought of reward has vanished. No, it is still present in the humility of the beginning, but vanished as a direct motive, and that to which autonomous virtue aspired but could not attain unaided is accomplished: pure good for its own holy sake. Never has purity of intent been more exalted than in the bearing of the saints, who completely overlooked themselves in their burning desire to be possessed by God for God's sake. Only by not aspiring to that purity which is his alone, were they able to avoid running amuck in delusion and pride.

CHAPTER III

POSSIBILITY AND IMPOSSIBILITY

We have just made an attempt to understand something of the uniqueness of the Sermon on the Mount: its revolutionary tidings; the energy with which it insists upon progression from the outer, specific act of virtue to the inner, all-permeating state of virtue; its demand that the degree of identification-of-self-with-neighbor be the sole measure for purity of intent, and consequently, its definition of love as the essence of man's new disposition.

Such demands necessarily raise the already mentioned question: is man capable of satisfying them? Can he be so minded, can he so act? To arrest and overcome violence in goodness; to respond to hate not with hateful deed nor even thought, but with love; to honor those of the opposite sex from the very core of one's being; to be so completely renewed by the divine tidings as to actually consider earthly sorrowing blissful and earthly rejoicing suspicious and dangerous—is this humanly possible?

The moment we accept the words of the Sermon not only emotionally or rhetorically but literally, the question becomes inevitable, especially when we read towards the end: "Enter by the narrow gate. For wide is the gate and broad is the way that leads to destruction, and many there are who enter that way. How narrow the gate and close the way that leads to life! And few there are who find it" (Matt. 7:13-14). Once we accept the question as justifiable, we find it cropping up again and again (see Matt. 13; 20:16, and 11:15), and we must face it. Is it possible to fulfill the demands of the Sermon on the Mount? Are the Christian tidings addressed to all or only to a few chosen ones? Of course, divine choice is made irrespective of the individual's natural traits, (ignoring the world's opinion that only he can perform great deeds who was born with a fearless heart and powerful will; that only he can produce masterpieces who bears within him the plumbless mystery of creative genius). Jesus did not come to bring his message to the particularly gifted, but to "seek and to save what was lost" (Luke 19:10). The "chosen" referred to here can only mean those upon whom God's grace is outpoured, enfranchising the human heart from the bonds of self, instructing it to differentiate between false and true reality, and fortifying it so that it may become capable of performing genuine deeds of faith.

What follows would depend on the nature of the individual. In one who is markedly talented, as was St. Francis, the outcome of grace would be a Christian greatness that is simultaneously worldly greatness. Grace, however, can also work in a person of the most ordinary make-up. Such an individual would live as inconspicuously as those about him, yet his heart would be in God. Whatever its "raw material," grace and its road are open only to those summoned by the autonomous decree of divine Providence. The idea that few are chosen is hard to accept and profoundly discouraging—more discouraging than the apparently harsher supposition that, strictly speaking, no one is capable of fulfilling the Christian demands.

For also this thought seems at times near—as in the conversation with the rich young man. By the end of the dialogue it is obvious that the would-be follower is loathe to sacrifice his belongings, and Christ seizes the occasion to demonstrate the "woe" that threatens the man of property. Logically enough the disciples conclude: If this is so, who can be saved? Christ looks at them and says: "With men this is impossible, but with God all things are possible" (Matt. 19:26). Here it is apparently question of the very essence of Christian existence, and the individual is shaken to hear that no one is exempt from the general impossibility of its realization. Then, one of the great mass of humanity, he calls upon God's mercy, knowing that after all, there must be good reason for Christ's coming: our salvation. In the Sermon on the Mount God demands fulfillment of his laws. We feel that he has the right to demand this; we concede that his demands are just—only to hear that what is expected of all can be fulfilled only by a very few: by those to whom fulfillment is given. This is indeed difficult to accept.

It is essential to remember that the truths of Holy Scripture should never be isolated. Always they must be fitted into the whole, where further truths develop or limit their sense, or balance them with some important counter-truth. For example, the message of the angels on Christ's birth night is one of peace to all who are of good will (Luke 2:14), and Jesus himself says he has come "to seek and to save what was lost." Again and again he pities the many who wander restlessly about "like sheep without a shepherd" (Matt. 9:36). This sounds quite different from the word about the few who are chosen. Yet it too must be included. Both are true. Intellectually we cannot unravel the contradiction; we must try to accept it as it stands, each as best he can before God. If we understand correctly, what Scripture asks is this: How do you know that you are *not* among the chosen? The choice is God's secret; no one knows whether or not he is included, but everyone has the right, no, duty to hold himself open to the possibility. Listen to the Word; weigh the full earnestness of a calling—then see if you dare to say you have not been chosen!

Perhaps you reply: How shall I know? I feel nothing! What is it like to be called? . . . To this Holy Scripture answers: You must not put the question that way. Your task is to accept the commandments of the Lord and to act accordingly. A vocation is no label marked "chosen" which can be fixed to a human existence once and forever. It is a living intention of God, efficacy of his love in the chosen one. Only through the action taken by that person can it become reality. . . . But surely one who is called must behave in a certain recognizable manner? In a certain manner—which? Where is the absolute norm that officially expresses the attitude of the Sermon on the Mount? Jesus once spoke of turning the other cheek when struck, yet when he was brought before the high priest and one of the officers struck him on the cheek he defended himself: "If I have spoken ill, bear witness to the evil; but if well, why dost thou strike me?" (John 18:23). He called upon the order of the court. This shows how little we can bind ourselves to any one point. No one has the right to judge whether or not another lives according to the spirit of the Sermon on the Mount. There is no specific outward behavior that expresses it. Indeed, not even the chosen one himself can be certain how things stand with him. St. Paul says it explicitly: God alone is judge. Dare then to hope that you are chosen! The chance is taken in faith, and neither from the world's point of view, nor from that of inner or outer experience, can there be any possible objection. But I cannot love my enemy! You can bring yourself to the point of no longer hating him. That is already the beginning of love. . . . I can't even do that! . . . Then try at least to keep your dislike out of your speech. That would be a step in the direction of love. . . .

But surely that would be watering the wine? Isn't it a question of everything or nothing? To be quite frank, the Either-Or people attitude often looks suspiciously like rhetoric. No, what the Sermon on the Mount demands is not everything or nothing, but a beginning and a continuing, a rising again and plodding on after every fall.

What then is the main thing? That we accept the Sermon on the Mount not as a fixed, inflexible decree to be carried out to the letter, but as a living challenge and activating force. It aims at establishing a contact between the believer and his God that is gradually to become effective; at instigating action geared to continual progress. But we still have no answer to our question. So far all that has been said is that we are concerned not with a program but with vital action, and that we should begin at once. Is there no cue that might help us at least intellectually to see what we're about? I believe there is, and I should like to explain how I have tried to clarify things for myself; it may be of help to others.

When Jesus preached his Sermon on the Mount—and not only that one sermon, but also others in the same powerful but simple vein—a tremendous possibility stood behind his words. Everything was keyed to the one great hope: "the kingdom of heaven is at hand" (Matt. 3:2). He said specifically that it was near; "at hand" cannot be solely an enthusiastic phrase or rhetorical warning—Jesus always means what he says, and if he says something is "at hand," it is. As far as God was concerned, Isaias' prophecy of the new existence stood ready to become reality. It is idle to try to imagine what that kingdom would have been like. The prophet suggests it in visionary words when he writes in his eleventh book of the calf that shall graze with the lion, of the lamb playing peacefully with the wolf. Then no hurt shall be done, no life taken, and knowledge of the Lord shall lie deep as ocean waters over the face of earth. From the all-renewing power of the Spirit a holy existence was to dawn. Everything was to be different. It is primarily in view of this great possibility that the commands of the Sermon on the Mount were given. The people to whom they are addressed are those who were to participate in this great renewal, and in the new existence these instructions were to be the generally obeyed commands of a God lovingly accepted by all. Such then, the kingdom that would have come if Christ's message had found belief—belief not only of a few individuals, but of the nation that had bound itself to God in the covenant of Sinai. Those in authority: the high priests and the Sanhedrin, the scribes and doctors of the faith should have accepted this belief; when they failed to do so, it was up to the people to thrust them aside and proclaim their faith for themselves. Instead, Christ was rejected by his entire race; so he turned elsewhere— to death. Not in a burst of faith and love and all-renewing spirit did salvation take place, but through Jesus' destruction. Thus he became the sacrifice of expiation. . . . Those addressed by him after this momentous refusal are no longer the same people to whom Jesus first spoke. Now they had become those responsible for Christ's death, the second fall—men from whom the kingdom had recoiled. The harshness of history remains unmitigated.

And still Christ upholds his demands. But now he balances them with something else—his Church, which stands in the closest possible relation to him. She is the continuation of the Reincarnation in history. She is, as St. Paul teaches, the eternal consummation of Jesus' saving and renewing vitality in time. Simultaneously she seems to stand in yet another relationship to him. The Church was founded on the Lord's final journey to Jerusalem, after the decision that he was to die had fallen. (Immediately afterwards he speaks of the violence awaiting him at the hands of the leaders of the people: Matt. 16:13-23.) The Church was established after the Son's return to his Father, upon the descent of the Holy Spirit of Pentecost, Spirit that continually forms Christian history. Christ seems to have made her our weakness' defendant, counter-poise of himself and his demands. She is the advocate of the possible, true mother; reminder, in view of God's tremendous requirements, that after all we are only human.

I am not referring to the limitations of the Church: to her indolence, intolerance, tyranny, narrowness, or to any other form of evil that might be present in her. All these are simply improper, and we shall have to answer for them before God. No. Here I wish to point out the specific task that the Church has been given to fulfill: to reconcile Christ's demands (which seem to exceed human strength), with man's present possibilities; to create a pass, a bridge between them; to come to our aid. Her role can of course become hazardous. It can endanger the purity of divine command; can allow the human element to take the upper hand. Precisely this qualifying element, the wish to mediate, seems to cloud the genuine spirit of the divine tidings. Nevertheless, Christ demands precisely this service of the Church, and it must be rendered in loyalty and humility. So much seems to depend on its proper interpretation and performance! There is a Christianity which stresses the harshness of Christ's demands. It says: everything or nothing and brands the slightest consideration of human weakness as apostasy. The result is that it is forced to conclude either that only very few indeed are capable of following Christ's trail (to the eternal damnation of all others), or it declares that man can do nothing at all by himself and therefore the only course open to him is to accept the consequences and fling himself upon the mercy of God. In both cases the Church must appear a human institution—worse, apostate.

All this sounds extremely Christian; however, on closer examination, we begin to suspect that we are dealing with a grave case of sur-exaltation—excess of so-called strength behind which weakness lies concealed—combined with an unconditional attitude founded on ignorance of human nature. Or worse: possibly it is an unconscious strategy of human nature which attempts to place Christianity in the absolute in order to distance it from the world, that the world be freer for worldliness. On the other hand, behind the Church's attitude, lies a profound sense of realism, a will to Christianize that begins with the possible in order to end on the peaks of sanctity. It is no accident that the 'absolutist Christianity' just mentioned implicitly denies the whole conception of sanctity as 'unchristian.'

Whatever the immediate questions that arise from all this: question of the enormity of the demands as opposed to the weakness of men; of the all or the few or none can live up to them; of absolutism or adaptation to human possibilities; of divine severity or divine tolerance—we must concentrate on the ultimate. Every one of these questions must be considered with a single end in view: God. It is to him that the Sermon on the Mount refers, to God the Father. Jesus focuses the attention on him, precisely here in connection with these difficult demands. Here he does not say as usual, "your Father" in the general plural sense of the adjective, but *thy* Father, thou specifically summoned one! Here God is no exalted and distant lawgiver heaping mankind with ponderous burdens in order to judge and condemn later; he commands in love and helps us to obey. He himself brings his laws to men, lives among them, with them, and is personally concerned with the problem of their acceptance. Here is the all-seeing Father who knows every need before it is expressed because his providential eye is constantly upon us. This the God we must keep in mind when we weigh these questions. Only then will they come into their own deepest sense, and the promise receive its answer: love.

CHAPTER IV

SEED AND EARTH

When we study the Sermon on the Mount—that purest expression of Christ's message preached at a time when there was yet no public opposition to him—we unconsciously ask ourselves: to whom essentially was it addressed, and what were its chances, from an earthly point of view, of being understood.

We moderns are inclined to answer: Jesus spoke first of all to the individual, then to mankind in general. Both answers are correct, for only since Jesus Christ does it exist, this double calling of the individual and of all men irrespective of race.

Nevertheless, the reply is a little too modern to be wholly true; its simultaneously individualistic and international conception must be readjusted and purified. Jesus himself thinks more historically. Primarily concerned with divine history, he never forgets that he was sent first of all "to the lost sheep of the house of Israel" (Matt. 15:24). His tidings especially concern those bound by the Covenant of Sinai, race whom the prophets have taught to expect the coming of the Messiah to the chosen people under the domination of regent and official. This then the nation Christ "officially" (the word used here in its fullest sense: as a charge and mission) calls upon to believe. Its Yes would have brought about the fulfillment of the jesajanic prophecy, the all-transforming dawn of the kingdom. When, instead, the people refused Christ, the repercussions were felt far beyond the limits of personal salvation, also beyond the historical confines of the Jewish nation. As the response of the people duty-bound to God, it was the response of the whole human race. What followed meant not only that the tidings were passed on to others, but that now the whole problem of salvation itself was profoundly altered. The failure of the Jewish people to accept Christ was the second Fall, the import of which can be fully grasped only in connection with the first.

Those who heard Christ during his life heard his voice across one and a half thousand years of history, a circumstance which simultaneously helped and hindered. Israel's history had been shaped by its faith in God. Through this faith the little nation had been able to assert itself against the surrounding empires of the Assyrians, Babylonians, Egyptians and Greeks. Secure in its monotheistic belief, it had been able to overcome the spiritual and religious forces around it. However, in this belief in the one-and-only God, it had also begun to grow harsh and rigid. Consequently, when Jesus' divine message was proclaimed, revealing a God so intrinsically different from the God they had conceived, the Jews were angered. With superhuman courage and tenacity they had fought for the Sabbath, for the temple and its rites; but in the process, Sabbath, temple and ritual had become idols.

Such then the background of the people Jesus was addressing.

How did the leaders of the people respond to these tidings? Negatively, from first to last. From the start we see the watching, suspicious faces of "the Scribes and Pharisees." The grounds for criticism are usually ritualistic: that Jesus heals on the Sabbath; that his disciples pluck handfuls of grain on this day; that they do not wash before eating and so on. The real reason, however, lies deeper. Jesus' opponents feel that here is a will foreign to their own. What they desire is the perpetuance of the old covenant. God's dominion is to be established in the world, to be established by his chosen race. Granted, some pneumatological event will bring it about, but so as to eternalize the victory of the old covenant in the world. When they notice that the new Rabbi mentions neither the temple nor the Kingdom of Israel; that he questions the world and the value of earthly existence, proclaiming the divine government of perfect freedom, they feel that he is an alien spirit, and cannot rest until they have him safely under ground. So much for the Pharisees, the strictly orthodox, nationalistic 'conservatives.' Their hated rival group, the Sadducees—liberal, progressive, and influenced by Greek culture—at first pay no attention whatsoever to the 'dreamer.' However, once the movement becomes suspiciously powerful, they join forces with their despised opponents long enough to put an end to the dangerous one.

And the masses? When those in authority failed, it was up to them to obey the impulse of Palm Sunday, and fired by the spirit that the prophet Joel calls Messianic, to recognize the Messiah and proclaim their allegiance to him. But this does not happen. The people do have a certain instinct for Jesus. They come to him for help in their need: they listen to his words, are shaken by his miracles. At times they sense the Messianic mystery that enfolds him and they try to make him king. But their conduct is confused. At the very beginning, in Nazareth, a wave of such jealousy sweeps them that they attempt to take his life (Luke 4:16-30). Later, in Gerasa when he heals the possessed boy, and the herd of swine plunges into the sea, they conclude that he must be dangerous and urge him to go elsewhere (Luke 8:22-37). When he passes through Samaria on his way to Galilee they receive him amicably (John 4:1-42); however, when he returns from the opposite direction on his way to hated Jerusalem, they do not allow him to enter the city. (See Luke 9:51-55.) The masses sense his power and significance, but indeterminately. What is felt is not coordinated into responsible action. For this a guiding hand is needed, and it is not there. How fittingly one of Jesus' friends or disciples might have bridged the gulf between him and the masses, might have gathered the hearts of the crowd and led them to decision! But Jesus' followers are afraid and remain in the background. Thus the people are delivered over to the Pharisees, who make easy game of them, deftly leading them from the enthusiasm of Palm Sunday to the apostasy of Good Friday.

The political forces of the day should also be mentioned; they remain neutral. The actual power was in the hands of the Romans. Pilate only learned of Jesus' existence through his denunciation and at first took the prisoner for one of the many hotheads of the times. He soon realized, however, that he was dealing with someone extraordinary—belief that higher beings or sons of God appeared on earth was not uncommon to the age, and he grew uneasy and tried to free him. But in the end he too conceded to the pressure of the accusers.

Then there are the local princes, among them Herod, tetrarch of Galilee and Jesus' immediate sovereign. His portrait is sketched clearly enough in the Gospels. He is one of the many small oriental despots who are simultaneously vassals of the Roman Empire. Weak and spoiled, he is apparently not shallow, for he loves to talk with his prisoner, John the Baptist, whom he takes seriously. But his depth is without character, for on the strength of a lightly given 'word of honor,' he orders the holy man's execution. When news of Jesus' miracles reaches him, he is seized by a superstitious fear that John has reappeared (Luke 9:7-9). Jesus mentions him once: When the Pharisees tell him he should leave the country, for Herod wishes to kill him: "Go and say to that fox, 'Behold, I cast out devils and perform cures today and tomorrow, and the third day I am to end my course' " (Luke 13:32). During the trial Pilate sends the prisoner to his sovereign. It is a gesture of courtesy by which Pilate hopes to rid himself of the disquieting affair. When Jesus remains mute before Herod, he ridicules him and sends him back in the trappings of a royal fool. The two authorities, formerly enemies, now become friends (Luke 23:12).

And what of the intimates of the Lord? Mary was linked closely with him. We have already spoken of their relationship; there is not much more to be said. With Jesus' next of kin, his "brothers," it is a different story. In chapter seven St. John describes a typical incident. The Pasch is approaching, and they are planning the customary annual pilgrimage to Jerusalem. Jesus' relatives try to persuade him to go with them: anyone who can do what he can should not remain in the provinces; he should go there where all really important events take place and make a name for himself! Jesus replies: My time has not yet come. Your time, it is true, is always there.

We feel the distance between them, even a hint of disdain. Finally, St. Mark reports how once, while Jesus was teaching, and the crowds streamed to him from all sides, his family try to restrain him: "But when his own people had heard of it, they went out to lay hold of him, for they said, 'He has gone mad' " (Mark 3:20-21). Pique, incomprehension, closed hearts and violence all the way along the line.

And the disciples? It must be admitted that during Jesus' lifetime not one of them suggests a great personality. Before Pentecost they are still all too human. It is depressing to see Jesus among them. Uncomprehending they degrade everything, are jealous of each other, take advantage of their position, and when the test comes, fail. Already in Capharnaum when Jesus introduces the Holy Eucharist, his followers begin to murmur among themselves. Many of his disciples declare: How can one listen to such things? And they turn away from him. At this the Lord asks the Twelve if they too want to go; the answer hardly rings with vital conviction. Shaken, bewildered, they rescue themselves in blind faith: "Lord, to whom shall we go? Thou hast words of everlasting life." (See John 6:60-69.)

Among these Twelve is Judas who has already lined his pockets from the common purse (John 12:6). And when it comes to the seizure, they all flee, and Peter denies his Master (John 18:15-27).

Who then was really open to Jesus' message? First of all, quiet individuals, people inclined by nature perhaps to enthusiasm or aloofness. They distanced themselves from the constant influx of political events in Jerusalem, from the differences of the Pharisees and Sadducees. They lived completely in the tradition of the prophets, quietly waiting for the fulfillment of God's promise. To these belonged Zachary the priest, Elizabeth, Mary's cousin, Simeon the prophet, Anne, the ancient seer, Lazarus with his two sisters, and a good many others. They came closest to understanding the Lord. But perhaps also not rightly—possibly for that they were too individualistic.

Then there were the social outcasts, the "publicans and sinners": the ones hated as the enemies of the people because they sided with the Romans for economic considerations, the others despised as dishonorable. What was otherwise their misfortune was perhaps here their salvation. Having no social position to lose, they were more open, readier for the out-of-the-ordinary. They considered Jesus an overthrower of worldly opinion, and they flocked to him; was he not accused of being a "friend of publicans and sinners"? But, of course, when it came to the ultimate decision, such people had no influence whatsoever.

And finally there is a third group: the heathen. Jesus' manner of speaking of them is notable. His words seem to take on a special warmth, almost longing. When the captain tells him it is unnecessary for him to come personally to his sick servant, he has but to command the illness to leave and it will obey, Jesus is both delighted and saddened. "Amen I say to you, not even in Israel have I found so great a faith" (Luke 7:9). Something similar occurs in the incident of the Chanaanite woman. Her faith is great enough and humble enough to allow her to understand that Jesus has been sent first of all to the children of the house of David: to the chosen people, and that she herself is like one of those little dogs that hope for the crumbs "that fall from their masters' tables" (Matt. 15:27). But her faith in divine abundance for all is unshakable. The general impression of the heathen that the Lord must have had is evident in the words with which he threatens the cities of Israel at the time of the Galilean crisis: "Woe to thee, Corozain! woe to thee, Bethsaida! For if in Tyre and Sidon had been worked the miracles that have been worked in you, they would have repented long ago in sackcloth and ashes" (Matt. 11:21).

It was among the heathen that Jesus found open souls and fresh, ready hearts. Only too often, ancient religious tradition, long training, and hard and fast usage stamp the ground hard. The spirit no longer takes any imprint; the heart remains cool or undecided, and rarely does feeling become that passion which demands absolute earnestness. So it must have been then with the Jews. The heathen, on the other hand, were rich virgin soil, frontier country of endless possibilities. But they too had little effect on the imminent decision, for it was not to them that Jesus had been sent. The ground on which Jesus' words fell was hard ground indeed.

We are accustomed to accepting the course of the Lord's life on earth as predetermined. Because it was as it was, we conclude that it was meant to be so. We judge everything by its outcome and forget how monstrous—in the eyes of both God and man—the means by which it was accomplished. We have entirely lost the middle ages' reaction of horror at thought of God's murder. We must strip ourselves of our customary callousness and realize how frightful the whole procedure was, how hardened men's hearts, how paltry Jesus' reception!

Not until we have felt our way back to this attitude will we understand Christ's word: "but this is your hour, and the power of darkness" (Luke 22:53). He knew that in the last analysis, mankind's unique, limitless possibility was not frustrated by human will alone. For this, humans, in spite of all their presumption and violence, are much too insignificant.

It is incomprehensible that things could go as they did when, after all, he was who he was! *Why* was none of those in power receptive and courageous? Why was no one there to lead the people to Christ? Why were his disciples, humanly speaking, so inadequate?

Who is this God who seems to lack the power to bring about his Son's due reception? What a strangely disturbing impression of weakness he makes! And what wicked, dogged power is this thing called "world" that is capable of hardening itself against God's summons and cold-bloodedly making an end of his envoy? What kind of God must this be to remain silent before such things!

We live so thoughtlessly that we no longer feel the impact of such unheard of conduct. How do men imagine the advent of divinity on earth? The myths suggest outpourings of dynamic radiance. Buddha is an ascetic, but he thrones in more than royal esteem. The sage Lao-tse is venerated as a god. Mohammed gallops across the world at the head of victorious armies. Here though, God himself becomes man. He has a divinely grave 'interest' in Jesus' human existence; his own honor is at stake, his omnipotence—and what happens! The long history of the Old Testament has been painstakingly directed towards the coming of the Messiah, yet when he does come, this mysterious hardening of people's hearts, this inexplicable fate! What God is this that such things could happen to his Son?

Surely we begin to feel the otherness of Christianity. Those other 'divinities' were earthly powers, and earth recognizes and loves what is hers. When something truly from elsewhere comes, how different the response! Gradually we sense what it must be to be a Christian: to be allegiance-bound to such a God in a world that is as it is. No wonder it means estrangement. And doesn't "world" in reality, mean ourselves—not only that which is about us? That in us which is close to the divine is somehow alien to us, and we have good grounds for the Christian fear that what happened once might be repeated in us: the second fall, the closing of our own hearts to God!

PART FOUR

CHAPTER XII

BELIEF IN CHRIST, IMITATION OF CHRIST

Among the instructions that Jesus gives the Twelve before sending them out into the world are the following: "Do not think that I have come to send peace upon the earth; I have come to bring a sword, not peace. . . . He who loves father or mother more than me is not worthy of me; and he who loves son or daughter more than me is not worthy of me. And he who does not take up his cross and follow me, is not worthy of me. He who finds his life will lose it, and he who loses his his life for my sake, will find it" (Matt. 10:34-39).

Jesus' message is one of good will. He proclaims the Father's love and the advent of his kingdom. He calls people to the peace and harmony of life lived in the divine will. Yet their first reaction is not union, but division. The more profoundly Christian a man becomes, the deeper the cleft between him and those who refuse to follow Christ—its exact measure proportionate to the depth of that refusal. The split runs right through the most intimate relationship, for genuine conversion is not a thing of natural disposition or historical development, but the most personal decision an individual can make. The one makes it, the other does not; hence the possibility of schism between father and son, friend and friend, one member of a household and another. When it comes to a choice between domestic peace and Jesus, one must value Jesus higher; even higher than the most dearly beloved: father and mother, son and daughter, friend or love. This means cutting into the very core of life, and temptation presses us to preserve human ties and abandon Christ. But Jesus warns us: If you hold "life" fast, sacrificing me for it, you lose your own true life. If you let it go for my sake, you will find yourself in the heart of immeasurable reality.

Naturally this is difficult; it is the cross. And here we brush the heaviest mystery of Christianity, its inseparableness from Calvary. Ever since Christ walked the way of the cross, it stands firmly planted on every Christian's road, for every follower of Christ has his own personal cross. Nature revolts against it, wishing to 'preserve' herself. She tries to go around it, but Jesus has said unequivocally, and his words are fundamental to Christianity: He who hangs on, body and soul, to "life" will lose it; he who surrenders his will to his cross will find it—once and forever in the immortal self that shares in the life of Christ.

On the last journey to Jerusalem, shortly before the Transfiguration, Jesus' words about the cross are repeated. Then, sharply focused, the new thought: "For what does it profit a man, if he gain the whole world, but suffer the loss of his own soul? Or what will a man give in exchange for his soul?" (Matt. 16:26).

This time the point plunges deeper. The dividing line runs not between one person and another, but between the believer or one desirous of belief and everything else! Between me and the world. Between me and myself. The lesson of the cross is the great lesson of self-surrender and self-conquest. Our meditations are approaching the passion of the Lord, so it is time that we turn to Christianity's profoundest, but also most difficult mystery.

Why did Jesus come? To add a new, higher value to those already existent? To reveal a new truth over and above existing truth, or a nobler nobility, or a new and juster order of human society? No, he came to bring home the terrible fact that everything, great and small, noble and mean, the whole with all its parts—from the corporal to the spiritual, from the sexual to the highest creative urge of genius—is intrinsically corrupt. This does not deny the existence of individual worth. What is good remains good, and high aspirations will always remain high. Nevertheless, human existence *in toto* has fallen away from God. Christ did not come to renew this part or that, or to disclose greater human possibilities, but to open man's eyes to what the world and human life as an entity really is; to give him a point of departure from which he can begin all over with his scale of values and with himself. Jesus does not uncover hidden creative powers in man; he refers him to God, center and source of all power.

It is as though humanity were one of those enormous ocean liners that is a world in itself: apparatuses for the most varied purposes; collecting place for all kinds of passengers and crew with their responsibilities and accomplishments, passions, tensions, struggles. Suddenly someone appears on board and says: What each of you is doing is important, and you are right to try to perfect your efforts. I can help you, but not by changing this or that on your ship, it is your course that is wrong; you are steering straight for destruction. . . .

Christ does not step into the row of great philosophers with a better philosophy; or of the moralists with a purer morality; or of the religious geniuses to conduct man deeper

147

into the mysteries of life; he came to tell us that our whole existence, with all its philosophy and ethics and religion, its economics, art, and nature, is leading us away from God and into the shoals. He wants to help us swing the rudder back into the divine direction, and to give us the necessary strength to hold that course. And other appreciation of Christ is worthless. If this is not valid, then every man for himself; let him choose whatever guide seems trustworthy, and possibly Goethe or Plato or Buddha is a better leader than what remains of a Jesus Christ whose central purpose and significance have been plucked from him.

Jesus actually is the Rescue-pilot who puts us back on the right course. It is with this in mind that we must interpret the words about winning the world at the loss of the essential; about losing life, personality, soul, in order to possess them anew and truly. They refer to faith and the imitation of Christ.

Faith means to see and to risk accepting Christ not only as the greatest teacher of truth that ever lived, but as Truth itself (John 16:6). Sacred reality begins with Jesus of Nazareth. If it were possible to annihilate him, the truth he taught would not continue to exist in spite of the loss of its noblest apostle, but *itself would cease to exist.* For he is the *Logos,* the source of Living Truth. He demands not only that we consent intellectually to the correctness of his proclamation—that would be only a beginning—but that we feel with all our natural instinct for right and wrong, with heart and soul and every cell of our being, its claims upon *us.* We must not forget: the whole ship is headed for disaster. It does not help to change from one side of it to the other or to replace this or that instrument. It is the course that must be altered. We must learn to take completely new bearings. What does it mean, to be? Philosophy goes into the problem deeply, without changing being at all. Religion tells me that I have been created; that I am continuously receiving myself from divine hands, that I am free yet living from God's strength. Try to feel your way into this truth, and your whole attitude towards life will change. You will see yourself in an entirely new perspective. What once seemed self-understood becomes questionable. Where once you were indifferent, you become reverent; where self-confident, you learn to know "fear and trembling." But where formerly you felt abandoned, you will now feel secure, living as a child of the Creator-Father, and the knowledge that this is precisely what you are will alter the very taproot of your being. . . . What does it mean to die? Physiology says the blood vessels harden or the organs cease to function. Philosophy speaks of the pathos of finite life condemned to aspire vainly to infinity. Faith defines death as the fruit of sin, and man as *peccator* (Rom. 6:23). Death's arm is as long as sin's. One day for you too its consequences and those of death's disintegration will have to be drawn. It will become evident how peccant you are and consequently moribund. Then all the protective screens so elaborately arranged between you and this fact will fall, and you will have to stand and face your judgment. But faith also adds, God is love, even though he allows sin to fulfill itself in death, and your Judge is the same as your Savior. If you were to reflect on this, over and over again until its truth was deep in your blood, wouldn't it make a fundamental difference in your attitude towards life, giving you a confidence the world does not have to give? Wouldn't it add a new earnestness and meaning to everything you do?

What precisely is this chain of acts and events that runs from our first hour through our last? The one says natural necessity; the other historical consequence; a third, something else. Faith says: It is Providence. The God who made you, saved you, and will one day place you in his light, also directs your life. What happens between birth and death is message, challenge, test, succor—all from his hands. It is not meant to be learned theoretically, but personally experienced and assimilated. Where this is so, aren't all things necessarily transfigured? What is the resultant attitude but faith?

Religion then! But there are so many, one might object; Christ is just another religious founder.

No; all other religions come from earth. True, God is present in the earth he created, and it is always God whom the various religions honor, but not in the supremacy of his absolute freedom. Earthly religions revere God's activity, the reflections of his power (more or less fragmentary, distorted) as they encounter it in a world that has turned away from him. They are inspired by the breath of the divine, but they exist apart from him; they are saturated with worldly influences, are formed, interpreted, colored by the historical situation of the moment. Such a religion does not save. It is itself a piece of "world," and he who wins the world loses his soul. Christ brings no "religion," but the message of the living God, who stands in opposition and contradiction to all things, "world-religions" included. Faith understands this, for to believe does not mean to participate in one or the other religions, but: "Now this is everlasting life, that they may know thee, the only true God, and him whom thou hast sent, Jesus Christ" (John 17:3). Men are to accept Christ's tidings as the norm of their personal lives.

My attitudes towards things to be done may be various. One follows the principle of maximum profit with minimum effort. This is the clever or economical approach. I can also consider a specific task in the light of duty, the fulfillment of which places my life on a spiritual and moral level. Christ teaches neither greater cleverness nor a higher sense of duty; he says: Try to understand everything that comes into your life from the viewpoint of the Father's will. If I do, what happens? Then I continue to act in accordance with cleverness and utility, but under the eyes of God. I will also do things that seem foolish to the world, but are clever in eternity. I will continue to try to act ethically, to distinguish clearly between right and wrong and to live in increasing harmony with an increasingly dependable conscience. All this, however, in the living presence of Christ, which will teach me to see things I never would have noticed alone. It will change my concepts and trouble my conscience—but for its good, stripping it of levity's self-confidence, of moral pride, and of the intellectual stiffness that results from too much principle-riding. With increasing delicacy of conscience will come a new firmness of purpose and a new energy (simultaneously protective and creative) for the interests of good.

Similarly, my attitude to my neighbor may be ordered from various points of view: I can consider others competition, and attempt to protect my interests from them. I can respect the personality of each. I can see them as co-sharers of destiny, responsible with me for much that is to come, and so on and so forth. Each of these attitudes has its place, but everything is changed once I understand what Christ is saying: You and those near you—through me you have become brothers and sisters, offspring of the same Father. His kingdom is to be realized in your relationship to each other. We have already spoken of the transformation that takes place when fellow citizens become brothers in Christ; when from the "you and me" of the world springs the Christian "we." Much could be said of the Christian's attitude to destiny and all that it implies in the way of injustice, shock and tragedy: things with which no amount of worldly wisdom, fatalism or philosophy can cope—and preserve its integrity. This is possible only when some fixed point exists *outside* the world, and such a point cannot be created by man, but must be accepted from above (as we accept the tidings of divine Providence and his all-directing love). St. Paul words it in his epistle to the Romans (Chap. 8): "Now we know that for those who love God all things work together unto good. . . ." This means an ever more complete exchange of natural security, self-confidence, and self-righteousness, for confidence in God and his righteousness as it is voiced by Christ and the succession of his apostles.

Until a man makes this transposition he will have no peace. He will realize how the years of his life unroll, and ask himself vainly what remains. He will make moral efforts to improve, only to become either hopelessly perplexed or priggish. He will work, only to discover that nothing he can do stills his heart. He will study, only to progress little beyond vague probabilities—unless his intellectual watchfulness slackens, and he begins to accept possibility for truth or wishes for reality. He will fight, found, form this and that only to discover that millions have done the same before him and millions will continue to after he is gone, without shaping the constantly running sand for more than an instant. He will explore religion, only to founder in the questionableness of all he finds. The world is an entity. Everything in it conditions everything else. Everything is transitory. No single thing helps, because the world as a whole has fallen from grace. One quest alone has an absolute sense: that of the Archimedes-point and lever which can lift the world back to God, and these are what Christ came to give.

One more point is important: our Christianity itself must constantly grow. The great revolution of faith is not a lump of reality fallen ready-made from heaven into our laps. It is a constant act of my individual heart and strength. I stand with all I am at the center of my faith, which means that I bring to it also those strands of my being which instinctively pull away from God. It is not as though I, the believer, stood on one side, on the other the fallen world. Actually faith must be realized within the reality of my being, with its full share of worldliness.

Woe to me if I say: "I believe" and feel safe in that belief. For then I am already in danger of losing it (see Cor. 10:12). Woe to me if I say: "I am a Christian"—possibly with a side-glance at others who in my opinion are not, or at an age that is not, or at a cultural tendency flowing in the opposite direction. Then my so-called Christianity threatens to become nothing but a religious form of self-affirmation. I "am" not a Christian; I am on the way to becoming one—if God will give me the strength. Christianity is nothing one can "have"; nor is it a platform from which to judge others. It is movement. I can become a Christian only as long as I am conscious of the possibility of falling away. The gravest danger is not failure of the will to accomplish a certain thing; with God's help I can always pull myself together and begin again. The real danger is that of becoming within myself unchristian, and it is greatest when my will is most sure of itself. I have absolutely no guarantee that I shall be privileged to remain a follower of Christ save in the manner of beginning, of being *en route,* of becoming, trusting, hoping and praying.

CHAPTER XIII

FORGIVENESS

The next to the last request of the Pater Noster runs: "And forgive us our debts as we forgive our debtors." Mark elaborates on the thought: "And when you stand up to pray, forgive whatever you have against anyone, that your Father in heaven may also forgive you your offences" (11:25). And Matthew adds directly to the words of the prayer: "For if you forgive men their offences, your heavenly Father will also forgive you your offences. But if you do not forgive men, neither will your Father forgive you your offences" (Matt. 6: 14-15). Thus God's forgiveness of our sins depends upon our forgiveness or refusal to forgive others for the injustices they have committed against us.

After Jesus has spoken of fraternal, mutual correction, the text continues: "Then Peter came up to him and said, 'Lord, how often shall my brother sin against me, and I forgive him? Up to seven times?' Jesus said to him, 'I do not say to thee seven times, but seventy times seven' " (Matt. 18:21-22). Forgiveness should be no occasion, but our habitual attitude towards others. To drive this fundamental point home, Jesus illustrates his teaching with the story of the king who audits his accounts. Finding an enormous deficit in the books of one of his administrators, he commands that his property, family and person be placed under custody until the debt is paid. The man begs for mercy, and his master, who is magnanimous, cancels the debt. But the administrator has hardly left the room when he encounters a colleague who owes him an incomparably smaller sum. He seizes him, and deaf to excuse or plea, drags him to the debtors' court—in those days notorious for its harshness. The king learns what has happened, and angered by the man's heartlessness submits him to the same fate he has inflicted upon his debtor. "So also my heavenly Father will do to you, if you do not each forgive your brothers from your hearts" (Matt. 18:35).

Earlier in the same chapter Christ discusses what is to be done with one who refuses to see or admit his wrongs. It is up to you to straighten him out. If it is you he has injured, you must not simply ignore him in a mood of irritated moral superiority, but must go to him and do everything possible to make him understand and willing to clear things up. This will not be easy. If you come to him condescendingly, or pedantically, or in the role of the ethically superior, he will only consider you presumptuous. His opposition to your claims will entrench itself against the real injustice of your Pharisaic attitude, and the end of it all will be worse than the beginning. Therefore, if you wish to obey Christ, you must first free yourself of all 'righteous' indignation. Only if you forgive entirely, can you contact the true self of the other, whom his own rebelliousness is holding back. If you can reach this better self, you have a good chance of being heard, and of winning your brother. This then the great doctrine of forgiveness on which Jesus insists as one of the fundamentals of his message. If we wish to get to its root, we must dig our way there question by question.

What must we overcome in ourselves to be capable of genuine forgiveness?

First of all, deep in the domain of the purely natural, the sentiment of having to do with an enemy. This sense of the hostile is something animals have, and it reaches as far as their vulnerability. Creatures are so ordered that the preservation of the one depends on the destruction of the other. This is also true of fallen man, deeply enmeshed in the struggle for existence. He who injures me or takes something valuable from me is my enemy, and all my reactions of distrust, fear, and repulsion rise up against him. I try to protect myself from him, and am able to do this best by constantly reminding myself of his dangerousness, instinctively mistrusting him, and being prepared at all times to strike back. . . . Here forgiveness would mean first that I relinquish the clear and apparently only sure defense of natural animosity; second, that I overcome fear and risk defenselessness, convinced that the enemy can do nothing against my intrinsic self. Naturally, this does not mean that I close my eyes to danger, and it is self-understood that I do everything in my power to protect myself: I must be watchful and resolute. But the crux of the matter is forgiveness, a profound and weighty thing. Its prerequisite is the courage that springs from a deep sense of intimate security, and which, as experience has proved, is usually justified, for the genuine pardoner actually is stronger than the fear-ridden hater.

The desire for revenge is slightly more 'human.' It is not a response to mortal danger, but to the danger of loss of power and honor. The fact that the other was able to damage me proves that he was stronger than I; had I been what I should be, he never would have dared to attempt it. The impulse to retaliate aims primarily at reestablishing my self-respect by humiliating my enemy. I would rise by the other's fall. . . . To forgive him would mean to renounce this satisfaction, and necessitates a self-respect independent of the behavior of others because it lives from an intrinsic honor that is invulnerable. Again experience has shown that such an attitude also better protects my reputation, for my freedom blunts the point of the insult, thus disarming the aggressor.

One step closer to spiritual value is the desire for justice: order not of things and forces, but of human relations. That the individual receive according to his deserts and remain with these in the proper relationship to others and their deserts; that is justice. When someone does me an injustice, he disturbs that order there where it most vitally affects me, in myself. This is what arouses me. In the elementary desire for justice there is much that is simply primitive fear, for the just order is primarily protective. Wounded pride and the desire to avenge it are different; they are satisfied when they can take justice into their own hands. Fundamentally, what they demand is treatment conforming to one's personal dignity, and its simplest expression is the ancient law, "eye for eye, tooth for tooth" (Ex. 21:24). What the other had done to me shall be done to him; thus the wrong will be atoned, and order reestablished.

Here forgiveness would mean renouncing the right to administer justice oneself. To leave it to the authorities, to the state, to destiny and ultimately to God is the beginning of self-purification. But pardon really worthy of the name is much more: it is relinquishment of the wish to see punishment meted out at all. Quitting the questionable territory of desired pain for pain, damage for damage, atonement for guilt, one enters the open country of freedom. There too order exists, but of a different kind. It is not the result of weights and measures, but of creative self-conquest. Magnanimity, man's premonition of that divine power known as grace, rises to the surface. Forgiveness reestablishes order by acquitting the offender and thereby placing him in a new and higher order of justice.

But why should we act thus? The question really deserves to be posed. Why forgive? Why not simply establish justice? Wouldn't it be better? One answer is: forgiveness is more human. He who insists on his rights places himself outside the community of men. He would be judge of men rather than one of them, sharer of the common fate. It is better to remain within the circle of humanity and broaden heart and mind. Prerequisite is an innate altruism, and if we know people who have it, we also know how often it is accompanied by negative characteristics, by weakness, lack of dignity, indiscriminate negligence, disregard for truth and justice, even sudden outbursts of cruelty and vengefulness. . . . It has been pointed out that in reality, insistence on justice is servitude. Only forgiveness frees us from the injustice of others. To understand this attitude too requires a certain characteristic impersonality towards oneself and others; again with its negative counterpart: the tendency to disregard the rights and dignity of the individual. Much more could be said about the nobility of forgiveness and its accompanying values: generosity and magnanimity, and so on. This would all be correct, but still far from the pith of the New Testament's teaching.

Christ's exhortations are founded neither on social nor ethical nor any other worldly motives. We are told, simply, to forgive men as our Father in heaven forgives us. He is the primary and real Pardoner, and man is his child. Our powers of forgiveness are derived from his.

We beg the Father to forgive us as we forgive those who have been unjust to us. When you begin to pray, says the Lord, and suddenly remember that you have a grudge against someone, forgive him first! If you do not, your unforgiveness will step between you and the Father and prevent your request from reaching him. This does not mean that God forgives us because kindness to our neighbors renders us 'worthy' of his generosity. His pardon is pure grace, which is not founded on our worthiness, but creates it. *A priori,* however, is the opening of the heart for divine magnanimity: our readiness to forgive "our debtors." If we close it instead, we shut God's forgiveness out.

Briefly, forgiveness is a part of something much greater than itself: love. We should forgive, because we should love. That is why forgiveness is so free; it springs from the joint accomplishment of human and divine pardon. Like him who loves his enemies, the pardoner resembles the Father "who makes his sun to rise on the good and the evil, and sends rain on the just and the unjust" (Matt. 5:45).

Pardon reestablishes Christian fraternity and the sacred unity of the I-you-he (God). He who reasons from this height considers his neighbor's welfare precious, and to know him in the wrong is painful, as it is painful to God to witness a man's fall from his divine love. And just as God longs to win the lost one back (possible only through his aid in the form of grace), the Christian longs to help his brother to return to the community of sacred life.

Christ is forgiveness incarnate. We search in vain for the slightest trace of any reaction of his incompatible with pardon. Nothing of fear in any form is in him. His soul knows itself invulnerable, and he walks straight into danger, confident "because the Father is with me" (John 16:32). Vengeance is farthest of all from his thoughts. He is forced to endure unimaginable injustices, not only against his human honor, but also blasphemously directed against the honor of his Father. His sacred mission is called a work of Satan! His anger does flare, but it is divine wrath that blazes at the sacrilege, not desire for revenge. His self-confidence is untouched by the behavior of others, for he is entirely free. As for the weighing and measuring of justice, Christ came precisely for this, but he elevated it to the unspeakably higher plane of grace beyond weight and measure, dissolving man's own injustice in the divine solvent of genuine pardon. His message could not have been more personally delivered. He not only taught divine forgiveness, but demonstrated it on himself. All man's sinfulness against God gathered and precipitated blood upon the head of the "sign that shall be contradicted" (Luke 2:34). And Christ neither attempted to withdraw from the terrible rain, nor did he take personal offense; he recognized the injustice for what it was: an offense against God. He sealed the divine forgiveness he had come to bring by his own act of pardoning, offering his Father as expiation for humanity's sin, his own acceptance of the injustice heaped upon him: "Father, forgive them, for they do not know what they are doing."

And now we touch bottom: God's forgiveness did not occur as a mere pardon, but came as the result of Christ's expiation. He did not cancel mankind's sin, but reestablished genuine justice. He did not simply tear up man's frightful debt, but repaid it—with his own sweat and blood and tears. That is what Christian salvation means, and it is no isolated incident deep in the past on which we are still capitalizing, but the foundation for our whole Christian existence. To this day we live from the saving act of Christ, but we cannot remain saved unless the spirit of salvation is actively realized in our own lives. We cannot enjoy the fruits of salvation without contributing to salvation through love of neighbor. And such love must become pardon when that neighbor trespasses against us, as we constantly trespass against God.

CHAPTER XIV

CHRIST THE BEGINNING

"I have come to cast fire upon the earth, and what will I but that it be kindled? But I have a baptism to be baptized with; and how distressed I am until it is accomplished!" (Luke 12:49-50). The words were probably uttered before Jesus crossed the Jordan to go to Jerusalem.

St. Paul speaks of the saving knowledge of Jesus Christ, which excels all else (Phil. 3:8). By this he does not mean knowledge in the sense of information or psychological insight, but that wisdom which springs from faith and love, fruit of the intimate contact with the soul of Christ when man's own soul suddenly becomes aware of whom it is embracing. And since Christ is power, the individual who so contacts him is transformed by the flow of divine strength. . . . If we call this central part of Christ's being his disposition, how, actually, is he disposed?

How can a man be disposed towards his fellow men? To start with the worst, he can despise them, taught by pride or disappointment, or sheer emotional exhaustion. He can fear them, or use them or benefit them. He can also love his fellows, and by giving himself to them, ripen to fulfillment of his own intrinsic being. Perhaps even creative love will stir in him, and he will venture everything, body and soul, breaking revolutionary paths for others to follow. What does Christianity say to all this? The answer is not easy to accept; indeed, for one without faith it is unacceptable. It runs: All these attitudes are enmeshed in the world, in the powers of evil, in the straits of fear and natural instinct, in intellectual and spiritual pride, in that which we over hastily define as "good." They can be good, even noble; but they are bonds nevertheless. The little freedom they enjoy is always limited by the borders of a world which is itself in chains.

Not so Christ. The purity of his disposition is not the result of a struggle against evil and victory over fear, nor is it instinctive physical purity or inborn spiritual nobility. In him the disposition of the Son of God is alive; purity which enters the world from above and is its new, spotless beginning. It is God's love that was made man. Not any man, but Jesus Christ, the Galilean, offspring of a specific race and age, of its social, political and cultural aspects, but so disposed that in the man Jesus faith finds the pure expression of divine sonship.

There is only one whom we might be inclined to compare with Jesus: Buddha. This man is a great mystery. He lived in an awful, almost superhuman freedom, yet his kindness was powerful as a cosmic force. Perhaps Buddha will be the last religious genius to be explained by Christianity. As yet no one has really uncovered his Christian significance. Perhaps Christ had not only one precursor, John, last of the prophets, but three: John the Baptist for the Chosen People, Socrates from the heart of antiquity, and Buddha, who spoke the ultimate word in Eastern religious cognition. Buddha is free; but his freedom is not that of Christ. Possibly Buddha's freedom is only the ultimate and supremely liberating knowledge of the vanity of this fallen world.

Christ's freedom is based not on negative cognition, but on the love of God; his whole attitude is permeated with God's earnest will to heal the world.

Everything in life is uncertain. The moment we demand more than mere probabilities, we are forced to admit that everything is questionable: people, things, works, knowledge. If we ask: Does anything really possess an ultimate, divine guarantee? the reply is: Yes, one thing does possess, *is* that guarantee, the love of Jesus Christ. It alone breathes such eternal purity, that the slightest doubt is equivalent to attack. What are the effects of this divine disposition?

What effects does one man have on another? His wickedness may destroy, his fear poison, his lust overpower and en-
slave. Or he may liberate, help, animate, create a sense of
community and good works. His best talents may bring into
being things of permanent splendor. All these are realities, and
it would be folly to underestimate a single one. Nevertheless,
there is a limit to man's possibilities: he can effect only things
within the world. He can develop given possibilities; change and
shape given conditions; he cannot change the world as a whole,
for he is part of it. . . . He has no influence over being as such
or its characteristics. He can change all manner of things on the
surface of earth; earth itself escapes his power. Only one person
ever seriously attempted to go farther: to lay hands on being—
Buddha. He desired more than mere moral progress or peace
outside the world. He attempted the inconceivable: himself
part of existence, he tried to lift all existence by its "boot-
straps." So far no Christian has succeeded in comprehending
and evaluating Buddha's conception of Nirvana, that ultimate
awakening, cessation of illusion and being. To do this one must
have become entirely free in the love of God's Son, yet remain
linked by a profound reverence to the great and mysterious man
who lived six centuries before the Lord. One thing is certain:
Jesus' attitude towards the world is basically different from that
of Buddha: Christ is the Establisher of absolute beginning.

Not only does Jesus bring new truth, new means of moral
purification, a doctrine of more crystalline charity to be established among men; his entry into this old world of ours launches
the new. And not merely in the intellectual sense through the
recognition of hitherto unknown truths, or in the psychological
sense of an all-renewing inner experience, but actually. "I came
forth from the Father and have come into the world. Again I
leave the world and go to the Father. . . . I have overcome the
world" (John 16). This is not the tone of one who have morally
or religiously worked his way through to another, higher plane
of existence. Nothing in the Gospels suggests that Jesus had to
struggle through worldly captivity or uncertainty to the complete freedom he enjoyed. This is what makes every attempt
to 'psychoanalyze Jesus' as ridiculous as it is impossible; in him
there is no such thing as 'development of personality.' His inner

life is the fulfillment of a fact: that he is simultaneously Son of Man and God. The person of Jesus is unprecedented and therefore measurable by no already existing norm. Christian recognition consists of realizing that all things really began with Jesus Christ; that he is his own norm—and therefore ours—for he *is* Truth.

Christ's effect upon the world can be compared with nothing in its history save its own creation: "In the beginning God created heaven, and earth." What takes place in Christ is of the same order as the original act of creation, though on a still higher level. For the beginning of the new creation is as far superior to the old as the love revealed in the incarnation and the cross is to the love which created the stars, plants, animals and men. That is what the words mean: "I have come to cast fire upon the earth, and what will I but that it be kindled?" (Luke 12:49). It is the fire of new becoming; not only "truth" or "love," but the incandescence of new creation.

How earnest these words are is clear from those that follow: "But I have a baptism to be baptized with; and how distressed I am until it is accomplished!" "Baptism" is the mystery of creative depths: grave and womb in one. Christ must pass through them because human hardness of heart does not allow him to take the other road. Down, down through terrible destruction he descends, to the nadir of divine creation whence saved existence can climb back into being.

Now we understand what St. Paul meant with his "excelling knowledge of Jesus Christ": the realization that this is who Christ is, the Descender. To make this realization our own is the *alpha* and *omega* of our lives, for it is not enough to know Jesus only as the Savior. With this supreme knowledge serious religious life can begin, and we should strive for it with our whole strength and earnestness, as a man strives to reach his place in his profession; as a scientist wrestles with the answer to his problem; as one labors at his life work or for the hand of someone loved above all else.

Are these directives for saints? No, for Christians. For you. How long must I wait? God knows. He can give himself to you overnight, you can also wait twenty years, but what are they in view of his advent? One day he will come. Once in the stillness of profound composure you will know: that is Christ! Not from a book or the word of someone else, but through him. He who is creative love brings your intrinsic potentialities to life. Your ego at its profoundest is he.

This is the literally all-excelling knowledge to which St. Paul refers. It springs like a spark from that "fire" Christ came to bring, streams like a wave from the "baptism" through which he had to pass. To know Christ entails accepting his will as norm. We can participate in the beginning which is he only by becoming one with his will. When we feel this we draw back, startled, for it means the cross. Then it is better to say honestly: "I can't, yet," than to mouth pious phrases. Slow there, with the large words "self-surrender" and "sacrifice"! It is better to admit our weakness and ask him to teach us strength. One day we shall really be able to place ourselves fully at his disposal, and our wills will really be one with his. Then we shall stand at the threshold of the new beginning. What that will mean we do not know. Perhaps pain or a great task, or the yoke of everyday existence. It can also be its own pure end; it is for God to decide.

Very likely after such an hour everything will seem to return to 'normal' and we will appear strange in our own eyes or fear that we have fallen from his love. We must not be confused, but hold fast to that hour or moment and continue our way. It will return; and gradually such moments will fuse to a permanent attitude something like that revealed in the words of the apostle: "For I am sure that neither death, nor life, nor angels, nor principalities, nor things present, nor things to come, nor powers, nor height, nor depth, nor any other creature will be able to separate us from the love of God, which is in Christ Jesus our Lord" (Rom. 8:38-39).

Karl Adam
1876-1966

"Karl Adam has shaped the view of Christ and Church held by a generation of German Catholics" (Laubach). More than that, he has had a lasting impact throughout Western Christian theology in our century. His powerful early work, The Spirit of Catholicism *(1924), is sampled in the volume on the Church; here we turn to his mature work published thirty years later, as his distinguished career at the University of Tübingen was drawing to a close.*

The Christ of Faith, *Adam tells us, is "in essence a summary of lectures I gave over a number of decades." Its 25 chapters cover the entire realm of Christology, touching on all the issues, classical and contemporary. The first 19 chapters deal with "The Person of Christ," and the last seven consider "The Work of Christ." The particular contribution and emphasis of Adam is reflected in the fact that no less than seven chapters of the first part are devoted to questions concerning the "consciousness of Christ." The impact of Nietzsche, Freud, and Jung was inescapable, and Adam viewed this positively as a challenge which the theologian had a responsibility to grapple with. A new age brings new outlooks, new concerns, new insights. A theology that cannot relate to its time and evaluate strengths and weaknesses is irresponsible and negligent.*

Psychology was not the only source from which new questions were being raised. Biblical studies also, with the application of newer, more probing methods, opened new avenues of speculation. Karl Adam, fully in touch with the spirit of the times, saw that what was needed in Catholic thought was a new stress upon the full humanity of Jesus. In the process there were those who were nervous about this emphasis. Was Nestorianism being revived? But Adam did not see this as the danger. As Jungmann and Congar had amply shown in their historical studies, Monophysitism has always been the greater temptation to the pious Western Christian. Modern secularism reduces Jesus readily to a mere man, but the typical Christian is much more likely to see Him so totally as "God walking the earth" as to forget His humanity entirely (Monophysitism).

As Chesterton so graphically expressed it, heresy is as easy as falling off a log; all you have to do is go to any extreme. Whereas the thrill of orthodoxy is in balancing opposites, maintaining in tension truths that seem to conflict. Classical Christology is the perfect example: Jesus is true God, Jesus is true man. It is far easier to proclaim one and forget the other than to maintain both in dialectical tension. If Adam at times seems to put more stress on the second than the first, that is only because the long-standing tendency in Catholic theology leaned the other way, and the new sciences that required confrontation were the ones that raised questions about the human nature more than the divine.

As a result, our selection from Karl Adam's The Christ of Faith *consists of two chapters (14 and 15). The first is "The Hypostatic Union and the Divine Nature of Christ," the second is "The Hypostatic Union and the Human Nature of Christ." Thus the opportunity is provided to see the "complete theologian" at work, to watch how he does justice to the tradition in one realm, then turns to give equal consideration to the other pole. He does this so well, of course, because of the unified vision he fosters of Jesus as the "Christ of Faith."*

THE CHRIST OF FAITH

CHAPTER XIV

THE HYPOSTATIC UNION AND THE DIVINE NATURE OF CHRIST

I n his classic *Epistola dogmatica ad Flavianum*, Leo the Great expounded the Church's dogma of the duality in Christ's unity so clearly that all the bishops gathered at the Council of Chalcedon in 451 were carried away, and cried with one voice: *per Leonem Petrus locutus est*, Peter himself has spoken through Leo's mouth. Taking Leo's epistle as its basis the Council defined not only the one person and substance, *una persona atque substantia (ἐν πρόσωπον καὶ μία ὑπόστασις)*, but also the two natures unconfused, immutable, indivisible, inseparable, *duae naturae inconfuse, immutabiliter, indivise, inseperabiliter (ασυγχυτως, ατρεπτως, αδιαιρετως, αχωριστως)*. We shall first discuss the divine nature in Christ in its relationship to the Trinity.

The incarnation of the second divine person

It is an article of faith (*de fide*) that only the *second person* of the Trinity became man. In opposition to the Patripassians, who ascribed the incarnation to the Father because they thought they were compelled to assume only one divine person, the Church's creed called upon the testimony of the Scriptures and the early Fathers, and demonstrated that the Trinity as a whole did not enter into the hypostatic union, nor yet the first or third person of the Trinity, but only the second person. The question immediately arises: Does not the consubstantiality of the three divine persons (they are not indeed substantially separable from the divine nature) mean to imply that the incarnation of the second person necessarily drew the other two divine persons in its wake? This conclusion seemed so inevitable to the Nominalist Roscelin (d. after 1120) and the philosopher Günther (d. 1863) that they abandoned the consubstantiality of the three divine persons in order to avoid the necessity of ascribing the incarnation to the Father and the Holy Spirit as well as to the Son. To this extent they were adherents of tritheism, which splits the divinity up into three separate persons, and denies their common substance. We shall not be far from a solution to our question if we follow the Church's definition of the relation of the person to nature. According to this, it is the person that first gives a substance its autonomy. It had already been decided by St. Thomas Aquinas with a simple *"distinguo."* He distinguished the effective principle of the incarnation and its goal, or object (*terminus*). The object of the union of both natures can be only a divine person, and not a divine nature. For what the incarnation is intended to effect is after all the unity of the divine person in two natures. Only the person gives the autonomy. And the substantial being of Jesus' humanity attains its end and its fulfilment only in the autonomy of the second divine person. Hence it is only one of the three divine persons, and not the triune divine substance, that in the incarnation can give the human nature its autonomy. The divine nature too exists with inner necessity only through the absolute autonomy of the three divine persons. It is not the divine nature that is the ultimate bearer, but the three divine persons in their relationship to one another. Thus Christ's humanity is not assumed into the unity of the divine nature, but into the unity of the divine person. The function of the Logos towards the human nature is purely ontological, and not dynamic. For all it shares of the divine substance with the human nature is its autonomy. The union is strictly hypostatic. So the object of the union can be only a divine person. The divine nature can also be described as the object of the union only to the extent that it has assumed the human nature in *persona Verbi*. It belongs to the human nature only *ratione personae Verbi*, only through the autonomy of the second person.

Though the object of the union can be only one divine person, its effective principle belongs to all *three persons* together. This is the express doctrine of the Fourth Lateran Council (1215): *Dei filius Jesus Christus a tota trinitate communiter incarnatus.* For it is through the power of the divine nature that the hypostatic union is wrought. This is the *principium quo* of all divine works (while the person, on the other hand, is the *principium quod*). All God's external works belong to the divine nature. For that which is not person in God, that which strictly speaking does not give the Godhead the autonomy of the Trinity, belongs to the divine nature. The real difference of the three divine persons is relevant only to the divine life within the Trinity. Outside the Trinity, the triune God works as the one omnipotent God, through the unity of his nature. So we must say that the hypostatic union takes place actively, to the extent that it is an *incarnare,* an act of incarnation brought about by all three divine persons. It is an *opus Dei ad extra,* an act of the divine essence. On the other hand, it is passive to the extent that it is an *incarnari,* a state undergone by the second divine person, and belonging to him alone.

The grounds for the incarnation of the Son

But why is the second divine person the object of the union, rather than the first or the third? Human reason is unable to illuminate the most profound sufficient reason. It can only show that the incarnation was most fitting for the Son alone. The Son is the eternal Word of the Father, the expression in personal form of his being, the quintessential personal form of all the divine ideas according to which the world—and man in particular—was created, *similitudo exemplaris totius creaturae,* the pattern and likeness of all creatures. The natural and supernatural image of man was formed after him, who was the likeness of the Father. And so it was fitting that when this image formed in the likeness of the Son was distorted by sin, it should once again be renewed and re-established in the Son, the eternal Word. If the creation was accomplished by means of the Word, and in its likeness, then it is fitting that the new creation should also be accomplished by the Son, and in his likeness. This is related to the idea that Christ is God's Son in a unique, physical sense. As far as the purpose of the new creation was to re-establish in man redeemed his filiation to God, to elevate him to the status of God's adopted son, it was fitting that the very person to restore man to this filiation and exalt him to be the son of God should have been the eternal and consubstantial Son of God himself. So we maintain that it is fitting that the Logos alone, as the image of all human and created perfection, and on account of its mysterious filial relationship to the Father within the Trinity, should have been the divine person to restore mankind to its lost likeness and filiation to God.

This may give us some modest insight into the supernatural motive for the mystery of the incarnation, and into those thoughts of God's that caused Christ to become man. When we speak of Christ's mediation, the first thing that comes to mind is his function of reconciling sinful mankind to God. But this function is only one single impulse in the entire idea of divine mediation. Essentially, it is rather the communication of the marvellous closeness of God's *union with his creation*. And the reconciliation of created beings is only one instance within this. As man, Christ is one with mankind; indeed with the entire created world, at whose head he stands. As God, he stands in a union of substance with his Father, from whom he comes, and with the Holy Spirit, in which he encounters the Father. Standing in the world, one with the world, he towers up into the very heart of the Godhead, he is God himself, one with the Father and the Holy Spirit. And so in his person, he draws the world up into the very neighbourhood of the eternal Father, while on the other hand he emanates over the entire world the union he has with his Father. He binds God and his creation into such a close reciprocal relationship that he cancels and overcomes not only every abyss between God and his creation but also the infinite disparity that separates them by their very natures; Christ conquers not only religious and ethical remoteness but also ontological distance. The God-man cancels out both the infinite remoteness of mere created being and the infinite remoteness of sinful being. So Christ is the substantial bond which brings together the most disparate antinomies. The Lord's sublime prayer that mankind "may be one even as we are one: I in them and thou in me; that they may be perfected in unity" is perfectly fulfilled in the God-man (cf. Scheeben, *Mysterien des Christentums,* pp. 350f.).

The peculiar significance of the incarnation

This makes it easy to understand the number of theologians who follow the Scotist doctrine in maintaining that the incarnation could have taken place *even without Adam's fall*, and quite independently of it. It has its end in itself. It is the most sublime fulfilment of Paul's words: "In him we live and move and have our being." If we were to recognize God as he is, in the innermost necessities of his being, then the incarnation would appear to our astounded eyes as God's most radiant revelation, in the added sense that it is the freest expression of his innermost essence, freely willed and outwardly wrought by the infinite power of his life and love. This inner beauty and sublimity of the mystery of the incarnation helps us to understand why the German Idealist philosophers (such as Fichte, Schelling, Hegel) described this very idea of the God-man as the "profoundest insight," and made it the basis of their philosophic speculation. It is true their interpretation of the idea has a pantheistic twist: for them, Jesus' significance consisted in the fact that he had led man as a species to the consciousness of the divinity of his humanity. In contrast to this, Christianity cherishes the certainty that just as no new development ever comes from the species as a whole, but only from single personalities, so the great new thing that was made manifest in Christ—especially the idea of God made man—was accomplished and fulfilled in one single man, Jesus of Nazareth, and not in the species man. However, these interpretations of the Idealists are testimony enough to the abundance of truth and value that lies within the Christian message, *"et Verbum caro factum est."*

Now that we have thrown some light upon Jesus' divine nature under the aspect of the hypostatic union, we shall proceed to discussing that union in its relationship to the humanity of our Lord.

CHAPTER XV

THE HYPOSTATIC UNION AND THE HUMAN NATURE OF CHRIST

The integrity of Christ's human nature

We have already pointed out that Pope Leo's *Epistola dogmatica ad Flavianum*, which was later confirmed by the Council of Chalcedon, stresses the proposition that the assumption of Christ's humanity into the person of the Logos took place without in any way diminishing the peculiar properties of either nature, *salva proprietate utriusque naturae et substantiae.* This expression was repeated in the dogmatic decision reached at the Council of Chalcedon. As we have learned, it was originated by Tertullian. By way of commentary, the Council added the explanation that the self-same Christ was contained unconfused and immutable (*inconfuse, immutabiliter*) in both natures. This decision was levelled against Eutyches, who defended the doctrine that both natures were transformed into the divine, which implied a unity and a homogeneity in the nature of Christ (μιά φύσις). Like Gregory of Nyssa, Eutyches made use of the metaphor of the sea and the drop of vinegar to illustrate his doctrine of transformation. Just as a drop of vinegar poured into the sea will take on the nature of the sea, just so the human nature was transformed into the divine. So Christ was certainly made up *out of* two natures originally, but after the union he no longer persists in two natures, but only in one. This Monophysite heresy recalls the Indian myth of the god Krishna, who has the power to transform himself into men, or even into beasts. There were other Monophysites, particularly Severus of Antioch (d. 538), who did not advocate this virtual transformation of human into divine nature, but maintained that the union brought about the formation of a new, third commingled nature that embraced both the divine and the human natures. Or they assumed at least that the unchanged humanity and divinity in Christ were so closely compounded that they made up one single "composite" nature, just as body and soul together make up the one human nature.

It is not necessary to refute the various versions of the Monophysite doctrine in the light of revelation. We have already advanced sufficient proof that the Holy Scriptures and the early Fathers maintained that both natures preserved their own integrity, and were not commingled, even after the incarnation. As we have seen, the image of Christ derived from the Synoptic Gospels, and from the Scriptures previous to them, stresses the humanity of Jesus. The very fact that the incarnate Logos remained truly human is the premise from which we conclude his capacity to suffer, and his power to save. The Fathers emphasized again and again that if Jesus' humanity were to lose the complete

integrity of its nature, its "naturality," it would not be able to
redeem our own nature in its entirety. Irenaeus of Lyons (d. 202)
had already established this principle. Gregory of Nazianzus
gave it the following formulation: "What is taken away from
the human nature remains unredeemed. Only what is united with
the Godhead is also redeemed" (*Epistola* 101). Besides the testimony of the Fathers, the very fact that our nature *was* redeemed
in its entirety is a further warranty that a complete individual
human nature persisted in the Incarnate One, and that Christ's
humanity did not in any way dissolve away into the divine nature.

Philosophical objections to Monophysitism

We intend here to throw some light on the philosophical
objections to Monophysitism, because they help to clarify the
Church's formulation of the dogma and reveal the keen dialectic
at its foundation. Monophysitism is a metaphysical impossibility,
because it violates the concept of God—the infinity and immutability of God. A finite nature can certainly receive its autonomy
and personality from the infinite divine person, but it can never
be commingled into becoming one with the divine nature. As
long as the infinite is to remain so, the finite can never be absorbed or compounded into it. Two orders of bearing confront
each other here, and they are simply not comparable. There is
no operation that will transform nought into a positive number.
Jesus' humanity, as a created contingency, is this kind of nought
in comparison with the absolute being of God. But the concept
of God is destroyed even by the more moderate theory of Severus. The Antioch theologian assumed that, by analogy with the
human soul in the body, Christ's divinity would be the forming
principle, the *forma substantialis,* of Jesus' humanity. In this way
this humanity of Jesus' would no longer remain pure humanity,
but would have become divine humanity, a new and specifically
different nature. But this theory too is a metaphysical impossibility. For God, who is infinite, can never be the *forma substantialis*
of a finite nature, as the soul is the *forma substantialis* of our
body. The infinite quite simply surpasses the bounds of the
finite in every way. There is no single point in the chain of being
which the infinite and the finite have in common. And so divinity

cannot join with humanity to form a third nature, because this would be a denial of the distinction between the infinite and the finite. Both parts of the new compounded nature would have to belong to a new order of being, and either the infinite would have to become finite or the finite would have to become infinite.

The Monophysites appeal for support to the expression "mixture" or "compound" ($\kappa\rho\tilde{\alpha}\sigma\iota\varsigma$), which is frequently used by the early Fathers. But in doing so they misinterpret patristic usage. Those Fathers, such as Irenaeus, Tertullian, Augustine, and Cyril of Alexandria, who speak of a *"commixtio,"* are perfectly clear that they advocate the continued integrity of both natures. They use the expression "compound" or "mixture" simply to stress the fact that the two natures come together in one divine person, and that the closest interpenetration of both natures is thereby achieved. What they mean is the circumincession, which we shall discuss later.

The Monophysite theologians also made frequent use, for their own ends, of the patristic allusions to the analogy of the union of body and soul in man; body and soul in man together make up a human nature, and, analogously, divinity and humanity could be united in Christ into a new divine-and-human nature. Even the Athanasian Creed made this simile. But in fact it was intended only as a simile, and nothing more. In one respect the comparison was exceedingly apt. Like the divinity and humanity in Christ, body and soul in man are also compounded into one unity of subject, into one individual person. And just as the unity of body and soul is not merely moral but also physical, that is, given by the nature of both substances, just so the unity of divine person and human nature in Christ is not merely moral and accidental but substantial. Moreover, like Christ's humanity and divinity, man's body and soul too remain after their union essentially different substances. And just as the divine Logos is the higher and dominant principle, possessing the human nature and endowing it with its ultimate perfection, just so is the soul the dominant principle in man, animating the body, and granting it a part in its spiritual life. But notwithstanding all these similarities between divinity and humanity in Christ on the one hand, and soul and body in man on the other, the differences are not to be overlooked. Divinity and humanity are *substantiae completae,* while body and soul are *substantiae incompletae.* Divinity and humanity together could never form a third nature common to them. On the other hand, the union of body and soul produces one single nature. Furthermore, the soul is the *forma substantialis* of the body. But, because the divine nature is infinite, it can never be the substantial form of a nature that is finite. Finally, body and soul are thus real parts of the human whole. Divinity and humanity, on the other hand, can never be regarded as parts of the God-man, for of course divinity can never be a part.

The duality of Christ's will and his exercise of will

More important than the proof of Christ's unimpaired humanity for our assessment of his inner life is it to establish in theological terms the conclusion that can be drawn from his duality of nature. This conclusion is the dogma of Christ's duality of will, and the duality of his exercise of will. For reasons of ecclesiastical politics, Sergius, the Patriarch of Constantinople, attempted to win over the Monophysites, and after the year 620 defended this formulation: "There are two natures in Christ, but only one will and one mode of activity" ($\xi\nu$ $\vartheta\epsilon\lambda\eta\mu\alpha$ $\kappa\alpha\grave{\iota}$ $\mu\acute{\iota}\alpha$ $\grave{\epsilon}\nu\acute{\epsilon}\rho\gamma\epsilon\iota\alpha$). This proposition was very soon repudiated at the Vatican Council in 649 under Pope Martin I. And later it was condemned by the dogmatic Epistle of 680 sent by Pope Agatho to the Emperor Constantine. This was confirmed by the Sixth General Council at Constantinople in 680-81, which promulgated the following doctrine: "We acknowledge in Christ two physical wills and two physical activities without separation, without transformation, without division, and without commingling." This definition alone is enough to make clear that the question at issue is not the moral unity of both natures, not whether Jesus' human will was, or could ever be, at variance with the divine will—for that was the very thing that made up the sanctity of Jesus' human will, that it should always be freely in harmony with the will of God. What was rather at issue was exclusively the question of the physical freedom of the wills and their activities, whether in fact after the incarnation two wills were present in the incarnate Logos, and whether the human exercise

173

of will was able to take effect after the human fashion, in complete freedom. Holy Scripture gives a clear and unambiguous answer to this question. Christ himself speaks expressly of his human will, and contrasts it to the divine will. He prays on the Mount of Olives: "Father, if it is possible, let this cup pass away from me; yet not as I will, but as thou willest" (Matt. 26.39; Luke 22.42). And in the Gospel according to St. John, Christ's words have a similar tenor (6.38). "For I have come down from heaven, not to do my own will but the will of him who sent me." Jesus' human will knows what infinities separate it from the holy will of God. That is why Christ prays to the Father. Christ is not only the object but also the subject of prayer. He himself prays. And sometimes this prayer comes from the depths of his desolate humanity. "My God, my God, why hast thou forsaken me?" (Mark 15.34). When the Gospels speak of our Lord's humility, and his reverence towards the Father, they are describing Jesus' purely human ways of exercising his human will. While the early Fathers emphasize the duality of natures in Christ, they are also indirectly—and sometimes expressly—stressing his duality of will. The only exception seems to be Pseudo-Dionysius the Areopagite. In fact, he seems to regard the conative powers of the God-man to be a specific kind of striving, unique and peculiar to God incarnate. Although he lived around 500, at the time of the Monothelete disputes he was regarded as a pupil of St. Paul, and the Monotheletes made use of his doctrines in this sense. In his Fourth Epistle, Dionysius makes this striking remark: Christ's divine activities were not wrought in divine fashion, nor his human activities in human fashion, but he exercised "a certain new activity," the activity of God incarnate, both divine and human ($\vartheta\epsilon\alpha\nu\delta\rho\iota\kappa\dot{\eta}\ \dot{\epsilon}\nu\dot{\epsilon}\rho\gamma\epsilon\iota\alpha$), or theandric. The expression "both divine and human" ($\vartheta\epsilon\alpha\nu\delta\rho\iota\kappa\dot{\eta}$), derived from Origen, who was the first to speak of the "God-man" ($\vartheta\epsilon\dot{\alpha}\nu\vartheta\rho\omega\pi\sigma\varsigma$). The Monophysite theologians interpreted this strange proposition to mean that the divinity and humanity in Christ composed a kind of new nature, as body and soul did, and that the activities of this compound theandric nature were peculiar and special activities. They understood that the moving principle in Christ was exclusively the divine will. The human will was purely passive in its relationship to it. It was simply a passive instrument in the

174

service of the divine will. What distinguished Christ's human will from the ordinary will of the rest of mankind was that it should be entirely assumed and solely activated by the divine will. According to the Monophysites, Dionysius leaves no doubt that the real initiative for Christ's actions is to be ascribed solely to the divine will of the Logos. But this interpretation of the Monophysite theologians does not entirely coincide with what Dionysius really taught. The Father simply meant that because Christ's two natures subsisted in the one divine person of the Logos, their volition and way of acting alike should be ascribed to this one divine person. So he does not derive the new quality in Christ's willing to a unity of nature and a commingling of both wills in Christ, but to the unity of person, and the uniqueness of the divine bearer of these two wills. According to the principle: *actiones sunt suppositorum*, that is, all activities are to be ascribed to the self that commits them, all Jesus' activities, divine or human, are the true activities of the self of the Logos. For this self is the *principium quod*, the agent or subject, of all the Lord's activities. But to the extent that these activities of the self of the Logos are accomplished only through the medium of Christ's humanity, that is, to the extent that this humanity is the *principium quo* of the Logos' activities, Dionysius believed he should describe them all as actions that were truly divine and human, or theandric ($\vartheta\epsilon\alpha\nu\delta\rho\iota\kappa\acute{\eta}$). Obviously, this is not directly relevant to our problem of whether we may establish two wills and two modes of exercising them in Christ. Dionysius is not calling the autonomy of both wills into question, but only emphasizing that the Lord's purely human activities belong to the Logos, and to that extent are theandric activities. Later theology too had no quarrel with this formulation. But it did attempt to distinguish the single activities of the incarnate Logos not only under the aspect of the divine person, the *principium quod,* but also under the aspect of the dual nature through which they were wrought, the *principium quo.* The kind of activity, after all, is determined not by the person, but by the nature from which the activity proceeds. Only the nature determines the *quale*, the kind or sort of act. And so ever since St. Thomas (*Summa Theologica*, III, qu. 19, a. 1 ad 1), Scholasticism has come to distinguish three kinds of activity in Christ. Firstly, the purely divine acts. These are the actions brought about by the Logos before its incarnation—for example, the creation. They were wrought exclusively by the divine nature as the *principium quo*. In distinction to these, there are the purely human acts. These are the actions which, by their very character, belong exclusively to Jesus' human nature, actions like seeing, weeping, suffering, and so on. These actions can be called theandric only in so far as their subject is the second divine person. Their *principium quo* is solely the human nature. The third kind of activity in Christ consists of those actions which are in fact accomplished by the Logos through the divine nature, but in such a way that in doing so he makes use of his human nature as an instrument. This is the category in which the miracles primarily are ordered. To the extent that these are supernatural in substance—for example, the raising from the dead—Christ can accomplish them only because he is God. But he works them with the help of his humanity—for example, when he says to the dead girl, "Talitha kumi," or when he touches the blind man's eyes with spittle. These activities are divine and human in the true sense.

We may conclude from this classification of Jesus' activities that Christ could also accomplish purely human activities, and did in fact do so. Even after the hypostatic union, his human will preserved its own peculiar properties and its own play of movement. This will was by no means impaired; it was by no means the passive object of volition. The psychological laws governing the course of the human will and its activities continue to function with complete self-sufficiency and independence even in the incarnate Son of God. And thus a psychological assessment of Jesus' inner life is made possible.

The freedom of Christ's human will

The most important conclusion to be drawn from the character of human volition is this: Christ's human will was *free*, as free as anyone else's human will. But we must be careful to set clear limits to the concept of human freedom. It is of the essence of human freedom that human volition should remain true to its innermost nature, that is that it can freely, unimpeded from without or within, strive to attain its specific object or not. The specific object of volition is what it regards as "good" or "valuable." Volition is, by its very nature, directed towards good. In theological terms, value is the formal object (*objectum propter quod*) of volition, just as truth is the formal object of our rational disposition, and beauty the specific object of our aesthetic disposition. That being which is so constructed as to strive for the objectively valuable, unimpeded by outward compulsion or inner susceptibility, and in the conscious affirmation of its own fundamental tendency, is in the most consummate sense free. This freedom is a "sweet necessity," as St. Augustine puts it. In this sense God is uniquely and absolutely free, because in the conscious working of his being he is in no way impeded by influences that are not divine, and because from within he affirms his own most perfect being as the highest value. Similarly, the angels and the saints in his Grace enjoy a relatively consummate freedom. For to be free means to affirm and fulfil the tendency of our being towards the objectively valuable, unimpeded from within or without. This freedom from external compulsion (*libertas a coactione*) and from inner constraints (*libertas a necessitate*) is essential to human volition, if it is to be exercised as a free activity. But on the other hand, the freedom to strive after what is of no value to its nature, to strive for what is objectively worthless (*libertas contrarietatis*), is not essential to volition, indeed, it is even a defect in it. When the human will strives after something that is only apparently valuable to it, only in its imagination, but not objectively, not in reality, it is clearly a will directed towards a false goal out of a false motive, a will that is a breach with the objective tendency of its being. This is a volition that is fundamentally unnatural, and an abuse of freedom. In this connexion, we will later establish that because of the hypostatic union, Christ was not liable to this abuse of freedom. The true freedom of his will lay rather only in the direction of what is objectively valuable. This is where he was free to choose and not to choose (*libertas exercitii*), and to choose one thing or another (*libertas specificationis*). This freedom of moral will is an essential premise of Jesus' power of redemption. By inwardly affirming what his divinely illuminated thought acknowledged to be objective good and the will of the Father, and by appropriating it to himself, and fulfilling it for the Father's sake, he endowed his action with a moral value, and made it an action of merit. Only his freedom and his responsible decision made him the *causa meritoria* of our justification (The Council of Trent, sess. 6, cap. F). Only this can explain his claim to a divine reward for what he has wrought: "I have glorified thee on earth; I have accomplished the work that thou hast given me to do. And now do thou, Father, glorify me with thyself, with the glory that I had with thee before the world existed" (John 17.5). Jesus' greatest moral strength and his concentrated affirmation of the Father's will is revealed in his suffering submission. "He humbled himself, becoming obedient to death, even to death on a cross" (Phil. 2.8). Jesus expressly stresses his freedom of volition. "No one takes it [my life] from me, but I lay it down of myself. I have the power to lay it down, and I have the power to take it up again" (John 10.18). John the Evangelist in particular is concerned to point out our Lord's divine glory even in his suffering, and he stresses this sovereign freedom of Christ's moral will in the passion. The Synoptic Gospels underline how Jesus submitted to his Father's will that he should drink the cup of sorrows only after an inner struggle, only after conquering the reluctance of his own natural desires. But John deliberately stresses that even this struggle was suffused with the triumphant awareness that "I lay down my life for my sheep" (John 10.15). In John's view, there was not a moment in our Lord's inner life when he would not have affirmed his Father's will, the *summum bonum* of his striving, with all the power of his own volition. The Evangelist does not hide the distress in Jesus' soul that caused him to cry out: "Father, save me from this hour." But it is significant that he immediately follows this appeal with another: "No, this is why I came to this hour. Father, glorify thy name" (John 12.27, 28).

Christ's incapability of sin

This absolute freedom of Jesus' human will necessarily led to a unique *moral unity* of the divine and human will in Jesus. The physical duality of Christ's will was cancelled out into a consummate moral unity. In his Epistle to Sergius, Pope Honorius had this moral unity in mind when he explained, "We acknowledge one will in our Lord Jesus Christ, because what was assumed

178

by the divinity was certainly not our guilt, but our nature. It assumed our nature in the state in which it was created before we sinned, and not in its corrupted state after our sin." With these words, Honorius meant to imply that Jesus' human will had not been corrupted by original sin, and that therefore he could never be at variance with the will of the Father. His human volition was animated by one purpose—the fulfilment of the Father's will. Obviously, Honorius did not recognize the problem that came to the fore in the Monothelete disputes, or he did not want to recognize it, and so he forbade any discussion of the problem of the two energies or activities at all. Such a question, he maintained, had no support either from the Bible or from ecclesiastical tradition. By this command, he aided the growth of the new Monophysite heresy, and was therefore excommunicated.

It is hardly necessary to give express reasons for the moral unity of the two wills in Christ from revelation. After all, it was Jesus' task to do the Father's will. "Thy will be done on earth as it is in heaven"—this is the very heart of his message. John tells us that he declares: "I seek not my own will, but the will of him who sent me" (5.30). On the Mount of Olives his created being, the natural instincts of his human nature (*voluntas ut natura*), protested against the terrible shape the Father's will threatened to take for him, and he begged, "Father, let this cup pass away from me." But even then, his heroic magnanimity made him add: "Yet not as I will, but as thou willest" (Matt. 26.39; Luke 22.42). He prayed to be saved from suffering, but only under the condition that this should coincide with the Father's will. However much his natural volition (*voluntas ut natura*) might instinctively turn to animal self-preservation, his moral volition (*voluntas ut ratio*) was subordinate to the will of the Father. His natural instincts protested against suffering and death as a physical evil. And his moral volition to a certain extent admitted this protest. This is why Augustine describes it as *ratio inferior*. But to the extent that it was not one with the divine will, it was overcome by the *ratio superior* of his free moral decision, and subordinated to the will of the Father. So Scholastic theology distinguished three wills in Christ's prayer on the Mount of Olives: the commanding will of the Father; the protesting will of Christ's animal nature; and the freely obedient, moral will of the Lord.

If we probe to the roots of this absolute moral unity of the two wills in Christ, we shall ascertain that its first immediate cause was the independent movement of the human will. Like all the movements of created beings, this independent movement too is brought about by the physical influence of the divine first cause. God as the creator and support of all being is the cause of this independent movement's taking place in complete freedom, corresponding to the free causality of the creator. But the independent movement of Christ's will towards the Father was simply *incapable* of departing from this course; every possibility that Christ's volition might oppose the working of God was excluded. This *incapability of sin (impeccabilitas)* was the necessary result of the inclusion of Jesus' human will in the hypostatic union. To put it more clearly, in fact, Jesus never consciously acted against the will of the Father. This inability to sin, *posse non peccare*, he derived from his moral freedom. But above and beyond that, he was incapable of sin, *non posse peccare*, and this he derived from his substantial relationship to the Logos. The theological schools have various explanations for this *impeccabilitas* brought about by the incarnation, which we shall discuss later. But on principle we may already accept the fact that because Christ's human nature had its autonomy in the divine person, his human will too was so much the possession of the self of the Logos that it was metaphysically unable to break out of the sphere of the divine will. It was the second divine person that gave our Lord's human nature its autonomy, and at the same time it was the Son that was the subject and support of all our Lord's human acts. This was why it was a metaphysical impossibility for the human will ever to deviate from the divine will. Otherwise we would be confronted by the inner impossibility that he who was God and the essence of sanctity was capable of sin.

But how is this incapability of sin to be explained? How can it be reconciled with the freedom of Christ's human will?

The Scotists' doctrine posits an *impeccabilitas externa*. They would have it that an external factor, divine Providence, preserved Jesus' will in advance from any fall. Indeed, according to the Scotist view, Jesus' will would in fact be capable of sin, like any other human will, for his human nature is human in every respect; and even if actual sin does not belong to human nature, the potential capability of sinning certainly does. And Jesus too possessed this capability. But his efforts were watched over and cared for by God's provision so powerfully that any fall was out of the question from the start. As we may see, the Scotist theory preserves the freedom of Jesus' human will in every respect. Pope Paul V expressly ensured its doctrine against the accusation of incorrectness, or even heresy. For however much it stresses Jesus' complete humanity, it still achieved the essential thing the theologians were concerned about: it acknowledged and preserved the *impeccabilitas* of his human volition. It is easy to see that this theory of Duns Scotus' is a direct conclusion from his view of the inner constitution of God incarnate.

In contrast to Duns Scotus' doctrine, Thomism advocated an *impeccabilitas interna.* According to this view, Jesus' humanity existed only through the Logos, so his human will too could exist only through and in the Logos. So his will is constructed and predestined in such a way that he himself in his peculiar structure and disposition is the most perfect human instrument of the Logos—so perfect that he is absolutely incapable of sin. Because Jesus' human will receives its existential being from the Logos alone, it possesses only those psychological potentialities and faculties that are directed towards the good, the best, the divine, and no capability of sinning at all. So in the Thomist view, Christ's freedom of human volition was not absolute, but had certain limits. The underworld of sin is out of his range. But according to Thomism, his scope in the realm of good is so much the more inclusive and intensive. Because he is free to will and not to will (*libertas exercitii*), Jesus is able to commit or omit a morally good action. He is able to undertake the healing of the sick, or not, speak or hold his peace, pray or not pray. And because he is free to will one thing or another (*libertas specificationis*), he is able to make the independent decision whether he should heal all ten lepers or only the one grateful Samaritan; or whether he should make his mortal journey to Jerusalem at once, in keeping with the wishes of his "brethren," or wait until his hour had come. So according to the Thomist theory, Jesus' human will was completely free to do good. The rhythm of his soul was a movement between the good and the better. It was the freedom of the saints and the angels, the existential affirmation of all that is holy and divine.

Jesus' freedom in face of his suffering

From this point of view, how are we to regard the freedom of Jesus' human will when confronted with his passion? If Jesus' will was so constructed that he was able to strive only after the good and the best, and if on the other hand he clearly acknowledged that it was his Father's will that he should die for mankind, is it still tenable to speak in Thomist terms of his sorrowing submission and the meritoriousness of his suffering? After all, Jesus knew that the prophets, Isaias especially, had all foretold his death for our salvation. Time and again he reminds us: "It is written that the Son of Man must suffer." So Jesus' human consciousness was confronted with a "must," the express will of his Father. But if his own will tended according to its very nature towards the consummation of this his Father's will, how can we still speak of any freedom or meritoriousness in his own will to suffer? Scheeben regards this problem as a crucial difficulty. He tries to clear it away by regarding the freedom of God incarnate as a kind of freedom that cannot be compared with ordinary human freedom. Its specific quality lies precisely in the fact that Jesus' moral will is not the will of an ordinary man, but the will of the Logos. But does this not take us back to the Monophysite error of Severus, who called Jesus' human nature a specifically new one, a compounded nature different from ours?

The Thomist view does not provide us with a complete solution to this problem. We might, however, mention one or two points that make this enigma less burdensome to the Thomists.

One thing is certain: Jesus' death for our salvation was from eternity determined in the divine ordinance. Because this divine ordinance concerned the ways of God in the outward world (*quoad extra*), it belonged not only to the Father but equally to the Son and to the Holy Spirit, in short, to the *unus Deus*. So God's divine ordinance that the Messias must suffer and die also belongs to the Logos. Therefore, the Messias' prayer known as *Speravi, speravi* (Psalm 39.7; Heb. 10.5 f.) should not be ascribed

to the Logos, as many Church Fathers have done, but only to
his human consciousness and human will. "Therefore in coming
into the world he says, 'Sacrifice and oblation thou wouldst not,
but a body thou hast fitted to me: In holocausts and sin offerings
thou hast had no pleasure. Then said I, "Behold, I come—(in the
head of the book it is written of me)—to do thy will, O God." ' "
St. Basil was of the opinion that this prayer of the Messias presupposed some task imposed upon the Logos by the Father, but
the kind of task that is not given to the Logos as if he were a
slave (δουγικῶς), but as a father would give it to his son (υἱκῶς).
In reality, when the Epistle to the Hebrews refers to this prayer,
it does not have the pre-existent Logos in mind, but the Logos
incarnate. It belongs to Jesus' human will. Following this, so
much is certain: The suffering and death of the Messias was
ordained in eternity by God, the *unus Deus*; the Logos had a
part in this decree just as the Father and the Holy Spirit had.
Furthermore, it is also certain that Jesus knew of this even in his
human consciousness. This consciousness was permeated with
the certainty that he was confronted with suffering and death.
"It is written that the Son of Man must suffer." When Peter tries
to dissuade him from his thoughts of suffering, he calls him Satan,
who does not mind "the things of God." Thirdly, it is certain
that for Jesus' human consciousness, the fulfilment of the divine
will was a categorical imperative every bit as forceful as any
other commandment of God's. His moral conscience had no
freedom of choice in the sense that he could ever have withdrawn
from this decision of God's will, which he recognized so clearly.
Such a flight from the will of God would have been impossible
to his moral conscience. Jesus had no *libertas contrarietatis* here
or elsewhere. A fourth certainty may be concluded from this:
The freedom with which Jesus acquiesced to the passion was
specifically the same freedom with which he always acquiesced
to the clearly acknowledged will of God. Because his human
intellect was filled and permeated by the absolute wisdom and
goodness of his Father, to a degree that we mere mortals may
never attain, here too his human will could make its complete
and unreserved affirmation out of its innermost freedom, although the circumstances under which this will might take shape
were as yet unknown to him. It was a free and unreserved, in-

ward affirmation of the Father's will. The freedom with which he uttered it was the same freedom with which he always affirmed the Father's will. By the power of his own volition, his moral will was forever bound to the Father's will. This was the personal freedom Jesus had in mind when he declared: "No one takes [my life] from me, but I lay it down of myself." For his affirmation of the Father's will came entirely of his own free personal decision to do his Father's will in everything. His incapability of sin secured immutably only the *goal* of his way, which was the fulfilment of the divine will. That he went his way as he did was for his human freedom to decide.

In the course of his passion, whenever Jesus found himself in a new situation demanding a renewed effort of will, he was able, and was compelled, to renew this affirmation of his Father's will, made on principle and out of his innermost personal freedom, on the empirical level. Or, more precisely, the empirical experience of his passion was a constant challenge to the initiative of his will to suffer. He must surely have had some anticipatory knowledge of the suffering that was awaiting him. On three great occasions he prophesied to his disciples about his coming sorrows. But to know a thing in theory is quite different from experiencing it in practice. After his experience upon the Mount of Olives, Jesus was able and was compelled to renew his position towards the Father's will constantly at every station of the cross, and so constantly preserve the freedom of his volition even when confronted with the ultimate terror.

Our conclusion is this: Jesus' clear awareness that his suffering as the Messias was the will of God could in no way prejudice the freedom of his decision—it could have as little effect as the knowledge of any other divine decree would have on the freedom of his moral action towards that decree. What distinguished his freedom from ours was simply the fact that it was not a *libertas contrarietatis*. But Jesus had no psychological apprehension of this fact—that it was impossible for his will to depart from the divine will. Metaphysically, it was certainly impossible for him to sin: But this metaphysical factor in his incapability of sin lay *beyond* his human consciousness. It is to be strictly distinguished from the psychological factor that he always clung faithfully to the will of the Father. He had no psychological means of knowing of his metaphysical incapability of sin. For such knowledge would have impeded the heroic ardour with which he exercised his freedom. All theologians are agreed that Jesus' humanity lacks the supernatural illumination and energy of God's absolute vision, in so far as it would have diminished the merit of his suffering or rendered it impossible. So he could not have had any direct, unfailing, supernatural certainty of his metaphysical incapability of sin either. This certainty issued from the power of his own natural human will alone.

This enables us to affirm that within the bond of the hypostatic union the human will was not merely passive; it was not a lifeless instrument upon which the Logos played at will. It was *active,* and *independent.* How sublime the divine synthesis is can be seen precisely in the human nature's independency. It is as mighty and all-embracing as it is gentle and tender. The closeness of its union with the divine self of the Logos never weakened the autonomy of human volition, not even in the question of Jesus' human freedom. This volition too preserved the *proprietas* of created being. So even from the Thomist point of view we may understand the extent to which even an *impeccabilitas interna* might make a truly free action on the part of Jesus' human volition possible. The solution of this problem is incomparably easier from the Scotist theory of an *impeccabilitas externa.*

The beginning and the duration of the hypostatic union

We may now return to our main problem of the relationship of Jesus' humanity towards the hypostatic union. We still have to answer the question: At what point did the miracle of the hypostatic union have its beginning in our Lord's humanity? How long did it last? How was it related to the personal, meritorious activity of Jesus' human will? This is the question that probes into the beginning, the duration, and the ultimate cause of the hypostatic union.

It is part of our dogma that the hypostatic union began at the moment when Christ's human nature was conceived, when God's triune creative power begat the Lord's human nature in the Virgin's womb. This is not to say that this generation of the human nature preceded the union with the Godhead, and that the union with the Logos took place only afterwards. The generation of Jesus' human nature was rather brought about by the power of the union, by the act of assumption into the divine person. All the Creeds of the Church are one in reciting: *qui conceptus de Spiritu Sancto, natus ex Maria virgine.* There was no moment when Jesus' humanity existed without being hypostatically united with the self of the Logos. We have already discussed the view, put forward by the Judaeo-Christian Ebionites in particular, that the divine principle did not descend upon Jesus' humanity until his baptism, and that this baptism was the hour of birth for his epiphany upon earth. As long as Christology remained undeveloped, this view raised its head now and again even in ecclesiastical circles. They were inclined to refer the words of the second Psalm, "this day have I begotten thee," to the commencement of Christ's career as the Messias, and not to the beginning of his natural life. The Nestorians referred it to the divine Pneuma's act of indwelling within Jesus the man. This presupposition could be the basis of avowing Christ as the God-man, but it would mean that there would be two selves within him, a divine and a human self, and the union would depend upon the meritorious works of the human self, and would be a merit, and not pure Grace. We can see here how closely Nestorianism and Pelagianism approach each other.

Our analysis of Jesus' self-consciousness has shown that from childhood Jesus knew himself to be the Son of the Father according to his natue. When his mother reproaches him, "Behold, in sorrow thy father and I have been seeking thee," he rejoins, "did you not know that I must be about my Father's business?" His description of himself as the Son of Man is a sufficient indication that he was conscious of his pre-existence. Jesus knew that he was the Saviour coming from heaven to set up the kingdom of God upon earth. Paul and John were both perfectly clear in their doctrine of his pre-existence as the Son of God. And Matthew and Luke furnish express testimony that the pre-existent Son of God was already incarnate in Mary's womb. This belief in Jesus' pre-existence was a common part of the Christian tradition from the very beginning. Both Ignatius of Antioch and Clement of Rome are completely at home in the ideas of Paul and John. Later Fathers of the Church expressly oppose the Ebionite doctrine that the divine Pneuma did not descend upon Jesus before his baptism. For example, Gregory of Nyssa says, "As the man first came into being, the divinity became one with him" (*Adversus Apollinarem*, 53). Leo the Great made it is his urgent teaching, "*natura nostra non sic assumpta est, ut prius creata, post assumeretur, sed ut ipsa assumptione crearetur*" *(Epistola* 35.3).

Origen too ascribed pre-existence to Christ's soul, and put forward the view that this soul had from eternity existed in union with the Logos even before the conception of the body. But he was building upon the false assumption, originally deriving from Platonic thought, that pre-existence was the property of all human souls. So in 553 this doctrine was repudiated by the Synod of Constantinople, with the agreement of Pope Vigilius.

The supernatural conception and the birth of Jesus according to Matthew and Luke

To be completely clear about this, let us look more closely at the accounts given in the New Testament of the supernatural conception of Jesus. The Gospel according to St. Luke gives us a detailed description of the annunciation (1.26-39). It reaches its culmination in the angelic tidings: "The Holy Spirit shall come upon thee and the power of the Most High shall over-shadow thee; and therefore the Holy One to be born shall be called the Son of God" (1.35). And the account concludes with Mary's reply: "Behold the handmaid of the Lord; be it done to me according to thy word" (1.38). This is Luke's description of Mary's experience. Matthew too gives us an account of Jesus' supernatural conception, but this time not from Mary's point of view, but from Joseph's. Because Joseph was disturbed that his betrothed was blessed with child, and in his distress was minded to put her away privately, an angel of the Lord appeared to him in a dream and said, "Do not be afraid, Joseph, son of David, to take to thee Mary thy wife, for that which is begotten in her is of the Holy Spirit. And she shall bring forth a son, and thou shalt call his name Jesus; for he shall save his people from their sins" (1.20 f.). Jesus' genealogy, which is set down from different traditions by both Matthew (1.1-18) and Luke (3.23-38), gives some help in interpreting the supernatural conception.

Without going into a discussion of the variations in the tradition (some assume that the account Luke gives is of Mary's descent), we may point out what they have in common: in both, Jesus is represented as the legally recognized son of Joseph, the descendent of David. In Matthew's account, the line of the generations stretches from David to Abraham. Luke extends this line back to Adam, in keeping with Pauline theology, to show that Adam and Christ are the two original created types of mankind. There is apparently a contradiction here between Jesus' supernatural, unfathered conception and his descent from the line of David, but this is resolved in Matthew's tendency to describe Jesus' relationship to David's line as legal and not natural, brought about by his adoption by Joseph. Joseph recognized him and accepted him as his child even while he was still in Mary's womb. His true father is God alone. Jesus did not have an earthly father, but only an earthly mother, Mary. This is expressed in Matthew's account of Jesus' descent when he writes: "And Jacob begot Joseph, the husband of Mary, and of her was born Jesus who is called Christ" (1.16). This text has been disputed, as we possess it in many variants. One of them runs as follows: "And Jacob begot Joseph, who was betrothed to Mary the maid. She bore Jesus, who is called Christ." The reference to "the husband of Mary" (Matt. 1.16), and hence to a bond of marriage, is lacking here. Jesus was born unfathered from the betrothed Virgin Mary. Now this variant was obviously intended to stress the *spiritual* character of Jesus' conception as much as possible, and to exclude any possibility of an earthly, natural origin. This tendency towards spiritualization puts this variant close to Tatian and his *Diatesseron.* Theodoret (*Compendium Haereticarum Fabularum,* 1.20) recalls that, in his *Diatesseron,* Tatian cut out the genealogies and everything else that might point to the birth of our Lord from the seed of David. So it would seem that our variant might be influenced by Tatian. The third variant has a different tenor. This is the one that is welcomed by the opponents of the miracle of the incarnation. It runs as follows: "Jacob begot Joseph. Joseph, to whom the virgin Mary was betrothed, begot Jesus, who is called Christ." In this passage, Joseph is referred to as Jesus' true father. But it is remarkable that the text nevertheless speaks of the *Virgin* Mary, and that she was merely betrothed.

We might well think that if the author of this variant seriously wanted us to regard Joseph as Jesus' real father, he would have had to omit the expression "virgin" as well as the reference to her betrothal. For if Joseph is Jesus' real father, the reference to Mary's state of virginity is simply meaningless, and so is the reference to her being Joseph's betrothed, for it was Jewish law and custom that the affianced bride should live as a virgin, and might not yet live in wedlock. So we are justified in concluding that in this variant we have to reckon with a very clumsy editor. Vogels' speculation is probably correct—that the editor deliberately tried to do away with the influence of Tatian clearly apparent in the previous variant, and therefore called Joseph Jesus' father, but without meaning to imply that Jesus was naturally begotten. His use of the expression "begot" was figurative, just as Matthew and Luke used it figuratively in one or two places in their genealogies. Be that as it may. This variant cannot in any way be regarded as clear and unequivocal evidence that Joseph was Jesus' natural father. If it really does contain a polemic thrust against the influence of Tatian in the previous text, then it certainly cannot be the original one. The genuineness of these variants is disputed even with the evidence of textual tradition by such distinguished commentators as Tischendorf, Westcott, Hort, Nestle, and Vogel.

The uninterrupted duration of the hypostatic union

Next we shall inquire as to the duration of the incarnation. It is dogma that the hypostatic union will never come to an end. On the other hand, it is not dogma, but *sententia certa*, that the hypostatic union was never interrupted. With reference to the latter, there were certain Gnostics and Manichees who assumed that the divine Pneuma left Jesus at the beginning of his suffering. As late as 418, the monk Leporius maintained that at Jesus' death, at least, the divinity departed from our Lord's body, if not from his soul. He based this argument upon Jesus' cry of grief upon the cross, "My God, my God, why hast thou forsaken me?" (Matt. 27.46). There were even some Fathers of the Church, such as Ambrose, Hilary, and Epiphanius, who were inclined to this idea. This was the only way they imagined that the utter depth of Jesus' suffering could be understood. Contemporary theology declares it is its "certain" opinion that in the three days of his death Jesus was no longer a living man, but that his body still belonged to the hypostatic union. They refer to St. Paul's words in his first Epistle to the Corinthians, *"Dominum gloriae crucifixerunt,"* "they . . . crucified the Lord of glory" (1 Cor. 2.8). This would imply that it was not our Lord's humanity, forsaken by God, that suffered, but "the Lord of glory." In any case, the Crucified One remained part of the hypostatic union even in his death, body as well as soul. But those Fathers of the Church who have confronted this problem—Gregory of Nyssa and Augustine, in particular—maintain above and beyond this that our Lord's dead body too remained in union with the Godhead, because it showed itself to be incorruptible. They are right in understanding the cry of the Crucified One to mean that Jesus saw he was destitute of all divine aid, but not of the divine presence.

Late Scholastic theologians were tormented by the question whether the blood shed on the cross left the hypostatic union with the self of the Logos. The Franciscan theologians of the fifteenth century maintained that this was so, while the Dominicans denied it. In 1464 the problem was disputed for three days before Pope Pius II, but with no final decision. As far as contemporary theologians are concerned with this thorny problem, the majority have come to the decision that only the blood that was reunited with the body in the resurrection remained in union with the self of the Logos while body and soul were separated. The blood that is now and again to be seen preserved in ampullae is no longer part of the hypostatic union, even it it were real blood of our Lord, and not that well-known blood bacillus *prococcus prodigiosus.*

We now proceed to the second question, whether the hypostatic union will ever come to an end. Origen betrays the extent to which he is a Hellenist and a follower of Plato in his view that the Lord would be divested of his body at the Last Judgement. To Origen, the body is something unspiritual and unworthy, and so he cannot imagine that this body could remain in eternal union with the divine spirit. In order to repudiate any possible inferiority of the Logos, Bishop Marcellus of Ancyra (d. 374) went so far as to maintain that at the end of time the Logos would be divested of all human nature, including the human soul. This was opposed by the proposition of the First Council of Constantinople in 381: *"cujus regni non erit finis."* Origen's view was repudiated in 553 at Constantinople. The dogma is supported by clear statements in the Holy Scriptures. The angel Gabriel announced to Mary: "The Lord God will give him the throne of David his father, and he shall be king over the house of Jacob forever; and of his kingdom there shall be no end" (Luke 1.32, 33). The doctrine of the Church Fathers followed this. Christ's incarnation would persist even in his transfiguration, because it is founded in his special position as the head and mediator of the universe. When St. Paul declares (1 Cor. 15.28), "When all things are made subject to him, then the Son himself will also be made subject to him who subjected all things to him, that God may be all in all," he is referring to the fact that the Son's active mediation as the Messias, which now upon earth is constantly taking up new saints into his holy body and extending the kingdom of Christ, will come to an end at the Last Judgement. Then Christ's messianic reign will be over. It will be succeeded by the reign of God.

Grace as the ultimate cause of the hypostatic union

We have still one question left to answer. What is the basis of the hypostatic union? Is it founded upon the merits of Jesus' humanity, or is it pure Grace? Should we refer the assumption of Jesus' human nature into the self of the Logos back to some meritorious action performed by that human nature and fore-ordained by God's omniscience, so that the humanity might claim its union with the Godhead as a kind of right? Or is the hypostatic union in every sense the unmerited Grace of God? As we have already shown, the primitive Christology of the Shepherd of Hermas established a causal relationship between the assumption of Christ the man into the filiation of God, and the consummate act of obedience, the probation of the "human servant" Jesus who dwells within the spirit of the Logos. Similarly, Nestorius based his doctrine of the two Sons of God upon the doctrine of probation. Christ's human self earned its union with the divine self because it demonstrated its obedience in life and in death. Contrary to Nestorius' doctrine of probation, it is regarded as *sententia communis* that the hypostatic union was in the full sense of the word *pure Grace* given to Christ's human nature, an unearned, supernatural gift of divine love. This is why theology refers to a Grace of union, *gratia unionis*. Logically speaking, it was impossible for Jesus' humanity to earn or deserve or merit its assumption into the divine Word, for before the union, of course, it did not exist at all. A causal relationship between Jesus' human probation and the union of divinity and humanity could be understood only by calling upon the concept of a *scientia media*, which was later used by Molina. This would offer the interpretation that God had foreordained this probation of Jesus' human will in eternity, and brought about the temporal realization of the union of the humanity with the Logos on the basis of this eternal prevision. It is certainly conceivable that this was the precise reason why God chose this concrete human nature for the union, because he had from eternity foreseen that it would exercise its free will perfectly. But in objection to this, the question immediately rises as to what necessary reason God could have for uniting this nature with his second person, taking into consideration its foreordained probation, in a way that in essence transcends every other supernatural relationship between God and his creation, and every other supernatural form of union that had been granted to other saints. This is not a question of an accidental union with the Godhead, as in the case of other men endowed with Grace, but a substantial union. In human terms, why was not God satisfied with ranging Jesus' humanity in the highest rank of the saints, as he did the Immaculate Virgin, on account of the foreordained sanctity of her person? Why did he translate Jesus' humanity into an entirely new and unique order of being, the hypostatic union? What was his purpose? If our reply is because from eternity God foreordained that Jesus' humanity should work together with divine Grace in a unique mode, then even this unique co-operation does not serve to make the prodigious miracle of the hypostatic union comprehensible. An infinite amount still remains that no activity of any created being, even under the mightiest influence of Grace, could ever merit or earn, and that is the elevation of this one creature out of its natural mode of existence, and its translation into the unity of the personal being of God. Only the infinite fullness of the divine essence is able to communicate divine being, and this is its sovereign action. The achievement of a mere creature cannot be intensified to such a degree that it surpasses the bounds of created being and claims the right to be assumed into the autonomy of the Logos. And so, however perfect we may conceive Jesus' humanity to be, it can *never earn* the hypostatic union on its merits. True, it would certainly be possible for God to foresee in eternity the pure and holy activities of Jesus' humanity, and for him thus to have predestined it to join in the hypostatic union. Then it would have been in the name of divine justice, and not as an act of God's free love. In this case too it would be a union of free Grace (*gratia unionis*). But all the same, it would still somehow be bound up with the foreordained merits of Jesus' humanity. And so this possibility too yields before the infinite miracle of the incarnation. This miracle penetrates so far into the depths of the divine substance, so deep into his mercy, wisdom, and omniscience, that it would be presumptuous for us to seek its foundation in created being. This is an act of God alone.

This throws new light upon the relation of our dogma to the Christian concept of Grace. The Christian concept of Grace is nothing but the application of the Christian concept of God. Because God alone is the essence of perfection and holiness, the effort of any created being to attain to God is conceivable only because it has been previously affected by God himself. Just as no created act comes about in the order of cosmic being without having been metaphysically supported and brought about by God, just so in the order of supernatural being no efforts towards the highest are possible that have not first been anticipated by the Grace of eternal sanctity and love. And so even the most consummate moral behaviour would be just an empty stammering, as long as it were not dominated in its totality by the Grace of the eternal God. So the empirical concrete humanity of Jesus is the purest work of God's Grace, the most sublime work of art formed by the All-Holy from the stubborn material of humanity. And the elevation of this work of art into the sphere transcending every mode of created being, into the circle of God's own life, is even more intensely God's personal act alone, pure Grace. It was St. Augustine, profoundly moved, who pointed to this miracle of love: *Natura humana sine ullis praecedentibus bonorum operum meritis Deo Verbo est in utero virginis copulata (De Trinitate*, 15.26).

If we wish to formulate the *gratia unionis* more precisely in Scholastic concepts, we must describe it as *uncreated, substantial Grace.* For the gift it makes to Christ's humanity is the autonomy of the Son of God. And so it is an eternal Grace, because it is identical with the personal being of the Son of God. And it is a substantial Grace, because it is the highest and most perfect substance, the Logos itself, that endows the human nature with its autonomy.

* * *

We have thrown some light upon the mystery of the hypostatic union in its peculiar properties, in the innermost foundation of its being, in its relation to the Trinity, and in the effect of this mystery upon the humanity of Jesus. But every thought we have uttered has made us realize that all our human speech is mere stumbling. To understand the hypostatic union would mean to understand God. Even here we cannot get beyond merely metaphorical concepts. But we are able to ascertain as much as we need for our own religious life. We have attained the apperception that in Christ we are confronted with the personal revelation of God, that he is the highest and holiest Word that God ever uttered into the world, and that all the boldest dreams and sublimest longings of mankind are united in him. The riddle of existence, and with it its narrowness and gloom, are solved for us in the Incarnate One. Christ lifts us out of the limitations and imperfections of our sinful nature up into the infinite breadth of the divine life. Our own life too draws its ultimate meaning and definitive form from the same pattern upon which St. Thomas based the divisions of his *Summa Theologica*: from God—to God—through Christ—in God.

We shall now go on to discuss the consequences that rose directly from the hypostatic union. As the first consequence, we shall take the Christological Perichoresis, or circumincession, that is, the profound penetration of Jesus' humanity by the presence of the triune God; and then we shall go on to discuss what is known as the *communicatio idiomatum*, the reciprocal exchange of divine and human properties in the God-man, and so we shall learn the right way of speaking of the mystery of Christ.

Walter John Burghardt
1914-

Walter Burghardt was born in New York City, entered the Jesuits in 1931, and was ordained a priest in 1941. His M.A., Ph.L., and S.T.L. were all from Woodstock College, where he became professor of patristic theology in 1946. He received his doctorate in theology from the Catholic University of America in 1957.

From his position as editor of Theological Studies, Fr. Burghardt has been in touch with the central developments in Catholic theology over the last few decades. Patristics has been his field of interest and specialization since before his doctoral dissertation on Cyril of Alexandria, published in 1957. That same year he brought out a volume showing The Testimony of the Patristic Age Concerning Mary's Death. He was given the Mariological Award in 1958 and was president of the Mariological Society of America from 1960 to 1962.

Ever since the time of Nestorius, it has been clearly realized that a theologian's "Mariology" was inseparable from his "Christology." It is not surprising, therefore, that in our century— with the growing accent upon the full humanity of Christ— attention would also focus on the role of Mary, His Mother. This development peaked in the middle of the century with the definition of her Assumption by Pope Pius XII in 1950, followed by the declaration of 1954 as a "Marian Year." But this very *trend, prompted in part by polemical considerations, held the danger of distortion, the threat of treating Mary in isolation from her Son and His Church.*

Vatican II dealt directly with this problem by making the treatment of Mary a chapter within the Constitution on the Church. But such action was made possible only because of the restoration of perspective that had been achieved by then, thanks to the labor of a group of theologians that included Fr. Burghardt. With the balance provided by his solid historical perspective, he led the way to viewing Mary in terms of the Church, a type of the Church, a member of the Church; he did this by making full use of the Pauline doctrine of the Church as Christ's Body. Other modifications would follow as the perspective spread and its implications were drawn out more fully, but coming at the time that it did, this was an important step.

The essay that follows originally appeared in 1956 in a collection entitled The Mystery of the Woman, *edited by Edward D. O'Connor and published by the University of Notre Dame Press. Whatever one's final evaluation of the approach, there is no denying the beauty and harmonious consistency that it provides. It ensures that the praise of the mother will always be derived from her association in the work of her Son. In that process, as this essay makes clear, any homage paid to Mary will always stem from a realization of the salvation achieved by Christ, the Word of God become incarnate through her.*

THE MYSTERY
OF THE WOMAN

THEOTOKOS: THE MOTHER OF GOD

One of the most significant sermons of antiquity was delivered fifteen centuries ago. The date: early September, 431. The place: the Church of St. Mary at Ephesus on the west coast of Asia Minor. The congregation: almost 200 bishops of the East. The occasion: the dying hours of the Council of Ephesus, at which a virgin of Nazareth was proclaimed Mother of God. The preacher: Cyril, Patriarch of Alexandria in Egypt.

Cyril opened his sermon with a startling eulogy: "Hail, from us, Mary, Mother of God, majestic treasure of the whole world . . . crown of virginity, sceptre of orthodoxy . . . dwelling of the Illimitable, mother and virgin. . . ." Cyril closed his sermon with a remarkable sentence: "May we . . . reverence the undivided Trinity, while we sing the praise of the ever-virgin Mary, that is to say, the holy Church, and of her spotless Son and Bridegroom."

The two facets of this essay are suggested by two appositive phrases with which Cyril dignifies Mary: (a) "Mary, Mother of God," and (b) "Mary, that is to say, the holy Church." More specifically, I submit that the significance of the divine maternity in 431, when it was equivalently defined, lay in its relationship to the *physical* Christ; and that its significance in 1960 lies in its relationship to the *mystical* Christ. In other words, the significance of the divine maternity in fifth-century Ephesus lay primarily in this, that it furnished a fresh insight into the *person* of Christ, into Christology; its added significance in twentieth-century America lies in this, that it suggests a fresh insight into the *work* of Christ, into soteriology.

I

First, then, 431. The Council of Ephesus is significant for a fact, and the fact itself has significance. The *fact* is simple enough. The title, Mother of God (*theotokos*), was expressly presented to the Council, in a letter of Cyril, as orthodox doctrine, and Cyril's letter was solemnly approved in the assembly. This impressive approbation did not fall like a thunderclap on the Christian world; it had been prepared by three and a half centuries of the theological development. That development is itself fascinating.

Strangely enough, what was first denied to our Lady after she left this earth was not the prerogative, Mother of God, but what her contemporaries never dreamed of denying, that she was Mother of *Jesus*. The early crisis was Docetic—the affirmation that our Saviour simply did not have a genuinely human body, or at any rate, as Tertullian sums it up, that "He was born *through* a virgin, not *of* a virgin—*in* a womb, not *of* a womb." In a word, He was not fashioned of Mary's substance. But there was a complementary denial. Where the Gnostics introduced a distinction between Jesus born of Mary and the Christ who descended into Jesus at baptism, they denied implicitly that the Child of Mary was God.

The Christian reaction in the first three centuries is expressive. Not that our Lady is categorically denominated Mother of God; there is no indisputable evidence for the title before the fourth century. But Ignatius and Aristides in the East, Justin and Irenaeus and Tertullian in the West, have a two-edged answer for the Gnostic position. On the one hand, they use expressions that equivalently affirm Mary's divine motherhood. On the other, they trumpet the twin premises for their conclusion: (*a*) Jesus was genuinely born of Mary; and (*b*) Jesus born of Mary is God.

With the fourth century the title, Mother of God, becomes a commonplace. As the evidence stands, we find it first in 319, when Alexander, Bishop of Alexandria, announces to his colleagues the deposition of Arius. But even then the word flows from his pen so naturally, so spontaneously—I might almost say, so nonchalantly—that it leaves an impression of everyday usage. And soon the Christian world echoes with it. Athanasius in Alexandria, Eusebius in Caesarea, Cyril in Jerusalem, Epiphanius in Salamis, Hilary in Gaul, Ambrose in Milan, and Jerome in Rome—none feels he must justify it, none feels there is something to explain. So welcome is the word that in 382 Gregory of Nazianzus can hurl anathema at Apollinaris: "If anyone does not admit that holy Mary is Mother of God, he is separated from the divinity." And while the theologian wielded the word as a weapon, the layman whispered it in accents of love. For from the same fourth century comes a precious papyrus leaf, from which we can reconstruct the original Greek of our lovely prayer, "We fly to thy patronage, O holy Mother of God"; and the word that stands out clearly is *theotoke*, Mother of God. More eloquent than this love-call of Christians is Julian the Apostate's cry of despair: "You [Christians] never stop calling Mary Mother of God."

Little wonder that, from 428 on, a rising reluctance to call Mary "Mother of God" provoked such violent reactions. Little wonder that, when Nestorius of Constantinople gave his blessing to a bishop who preached, "If anyone says that holy Mary is Mother of God, let him be anathema," Cyril of Alexandria retorted, "If anyone does *not* confess that . . . the holy Virgin is Mother of God . . . let him be anathema." Little wonder that, when the Council of Ephesus convened in 431, Cyril could write of that first session to his flock in Alexandria:

"Know, then, that on the [22nd of June] the holy Synod met at Ephesus in the great Church . . . of Mary, Mother of God. We spent the whole day there, and finally . . . we deposed . . . Nestorius and removed him from the episcopal office. Now there were about 200 (more or less) of us bishops gathered together. And the whole populace of [Ephesus] was waiting tensely, waiting from dawn to dusk for the decision of the holy Synod. When they heard that the unfortunate fellow had been deposed, with one voice all started to shout in praise of the holy Synod, with one voice all began to glorify God, because the enemy of the faith had fallen. When we left the church, they escorted us to our lodging with torches; for it was evening. Gladness was in the air; lamps dotted the city; even women went before us with censers and led the way."

That is the *fact* of Ephesus, and on the surface it is simple enough. A bishop had questioned Mary's most precious prerogative, and his brother bishops had banned him from their fellowship. But that is not quite the *significance* of Ephesus. Nestorius' concept of Mary stemmed from his concept of Christ. Similarly, what Ephesus determined with respect to Mary's motherhood was rooted in what Ephesus believed with respect to Christ's sonship. That is why Nestorius, for all his reluctance, could say to Cyril in all honesty: "It is not on the ground of a [mere] name that I part from you; it is on the essence of God the Word and on the essence of the Man." What was at stake was the Incarnation itself. In what sense did God become man? In what sense can we say with St. John, "the Word was made flesh"? How were God and human nature made one in the womb of a virgin?

The solution of Nestorius is shrouded in uncertainty. How he conceived that incredible union is not at all clear; somehow God dwelt in flesh as in a temple. What is clear is the set of conclusions he drew therefrom. "Does God have a mother? [He does not.]" "I say it is the flesh that was born of the Virgin Mary, not God the Word. . . ." "It is not right to say of God that He sucked milk. . . ." "I do not say that God is two or three months old." "A born God, a dead God, a buried God I cannot adore."

The answer of Ephesus was unequivocal. The flesh which Mary fashioned of her flesh, that flesh the Son of God took to Himself, took as His own, at the moment of its fashioning. At that instant, and forevermore, this flesh was as much God's flesh as my flesh is mine. This union of God's Son with a human nature was a far different thing from the presence of God in every corner of His universe, far different from His presence in my soul through grace, far different from His presence in my body through Communion, far different even from the Nestorian idea of God dwelling in a temple. This flesh fashioned of Mary is the only flesh that is strictly God's own. When Mary murmured, "Be it done unto me according to thy word," at that moment there were not two individuals, two persons in her womb: one of them God, the other a man. There was one individual, one person: the God-Man. The Man was God, the God was the Man.

That is why Ephesus could believe, against Nestorius, that *God* was conceived in Mary's womb and lay for nine months beneath her heart; that *God* was laid in a feeding-trough and exiled to Egypt; that *God* worked with His hands, learned what hunger tastes like, and thirst; that *God* was tired enough to sleep out a storm in an open boat; that *God* was slapped and spat upon, mocked for a fool, whipped like a dog, and nailed to a tree.

The man was God, and God was the Man. That is why Ephesus had to believe that the thoughts of Christ which cover the pages of the Gospel, the words which fell for thirty years from the lips of Christ, are God's thoughts and God's words. Not that God somehow reached out and claimed them, called them His own; but that these thoughts were framed in the human mind of God, these words hung on the human lips of God. It was not a man linked to God like other men, who whipped traffickers from a temple, who loved Martha and her sister Mary, who wept over Jerusalem and over Lazarus. It was God enfleshed.

It is only if you hold fast to this concept of Christ that you can call Mary unconditionally Mother of God; Nestorius saw that. And conversely, it is only if you cling unequivocally to the title, Mother of God, that you can find the Son of God in a human womb; Nestorius saw that too.

That is why Ephesus canonized the letter to Nestorius in which Cyril declared: "We must not . . . sever into two sons the one Lord Jesus Christ. Such severance will be no help at all to the correct expression of the faith, even if one allege unity of persons. Scripture, you see, has not said that the Word united to Himself the person of a man, but that He has been made flesh. Now the Word's being made flesh is nothing else than that He partook of flesh and blood in like manner with us, and made our body His own, and proceeded Man of a woman, without having cast away His divinity. . . . This is what the expression of the exact faith everywhere preaches; this is the mind we shall find in the holy Fathers. In this sense they did not hesitate to call the holy Virgin God's Mother (*theotokos*)—not as though the nature of the Word or His divinity took beginning of being from the holy Virgin, but that of her was begotten the holy body animated with a rational soul; to this body the Word was united personally, and so He is said to have been born according to the flesh."

Briefly, then, Mary is Mother of God. She is Mother, because the flesh God took, He took from her flesh; and because Mary gave to her Son everything any mother gives to her child in its fashioning. She was pregnant with Christ. And she is Mother of God, simply because the human being who came forth from her womb was and is God.

It is understandable, then, why Ephesus was so exercised over a single word, *theotokos*. True, in the minds of some reputable historians Ephesus is synonymous with imprudence, intrigue, ecclesiastical politics. But, to its credit, Ephesus recognized that the denial or even the abandonment of *theotokos* was equivalent to a disavowal of Nicaea. Not that the Council of Nicaea had called Mary "Mother of God"; but that, unless Mary is God's Mother, you cannot confess, with the Fathers of Nicaea, "I believe in . . . Jesus Christ, God's Son . . . who for us men and for our salvation came down, was made flesh, became man. . . ."

Call Ephesus, if you will, a war of words; we need not blush. For us, a word is the incarnation of an idea. A century before, in the Arian crisis, the Christian world had been ruptured by a word. With that word, *homoousios*, "consubstantial," Athanasius summed up orthodox belief on the Eternal Word, the Son of God. In the Nestorian controversy the Christian East was sundered once more by a word. With that word, *theotokos*, "Mother of God," Cyril summed up orthodox belief on the Word Incarnate, the Son of God made flesh. That is why Cyril could thunder: "To confess our faith in orthodox fashion . . . it is enough to . . . confess that the holy Virgin is Mother of God." And three centuries later St. John Damascene, whose glory it is to have summed up in himself the theology of the Greek Fathers, wrote so simply: "This name contains the whole mystery of the Incarnation."

It is a striking thing that a Mariological term should have been selected as the ultimate test of Christological orthodoxy. Striking, but not surprising. Our Lady's role at Ephesus is the spontaneous outgrowth of her role at Nazareth, of her role throughout history. Her deep significance has always been her relationship to Christ. At Ephesus it was the *physical* Christ her divine maternity revealed. In this human mother the Christian mind caught a vision of her divine Son.

II

So much for 431. It is the contention of this essay that in 1960 the divine maternity has an added significance. In 431 the significance of Mary's motherhood lay in its relationship to the *physical* Christ; in 1960 its significance lies in its relationship to the *mystical* Christ. At Ephesus the divine maternity furnished a fresh insight into the *person* of Christ, into Christology, into the fact of the Incarnation; in 1960 it suggests a fresh insight into the *work* of Christ, into soteriology, into the task of the redemption.

You see, in theological circles today there is a remarkable Marian movement. What this movement yearns for is a deeper penetration into the mystery that is Mary, the mystery that makes Mary the unique creature she is. It is not content to see in the Mother of God simply the object of a special veneration, of a warmer flame of love. It wants to insert our Lady in her proper place in the divine dream for our redemption.

To achieve this, theologians are unaware that it is not sufficient to range privilege alongside privilege, mystery beside mystery, and say: that is Mary. It is not enough to plumb the depths of Mary's immaculate Conception, her perpetual virginity, her divine maternity, her utter sinlessness, her glorious Assumption; it is not enough to penetrate the meaning and the beauty of each of these if you are to say: I know our Lady. For beauty and truth lie not so much in the isolated fragments as in the harmony of the whole. What is needed is a basic idea which gives meaning to all the rest, some tremendous insight into the mind of God which, while it welds together the scattered prerogatives that spell Mary, will, above all, explain her role in the divine design we designate redemption.

Basically, I believe, this insight will have to be achieved in terms of the divine maternity; that prerogative is, in some genuine sense, fundamental. But the contemporary theologian is asking: Is there something still more fundamental? What is it that lies at the core of Mary's motherhood? Why, for example, did God fashion Mary precisely as bridal Mother of God—as God's Mother and His bride as well? God wills it, yes; but God's will is not whim. It may be that we shall end by bending low before mystery. The point, however, is this: theologians believe they have caught a glimpse of the divine idea that gives ultimate meaning to the divine maternity, that sets the Mother of God in the center of God's plan for man.

The solution to the problem was suggested towards the close of the fourth century by St. Ambrose, Bishop of Milan, when he wrote: "Mary is type of the Church." To have a type— as we are using the word here—four elements are desirable. In the first place, you have concrete representation, even at times personification. An idea, a spiritual reality is represented by something concrete, is represented by some palpable form, is made present at times by a human figure. Somewhat as we represent, personify the abstract idea of justice by a blindfolded lady with scales and a sword, so the early Christians represented, personified the inner life of the Church by the human figure of our Lady.

The second requisite: a real relationship that links the two, an objective foundation for this representation. The relationship that links Mary and the Church, the relationship that makes Mary a type of the Church, is not a creation of the human mind, as is the case with justice and the visionless lady in white. It is not a casual, accidental likeness which invites the meditative mind to oscillate between Mary and the Church. The resemblance between the Church and the human figure of Mary is the consequence of an inner tie that is real, a deep-seated relation that is objective. The resemblance between the two is not put there by the human mind, it *is* there. The relationship is not invented; it is discovered.

The third requisite is the most significant, if only because it concretizes the second. A type cannot rest satisfied with two terms, the type and the antitype, the figure and the thing it prefigures, the human person and the spiritual reality it personifies. It demands a third term, a design which envelops the other two, a master plan which finds its first realization and revelation in the person who is the type, and its second revelation and realization in the antitype. In the concrete, when we say that

Mary is type of the Church, we do not isolate Mary and the Church, as though they were related in some sort of vacuum. Mary is type of the Church in virtue of a divine design, an eternal plan in the mind of God which finds its realization first in bodily form in the person of Mary, then in the spiritual reality that is the Church. The resemblance between Mary and the Church is rooted in the divine dream of redemption. The third term is God—God's plan for man.

The fourth element follows from the second and third: the prototype is a moral pattern for the image. A *moral* pattern. The prototype, Mary, is a living individual. The image, the Church, is a collectivity, is actualized in the individuals who make up the Mystical Body of Christ. If Mary, as type of the Church, personifies the inmost essence of the Church, if the Church that unfolds in space and time exists in germ in Mary, then Mary is the model for the conduct of the Christian, the pattern of Christian living. Briefly, if by divine design Mary realizes in her own person what the Church is destined by God to be, then by divine design Mary realizes in her own life what the Christian is destined by God to do.

That much premised, the present essay will put forward a fact and an explanation. The fact: Mary is, in God's redemptive design, a prototype of the Church. The explanation: what this means in the concrete, how the Mary-Church idea lends meaning to the Mother of God and to her role in redemption.

First, then, is Mary a prototype of the Church? Did God plan redemption in such a way that, before the Church came forth from the pierced side of God's Son on Calvary, this Church somehow found its first realization in God's Mother? The answer will issue not from speculation but from revelation. God's mind is manifest in God's word.

In the twelfth chapter of the Apocalypse St. John has his celebrated Vision of the Woman. "In heaven a great portent appeared: a woman that wore the sun for her mantle, the moon under her feet, and a crown of twelve stars about her head. She had a child in her womb, and was crying out as she travailed, in great pain of her delivery. Then a second portent appeared . . .: a great dragon . . . fronting the woman . . . ready to swallow up the child as soon as she bore it. She bore a son, the son who is to herd the nations with a crook of iron. . . . In his spite against the woman, the dragon went elsewhere to make war on the rest of her children, the men who keep God's commandments, and hold fast to the truth concerning Jesus."

Many Scripture scholars insist that in the woman of Apocalypse 12 you have the Church of God personified. This woman, who has a vast progeny, whose children are the human beings who believe in Christ and live that belief, must be the Church of God. But this woman, who personifies the Church, is apparently the Mother of Christ: her son, says John, "is to herd the nations like sheep with a crook of iron." The Church of Christ, then, is personified by a woman, and the woman is the Mother of Christ. Somehow, therefore, in God's eyes, the Church and Mary are one.

This basic idea, that Mary is a type of the Church, recurs in patristic literature, in the theology of the first seven centuries, with an impressive constancy. In the first place, the Fathers frequently describe the Church in language borrowed from the person of Mary. The Church, like Mary, is a virgin. The Church, Origen insists, "is a chaste virgin, by reason of her rectitude in belief and in morality." The Church, like Mary, is a virgin mother. "Mary," says Augustine, "gave birth in body to the Head of this body; the Church gives birth in spirit to the members of that Head. In both [Mary and the Church], virginity is no hindrance to fertility; in both, fertility does not displace virginity." The Church's virginal motherhood, like Mary's, involves a sponsal relationship: the Church, like Mary, is bride of God. Christ our Lord, Jerome remarks, "is bridegroom of the virgin Church—the Church which has neither spot nor wrinkle." And though the Church's childbearing is consummated externally in baptism, as Mary's was in Bethlehem, at the basis of both is an inner act of conception: Christ is conceived in the soul of the Christian, as He was conceived in the body of Mary, in that the soul, like Mary, hears the word of God and believes it. In both there is a pregnant fiat: "Be it done unto me according to thy word." "That," as Chrysostom has it, "that is how the Church is wed to God."

But the Fathers go further. They are not content to dignify the Church with the prerogatives of Mary; such a manner of speaking might be sheer metaphor. The Fathers are more explicit than that; they tell us it is more than metaphor. Some insist that God deliberately made the Church like His Mother. As Augustine puts it: "The most beautiful among the sons of men [is] the Son of holy Mary, the Bridegroom of holy Church. Her [the Church] He made like to His Mother, for He made her our mother and keeps her His virgin." "Our Head," he claims, "Had to be born of a virgin . . . in the way of the flesh, as a sign that His members were to be born of a virgin Church in the way of the spirit." Some Fathers are more explicit still; they declare expressly that our Lady is type of the Church. Listen to Ambrose: "It is well that [Mary] is betrothed and yet a virgin, for she is type of the Church, which though wed is spotless." And Ephraem, the most distinguished representative of Syrian Christianity: "The Virgin Mary is a prototype of the Church, because she received the beginnings of the Gospel." And with no hesitation, no equivocation, comes the uncompromising affirmation: Mary and the Church are one; somehow Mary is the Church. Ephraem, for example, emphasizes the fact that beneath the cross Christ "gave to John Mary, His Church." Cyril of Alexandria we have heard at Ephesus: "May we reverence the undivided Trinity, while we sing the praise of the ever-virgin Mary, that is to say, the holy Church."

What Scripture hints at darkly, what the Fathers declare implicitly and explicitly, the Latin Middle Ages develop almost without interruption. Mary is type of the Church; she is its figure; she signifies it. The mystery of the Church is contained in the mystery of Mary as in its prototype and perfect exemplar. It is at once still hidden there and already revealed in advance, because it finds there its first and ideal realization. Our Lady, therefore, announces the Church and precedes it. She is its anticipation, and the remarkable things God accomplished in her He does not cease to reproduce in the Church. From the one to the other there is a real continuity; we cannot separate them; Mary and the Church are inseparably linked, because the same Christ links them to Himself.

The fact, therefore, seems beyond dispute. In Christian tradition Mary is type of the Church. So was she destined by God; so was she in actuality. The more difficult question remains: what does this mean in the concrete? How does the Mary-Church analogy lend meaning to the Mother of God and to her role in the drama of redemption?

The fundamental principle which dominates this whole discussion was formulated by St. Augustine: "He who made you without your co-operation does not justify you without your co-operation." It is the principle of human co-operation in the divine task of redemption: God has determined to save man by means of man. As in Paradise, so on earth, as in man's original fall, so in his later restoration, God would respect the inmost nature of His human creation, man's perilous power to say no. That divine decision spangles the pages of the Old Testament. Salvation is presented as a covenant, a pact, a contract offered by God and accepted by man. Or it is a marriage, wide-eyed and free, nuptials of love between God and Israel, and, in the New Testament, between Christ and the Church. The basic datum of this symbolism, exploited in Christian tradition till the Renaissance, is significant. In this marriage God is everywhere and always the man, the bridegroom; humanity is everywhere and always the woman, the bride. In this inspired figure of salvation it is the male who symbolizes the initiative and the power of God; it is the female who symbolizes the active receptivity of humanity and the fruitfulness which union with God communicates to it.

God saves man by means of man. In line with that design, God *became* man, asked of humanity the free gift of its flesh and blood. In harmony with that plan, Christ leaves His Church, the prolongation of His Incarnation, in the hands of men. The book that bears His name—the word of God—comes line by line from the pen of men. The grace He has won with His own body is communicated through the hands and lips of men. Nor will He come to the human heart unless the human heart whispers, "Come."

Now this co-operation of man with God is exercised in two ways: by faith and by ministry. Faith is primarily an interior thing, a drama within the soul; ministry is an exterior thing, a communication, an administration of words and sacramental signs whereby faith is born and grows. Faith is the task of the whole Christian community; ministry is the privilege of a segment within that community. Faith is receiving, an active receptivity; ministry is giving, an exercise of power in the name of God.

Precisely here we reach a conclusion of supreme significance. Mary cannot be a type of the ministering Church, of the Church in its hierarchical function. The hierarchical aspect of the Church is rather a prolongation of Christ's own activity, Christ's own power. It is the divine in the Church. Our Lady is type of the human element in redemption; she represents the believing Church, the whole community of Christians, men and women, hierarchy and laity, in so far as it hears the word of God and welcomes it within.

This personification of the Church finds its crucial hour at the Annunciation. That first Angelus, so simply told by St. Luke, veils a tremendous truth. It was not simply that God wanted Mary's motherhood to be a voluntary thing, uncompelled, unconstrained. Gabriel's role is more profound than that. The Son of God was about to wed human nature to Himself. Therefore, as St. Thomas phrases it, "what God was asking through the Annunciation was the consent of the Virgin *in the name of all humanity.*" Or, in the lovely sentence of Leo XIII: "The eternal Son of God, when He wanted to take to Himself man's nature, and so enter a mystical marriage with the whole human race, did not do so before obtaining the perfectly free consent of His Mother-to-be, *who played as it were the role of the human race itself.*" And, while a world waited breathlessly, Mary answered, "Be it done unto me according to thy word." Mary said yes. That whispered yes may well have been, in God's eyes, Mary's finest hour. At that moment she became bride of God and His Mother too: bride of God by her fiat, Mother of God whom she welcomed in her womb. At that instant was realized in Mary the substance of the mystery of the Church to come: the union of God and man in the Mystical Body of Christ.

This welcome given God by Mary was not a sheerly passive thing; it was incredibly active on all levels. In the spiritual order her faith, like all genuine faith, was the quickening response of her mind to a manifestation of God. In the moral order her consent was the loving response of her will to an invitation of

211

God. In the physical order her conception was the living response of her body to the activity of God: "the Holy Spirit shall come upon thee."

Briefly, our Lady, as Mother of God and His bride, has a representative function. The task of the believing Church is to continue through space and time the sponsal fiat of Mary, her whispered yes. This community of the redeemed has for vocation to co-operate in the work of redemption by loving faith, and so bring God to birth in the human frame. The Church, therefore, is a collective Mary, and Mary is the Church in germ.

This vision of Mary's motherhood as a representative thing becomes clearer still if we see it in its virginal aspect. In our synthesis it is no longer satisfying to see in our Lady's virginity before and after Bethlehem little more than a privilege highly appropriate, perhaps indispensable in a girl who is God's Mother. It will not do to ask with St. Ambrose: "Would the Lord Jesus choose for Himself a mother who could defile heaven's court with the seed of man?" From the vantage ground of history the answer is no. But the question is perilous. It might well leave the impression that the marital relationship is something less than good. Or it might, in reaction, revive a seductive fourth-century error, to the effect that marriage and virginity are equal in honor, that (as Helvidius claimed) Mary is doubly admirable for having been, in turn, virgin and mother: virgin till the birth of Jesus, then mother of the "brothers and sisters of Jesus" spoken of in Scripture. In any event, though the rhetoric of Ambrose may stimulate piety, it does not satisfy theology. The divine design goes deeper than that. Even in her virginity Mary is type of the Church; she represents the community of believers; her virginal motherhood is a first, a concrete, a symbolic realization of God's plan for redeemed humanity.

Womanly virginity, you see, has two facets. Negatively, it denies that intimate relationship with man which we term marital; it denies the initiative of man with respect to woman and woman's fruitfulness. But virginity, in the Christian concept, is not sheer negation, the absence of something. The negative aspect of virginity stems from something positive. The denial to man of any initiative in her fruitfulness must, if it is to be Christian, stem from a woman's total dedication to God, a complete openness to the divine, receptivity to God and to God alone. The denial of a bridal relationship to man is rooted in the affirmation of a bridal relationship to God.

And so it was with Mary. Her virginity meant, on the one hand, that no human being, no man, took the initiative in the bridal relationship which issued in the Son of God made flesh: "the Holy Spirit shall come upon thee." It meant, on the other hand—in fact, the denial of human initiative stemmed from—the total consecration of Mary to her Bridegroom, utter co-operation with God, an unfailing fiat, complete and exclusive.

And in this Mary is type of the Church; she represents the community of believers; she realizes in her own person what God intended for redeemed humanity. On the one hand, this union of God with man which is the Church denies to man the initiative in the task which links man to God. Not that man is purely passive; he must co-operate, else oneness with God is impossible. But his co-operation is a response—a response to grace, a response to God's invitation. "If we but turn to God," Augustine insists, "that itself is a gift of God." And that is the other aspect, the positive side, of the Church's virginity. The Church is linked to Christ as bride to groom. Her role, like that of Mary, is total consecration to Christ, a complete openness to the divine, a sensitiveness to the action of God's Spirit, an incredible readiness to respond, "Be it done unto me according to thy word."

The paradox is this. It is not simply that, as Augustine said, Mary's "virginity is no hindrance to fertility." For the Church as for Mary, it is only by reason of her virginity that she can achieve fertility. It was only by Mary's total response to God's invitation alone that the Son of God became flesh; it is only by prolonging this response through space and time that the Church, impregnated with the Spirit, is fruitful for the formation of Christ in individual souls. The words of Gabriel are expressive: "The Holy Spirit shall come upon thee, and the power of the Most High shall overshadow thee; and *therefore* the Holy One to be born shall be called the Son of God."

This vision of Mary's virginal motherhood as a representative thing grows clearer still if we ponder her Immaculate Conception. Here, too, our Lady is type of the Church. The Church, remember, is the Body of Christ. But it is a body redeemed; the members of that body have been touched with redemption. In the concrete, a human being enters the Church at a specific moment in time, by a baptism which weds him to Christ as it incorporates him into the Body of Christ. At that instant he *is* a person redeemed—at the instant he enters the Church. His redemption, however, has twin facets. Positively, he has captured Christ's life; negatively, he no longer has original sin. The two cannot coexist in the human soul: Christ's life and original sin. But notice: As God planned it, the Church does not take the human being, incorporate him into the Body of Christ, into the Church, and *then* remove original sin. At the moment he enters the Church he *is* free of original sin. That is why we say: the Church is a community of the redeemed, not a community of those who are to be redeemed.

But if it is of the Church's essence to be a community of the redeemed, of those who are free from original sin, then the Church herself has no part in original sin. That is her God-given nature. Therefore, at the first moment of her existence, at the instant of her incarnation on Calvary, she was sinless. In the womb of humanity, in the midst of a world estranged from God by the sin of Adam, the Church was conceived without original sin.

Here, too, in God's staggering design, the Mother of God is type of the Church. For, if the Church is to be personified, the human figure who personifies it must, like the Church, be free of Adam's sin. And not simply freed after being burdened with it. If it is of the Church's essence to be without original sin, to have no part in it, then the individual who is type of the Church must be without sin from the first moment of her existence; she must be immaculately conceived. That person, alone among the children fashioned of human seed, is God's Mother. Mary conceived without sin is Mary redeemed; and Mary conceived without sin, Mary redeemed, prefigures the whole community of the redeemed which is the Church, fashioned without sin from the lanced side of the Crucified.

This vision of God's Mother as type of the Church grows in clarity if we study her perfect sinlessness, her freedom from actual sin. The inner essence of the Church, as community of

214

the redeemed, means the participation of men in the redemption effected by Christ. All men who have been touched with redemption in baptism and are linked to the Church in submissive faith belong to this community of the redeemed. But redemption is a gradual process, a lifelong thing; it is not complete in baptism. We belong to this community of the redeemed more or less perfectly, we are more or less perfect members of the Church, to the extent that redemption has taken hold of us, in proportion as grace or sin dominates in our soul.

Because the redemption of humanity—in fact, the redemption of the individual—is not yet complete, the Church is not without sinners. Pius XII put it well: "One must not imagine that the Body of the Church, just because it bears the name of Christ, is made up during the days of its earthly pilgrimage only of members conspicuous for their holiness. . . . It is the Saviour's infinite mercy that allows place in His Mystical Body here for those whom He did not exclude from the banquet of old."

The Church is not without sinners, but it is without sin. "I believe in the holy Catholic Church." This is the Church which Paul saw Christ summoning into His own presence, "the Church in all its beauty, no stain, no wrinkle, no such disfigurement . . . holy . . . spotless." A paradox, yes: a Church of the sinful, yet herself without sin. But nonetheless true. Where the Church is, there sin is, because man, though redeemed from sin, is still free to sin. Sin, however, stands in contradiction to the Church's essence, and the Church's essence stands in contradiction to sin. But her essence, as community of the redeemed, will be fully realized only when redemption is complete, and sin is no more, and the Church looks upon her Head in glory—the day when, as Augustine said, "there will be but one Christ loving Himself."

Here again God's Mother is type of the Church. In her soul redemption found its perfect realization; in her soul there was never sin, there was only God. In our Lady we see God's design for redeemed humanity; in her we discover in its ideal state the sinlessness which is of the Church's essence, yet is realized not at once, but from day to day, through sin upon sin, till humanity be gathered up in Christ.

This vision of God's Mother as personification of redeemed humanity finds a final clarity in her bodily Assumption. There is a popular misconception among Christians with respect to the human body. For some, the body is nothing but an instrument, a tool of the soul. For others, the body is a burden from which the soul cries for release. All this is an echo of the third-century theory of Origen that the soul has been imprisoned in matter because it sinned in an earlier existence. Such an attitude pays slender homage to God. It fails to recognize that the body is an essential part of man; that without the body man is a creature incomplete; that, whether in heaven or purgatory or hell, a separated soul, as Jean Mouroux phrased it, "still longs for its body with a purely natural impulse of love."

In somewhat the same way the visible structure of the Church is an essential part of the Church. Not merely because it is an instrument through which God's life is communicated to men. It is that, of course; but it is more. The Church is visible of her very nature because everything which is to absorb redemption must somehow be absorbed into the Church. As the body played its part in the first sin, as the body fell with the soul from God, so does the body yearn for redemption. In the inspired language of Paul, we "groan in our hearts, waiting for that adoption which is the ransoming of our bodies from their slavery."

This redemption of the body, like all redemption, is achieved through the Body of Christ, through the Church. What is redeemed is absorbed into the Church, helps constitute her essence. That is why the Church is not simply a spiritual thing; she is visible, tangible, sensible, material. And when the body of man is absorbed into the visible structure of the Church, it ceases to be what St. Paul termed "the body of death"; it comes spiritually alive, because it is quickened by the Spirit of God. And the more fully grace permeates the Church and each member, the more intimately does the body partake of redemption, and the less the "law in my members" wars against the "law of my mind." This, however, is but the beginning of redemption. Redemption will find its consummation, its perfection, in the glory of the life to come—not merely in the soul's vision of God, but in the transfiguration of the body, when the whole material world will share in the perfection of redemption, and there will be "a new heaven and a new earth."

If Mary is type of the Church, of redeemed humanity, then this redemption of the body must appear in its perfection in her. The redemption operated by the Church will be consummated only after the general resurrection, when the body will be transformed, and the whole man, soul and body, will confront his Creator in an eternity of knowledge and love. That perfection of humanity redeemed, that consummation of the Church, finds its first purely human realization in the Mother of God, in Mary assumed into heaven, soul and body.

This vision of God's Mother as type of the Church has much to recommend it. To begin with, it preserves a perfect balance between Mary's humanness and her uniqueness. On the one hand, it curbs the anguished accusation, Mariolatry. Our Lady is seen as fully human. She is not equated with divinity, because she is essentially representative of humanity. She is not on a par with God the Redeemer, because she personifies man the redeemed. In her we glimpse not so much God's design for a single human being, as His plan for all human beings. If there is glory here and divinization, it is all humanity that is glorified in her, all humanity that is divinized. Granted she is, in Augustine's word, "supereminent" member of the Church; she remains, for all that, a member. And still she is not depreciated. If it is true that she symbolizes humanity redeemed, that she represents in her person what God intended for the whole Church, it is equally true that redeemed humanity, God's plan for His Church, is realized in its perfection in no individual save her.

Secondly, this vision of Mary as type of the Church clarifies and unifies her role in redemption. In this synthesis there is no Marian prerogative that is merely "fitting," no need to range privilege alongside privilege with a more or less tenuous tie. Mary is the unique creature she is, because redemption is the unique program it is. Redemption is a master plan, divinely conceived, divinely executed. It finds its first, its ideal, its perfect realization in a single human being: Mary redeemed. It finds its ultimate realization in a community of human beings: humanity redeemed. What the Mother of God is, that the

Church is destined to be. And what the Church is, that is already discoverable in God's Mother. When Léon Bloy saw the lesson of the Immaculate Conception in this, that the redemption was successful at its very outset, because it produced a Mary, he spoke more truly than he knew. For Mary is not simply redeemed; she is redeemed humanity.

Thirdly, this vision of Mary makes for authentic devotion. In attachment to the immaculate Virgin-Mother of God in glory, we are not simply bent low before mystery—mystery that is meaningless as far as contemporary living is concerned. We are not lost in wonder at an Immaculate Conception which can never be ours; at a wedding of perpetual virginity and physical motherhood unique in history; at a glorious resurrection not preluded, like ours, by the corruption of the tomb. Our devotion to God's Mother is the fruit not so much of mystery as of insight. In the Mother of God we encounter in human form the plan of God for man. In this one woman we see what the community of believers is and is destined to be. In her virginal maternity we glimpse in its perfection the role in which God casts every human being. What He asks of you and me is active receptivity—that, when we hear the word of God, we welcome it within. For on this depends our holiness, our oneness with God—the openness, the freedom with which we can respond, "Be it done unto me according to thy word."

Bernard J. F. Lonergan
1904-

*"Lonergan is one of the greatest minds of Christendom"
(Langdon Gilkey). "Lonergan is The Christian Thinker of the
20th century" (Bernard Tyrrell). Such statements indicate the
high esteem with which Bernard Lonergan is regarded by many
contemporaries. He was born in Buckingham, Quebec, Canada.
After two years at Loyola College in Montreal he joined the
Jesuits in 1922. His first trip to Europe was to study philosophy
for three years at Heythrop College in England. Three more
years were spent back in Loyola as a teacher of freshmen, then
he went to the Gregorian University in Rome for theology. He
finished the work for his doctorate in 1940. From 1940 to 1953
he taught theology in Jesuit seminaries in Montreal and Toronto,
and then was assigned to the Gregorian University, where he
taught for twelve years.*

*After the removal of one lung due to cancer, Lonergan
returned to Canada in 1965, taking up residence at Regis College
in Willowdale, Ontario, and concentrating on writing. In 1970
his thought was the subject of special attention in the First
International Lonergan Conference, held at St. Leo's College
in Tampa, Florida, and attended by 75 distinguished scholars
from various disciplines.*

*Lonergan's two most important works were separated by
fifteen years.* Insight *came out in 1957 and* Method in Theology

appeared in 1972. Both have been acclaimed as among the most important works of our era. He has contributed greatly to overcoming the old notion of Catholic theology as made up of unchangeable knowledge; this notion ignores the role of the knowing subject, whose understanding changes as his horizon changes, putting things in different perspective. More than anyone else, Lonergan has helped Christian theologians to appreciate the importance of "moving horizons."

The essay that is presented here is the rebuttal Lonergan wrote when, in Rome in 1958, an Italian Jesuit, A. Perego, reviewed and attacked his work on the consciousness of Christ. In a way it was fortunate that Fr. Perego misunderstood and distorted Lonergan's thought, for this served to elicit from Lonergan a more fully elaborated response which is a model of theological thinking. It is easy enough to speak theoretically about the validity and desirability, even the necessity, of doctrinal development in a Church that is alive and living its beliefs. But seldom is so clear an example provided as in this essay. Arguing the "parallelism" of the ontological and the psychological statements about the incarnate Word, Lonergan presents forcefully the grounds for incorporating the understanding of "Christ as Subject," which Karl Adam and Romano Guardini had been probing toward.

This single contribution hardly conveys the importance and impact of Bernard Lonergan on contemporary Catholic theology, but at least it serves to recognize the value and benefit that comes to all when intelligence such as his is brought intensely to bear upon understanding and appreciating the depths of Christian faith. He has given not only the book but also the reality of "Insight" to innumerable contemporaries in their search for a fuller vision of the meaning of Christ as Savior.

COLLECTION

CHAPTER 11

CHRIST AS SUBJECT: A REPLY

A few years ago I yielded to necessity and put together for my students some supplementary notes in speculative Christology. The booklet happens to have come to the attention of the Reverend A. Perego, S.J., and he has offered the readers of *Divinitas* a presentation and a critical evaluation of my views on the consciousness of Christ.

As the position imputed to me, both in the presentation and in the critical evaluation, is one that I fail to distinguish from heresy, I feel called upon to supplement Fr. Perego's animadversions and, at the same time, to correct his imputation.

My notion of the subject and of consciousness is alleged to be incomprehensible, and so I shall offer a simplified version of the matter and a solution of the arguments presumably thought to be decisive.

The intimate relation between the articles of faith and theological thought appears to me to be slighted, and so I shall reiterate in simple terms my conviction that the physical pain endured by Jesus Christ has a significant bearing on theological accounts of the consciousness of Christ.

My remarks, then, come under three headings: Part I, A Misrepresentation; Part II, the Notion of the Subject; Part III, Christ as Subject. To these I append a brief conclusion and readers wishing to know at once where I stand, should make a beginning where I end.

Part I: A Misrepresentation

According to Fr. Perego I hold the remarkable view that in Christ, ontologically and psychologically, there is a real duality of subject, *ego*, and *principium quod* (principle-which), and no more than an abstract unity. This is so odd that, perhaps, I had best quote the various passages in which this interpretation takes shape and is exploited. At the bottom of page 412 there occurs the sentence, which for convenient reference may be named quotation *A*. It reads:

> . . . If in fact the subject is considered in abstraction from the natures in which it subsists and from the consciousnesses by which it is manifested, we have to admit a *single* "I" in Christ, because there is only the single person of the Word and no other; but in so far as the "I" is referred instead to the nature in which it subsists, and to the consciousness by which it is manifested, we have to distinguish two "I's"—one divine and the other human.

The pattern seems clear: one in the abstract, two in the concrete. This is followed immediately at the top of page 413 by the complementary statement, quotation *B*, which reads:

> And the same must be said of the *principium quod* of the operations of Christ. If the person of the Word is considered without reference to the natures in which it subsists, we must say that in Christ there is one *principium quod*; but, if instead we take account of the nature in which it subsists, we must affirm that in Jesus the *principium quod* is double.

The pattern has recurred: one in the abstract, two in the concrete. Next we are told [quotation *C*] : "it is a mere abstraction to consider the person of the Word without reference to its natures (p. 118)." There follows an inference, indicated by the word, *consegue,* where the minor premise seems to be supplied by quotations *A* and *B* and the major by quotation *C*. One of the conclusions (quotation *D*) reads:

> . . . the duality in Christ of the *principium quod*, of the subject and of the "I," whether in the ontological order or in the psychological, corresponds to the reality, while on the contrary their uniqueness is nothing but an abstraction founded on another abstraction, namely, on the "person of the Word considered simply as such" (pp. 117, 118 and elsewhere).

Bernard J. F. Lonergan

Once more the pattern: one in abstract, two in the concrete. Accordingly, in Christ, on the view imputed to me, in both the ontological and the psychological order, there is a real duality of *principium quod,* subject, and *ego,* and the only unity is one abstraction founded on another. Perhaps it is superfluous for me to prove that, between such a view and Nestorius' *persona unionis,* the differences are negligible. If ontologically the only unity of the *principium quod* and the subject is just an abstraction, then the unity of the person is just an abstraction; if the unity of the person is just an abstraction, our Lady is not the Mother of God.

The imputation recurs at the bottom of page 415. After presenting my view that there is a single subject of both the divine and the human consciousness in Christ, the writer adds, (quotation *E*):

> ... However, that holds "according to the abstract consideration of the mind" (p. 118), since, if the conscious subject in Christ is considered with reference to the nature in which it subsists, then we have to say that the person of the Word *qua* subsisting in the divine nature and operating with the uncreated consciousness, constitutes the divine "I," which is not to be confused with the human "I" (pp. 116-117).

Naturally enough, this imputation is repeated once more when a *valutazione critica* of my position is attempted. So from page 423 there comes quotation *F*. It reads:

> Finally, we have to draw attention to this, that, while Lonergan on the one hand affirms the uniqueness of the psychological and ontological subject in Christ when he considers the divine person abstractly, that is, without reference to its two natures, on the other hand, when he considers the person in the concrete, with reference to its two natures, he introduces a true and proper psychological duality into the Savior.

So much for the statements I believe in need of explicit correction.

In speaking of Christ one may refer to the person, *principium quod,* subject, or *ego,* in four manners. Thus, one can speak

223

(I do not say, *think*) of the person or *principium quod* (1) with both natures, (2) with the divine nature, (3) with the human nature, or (4) with neither nature. Similarly, one can speak of the subject or *ego* (1) with both the divine and the human consciousness, (2) with the divine consciousness, (3) with the human consciousness, or (4) with neither the divine nor the human consciousness.

The reader will be familiar with the fourth of these manners: it is the view imputed to me. But he will be far more familiar with the first manner: it is Chalcedon's

> . . . we all with one voice profess our faith in one
> and the same Son, our Lord Jesus Christ, the same one
> perfect in deity and the same one perfect in humanity,
> truly God and truly man. . . .

Nor will a theologian be any less familiar with the second and third manners, for there is in common use the distinction between *Christus ut Deus* and *Christus ut homo*.

Now, on the strength of the references given in quotations *B* and *E*, let us turn to page 116 in my booklet and read:

> Therefore, insofar as the same subject is mani-
> fested to itself through the divine consciousness as
> well as through the human consciousness, there is
> simply one "I" in Christ just as there is one person.

> But, insofar as "I," or the psychological subject,
> not only denotes the subject itself but also implies a
> relation to the nature and the consciousness of which
> it is the subject, then, since there are two natures and
> two consciousnesses in Christ, we have to distinguish in
> him between the "I as divine," which is manifested to
> itself according to its infinite perfection, and the "I as
> human," which experiences itself according to the
> limitations of the assumed nature. Of course, to make
> this distinction is merely to transfer to the psycholog-
> ical field the familiar distinction between Christ as
> God and Christ as man.

I submit that the first paragraph (*Therefore, insofar as* . . .) does not abstract from both the divine and the human conscious-ness, that on the contrary it includes both. Hence, so far from

224

employing the abstract, fourth manner, imputed to me, I employ the concrete manner evident in the decree of the council of Chalcedon. There is, then, a discrepancy between quotation *A* and my text. Similarly, there is a discrepancy between the conclusion, given in quotation *D*, and my text. In like manner, there is a discrepancy between quotation *F* and my text.

Again, I submit that *simpliciter* (simply) is opposed to *secundum quid* (according to some aspect). There is, then, a discrepancy between my "unum 'ego' simpliciter" (one "I" simply) and on the other hand, the "secundum abstractam mentis considerationem" (according to the abstract consideration of the mind) of quotation *E*.

If now we turn to the second paragraph (*But, insofar as* . . .), we find it explicitly stated that my "ego ut divinum" (the "I" as divine) and "ego ut humanum" (the "I" as human) are to be taken in the same sense as "Christus ut Deus" (Christ as God) and "Christus ut homo" (Christ as man). But no one fancies that the latter distinction implies "due Cristi, quello divino e quello umano" (two Christs, one divine and the other human). By parity of argument, no one should fancy that the former distinction means "duo 'io'; quello divino e quello umano" (two "I's," one divine and the other human), as stated in quotation *A*, inferred in quotation *D*, put in other words in quotation *E*, and applied to the subject in quotation *F*.

So much for the first of the apparent minor premises. Let us now direct our attention to the other minor represented apparently by quotation *B*. If one turns, on the strength of the references supplied, to pages 117 and 118 of my booklet, one may read:

> In Christ, God and man, there are without mixture and without interchange two natures and two operations, and on this basis we formulate the notions (1) the divine nature as *principium quo* (principle-by-which) of the divine operation, and (2) the human nature as *principium quo* of the human operation.

> But in the same Christ, God and man, there is only one person which exercises both the divine and the human activity, and so on the basis of this unity of person there is to be admitted only one *principium*

quod of activity, namely, the divine person itself.

When this is grasped and firmly held, we may go on to ask whether that *principium quod* is to be conceived as the divine person simply as such, while we prescind from each nature, or is to be conceived as the divine person isofar as it subsists in a nature.

Here, clearly enough, after speaking in the first, concrete manner of the one person that operates both *divina* and *humana* and so is a single *principium quod*, there is raised the question of the fourth manner. Is this one *principium quod* to be conceived in abstraction from both natures? The answer follows on page 118:

> The answer is that the *principium quod* of activity is always the person with reference to a nature; hence the one exercising the activity is always either Christ as God or Christ as man; or, in other words, it is always the divine person either as subsisting in the divine nature or as subsisting in the human nature.

There follow three arguments to prove the contention that the *principium quod* is not to be taken in abstraction from both natures.

Now I submit that to attribute to me the position that the one *principium quod* in Christ is just an abstraction is to attribute to me a view that (1) I explicitly reject and (2) I give three arguments for rejecting. There is, then, a discrepancy between my text and quotation *B*, between my text and the conclusion given in quotation *D*, and between my text and the reference to page 118 given in quotation *E*.

Further, when I say that the "operans semper est aut Christus ut Deus aut Christus ut homo" (the one operating is always either Christ as God or Christ as man), I am employing language that is familiar to every theologian. That expression does imply a duality, not however in the *principium quod*, but in the *principia quibus* (principles-by-which). There is, then, a discrepancy between my text and the imputation of a double *principium quod* in the statement given in quotation *B*. There is a similar discrepancy between my text and the duality of the *principium quod* concluded in quotation *D*.

Bernard J. F. Lonergan

To complete the picture, let us note that, when in quotation *E* the reader is assured that the single subject of both the divine and human consciousness is just an abstraction, the reader of the corresponding passage in my booklet is assured of the contradictory. Having treated the divine consciousness of Christ on pages 100-106 and the human consciousness of Christ on pages 106-124, I began my answer to the question of the one subject of both the divine and human consciousness with the remark that follows:

> . . . after the abstract consideration in which there were discussion by turns of Christ insofar as he is God and Christ insofar as he is man, we have to undertake the concrete consideration in which we study Christ as he really is, namely, at the same time both God and man.

Since quotation *F* is adorned with no references, its value would seem to derive simply from the evidence provided by quotations *A, B, D,* and *E* with their references to my pages 116-118. There is however in quotation *D* a further, if vague, reference to *altrove*. It perhaps may be met in a more simple fashion than quotations from every relevant sentence in my booklet. The author of some reflections on my views in the *Revue thomiste* had little use for my metaphysical and psychological opinions. None the less, he felt able to write: "He firmly defends the psychological unity of Christ, and there one can have a sense of agreement with him."

To conclude, the view imputed to me in the quotations I have given is about as different as possible from what I actually state. I consider (1) Christ as both God and man, (2) Christ as God, and (3) Christ as man. I exclude a consideration of the *principium quod* considered apart from both natures. On the contrary, on the view attributed to me, there vanishes the consideration of Christ as both God and man; there is substituted the abstraction I reject; and for my legitimate prescinding, parallel to 'Christ as God' or to 'Christ as man,' there is introduced a real duality of the *principium quod*, subject, and *ego*.

Some reader, however, may wish to raise a question. It is one thing to be conscious of oneself as God; it is quite another

227

to be conscious of oneself as man. How, then, is it that divine consciousness and human consciousness can reveal one and the same subject?

If the hypothetical reader wishes an explanation of the mystery, he is asking too much. If he will be content with an imperfect analogy, that can easily be supplied. It is one thing to enjoy a good dinner; it is quite another to be flogged; but the same individual can first enjoy the one and then undergo the other. In brief, consciousness reveals not only acts and states but also the subject and, while acts and states vary, the subject remains consciously the same.

The difficulty, however, may be pressed. On my view the meaning of such names as *subject, principle,* includes a relation. If I speak of subject, I mean subject of consciousness. If I speak of principle, I mean principle of operation. If then it is one thing to be the subject of divine consciousness and another to be the subject of human consciousness, it follows that there are really two subjects. *A pari,* it follows that the principle of divine and human operations is really two principles.

The answer is *Non sequitur.* Relatives are not multiplied by the multiplication of correlatives. The father of two sons is not two fathers; similarly, he is not one father in the abstract and two in the concrete; he is just one father. Again, the teacher of one hundred pupils is not one hundred teachers; similarly, he is not one teacher in the abstract but the concrete one hundred teachers, drawing one hundred salaries, and enjoying one hundred paid vacations. Concretely, he is one and only one teacher.

Part II: The Notion of the Subject

The notion of the subject is difficult, recent, and primitive.

It is difficult. St. Thomas once remarked that everyone knows he has a soul, yet even great philosophers go wrong on the nature of the soul. The same is true of the subject. Everyone knows he is a subject, and so everyone is interested in the consciousness of Christ. Not everyone knows the nature of the subject, and so there is a variety of opinions.

The notion is also recent. If one wishes to find out what a soul is, one has only to read St. Thomas. If one wishes to find out what a subject is, it is not enough to read ancient or medieval writers. They did not treat the matter explicitly. They did not work out systematically the notion of the subject. They did not integrate this systematic notion with the rest of their philosophic and psychological doctrine.

In the third place, the notion is primitive. It cannot be reached merely by combining other better-known concepts. It can be reached only by directing one's attention to the facts and to understanding them correctly. Nor is this enough. A difficult, recent, and primitive notion is not theologically useful until it has been transposed into the classical categories of scholastic thought; and obviously such a transposition supposes some research into the exact meaning and the latent potentialities of classical writers such as St. Thomas.

Needless to say I did not attempt all this in a set of notes for theological students. I had explored Thomist intellectual theory in a series of articles published in *Theological Studies*. I had explored the complex speculative issues in a book, *Insight*. In my *De constitutione Christi* I was simply making available in Latin and for my students the conclusions I had reached in other studies.

My procedure was to present two opposed notions of consciousness: the first I named *conscientia-experientia* and I employed it as the basis of my view of the consciousness of Christ; the second I named *conscientia-perceptio* and I employed it to account for the opinions of those with whom I happened to disagree. Since the former met dogmatic requirements and the latter, I believed, did not, there seemed to me no need to leave the properly theological level of thought and to enter into philosophic and psychological questions.

Still, what precisely is the difference between the two positions, between consciousness conceived as an experience and consciousness conceived as the perception of an object? In my booklet I set forth these differences at length (pp. 130-34), but for present purposes it will be sufficient, perhaps, to select the fourth difference (*ad*) out of six, namely, that if consciousness is conceived as an experience there is a psychological subject, while if consciousness is conceived as the perception of an object there is no psychological subject. To establish this point I shall begin by indicating one manner in which the notion of *conscientia-*

perceptio may arise; I shall next point out the defect in this notion; thirdly, I shall indicate the essentially opposed character of *conscientia-experientia*; and finally I shall turn to Fr. Perego's objections.

Consider, then, the two propositions, John knows his dog, John knows himself. In both, the subject is John. In the first, the object is John's dog. In the second, the object is John himself. It follows that knowing is of two kinds: there is direct knowing in which the object is not the subject; there is reflexive knowing in which the object is the subject. Name reflexive knowing consciousness. Define the subject as the object of consciousness. Then it cannot be disputed, it seems, that consciousness is a reflexive knowing, for in consciousness the knower himself is known; and it cannot be disputed, it seems, that the subject is the object of consciousness, for whatever is known, is an object. Nothing, it seems, could be simpler or clearer or more evident.

Still, it may be well to attend to a difficulty that could be raised. A cognitive act exercises no constitutive effect upon its object; it simply reveals what the object already is; it exercises no transforming power over the object in its proper reality, but simply and solely manifests what that proper reality is. Accordingly, if consciousness is knowledge of an object, it can have no constitutive effect upon its object; it can only reveal its object as it was in its proper reality prior to the occurrence of the cognitive act or function named consciousness.

Thus, to illustrate this aspect of *conscientia-perceptio*, if without consciousness John is simply a prime substance (such as this man or this horse) then by consciousness John is merely revealed to himself as a prime substance. Again, if without consciousness John has no other psychological unity beyond the unity found in the objects of his knowledge, then by consciousness John is merely manifested as having no psychological unity beyond the unity found in the objects of his knowledge. Again, if without consciousness John cannot possibly be the conscious subject of physical pain, then by consciousness John is merely manifested as being incapable of suffering. Similarly, if without consciousness John cannot be the consciously intelligent or the consciously rational or the consciously free or the consciously responsible principle of his own intelligent, rational, free, or responsible acts, then by consciousness as knowledge of an object John merely knows himself as neither consciously intelligent, nor consciously rational, nor consciously free, nor consciously responsible.

My difficulty, then, with the simple, clear, and evident view, which I named *conscientia-perceptio,* is that it is *simpliste.* It takes account of the fact that by consciousness the subject is known by the subject. It overlooks the fact that consciousness is not merely cognitive but also constitutive. It overlooks as well the subtler fact that consciousness is cognitive, not of what exists without consciousness, but of what is constituted by consciousness. For consciousness does not reveal a prime substance; it reveals a psychological subject that subsequently may be subsumed, and subsumed correctly, under the category of prime substance. Similarly, consciousness does not reveal the psychological unity that is known in the field of objects; it constitutes and reveals the basic psychological unity of the subject as subject. In like manner, consciousness not merely reveals us as suffering but also makes us capable of suffering; and similarly it pertains to the constitution of the consciously intelligent subject of intelligent acts, the consciously rational subject of rational acts, the consciously free subject of free acts, and the consciously responsible subject of responsible acts.

How, then, can one account for this constitutive function of consciousness? One cannot reject the principle that knowing simply reveals its object; one cannot suppose that knowing exercises a constitutive effect upon its object. It is true that the mode of the knowing may and does differ from the mode of the reality known. But it is fantastic to suggest that knowing an object changes the mode of reality in the subject.

The alternative, I suggest, is to deny that consciousness is a matter of knowing an object; the alternative is to deny that only objects are known; the alternative is to reject the tacit assumption that *unumquodque cognoscitur secundum quod est obiectum* (everything that is known, is known insofar as it is an object), and to put in its place the familiar axiom that *unumquodque cognoscitur secundum quod est actu* (everything that is known, is known insofar as it is in act). On the basis of this axiom, one can assert that whenever there is a *sensibile actu* or an *intelligibile actu,* an object is known; and whenever there is a *sensus actu* or an *intellectus actu,* the subject and his act are known. On this view the subject in act and his act are constituted and, as well, they are known simultaneously and concomitantly with the knowledge of objects; for the *sensibile actu* is the *sensus actu,* and the *intelligibile actu* is the *intellectus actu.* Again, on this view the object is known as *id quod intenditur* (what is intended), the subject is known as *is qui intendit* (he who intends), and the act is known both as the *intendere* (intending) of the subject and the *intendi* (being intended) that regards the object.

On this position, which for other reasons I named *conscientia-experientia,* the constitutive as well as the cognitive aspects of consciousness are satisfied. For cognitive acts certainly constitute a prime substance as actually knowing sensible and intelligible objects; on the view I favor, they also constitute the prime substance as consciously sentient, consciously intelligent, consciously the one principle of many acts, consciously rational when one act supplies the known reason that motivates another act, consciously free when one act is the principle of other alternative acts, consciously responsible when the consciously free subject knows by other acts the consequences of his free choice.

Such, then, is one difference between *conscientia-perceptio* and *conscientia-experientia.* It remains that we listen to Fr. Perego's objections.

First, ". . . above all one fails to understand what consciousness conceived as experience is, this consciousness which grounds a confused notion on the side of the subject without that subject becoming an object or a term of consciousness. . . ."

R. I grant that there is no cognitional act without a content. I grant that there is no cognitional act without an object. I grant that there is no cognitional act without a term. I deny that that the sole content of a cognitional act is its object.

My position cannot be understood if it is true to say that whatever is known is an object. Again, my position cannot be understood if it is true to say that *unumquodque cognoscitur secundum quod est obiectum.* I deny however that either of those assertions is true. I should say that *unumquodque cognoscitur secundum quod est actu.* Further, I should say that one and the same act is at once the act of the object and the act of the subject; inasmuch as there is a *sensibile actu* or an *intelligibile actu*, an object is known; inasmuch as there is a *sensus actu* or an *intellectus actu*, the subject in act and his act are constituted and known. Nor do I believe that Fr. Perego can prove this position to be a contradiction in terms.

Moreover, while I do not believe that St. Thomas worked out a theory of the subject and consciousness, still one can learn a thing or two from him. He holds that intellective soul knows itself by its act. He holds that that act supposes a *species* received in possible intellect. He holds that *actus specificantur per obiecta* (acts are specified by their objects). He does not hold that the *species* of the act, by which intellective soul knows itself, is abstracted from the soul or a similitude of the soul. One might infer that, according to St. Thomas, when intellective soul knows itself by its act, the relevant act has an object and that object is not the subject.

Secondly, I had explained that consciousness is knowledge of the subject *sub ratione experti* (under the formal aspect of "the experienced") and not *sub ratione entis, vel quidditatis, vel veri* (under the formal aspect of being, of quiddity, of the true). Fr. Perego concludes that, on my view, consciousness cannot be intellectual.

R. I grant that any object known by intellect is known *sub ratione entis, quidditatis, veri.* I deny that what is known by intellectual consciousness is known under those formalities. My reason is simply that consciousness is knowledge, not of the objects of acts, but of the acts themselves and their subject.

Thus, any object, to which intellect attends, falls under the *intentio entis intendens* (intending intention of being). That intending is conscious; it is simply the wonder Aristotle said was the beginning of all science and philosophy. Still, it is one thing to wonder about sensible objects: it is quite another to wonder about intellectual wonder itself. Only in this second case does our own *intentio entis intendens* fall under our own *intentio entis intendens;* and only then is it considered *sub ratione entis.*

Again, what we understand and conceive, is known *sub ratione quidditatis.* Such understanding and conceiving are conscious. But it is only when we understand and conceive understanding and conceiving that we know understanding and conceiving *sub ratione quidditatis*. Hence, St. Thomas insisted that it is one thing to know our souls by their presence and quite another to know the nature of soul.

Finally, what we rationally affirm is known *sub ratione veri*. That rational affirming is conscious. But that consciousness is not a rational affirming of rational affirming.

Thirdly, Fr. Perego contends that according to the explicit doctrine of St. Thomas human psychological and moral consciousness is exclusively a matter of intellectual acts.

R. I grant that moral consciousness is principally intellectual. I grant that psychological consciousness is intellectual as well as sensitive. I grant that St. Thomas denies reflection to sense, but I am not so certain that he denies consciousness to sense. He wrote: "A sense faculty . . . does indeed begin to turn back to its essence, because it not only knows the sensible object, but also knows itself to be sensing; still the return is not complete, because the sense faculty does not know its own essence." He also wrote: ". . . it belongs to the same faculty to see a color and to see the modification produced [in sight] by the color, to see the thing that is actually the object of sight and to see the seeing of that object. Hence that faculty by which we see that we see is not extrinsic to the seeing faculty, but differs from it only by a mental distinction." Above all, since Christ suffered physical pain, it is to be noted that pain is an "experimental perception of injury" and that "pain . . . begins in injury to the body and terminates in apprehension by the sense of touch, because pain is in the sense of touch, as in the apprehending faculty." This seems to me very much like *conscientia-experientia*: the pain is in the sense of touch; the pain is, not in the whip that is felt by the sense of touch, but in the subject that feels the whip; it is *ut in apprehendente*.

I suggest, then, there is some reason for doubting that St. Thomas absolutely excluded sensitive consciousness. In any case, whatever may be the difficulties of Thomist exegesis, I feel that the issue in itself is quite clear. Pains are not objects of sense, *sensibilia propria*. There are no unconscious pains. The subject of the pain feels the pain. The subject of the pain is not unconscious but conscious. His consciousness does not consist in reflecting on his pains; he has to feel them before he can reflect on them;

if it is not *he* that does the feeling, if what he feels is not pain, then he has no pains to reflect on.

Fourthly, Fr. Perego urges, "St. Thomas is explicit also in asserting a real distinction in men between the direct cognitive act and the reflexive cognitive act which pertains to consciousness. He writes: 'It is one act by which the intellect perceives a stone, and another by which it understands itself to perceive a stone'."

R. I have no doubt about the real distinction between the two acts. I grant the legitimacy of naming the first act direct and the second reflexive. I fail to see the explicit evidence for naming the second act *coscienziale* or for suggesting that the first act is not *coscienziale*.

Further, I do not believe that a denial of consciousness in direct acts can be reconciled with affirmations that we experience what seem to be direct acts. St. Thomas wrote:

> ... Anyone can experience in himself the following, that when he tries to understand something, he forms images for himself by ways of models, and in these he inspects, as it were, what he is striving to understand.
>
> ... For man abstracts the intelligibles from images and receives them into his mind in their actuated state; for in no other way would we have come to knowledge of these acts, did we not experience them in ourselves.
>
> ... according to the opinion of Aristotle, which is more in accord with our experience ... according to the way of knowing that we experience.

Fifthly, Fr. Perego shifts his ground. Modern authors, anticipated by Suarez, distinguish between a direct consciousness had in the very exercise of sensitive and rational acts and, on the other hand, a formal reflexion that occurs in intellect alone. Only in the latter, he urges, is the subject known as subject, and so only the latter is human consciousness properly so called. This formal reflexive, he believes, must consist in a "second or reflexive intention of the mind, by which we turn fully back to ourselves, and behold our existence and our modifications in their presence to us." Consequently, he concludes, consciousness must be a *cognitio* and a *perceptio* with a proper term and content.

R. I have no doubt that consciousness has a content; I defined it as "an internal experience, in the strict sense of that word, of the self and of its acts." I grant that all cognitive acts have terms, but I believe they also have principles, and I should say that consciousness is of the principle not the term. Also, I have no doubt that Suarez is correct in distinguishing between *cognoscere proprie* (knowing in the proper sense), where one cognitive act is the object of another, and *cognoscere minus proprie* (knowing in a less proper sense), where each cognitive act is known by the very exercise of the act iself. Further, I think I have good reasons for being more precise and saying *sub ratione entis, quidditatis, et veri* instead of *proprie,* and saying *sub ratione experti* instead of *minus proprie.* Finally, I have no doubt that consciousness is a *cognoscere sub ratione experti.*

I should say, however, that in direct consciousness not only acts are known *sub ratione experti* but also the subject. I should add that in direct consciousness the subject is known not as object but as subject, for these acts already have their own objects, and *ex hypothesi* these objects are not the subject. On the other hand, I should say that the superfluous intuition postulated by Fr. Perego has as its object the subject and so knows the subject not as subject but as object.

Sixthly, Fr. Perego feels that I am somewhat confused in my thinking when I claim that (1) consciousness is had in all sensitive and intellectual acts and (2) consciousness is a presupposition of reflexive activities.

R. I think that one will find my position clearer when one discovers that one need not assume that only objects are known. Meanwhile, the following passage, which I transcribe from a recent article by Prof. Georges Van Riet, may be found helpful:

> In our opinion, every conscious activity is necessarily present to itself without reflexion, or, as Sartre writes it, is conscious (of) itself. What characterizes this consciousness (of) self, is the fact that it is still unexpressed; it is presence to self, not knowledge of

self; it does not use concepts, or judgments, or words; it is silent, it does not speak. From the moment it reflects, it speaks; to reflect is in fact to elucidate through expression; the fruit of reflexion is the judgment. The paradox of human consciousness, which is incarnate and not angelic, is that even the elucidating act is unreflected for itself, conscious (of) self. It expresses something not reflected on, something lived or perceived, it does not express itself. Only a new act of reflexion will elucidate it by giving it expression, but this new act will in its turn remain unreflected.

Seventhly, Fr. Perego feels that not only the distinction but also the relation between consciousness and reflexive activity is obscure.

R. Let us begin by putting the difficulty clearly. The data of consciousness are not imaginable. But St. Thomas holds that no mere man in this life can understand anything at all at any time without conversion to phantasm. How can one get intellect to operate with respect to data that are not imaginable?

Recall that acts are known by their objects, potencies by their acts, and the essence of the soul by its potencies. There exists, then, an associative train linking imaginable objects with conscious experiences. It is by exploiting that link that intelligence investigates the nature of sense, imagination, intellect, will, and the soul.

This, of course, is no more than a general directive, but it is easy to see that no more than a general directive can be given. Just as a blind man cannot understand a disquisition on colors, so a person with no experience of direct understanding cannot be expected to reach by introspection an understanding of what direct understanding is; and similarly a person without experience of introspective understanding cannot be expected to reach by an introspection of the second order an understanding of what introspective understanding is. One must begin from the performance, if one is to have the experience necessary for understanding what the performance is. Hence, if anyone cares for clarity on this issue, he can begin from the statement, "non si riesce a comprendere" (one fails to understand). He can contrast that experience of not understanding with other experiences in which he felt he understood. Then he can turn his efforts to understanding his experiences of understanding and not understanding. Finally, when proficient at introspective understanding, he can move to the higher level and attempt to understand his successful and unsuccessful efforts at introspective understanding.

I have dwelt on this point, because I believe it of utmost importance. We have seen that St. Thomas prefers Aristotle's cognitional theory because it accords with experience. We have seen that St. Thomas considered it to be a matter of experience that (1) we try to understand, (2) form relevant images, (3) inspect solutions in the images, (4) receive the intelligible in act, (5) abstract from phantasm. But this is far from the whole story. Aristotelian and Thomist intellectual theory is essentially a matter of understanding experience. St. Thomas wrote:

> . . . The species therefore of the thing actually understood is the species of the understanding itself; hence it is that understanding can understand itself through this species. Thus the philosopher in an earlier passage studied the nature of possible intellect by studying the very act of understanding and the object that is understood.

By the act of understanding and by the εἶδος, the τὸ τί ἦν εἶναι, the αἴτιον τοῦ εἶναι, grasped by understanding in sensible data, Aristotle worked out the nature of possible intellect. Without repeating the Aristotelian process in oneself, one may use the words *intelligere* and *quid sit*, but one does not know what they mean. Further, one has not a proper grasp of the nature and virtue of the human soul. Aquinas also wrote:

> . . . the human soul understands itself by its understanding, which is its proper act, perfectly demonstrating its power and its nature.

There is little in philosophy or in speculative theology that ignorance in these matters does not corrupt.

Eighthly, Fr. Perego insinuates that if certain expressions of mine are taken literally, they would imply pantheism, the denial of natural theology, and the denial of a natural, human beatitude.

Bernard J. F. Lonergan

R. The fact is that in his exposition, page 416, lines 6 to 24, Fr. Perego begins with a misstatement; he shifts from Italian to Latin to repeat his misstatement; the Latin is part of a sentence in my booklet, with the significant difference that that part by itself is false, while my statement is true. Next, instead of showing some concern for the *sensus auctoris,* he proceeds to insinuate that I omit what I do not omit. On the basis of this insinuated omission there arise the alleged consequences of pantheism, the denial of natural theology, and the denial of a natural human beatitude. Finally, he handsomely refuses to believe that I mean what he concludes from the statement he falsely inputed to me.

Now there is no need to demonstrate *twice* that Fr. Perego's presentation of another's views can leave something to be desired. The interest of the present misrepresentation lies in the fact that, if it bore any relation to my text, it could arise only from three simultaneous and incompatible misinterpretations. One might deny the unrestricted range of human intellect as intellect, and so deny the possibility of natural theology. One might deny the natural limitation of human intellect as human, and so conclude to pantheism. But no one would simultaneously deny both. Moreover, it is only by affirming both that there arises any problem about natural human beatitude.

Ninthly, a hypothetical reader may interpose that he too finds quite odd my meaning when I employ such terms as *intelligere, quidditas, quid sit, quidditative,* and even *ens.*

R. The act that occurs when the teacher teaches and the learner learns is from the teacher and in the learner; it is named understanding, *intelligere.* It occurs frequently in the intelligent and rarely in the slow-witted. When it has occurred, one finds things clear; when it has not, one finds things obscure; thus one and the same mathematical theorem can be a masterpiece of elegance to one man and an insoluble puzzle to another. Further, once a man has understood, he no longer needs the teacher; he can operate on his own; he can repeat similar and cognate acts of understanding with ease, promptitude, and pleasure; he has an acquired habit.

The object of the act of understanding is the intelligible; the intelligible is expressed in concepts, but its basic occurrence is prior to the occurrence of the concept. When one finds things obscure, one cannot conceive them, define them, think them; they are for one, unless one is modest, inconceivable, indefinite, unthinkable. Hence, before one can conceive, one must understand; and, of course, unless one is rash, before one can judge, one must both understand and conceive.

The intelligible, grasped by human understanding, is known in the sensible, in what is imagined; it is the ground of universal concepts; none the less, it is related intrinsically to the concrete. Such intelligible-in-the-sensible is the *proper object* of human intellect: it is proper in two senses, first, in the sense that man in this life understands no intelligible whatever except as a derivative of that proper object and, secondly, in the sense that no pure spirit has as its proper object, its basic source of all intelligibility, the intelligible-in-the-sensible.

Besides the proper object of human intellect, there is its formal object. The proper object pertains to human intellect as human, as specifically different from other types of intellect. The formal object pertains to human intellect as intellect, as having something in common with every type of intellect. This formal object of intellect is being, where being means everything. The fact that being, everything, is the formal object of human intellect cannot be demonstrated by showing that man does understand everything. But it is clear from the fact that man wants to understand everything about everything, that to answer any number of questions is only to invite more questions, than man's intellect does not come to a complacent stop until it understands everything about everything. Again, the same point can be made negatively. If the formal object of human intellect were not being, then it would be some genus; and if it were a genus, then intellect would be completely confined to that genus, as sight is to color, and hearing is to sound; but human intellect is not completely confined to any genus; it can raise questions about absolutely everything that exists or even could exist, and so it cannot be completely confined to some single genus.

Now human intellect is not the only intellect. Each different type of intellect has its own proper object. But there can be only one intellect in which the proper object is also the formal object. For, when the proper object is also the formal object of an intellect, then its natural act of understanding is infinite; it understands in act itself and as well everything else that does exist or could exist; such unrestricted understanding must be God, the principle and end of all actual being and, as well, the ground of all possible being.

There results the well-known paradox of finite intellect. Because its formal object is being, it is orientated towards infinite understanding; and without this orientation, it would not be an intellect. Because it is finite, it cannot be infinite understanding; for that would be a contradiction in terms; and so its proper object must differ from its formal object. Further, it cannot be said that finite understanding, while it is not infinite, none the less has an exigence for the infinite. If one says "exigence," one means necessity or one means nothing; but so far from being necessary, it is impossible for the finite either to be or to become the infinite; what necessarily is infinite, already is infinite; and what is not infinite, cannot become infinite, for the infinite cannot become. Nor does the revealed mystery of the vision of God change things in the least, for not even the beatific vision of Christ is an act of understanding everything about everything; and so not even in Christ is the alleged exigence fulfilled.

If the meaning of the foregoing has been understood, it is not difficult to learn the words. One has only to read St. Thomas and understand what is said. An intellect completely in act with respect to being is God. The proper object of our intellects is "quidditas sive natura in materia corporali exsistens" (the quiddity or nature that exists in corporeal matter). God is not a material substance, and so we do not know *quid sit Deus*. God is being and, since we do not know *quid sit Deus,* we do not know *quid sit ens;* in both cases our knowledge is analogical. We naturally desire to know *quid sit Deus*; actually knowing it, however, is perfect beatitude, natural to God alone, beyond the natural capacity and the natural will of any possible creature.

Tenthly, to return from the hypothetical reader to Fr. Perego, he advances that there is an obscurity in my view of the relationship between Christ's human consciousness and Christ's beatific vision.

R. I grant that the relationship is quite obscure if one is unfamiliar with the meaning of the question, *quid sit,* and also with the admiration that is the origin of all science and all philosophy. Otherwise, the relationship is plain as a pikestaff. By consciousness we are aware of ourselves but we do not understand our natures; because we know ourselves only *sub ratione experti,* we wonder what we are; and that wonder gives place to knowledge when we understand *quid sit homo.* But Christ as man was similar to us in all things save sin. He was aware of himself by consciousness, yet by that consciousness he did not know *quid sit;* moreover, since he had two natures, he had a twofold wonder, *quid sit homo* and *quid sit Deus;* the answer to the second was the beatific vision.

Let us end this section on the notion of the subject. My contention was that consciousness is not only cognitive but also constitutive of the subject. My contention was that an adequate account of consciousness is had by making more explicit the familiar Aristotelian-Thomist doctrine of the identity in act of subject and object. Perhaps the reader will agree with me when I say (1) that Fr. Perego does not seem to know what consciousness is and (2) that his many objections are just *solubilia argumenta.*

Part III: Christ as Subject

The function of theology is to state clearly and unequivocally the full meaning of the articles of faith. The theology of Christ as subject includes an explicitation of the article of the creed, that Jesus Christ, his only Son, our Lord, . . . suffered under Pontius Pilate. Consider, then, the following series of questions and answers that, were they not so elementary and so obvious, might be included in a catechism.

Q. Who suffered under Pontius Pilate?

A. Jesus Christ, his only Son, our Lord.

Q. Did he himself suffer, or was it somebody else, or was it nobody?

A. He himself suffered.

Q. Did he suffer unconsciously?

A. No, he suffered consciously. To suffer unconsciously is not to suffer at all. Surgical operations cause no pain, when the patient is made unconscious by an anesthetic.

Q. What does it mean to say that he suffered consciously?

A. It means that he himself really and truly suffered. He was the one whose soul was sorrowful unto death. He was the one who felt the cutting, pounding scourge. He was the one who endured for three hours the agony of the crucified.

Q. Do you mean that his soul was sorrowful but he himself was not sorrowful?

A. That does not make sense. The Apostles' Creed says explicitly that Jesus Christ, his only Son, our Lord, suffered under Pontius Pilate.

Q. Do you mean that his body was scourged and crucified but he himself felt nothing?

A. No, he felt all of it. Were our bodies scourged and crucified, we would feel it. His was scourged and crucified. He felt it.

Q. Is not Jesus Christ God?

A. He is.

Q. Do you mean that God suffered?

A. In Jesus Christ there is one person with two natures. I do not mean that the one person suffered in his divine nature. I do mean that the one person suffered in his human nature.

Q. It was really that divine person that suffered though not in his divine nature?

A. It was. He suffered. It was not somebody else that suffered. It was not nobody that suffered.

Such is the doctrine we have all believed from childhood. Still, as an object of faith, it is apprehended, not in terms of an understanding of the nature of the subject and of consciousness, but in the more elementary fashion that rests on our own experience of ourselves as subjects and as conscious. There remains, then, the theologian's task, and it consists simply in making explicit what already is implicitly believed.

Moreover, for present purposes there is no need for the theologian to master accurately what is meant by the consciously intelligent, consciously rational, consciously free, consciously responsible subject. His introspection can be limited to the simplest and most obvious of all instances, the suffering of physical pain. Can anyone suffer physical pain without being the subject of the pain? Can anyone suffer unconsciously? Can one be the conscious subject of physical pain without being constituted as conscious subject? Can one be constituted as conscious subject if one is merely known to an ontological self as an object, where that knowing involves no real modification in the object? I find the answers to these questions obvious.

It follows, then, since Jesus Christ, his only Son, our Lord, suffered physical pain, therefore he was constituted as the conscious subject of physical pain.

It follows *a pari* that the Word as man was the conscious subject of all his human acts, for he was similar to us in all things save sin. For if Christ was the conscious subject of physical pain, surely he also was the conscious subject of looking and listening, of imagining Solomon in all his glory and seeing the lilies of the field, of the acts of his *scientia beata, infusa, acquisita,* of the free and responsible acts of will by which he merited our salvation.

So simple a solution does not please Fr. Perego, and he objects that Christ as man cannot be a conscious subject in virtue of the hypostatic union as such.

I grant the contention and deny its supposition. My argument for the human consciousness of Christ was drawn, not from the hypostatic union as such, but from the definition of Chalcedon, *per omnia nobis similem absque peccato* (like us in everything, but without sin). If Christ was similar to us *in all things,* then he did not spend his entire life in a state of coma or of dreamless sleep.

Further, I wish to deny what the argument insinuates, namely, that by the hypostatic union Christ was not constituted as potentially a conscious subject. By that union the Word was made flesh, and the Son was really and truly a man. A man, by the mere fact that he is a man, is able to see, hear, feel, understand, judge, will, enjoy, suffer; *eo ipso*, he is able to be the conscious subject of these activities.

But Fr. Perego has a further objection. Such acts involves no actuation in the intentional order with respect to the Word. Therefore, they cannot constitute the Word as conscious of himself, a divine person.

I distinguish. There is no actuation in the intentional order with respect to the Word as object, as *id quod intenditur,* I transmit. There is no actuation in the intentional order with respect to the Word as subject, as *is qui intendit,* I deny.

Finally, Fr. Perego objects that if Christ as man, in exercising his sensitive and intellectual acts, is conscious of himself, a divine person, then these acts must be supernatural.

Either this is *ignoratio elenchi,* or else Fr. Perego is introducing a new principle that he has not proved.

It is *ignoratio elenchi,* if Fr. Perego fancies that I hold the Word as man to be conscious of himself inasmuch as he knows himself as object.

On the other hand, if Fr. Perego is objecting against the Word's self-awareness as subject, he has yet to prove that *actus specificantur per subiectum.* The Word himself is God and stands in no need of a supernatural elevation; by the *gratia unionis* the Word is a man and a potential conscious subject of a human consciousness, and the *gratia unionis* is already entitatively supernatural; to demand a further supernatural elevation of the acts exercised by the Word presupposes what has not been proved, namely, that acts are specified by their subject.

Conclusion

A subject is a conscious person. A person is conscious by being the *principium quod* of acts of sense or intellect. In so far as there is in man a *sensibile actu,* there is by that very act a *sensus actu* and a *subiectum actu*; in so far as there is an *intelligible actu,* there is by that very act an *intellectus actu* and a *subiectum actu.* Finally, the *subiectum actu* is the *principium quod* of the act.

There follows an *analogia fidei*: a parallelism to be recognized betwen ontological and psychological statements about the incarnate Word. The main parallel statements are that, as there is one person with a divine and a human nature, so there is one subject with a divine and a human consciousness. As the person, so also the subject is without division or separation. As the two natures, so also the divine and the human consciousness are without confusion or interchange. As the person, so also the subject is a divine reality. As the human nature, so also the human consciousness is assumed. As there is a great difference between "being God" and "being a man," so also there is a great difference between "being conscious of oneself as God" and "being conscious of oneself as man." As the former difference is surmounted hypostatically by union in the person, so the latter difference is surmounted hypostatically by union in the subject. As the two natures do not prove two persons, so the divine and the human consciousness do not prove two subjects.

The two sides of the parallelism have not, at present, the same theological note. The ontological side was developed centuries ago, and it has the authority of the decrees of Chalcedon and of the third council of Constantinople as understood by all Catholic theologians. The psychological side is an opinion on a question raised by contemporary theology; still, this opinion has in its favor arguments that seem rather peremptory.

First, one cannot accept "eundemque perfectum in deitate, et eundem perfectum in humanitate" (the same one perfect in deity, and the same one perfect in humanity) in an ontological sense to the exclusion of a psychological sense. The councils do not make any such reservation. On the contrary, they seem to me to exclude any such reservation (1) by the word *perfectum,* (2) by the phrase *per omnia nobis similem absque peccato,* and (3) by speaking of two wills and two operations. Now, if the foregoing distinction between the ontological and the psychological is excluded, then the councils define both sides of my parallelism. Further, while all theologians do not as yet recognize this, that hesitancy arises simply because theology develops in time with the theology of the ontology of Christ preceding the theology of the psychology of Christ.

Secondly, the article of the Apostles' Creed, which I have stressed, has a clear meaning in the minds of all the faithful including the theologians *qua fideles.* That clear meaning seems to me to exclude in rather peremptory fashion theories of the subject and of consciousness that, instead of explaining what everyone believes, not only seem to be reluctant to consider an article of faith with a clear connotation of consciousness but also seem to be incapable of being reconciled with what everyone believes.

Bernard J. F. Lonergan

Thirdly, the account of consciousness, which my position presupposes, fits easily into the framework of Aristotelian and Thomist thought. Moreover, while I have here given an argument drawn from the constitutive function of consciousness, I do not rest my case on that argument; my case rests on the facts of consciousness, and they are extremely numerous, extremely complex, and far too delicate to be exposed when one has to deal with somewhat unperceptive charges of incomprehensibility.

Edward Schillebeeckx
1914-

Edward Schillebeeckx, a Belgian Dominican, taught at Louvain for fourteen years before his appointment in 1958 to the University of Nijmegen in Holland. Since that time he has been one of the most prominent figures on the Dutch Catholic scene. Along with Karl Rahner and Hans Küng, he was one of the most active and influential northern European theologians at Vatican II.

His book, Christ the Sacrament of the Encounter with God, *quickly established itself as a milestone and was soon translated into German, French, and English. What made it so unusual was that the author was so thoroughly familiar with traditional scholastic theology but at the same time infused new life into it by relating it to contemporary thought. In the process Schillebeeckx achieves one of the richest syntheses imaginable. The book is about Christ, it is about the Church, it is about the sacraments, but it is about each of these as inseparable from the others.*

The most attractive trait that immediately won a wide audience for this approach was its pronounced personalism. The polemics of post-Reformation theology had taken their toll, and seminary manuals passed on the shortcomings induced by battle. Schillebeeckx forced a redirection, a raising of the sights; he instilled new meaning into old formulae and, in an age faced with the growing anonymity of technology, he insisted on a recovery of the profoundly personal dimension of Christian faith and life.

One of the trends to which Schillebeeckx gave great impetus was the broadening of the use of the word "sacrament" in Catholic vocabulary. For centuries the word had been restricted to seven major rites in Catholic worship and had been viewed in this limited horizon. But one of the basic insights to emerge from the biblical and liturgical movements was the realization that the seven "sacraments" were derivative from the one sacrament, the Church, which in turn was itself derivative from the prime Sacrament, Christ. Most of the book is devoted to the elaboration of this notion. Its beauty and power are quickly apparent: if a sacrament is a sign that causes what it signifies, consider the implications when applied to Jesus and the Church.

The book consists of seven chapters, the first of which is called "Christ, Sacrament of God," and the second is "The Church, Sacrament of the Risen Christ." Thus it is the first chapter which is found in the following selection, since the focus of this volume is Christology. In reading it one cannot help but be struck by the difference in emphasis from many of the other selections. Here is a scholar who is thoroughly at home with the Thomistic synthesis and greatly appreciates its achievement, but who realizes that contemporary concerns and insights must also find expression in any living and effective theology. The important thing is not just to utter correct formulae about the being of Christ, but to show the world His role in the human encounter with God.

CHRIST THE SACRAMENT
OF THE ENCOUNTER
WITH GOD

CHAPTER 1

CHRIST, SACRAMENT OF GOD

1. Humanity in Search of the Sacrament of God

S t. Augustine explains in a masterly manner how that
service of God which we know and practise in the
Church is as old as the world. He has divided the
gradual coming into being of the Church in the course of human
history into three great phases: the "Church" of the devout
heathen; the pre-Christian phase of the Christian Church in the
form of the chosen race of Israel; and finally the emergence of
the mature Church, the "Church of the first-born." (Heb.
12.23.) This development already gives us a first insight into the
meaning of a sacramentality of the Church.

1. Sacrament in Pagan Religion

In a nebulous but nonetheless discernible fashion the
sacramental Church is already present in the life of the whole
of mankind. All humanity receives that inward word of God
calling men to a communion in grace with himself. This obscure
call causes those among the heathen who listen to it in uprightness of heart dimly to suspect that there is a redeeming God
who is occupying himself personally with their salvation. Such
an inward religious experience produced by grace does not yet
encounter the visible embodiment of that grace, the fact of
which remains unknown, hidden in the depths of the human
heart.

Nevertheless, life in this created world gains a new and
deeper meaning when man lives in the world as one who has
received this call from God in his inmost being. The world of
creation then becomes an actual part of the inner yet still
anonymous dialogue with God. If the God who wants to enter
into a bond of personal relationship with us is the creator of

heaven and earth, it implies that our being confronted with the world, existence in this world, is going to teach us more about the living God than the world alone can teach us, more than merely that God is the creator of all things. Life itself in the world then belongs to the very content of God's inner word to us. It interprets dimly at least something of that which God personally, by the attraction of his grace, is whispering in our hearts. However vaguely, life itself becomes a truly supernatural and external revelation, in which creation begins to speak to us the language of salvation, in which creation becomes a sign of higher realities. The course of nature, human life in the world and with the world, tells us more because of God speaking within us than ever it could of itself. All is seen to have an extraordinary, indeed a personal, purpose; a purpose which lies beyond the possibilities of nature and of earthly life. Thus in paganism, too, the inward grace achieves a certain visible manifestation.

Heathen religion itself was striving to give outward shape to its inner expectations. Man cannot sever himself from God, because God will not let him go. As an outcome of the quest for some manner of expressing the deeply hidden but authentic religious urge, there has arisen among pagan peoples a motley collection of religious forms and aspirations which in its queries and in its beliefs, and through all its diversity, can still be traced back to a few particular fundamental religious motives. It is not easy for the human mind correctly to disentangle these motives, to tell what is genuine in all this, and what on the other hand is false. Precisely because they did not have the support of a special, a visible divine revelation, they became a mixture of true devotedness to God, of elements of an all-too-fallible humanity, of dogmatic distortion, moral confusion and finally even of diabolical influence; yet in all of this there was a spark of real holiness which now and again managed to shine forth. Only in their fulfilment in the Old Testament, and eventually in the New, does it become clear to us that God was showing us his active concern for the heathen too. His revelation has enabled us to appreciate the motives behind the pagan reaction to his concern: Man exists in an I-Thou relationship, in a situation of dialogue with God. Man had lost his living contact with God, the attitude of child to father, and of himself he could not regain it. Life in this world made this quite clear to him. But it is only in its visible fulfilment, first in the holy ones of Israel, and then definitively in the man Jesus, that we see the substance of truth which lay hidden in the tortuous myths of heathen religion. For that which was given distorted shape in these myths—projections of human experience in which grace was nevertheless obscurely active—at the same time faintly foreshadowed what was to come. It was in the visible form of something tangibly holy (Israel and Christ) that it received its true shape. Pagan religious society, frequently revitalized by great religious leaders which supported the heathen in his religious life and upon which that life was nourished, was the first providential sketch of the true Church of Christ which was to come. Thus this "Church," as the visible presence of grace, is a world-wide reality. More than this: as even the Fathers suggested, it is a fragment of unconscious Christianity. For every grace in the order in which we live is a grace that comes from the one mediator, Christ Jesus. In general we can therefore say that there is no religion if there is no Church. Grace never comes just interiorly; it confronts us in visible shape as well. To separate religion from Church is ultimately to destroy the life of religion. If one is to serve God, to be religious, one must also live by Church and sacrament.

2. Israel as Sacrament of God

It is seen from the foregoing that in the life of all mankind open to the inward call of salvation, God caused that to be foreshadowed which he was to bring to fulfilment in Israel and later in Christ. But grace, in the visible manifestation of its presence in the pagan world, remained strictly anonymous (this is equally true today concerning such religion as is to be found in "modern pagans"). The clear shape of this life-giving grace became explicit only in special divine revelation, and this occurred first of all in Israel.

A group of Bedouin of various ethnological origins, whose forefathers had been enticed into the region by the fertile abundance of the Nile Delta, wearied beyond endurance by the forced labour which Egypt imposed, formed themselves into the caravans of the Exodus. Out of the different clans thrown together in this way, each of which seems to have had its own religion, there grew one people which united itself in the desert under the name of the God Yahweh who had appeared to Moses. This was the birth of Israel, the people of God. As the Bible sets it forth, the account of God's appearing to Moses is evidently intended to show that this people had become a unity through the personal intervention of Yahweh the living God. When Israel had taken possession of their new land Canaan, prepared by God for the new nation, Joshua reminded the people of the strange god they had served "beyond the river [referring to Abraham in Mesopotamia] and in Egypt." Yahweh alone made the nation to be what it was. In blunt but moving terms the prophet Ezekiel describes the metamorphosis of a crowd of nomad Bedouin into the Church of God: "Thus saith the Lord God to Jerusalem: Thy root and thy nativity is of the land of Canaan. Thy father was an Amorrhite and thy mother a Cethite [which is to say, they were heathen]. And when thou wast born, in the day of thy nativity thy navel was not cut, neither wast thou washed with water for thy health nor salted with salt [an ancient method of purification and disinfecting], nor swaddled with cloths. No eye had pity on thee to do any of these things for thee, out of compassion to thee; but thou wast cast out upon the face of the earth in the abjection of thy soul [i.e., because you were found worthless], in the day that thou wast born. And passing by thee I [Yahweh] saw that thou wast trodden under foot in thy own blood. And I said to thee when thou wast in thy blood: Live . . . And I washed thee with water and cleansed away thy blood from thee, and I anointed thee with oil . . . And I clothed thee with fine garments. And thou wast adorned . . . and advanced to be a queen." Israel, the first phase of the Church, is the fruit of God's merciful intervention, a foreshadowing of that which St. Paul would say of the Church of Christ: ". . . Christ loved the Church, and delivered himself up for it, that he might sanctify it, cleansing it by the laver of water . . . that he might present it to himself, a glorious Church, not having spot or wrinkle or any such thing, but that it should be holy and without blemish." Israel's visible religion, its faithful people, its cult, sacraments, sacrifices and priesthood, was the first phase of the great Church.

This Church was already a visible presence of grace, a sign of saving grace which at the same time bestowed grace, not on account of a kind of anticipated effect of the mystery of Christ yet to come (such an anticipation is not easy to understand), but rather because Israel itself was already a partial realization of the mystery of Christ, it was the "Christ-event" in process of coming to be. The Church of the Old Testament was a sign and cause of grace insofar as in it the Christian age had really begun. Since it was as yet an incomplete presence of the mystery of Christ, the Church in Israel could not bestow the fullness of grace, but only the grace of a perfectly open readiness for the awaited Messiah; a saving Advent-grace of messianic expectation, a religion of the "God who is to come." The quintessence of divine revelation in the Old Testament is expressed in various places thus: "I will be your God, and you will be my people." For Israel's good, God would remain faithful to the Covenant, together with and at times even in opposition to Israel. But Israel in its turn had to keep faith with the Covenant; it had to live as God's true people. Such is the commission of the Church.

The whole of the Old Testament revelation is simply the historical process arising out of God's fidelity and the often repeated infidelity of the Jewish people. In the development of this situation, revelation was gradually perfected. God's ultimate purpose was to call a faithful people into life. Broadly speaking, there would be continual failure, until God himself raised up a man in whom was concentrated the entirety of mankind's vocation to faithfulness, and who would himself keep faith with the Covenant in the perfection of his fidelity. This man was Jesus. In him there was a visible realization of both sides of faith in the Covenant. In the dialogue between God and man, so often breaking down, there was found at last a perfect human respondent; in the same person there was achieved the perfection both of the divine invitation and of the human response in faith from the man who by his resurrection is the Christ. The Covenant, sealed in his blood, found definitive success in his person. In him grace became fully visible; he is the embodiment of the grace of final victory, who appeared in person to the Apostles. Christ himself is the Church, an invisible communion in grace with the living God (the Son made man with the Father) manifested in visible human form. For this is what he is as the "first-born" and Head of all creation. Consequently the whole of humanity is already, in its Head, "assembled" into communion with God (in Hebrew "Church" is *qahel,* the great assembly).

We have first to analyse this visible presence of grace which Christ is personally, in order to work from it towards an insight into the sacramentality of the Church.

2. Christ the Primordial Sacrament

1. Encounter with the Earthly Christ as Sacrament of the Encounter with God

The dogmatic definition of Chalcedon, according to which Christ is "one person in two natures," implies that one and the same person, the Son of God, also took on a visible human form. Even in his humanity Christ is the Son of God. The second person of the most holy Trinity is personally man; and this man is personally God. Therefore Christ is God in a human way, and man in a divine way. As a man he acts out his divine life in and according to his human existence. Everything he does as man is an act of the Son of God, a divine act in human form; an interpretation and transposition of a divine activity into a human activity. His human love is the human embodiment of the redeeming love of God.

The humanity of Jesus is concretely intended by God as the fulfilment of his promise of salvation; it is a messianic reality. This messianic and redemptive purpose of the incarnation implies that the encounter between Jesus and his contemporaries was always on his part an offering of grace in a human form. For the love of the man Jesus is the human incarnation of the redeeming love of God: an advent of God's love in visible form. Precisely because these human deeds of Jesus are divine deeds, personal acts of the Son of God, divine acts in visible human form, they possess of their nature a divine saving power, and consequently they bring salvation; they are "the cause of grace." Although this is true of every specifically human act of Christ it is nevertheless especially true of those actions which, though enacted in human form, are according to their nature exclusively acts of God: the miracles and the redemption. Considered against the background of the whole earthly life of Jesus, this truth is realized in a most particular way in the great mysteries of his life: his passion, death, resurrection and exaltation to the side of the Father.

That is not all. Because the saving acts of the man Jesus are performed by a divine person, they have a divine power to save, but because this divine power to save appears to us in visible form, the saving activity of Jesus is *sacramental.* For a sacrament is a divine bestowal of salvation in an outwardly perceptible form which makes the bestowal manifest; a bestowal of salvation in historical visibility. The Son of God really did become true man—become, that is to say, a human spirit which through its own proper bodiliness dwelt visibly in our world. The incarnation of the divine life therefore involves bodily aspects. Together with this we must remember that every human exchange, or the intercourse of men one with another, proceeds in and through man's bodiliness. When a man exerts spiritual influence on another, encounters through the body are necessarily involved. The inward man manifests itself as a reality that is in this world through the body. It is in his body and through his body that man is open to the "outside," and that he makes himself present to his fellow men. Human encounter proceeds through the visible obviousness of the body, which is a sign that reveals and at the same time veils the human interiority.

Consequently if the human love and all the human acts of Jesus possess a divine saving power, then the realization in human shape of this saving power necessarily includes as one of its aspects the manifestation of salvation: includes, in other words, sacramentality. The man Jesus, as the personal visible realization of the divine grace of redemption, is *the* sacrament, the primordial sacrament, because this man, the Son of God himself, is intended by the Father to be in his humanity the only way to the actuality of redemption. "For there is one God, and one mediator of God and men, the man Christ Jesus." Personally to be approached by the man Jesus was, for his contemporaries, an invitation to a personal encounter with the life-giving God, because personally that man was the Son of God. Human encounter with Jesus is therefore the sacrament of the encounter with God, or of the religious life as a theologal attitude of existence towards God. Jesus' human redeeming acts are therefore a "sign and cause of grace." "Sign" and "cause" of salvation are not brought together here as two elements fortuitously conjoined. Human bodiliness is human interiority itself in visible form.

Now because the inward power of Jesus' will to redeem and of his human love is God's own saving power realized in human form, the human saving acts of Jesus are the divine bestowal of grace itself realized in visible form; that is to say they cause what they signify; they are sacraments.

2. The Actions of Jesus' Life as Manifestations of Divine Love for Man and Human Love for God: Bestowal of Grace and Religious Worship

"As the Father has sent me, I also send you. When he had said this, he breathed on them and he said to them: Receive the Holy Spirit; whose sins you shall forgive, they are forgiven them." Thus it is as a revelation of God's merciful redeeming love that we are to understand the sending of the Son on earth. By the incarnation of the Son God intended to divinize man by redeeming him; by being saved from sin man is brought into a personal communion of grace and love with God. This implies two things. First, the fullness of grace which properly belongs to the man Jesus in virtue of his existence as God was intended by God to be a source of grace for others; from him all were to receive. Christ's love for man thus manifests God's love for men by actually bestowing it; it is the redeeming mercy of God himself coming to meet us from a human heart. But as well as this movement down from above, coming to us from God's love by way of Jesus' human heart, there is in the man Jesus also a movement up from below, from the human heart of Jesus, the Son, to the Father.

The human actions of Jesus' life as they come from above show us their character as acts of redemption of his fellow men; these acts, in the mode of a human love, are the merciful redeeming love of God himself. As coming from below they show their character as acts of worship; these acts are a true adoration and acknowledgement of God's divine existence; they are a service of praise or cult, religion, prayer—in a word, they are the man Jesus' love of God. Thus Jesus is not only the revelation of the redeeming God; he is also the supreme worshipper of the Father, the supreme realization of all religion. Jesus became the Redeemer in actual fact by freely living his human life in religious worship of and attachment to the Father. In Christ not only were God and his love for men revealed, but God also showed us in him what it is for a man to commit himself unconditionally to God the invisible Father. In this way God revealed to us the embodiment of religion, the countenance of a truly religious man. The living and personal relation of Jesus to the Father reveals to us what is meant by the majesty and mercy of God. In and through the religious service of Jesus, God has revealed himself.

If we now consider that this humanity of Jesus represents us all, then it also becomes clear that the movement up from below is a movement to the Father ascending, by way of Jesus' humanity, from the whole of mankind. Therefore Jesus is not only the offer of divine love to man made visible but, at the same time, as prototype (or primordial model) he is the supreme realization of the response of human love to this divine offer: "in our place" and "in the name of us all," as Scripture repeatedly says. Whatever Christ does as a free man is not only a realization in human form of God's activity for our salvation; it is also at the same time the positive human acceptance, representative for all of us, of this redeeming offer from God. The man Jesus is personally a dialogue with God the Father; the supreme realization and therefore the norm and the source of every encounter with God. As a reality religion can only be understood in the context of the incarnation of God the Son. For since redeemed existence means that through the intervention of God mankind itself is once more turned towards God in close communion of life with him, then the whole of mankind is already truly redeemed objectively in the man Jesus, as in its Head.

The foundation of all this is the incarnation. But this incarnation of God the Son is a reality which grows. It is not complete in a matter of a moment; for example, at Jesus' conception in Mary's womb or at his birth. The incarnation is not merely a Christmas event. To be man is a process of becoming man; Jesus' manhood grew throughout his earthly life, finding its completion in the supreme moment of the incarnation, his death, resurrection and exaltation. Only then is the incarnation fulfilled to the very end. And so we must say that the incarnation in the Son itself redeems us. This mystery of Christ or of redemption we can call, in its totality, a mystery of saving worship; a mystery of praise (the upward movement) and of salvation (the downward movement).

This ascending and descending dynamism pervades the whole human life of Jesus. For although Jesus in his earthly life was always the humiliated "Servant of God," he remained even in his humiliation the Son of God, the grace-abounding revelation of God. And although in his glorification Christ can bestow grace in full measure, there too he remains a man who, in religious and filial service, adores and honours the Father from whom he must receive all. Nonetheless we can trace a development in the course of the saving history of the mystery of Christ. By the fact that he became man, the Son of God is fundamentally already the Christ. But we must also realize that it was only upon his rising from the dead that, because of the love and obedience of his life, the Father *established* him absolutely as the Christ. We must look closely into this growth towards the fullness of redemption, for in it we are confronted with the mystery of Christ's life, which is this: The man Jesus, as "Servant of God," by his life of obedience and love on earth, even unto death, earned for us that grace of salvation which he, in glory with the Father, can himself as Lord and Christ, bestow upon us in abundance. This saving reality calls for the closest consideration, for in it we find the key to the sense of the sacramentality of the Church in its relation to the *Kyrios*, the risen and glorified Lord, and so also to the Holy Spirit.

3. Jesus' Humiliation in the Service of God and
 His Heavenly Exaltation: The Redemptive
 Mystery of Christ

"It was God who reconciled us to himself in Christ." This must underlie every consideration of our redemption. The living God himself, Father, Son and Holy Ghost, is our redeemer. But he brought about the redemption in the human nature of the second person, the Son of God, who in union with the Father and together with him is the source of the life of the Holy Spirit. It is this in its human embodiment—from Jesus' conception in Mary's womb, in and beyond his death, to his "establishment in power" as the risen Christ—which constitutes his redemptive mystery. We can distinguish four phases in this redemption:

First: The initiative of the Father through the Son in the Holy Spirit. This initiative is the trinitarian background within the Godhead which, though veiled, can be discerned through the temporal order of salvation in the incarnate Son, "who through the eternal Spirit offered himself without blemish to the Father."

Second: The human response of Christ's life to the Father's initiative in sending him: ". . . becoming obedient unto death, even to the death of the cross"—in other words, the religious obedience of the "Holy One of Yahweh" or of the "Servant of God."

Third: The divine response to Jesus' obedience in the humiliation of his life. "For which cause also God [i.e., the Father] has exalted him exceedingly, and given him a name which is above all names," that is, given him might above all powers: Jesus has become the Lord, the *Kyrios,* meaning "the Mighty," he who exercises lordship—"God has made him *Kyrios.*"

Fourth: The sending of the Holy Spirit upon the world of men by the glorified *Kyrios* or Lord. Christ, "having reached the consummation [only now] became . . . the source of eternal salvation" for us. The force of the redemption came fully into operation only when Jesus was exalted at God's right hand. "And I, when I am lifted up . . . will draw all things to myself." The last phase of the mystery of Christ, between the ascension and the *parousia,* is therefore the mystery of the sending of the Holy Spirit by Christ as the climax of his work of salvation.

261

We must consider the whole of this in detail. First of all we shall enquire what Scripture teaches about the Passover, the Ascension, and Pentecost, as a foundation for our further analysis.

(a) Passover, Ascension and Pentecost

At the Last Supper, Christ clearly gave his death the significance of a sacrifice of himself to God for all. This gift of himself to God was essentially an act of love. But this was realized and embodied in the death he suffered at the hands of sinful humanity. He offered himself sacrificially for us to the Father, and the particular way in which this came to completion was by his laying down his life. The words of interpretation which Scripture uses in connection with the bread and wine show us Christ's approaching death as a true sacrifice of reconciliation that reinstates the covenant with God. The body of Christ, the "Servant of God," is given in a death of vicarious reconciliation. "The blood of Christ" is a theme that is truly central in the primitive Church, as Scripture shows it to us. This death sanctifies mankind, reconciles, establishes peace, redeems, constitutes the Church, and therefore unites man in communion with God and his fellow men. We are redeemed *in sanguine,* through the blood of Christ—this we find on almost every page of Scripture. It is impossible therefore to "spiritualize" Christ's sacrifice, to make of it merely an internal act of love. There was indeed the act of love, but it was embodied in the sacrifice of blood. Because of Jesus' free acceptance of it, death has an essential part to play in the redemptive event. For the incarnation through which we are redeemed is not, as we have seen, something that was complete all in one instant. It embraces the whole human life of Christ, including his death. And in this human life, and thus also in this death, Christ lives his sonship of the Father in fidelity and loving attachment to the Father.

At the same time this death is the utmost effort of Satan and sinful man to stamp out everything godly in the world. But no sooner had sin put Christ to death than God called him back to life. Such is God's victory over man's sin. The resurrection therefore enters into the essence of the redemption. But God the Father not only raised Christ to life: he also made him Lord or *Kyrios.* "Let all the house of Israel know most certainly that God has made both Lord and Christ this same Jesus whom you have crucified." In this text we find a fundamental *credo* of the primitive Church: we have killed Jesus of Nazareth, but God has raised him to life again. The Passover is thus our actual redemption, the expression of the "Ego vici mundum," "I have overcome the world." In and through Christ's rising from the dead, God himself has called "the new earth" into being in this world.

In the resurrection, then, as the eternally enduring act of salvation, there is also included Christ's ascension and establishment as Lord, the sending of the Holy Spirit which is Christ's actual exercise of lordship, and to a certain extent the *parousia* as well. In their essential core all these together form the single enduring mystery of salvation: the person of the humiliated and glorified Christ who is the saving reality. However, as they are shown forth in being given to us, the riches of this mystery enter one by one into the sequence of saving history. It is precisely for this reason that the New Testament indicates separate phases of the redemption which, included as they all are in the resurrection from the dead, nevertheless possess distinct meanings for salvation and manifest themselves in time in different ways. Thus we may state the dogmatic content of the Passover, the Ascension and Pentecost as follows:

(1) The Passover is the mystery of Jesus' loving attachment to the Father unto death itself; it is the fidelity to the Father of the Son made man despite the condition proper to fallen humanity in which he had found himself because of our sinfulness. But at the same time it is the mystery of the divine response to this loving fidelity; the answer of divine mercy to the sacrifice of love, and the nullifying or the destruction of the power of sin: the resurrection.

(2) The Ascension is: (a) the investiture of Christ risen from the dead as universal Lord and King, with which is connected (b) the glorification of Christ which constitutes him definitively and fully the Messiah and the eschatological "Son of Man." The Ascension is the change from *exinanitio* to *glorificatio,* from humiliation to exaltation; it is the eternally enduring goal of the incarnation of the Son of God. We may say

the Ascension is the incarnation itself in its completion, which precisely is the redemption. (c) Thus the Ascension is the prelude to the giving of the Spirit and the termination of Jesus' earthly mission. All these divine prerogatives of the man Jesus come to him through the fact that by the Ascension he is "with the Father," taken up in the cloud of the divine presence which "makes all things new"; this Jesus of Nazareth is the king of the universe, the *Christus Victor*. It is clear that according to Scripture Christ had to *become* king. But this does not exclude the fact that the foundation of it all was given in the incarnation itself. St. John, especially, emphasizes this point. But the incarnation of Christ is not something static. Christ's redeeming action, though a single reality, grows and develops so that, in the context of his whole human life, we can distinguish in it three principal elements: (a) his death and descent into hell; (b) the resurrection from the dead; (c) his glorification or his being established by the Father as Lord and thus sender of the Holy Spirit. St. John sees this progressive action as all one process of *glorification*.

Since all this came to completion in Christ as the first-born and precursor of all mankind, in his ascension we too are already in principle "with the Father."

(3) Pentecost is the eternally continuing actuation or application of this mystery in and through the Holy Spirit who now realizes and perfects *in us* that which was completed in Christ. Only through the Spirit whom Christ sends us does what is a reality in Christ—that in him all the faithful sit at the right hand of the Father—become actual in ourselves. The Spirit makes actual in us that which Christ achieved for us once and for all. Thus the action of the Spirit, after the earthly activity of Jesus, is truly proper to him as third person of the Trinity. But all that he does he draws out of Christ's work of redemption; Christ said, "He shall receive of mine. . . ." Christ is therefore not idle in heaven. For as well as praying and interceding for us, it is he who out of his love for the Father sends the Holy Spirit upon us. And it is the Father who remains the ultimate source of the saving activity of both Christ and the Holy Spirit, for "it was God [viz., the Father] who reconciled us to himself in Christ."

(b) The Significance of the Saving Mysteries
   of Jesus, the Christ

"I came forth from the Father and am come into the world; again I leave the world and I go to the Father." (John 16.28.)

(1) The Mystery of the Earthly Adoration of
   God the Father by God the Son Incarnate

The incarnation is the whole life of Christ, from his conception in the womb, through all his further life of action, completed finally in his death, resurrection and being established as Lord and sender of the Paraclete; it is prolonged everlastingly in his uninterrupted sending of the Holy Spirit. In this incarnation there is outwardly realized that mystery which St. John has expressed in the words "If I go not, the Holy Spirit will not come to you." Christ can send us the Spirit only "from the Father," only when he is "with the Father." There is a sense in which the earthly Christ is not "with the Father," no matter how closely he, as man too, may be united to the Father in loving attachment. This is not a question of some kind of local separation that supposedly would be involved in Christ's being on earth while the Father is "in heaven." But still it does mean some kind of "absence from home" or "estrangement" from God. For "while we are at home in the body [the actual meaning is, "while we are men existing in the fallen state"] we are away from the Lord." And Christ really did become thoroughly *sarx;* the Word, says St. John, was made flesh *(sarx);* that is, he became man not merely in the sense of "human being," but man in the existential condition of the children of Adam. Becoming man, God the Son entered into a humanity that had made its history one of condemnation, and that was branded with the sign of disobedience and alienation from God: death. By the concrete reality of his incarnation, St. Paul says in his own blunt way, God has "made Christ to be sin." Although personally sinless, the earthly Christ lived in a situation of "estrangement from God," not so much personally on his own account, but rather because, as our representative, he personally took the place of sinful mankind before the Father.

This was no mere "acting as if. . . ." Although we cannot plumb the depths of this saving reality with our human minds, for Christ it must have been a vivid and fearful experience, reaching its climax in the Garden of Olives and on the Cross. In the human core of his personal existence, Jesus is truly he who is laden with our sins; it is thus that he confronts his heavenly Father. "We all have sinned and lack the glory of God," that is, we do not have the Spirit of God. Thus too the glory of God was wanting in Jesus' humanity here on earth, and so, shortly before his death, he could pray to the Father with urgent insistence: "Father . . . glorify thy Son," which is to say "give thy glory to this man Jesus." During Jesus' earthly life, St. John says, "the Spirit was not given, because Jesus was not yet glorified." If indeed there is strife between the spirit and the flesh, the *pneuma* and the *sarx,* it means that the Spirit has first to overcome the unsaved state of humanity of Jesus, its condition as *sarx,* and has to deify and to renew the whole of his humanity through and through, including its very bodiliness. Only when this is done can the man Jesus, who is God, give the Spirit of God to us, too, in a sovereign way: "Now that he is exalted at the right hand of God, and having received of the Father the promise of the Holy Spirit, he has poured forth this which you see and hear."

In his earthly life Jesus, as Messiah or representative of sinful mankind, did truly go forth from the Father. So truly, in fact, that he can pray with us, "Out of the depths have I cried to thee, Lord"—not in a local but in a qualitative sense: "Out of the depths of the miserable state of fallen mankind, I call upon you, my God." This cry echoes above all from the Cross. It is the outburst of a man who, even though knowing himself personally bound to the Father in love from the depths of his human heart, was nevertheless living in utter truth, through to the very end, the experience of the estrangement from God belonging to *our* sinfulness, identifying himself with everything there ever was, or will be of sin-spawned alienation from God in the world. He had to pass through the helplessness of this alienation from God to receive the glory the Father would give him. In dispossessing himself of himself, Jesus hallowed himself to the Father in whom he finds his exaltation and glory. And behind all this there lies a mystery of unfathomable depth.

In Jewish family life "to go out from the father" is a technical term denoting that the son is sent on some mission by the father who is in charge in the home. The mission we are considering is the *redemptive* incarnation. But then the going forth from the Father implies at the same time the Son's entry into sinful humanity. The Father, it is true, continues to love the Son; the Son himself is never forsaken by the Father, not even on the Cross (as some have mistakenly suggested); he is never alone. But neither is he merely "himself"; he is also "all of us"; he takes our place in the most real sense of the phrase. And we are sinners. In this connection, the meaning Jewish tradition gives to the term "to go out from the father" is that family relations are ruptured (compare the parable of the Prodigal Son). According to this second meaning, the Son's going out from the Father into this world at enmity with God because of its sins is a commission given to Jesus, that he should bear witness in estranged, ungodly humanity to mankind's dependence on the Father, right up to the bitter end.

Here our prospects open upon God himself. For within the life of the Trinity, the Son is pure self-giving to the Father. Within God, this self-giving does not involve any giving-up, any self-dispossession. But on the level of the incarnation, Christ's self-giving to the Father does become a giving-up; it becomes the sacrificial offering of his life. Only a creature can sacrifice, because to be a creature is to be dependent. The Epistle to the Hebrews discloses to us a perspective in mystery that opens out upon the unfathomable mystery of the life of God itself: "... and whereas indeed he was the Son of God, he learned obedience by the things which he suffered." In his sacrifice Christ consecrated himself entirely to the Father. The result of this is that "being made perfect, he became to all that obey him the cause of eternal salvation." Christ's obedience and his attachment to the Father are therefore the essential precondition for the sending of the Spirit of Sanctification. In this the most profound significance of the incarnation is revealed; in Jesus' earthly humanity there is made known to us, in the first instance, that

Christ is the Son of God through and through, even in his humanity, filial and obedient in all things to the Father. This is the interpretation in human reality of what he is in the heart of the Trinity: "from the Father." And only when he has lived his sonship through to the very end in his human life, and lived his life in utter obedience to the Father even to death itself, is his divine sonship fully realized and fully revealed on the level of the incarnation. Let us examine this in greater detail.

As God, Christ is equal in all things to the Father; in such a way, however, that it is through the Father that he is *himself.* Receiving all from the Father, he is in accord with the Father in all. Nonetheless there is no genuine dependence of the Son on the Father in the strict meaning of the word. The truth of the matter is this: Between the Father and the Son there is an intimacy of life. Within the equality of the persons and the divine unity the Father is the origin of this life, in such a way that the Son, although equal to the Father, is beholden to him in all things by a perfect active receptivity.

The human existence of Jesus, as the humanness of the divine Son, is the revelation of these relations in the life of God; their transposition and interpretation into human forms— incarnation. Hence in the incarnate Son, the Son's intimacy of life with the Father enters into the sphere of creation and therefore of true dependence. For indeed to be man is to be a creature. This also means that the man Jesus' intimacy of life with the Father becomes, in Christ, truly a loving obedience. Dependence now enters the relation of love. As the revelation of this reality-within-God, the human life of Christ is the expression of adoration of God. As man, Christ *is* supreme worship of the Father. Christ was to live this worship of God in a human way, in the world of fellow men and things. The whole of the earthly life of Christ is loving obedience to the Father, lived in all the common situations of the life of man. In its actual content his human life becomes the religious expression of his abiding submission to the holy will of the Father, in spite of everything, in spite of death itself. This is the *whole* content of his human life; not something outside it or over and above it. Among all the acts of the life of this man, his death is the supreme expression of his religious surrender to the Father.

Christ as man realizes his divine sonship in this living human form.

He does this as the Messiah, in our name and in the place of all of us, as a prototype. The supreme moment in his life, the death to which he freely assents, is a messianic death; a death thus for the good of the people. As an act of messianic adoration of God, this is "liturgical." For in Christ our head and representative the sacrifice of the Cross, as that in which Jesus' inward adoration of God becomes an external reality and constitutes itself a real sacrificial cult, is an "act of the community" (*leiton ergon:* an act of the people), not yet performed by the people itself, but offered by the representative of the whole family of man and thus in the name of all and to the advantage of all. The sacrifice of the Cross itself is the great *liturgical mystery of worship,* through which Christ pleads with the Father for the grace of redemption for every man. It is in this way that Christ, in our name and in our place, makes reparation to the Father for our disobedience and for our irreligion.

The fact that he makes reparation to God means that in his human life, prototype of our lives, he makes God truly *God;* by his surrender he certifies God's infinite superiority to man ("oblation"): "The Father is greater than I," and in this he perfects his renunciation of self as the greatest of all values ("immolation"): "He offered himself without blemish to the Father." This self-giving, in the manner of self-dispossession, is the essence of all religious life, life in the service of God. Along with this it should be remembered that the Son of God became man precisely in order to be able to give himself in this sacrificial, self-dispossessing way. For however much the Son as God is pure self-giving to the Father, on the divine level it is nevertheless not possible for this to be in the mode of a giving-up, a dispossession of self or a sacrifice, as certain Russian Orthodox theologians (Bulgakov, Lossky) have wanted to suggest. Only in his human existence can the Son's eternal giving of himself to the Father be realized in the true form of a sacrifice and of self-dispossession. This is the reason why the Son, entering into the fallen world of mankind, has taken to himself precisely the *sarx;* a human existence which is branded with the sign of sin, condemned to suffering and to death. This he has done to make

269

the curse itself, the sign of condemnation, into a sign of supreme adoration of God. Thus his death becomes a death to sin. As the earthly Messiah or head of *fallen* mankind, whose sinfulness he takes upon himself, he had to win mankind to himself by that adoration of the Father which formed his whole human life, so making of mankind a redeemed messianic People of God. Thus Christ, by the religious service of his human life culminating in the sacrifice of the Cross, *becomes* the head of redeemed mankind. "Christ . . . loved the Church [the messianic People of God] and delivered himself up for it, that he might sanctify it . . . That he might present it to himself, a glorious Church, not having spot or wrinkle or any such thing, but that it should be holy and without blemish."

In and through the liturgical mystery of worship that is his sacrifice on the Cross, against the background of the whole of his life in God's service, the being of the Son of God as "from the Father" and "to the Father" is fully revealed and given reality on the human plane of his sonship. The divine procession of the Son from the Father and his eternal return are completely revealed and made human reality in the man Jesus in the supreme moment of his life: "Father, into thy hands I commend my spirit"—into thy hands I lay down my life. "I came forth from the Father and am come into the world; again I leave the world and I go to the Father." In and through his death for love, as the human interpretation of his divine attachment to the Father, in a messianic, redeeming act of love, to the very end Jesus sacrificially uttered his human love to the Father.

(2) The Father's Response to the Son's Life of Worship on Earth: The Resurrection and Glorification of Jesus and His Establishment as Lord and Sender of the Holy Spirit

The divine acceptance of the sacrifice belongs to the essence of this sacrificial offering up of life. The Father's acceptance of Jesus' sacrifice is the resurrection of Christ. The resurrection is the sacrifice of the Cross heard and answered by the Father. And answered precisely as a messianic sacrifice; as the sacrifice, therefore, of all mankind. Only in this response does the "objective redemption" become a reality; only then are we all already redeemed in principle (*in principe*), i.e., in Christ our Head. The Father exalted Christ as a result of his sacrifice—"Sit at my right hand"—this is Christ's enthronement by the Father as *Kyrios*. "The government is upon his shoulder." Only in his resurrection and exaltation with the Father does Christ become unconditionally Messiah: he is then, *in* his humanity, "the Son of God in power." Through this acceptance by the Father of the whole life of Jesus lived as the expression of his adoration of God, the entire cycle of mutual love between the Father and the Son is fully incorporated in the sphere of Christ's humanity. Only in this does Jesus reach his consummation. Thus, in virtue of Jesus' sacrificial love for the Father, the Father, through the resurrection, calls a "new creation" into being in the *sarx* of Christ: humanity in glory. Only in this is the redemption of humanity a reality.

(3) The Christ of Heaven, Sender of the Spirit of Sanctification

"When the Paraclete cometh, whom I will send you from the Father." (John 15.26.)

According to the insight the New Testament affords us, Christ can send forth the Spirit upon us only after his exaltation. This fact can be appreciated now in its most profound trinitarian significance. As God, the second person of the Trinity is not only the Son of the Father, but as Son in union with the Father he is at the same time the principle of the Holy Spirit: ". . . qui procedit a Patre per Filium." Within the triune God, the Father and the Son are pure giving and re-giving, and the life of these two persons in their giving and returning is so intense that, within the one divinity, it goes forth from their own persons and in a receptive returning is the fount of life of the Holy Spirit. The third divine person is thus conceivable only in terms of the reciprocal love of Father and Son.

Within the Trinity it is in his infinitely perfect belonging to the Father that the Son himself is the principle of life of the Holy Spirit; and therefore on the plane of the incarnation—as man—he can give us the Holy Spirit only when his sonship is consummated in his humanity too, which is only when he has freely and humanly given himself in love to the Father, who responds to this gift by the resurrection. The cycle of mutual love of Father and Son, as the origin of the Holy Spirit, is translated in the man Jesus by his sending the Spirit upon us. Only in the perfecting of the religious obedience of the man Jesus to his Father, who accepts this sacrifice of life out of love for his Son, out of love indeed for his Son as the representative of all mankind (as Messiah)—only in this can the man Jesus, "established in power," also be a co-principle of the sending of the Holy Spirit upon us. The *Kyrios* in his *humanity* is the sender of the Spirit. For this reason Pentecost can be understood only in terms of the Passover as a "passage from death to life." In its essence Pentecost is an Easter event. This is how St. John sees it; he does not speak of the pentecostal event peculiar to Luke on the fiftieth day after Easter. According to St. John, the first sending of the Holy Spirit took place on Easter Day itself, after the Easter-Ascension. After Christ had said to Mary Magdalen that he was about to go to the Father, and that she must tell this to the Apostles, he appeared to them. His first act as the risen and glorified Christ is, then, immediately to send the Holy Spirit upon the Apostles: "As the Father has sent me, I also send you. When he had said this he breathed on them; and he said to them, Receive the Holy Spirit." We can call this quite simply the Johannine Pentecost motif, in which it appears just as clearly as in Luke that the Ascension is the immediate condition for the sending of the Holy Spirit. The essential Christian Pentecost is an Easter event.

But with this first bestowal of the Spirit the manifestation of the Lord established in power is not at an end. Pentecost is a continuing event. Nevertheless, among the various unceasing bestowals of the Holy Spirit upon the primitive Church, we can point to several that stand out from the rest. This is already done in the New Testament itself. The first sending of the Holy Spirit, on Easter Day, is the one St. John emphasizes. St. Luke, on the contrary, places the pentecostal event on the fiftieth day after Easter, stressing the sending of the Holy Spirit upon the community of the first Church, the Church of Jerusalem. This is the inauguration of the christianizing of the Jewish people, and through this "christened" people (or some of them), of the whole world. We may call this the Lucan Pentecost motif. Finally, it is also possible to indicate a Pauline Pentecost motif, in the passage where the sending of the Holy Spirit upon the Church of Ephesus is seen by the same St. Luke as the starting-point of the christianizing of the pagan world. The account is clearly built up on the same lines as the account of the sending of the Spirit upon the Church of Jerusalem. This already indicates that to a certain extent there is something arbitrary in the promotion of the fiftieth day after Easter to the feast of Pentecost, or the feast of the sending forth of the Holy Spirit. It is obviously a case of thematic presentation (based on historical fact, and in the present instance also in connection with the Jewish Pentecost). Pentecost remains essentially an Easter reality; through his establishment as *Kyrios* (the Ascension motif, at least logically distinct from the Resurrection understood precisely as arising from the dead), Christ is the sender of the Holy Spirit. For this reason too, the givings of the Holy Spirit begin from Easter Day. Nonetheless, certain historical gifts of the Spirit are placed thematically at the origin of the founding of the Church and of particular Church communities.

As far as the Liturgy is concerned, the Lucan Pentecost motif has prevailed over the others. The reason for this is quite understandable, for the establishment in power of the Mother Church of Jerusalem does indeed definitely introduce the Church's period of salvation, the history of the Church as the saving community of the risen Lord, who through his apostolic college and through his Spirit extends the Church in space and time.

Conclusion

In this brief analysis we can see sufficiently clearly that the mysteries of the Passover (death, resurrection and exaltation) and of Pentecost are the representation in human form, realized in the mystery of Christ, of the mystery of the redeeming Trinity. Passover and Pentecost are the interpretation on the human plane of the divine relations of Son to Father, and of the Son in unity with the Father to the Holy Spirit. For within the life of the Godhead, that the Son should be the principle of the Holy Spirit is something which he receives from the Father. In the sphere of the incarnation this gift of the Father is represented in the commission of the man Jesus to be Christ, to be the *Kyrios* and the sender of the Holy Spirit upon the world of men.

(4) The Mystery of Christ's Love for the
   Father as the Foundation of His Unfailing
   Gift of Grace

The mystery of Christ, seen in this way, is the mystery of Christmas that reaches its fulfilment, by way of the whole human life of Jesus, in a mystery of Passover and Pentecost. This whole forms for us the revelation of the redemptive mystery of the Trinity, being progressively realized in human form. Through the earthly mystery of worship in his life Christ "merited" or obtained for us from the Father the grace of redemption which now, as the *Kyrios,* he can in fact give us to the full. All the Lord's activity in heaven is still a filial intercession with and adoration of the Father, but it is also a continual sending out of the Holy Spirit upon mankind. We must appreciate the order in which this takes place. The salvation of humanity is brought about in Christ's life of service as the Father's Son incarnate. For in his divine union with and total orientation towards the Father, the Son is the principle of the Holy Spirit. This relationship within God is exhibited in the plane of Christ's glorified messianic humanity in the following manner: because of his love for the Father, on the Father's initiative, the Lord sends us the Spirit of sonship. Hence the mystery of worship, which is Christ, is at the same time our salvation: a mystery of saving worship.

As we have said, these are two inseparable aspects of all the activity of Christ's life, both in his humiliation and in his glory, although in his humiliation we see his redemptive worship of the Father more plainly, while in his glorification it is rather his gift of grace that strikes us. This implies no contradiction, for though Christ before his glorification had still to realize actual redemption, and was not yet in reality a sender of the Holy Spirit, even in his humiliation, he was nevertheless the Son always beloved of the Father. In this we see how encounter with the earthly Jesus was already a grace. For in his heart Jesus already bore his sacrifice, with which, in anticipation, the Father was well pleased: "Thou art my beloved son. In thee I am well pleased." But this does not eliminate the fact that the great "pouring forth" of grace could take place only after the resurrection from the dead. So therefore we say that, on the foundation of his earthly mystery of worship, the Lord himself does in fact bestow the grace of redemption on us, at the same time not forgetting that his earthly mystery of worship had already touched hearts with grace and that the heavenly sending of the Spirit is founded upon the heavenly liturgy of Christ, who in his worship of the Father "is always living to make intercession for us."

Thus Christ is and remains the "high priest for ever." In our name and in the place of all of us he is ever praying the Father for grace for us, and then in actual fact giving us the grace for which he has prayed. For his prayer is unfailingly heard, because even in his humanity he is the well-beloved Son. He is unfailingly heard, it used to be said, because of his "meritorious" work of redemption on earth. But what this means is that he is heard because of his existence as Son, the existence which through his earthly activity he lived freely and faithfully to the end. The so-called "merit" is his service; is the free realization in human form of Jesus' divine love as the Son. Thus Christ's earthly and heavenly mystery of worship (i.e., the human religious shape of his sonship) is the foundation of the Lord's unfailing gift of grace. It is the expression in human form of the mystery of divine love; a mystery which in the Godhead manifests itself as mutual gift within the unity of love.

Thus, when we speak of Christ's mystery of saving worship or about his work of salvation-through-worship, we must not lose sight of the fact that Jesus' human adoration of the Father is itself the revelation of the divinity which he receives from the Father. Jesus' human love is the translation of divine love itself into human form. And this love from the human heart of God the Son drove him to the redeeming adoration of his death on the Cross. This adoration arises therefore from God's own love. For the man Jesus this means that even his adoration itself is a pure gift and grace from the Father without whom he can do nothing. Our salvation through Jesus' adoration is thus intelligible only in virtue of the fact that Jesus as man was himself sanctified by the Spirit of God; the redeeming activity of love of the man Jesus is a personal worship-through-salvation, and so, in our regard to our Christological redemption through the man Jesus. That absolute generosity which the Trinity simply *is* remains the universally dominant background of the mystery of saving worship in Christ.

The result of the redeeming incarnation, as an enduring heavenly reality, is that we are children of the Father in Christ. By the incarnation of his divine life of love, Christ earned for us that his Father should also be our Father; and by the same incarnation, but now through its fulfilment in glory, Christ in actual fact bestows upon us the Spirit which makes us children of the Father, so that we, too, truly are children of the Father. Thus we become by grace what Christ is by nature: Son of God. As *filii in Filio* we are thus caught up into the special providential relationships which hold between the Father and the incarnate Son, and the Father proves himself, in his Son's continual sending of the Holy Spirit, truly our Father all our life long. That which was brought to realization under the providence of the Father in the exemplar or prototype, the man Jesus, by the way which led from his humiliation to his glory, must now be renewed in the reproduction or antitype, the messianic family of the Church. But how in actual fact will this come about?

3. The Necessity for the Extension to Earth of the Glorified Christ, the Primordial Sacrament

1. Our Need to Encounter the Christ of Heaven

In the preceding pages we have been clarifying the meaning of the saving reality which is Christ, the one and only saving primordial sacrament. But it is precisely this, proper to Christ as the one and only "Sacrament of God," that confronts us with a problem from the moment that Jesus by his resurrection and glorification disappeared from the visible horizon of our life. For on the foundation of God's economy of salvation the gift of grace, or the encounter with God, remains bound up with our personal encounter with the man Jesus who is our only way to the Father. Now how can we encounter the glorified Lord, who has withdrawn himself from our sight? For Jesus' bodiliness, as the means of immediate communication, has vanished from our earthly life. The difficulty is even accentuated by Christ's words: "It is the Spirit that gives life; the flesh profits nothing." Still more pointedly, in flagrant contradiction of all that has been said so far, it would seem that bodily mediation in our encounter with Christ is meaningless, since Jesus himself has said, "It is good for you that I go." It would seem that it is rather Christ's bodily absence that is conducive to actual encounter with him.

It is true that Christ had to go away to where we are not able as yet to follow him. He has risen and thus disappeared from all our visible walks of life. But it was not his disappearance in itself that was "best for us," but rather his glorification at the Father's side, which of course implied that he had to disappear from those who are still not glorified. But at the same time this means that being in body together with the Lord in glory, which will happen at the *parousia,* is the eternally enduring and supreme realization of Christian living. Christ's incarnation is, as it were, some paces ahead of our deification, so that for a time he has passed out of sight beyond the visible horizon; but from there he is preparing the perfect reunion in bodily life and remoulding us from within, so that when our hearts are pure enough we, ourselves glorified, may see him face to face in the bodily encounter of the *parousia.* It is precisely for this reason that Christianity, as life between Passover and *parousia,* is so markedly eschatological. In part we have indeed to manage now without encountering Christ in the body. Precisely on this account Christian life is an Advent. We must be on the lookout, waiting for the encounter which has yet to come. Christianity is the religion of the *Maranatha:* "Come, Lord Jesus."

But in this we do not have the whole picture. For it is not possible to understand this expectation of the ultimate perfect encounter except in virtue of the fact that we have already in some way encountered the glorified Lord, not in the mere commemoration of something that happened ages ago in Palestine, nor even simply by our faith in him as now living, glorified and invisibly active in our lives. This is not all: Christ makes his presence among us actively visible and tangible too, not directly through his own bodiliness, but by extending among us on earth in visible form the function of his bodily reality which is in heaven. This precisely is what the sacraments are: the earthly extension of the "body of the Lord." This is the Church. But before we go on to study the character as Church of the earthly "body of the Lord" we must have a clear insight into the general meaning of an earthly prolongation of Christ's glorified humanity.

For why in fact this sacramental extension? Without it one of the profoundly human qualities of the incarnation of God would be lost to us. Now God has always remained faithful to his own methods of teaching us salvation. Because God loves man and has a sovereign respect for our earthbound humanity—for our reality as persons who in their own bodiliness live in a world of people and of things, and thereby grow to spiritual maturity—God always offers us the kingdom of heaven in an earthly guise. So he did in the Old Testament. So it was in the *ephapax:* the appearance once and for all of God the Redeemer in human shape. So, too, finally, does he continue to teach us in the sacramental Church which is the visible organ on earth of the living Lord. We shall now try to bring out the inner significance of this fact.

2. The Real Possibility of This Encounter from Christ's Side

Mutual human availability is possible only in and through man's bodiliness. Therefore men who are dead and not yet risen again can exercise no direct influence upon us by mutual human contact. If the dead are holy and already with the Lord, they can influence us only through their prayerful intercession with God, and not directly from man to man. This already makes it clear that on the side of Christ the man it is the resurrection which makes it possible for him precisely *as man* to influence us by grace. This is of capital importance. For we are ever inclined to pass cursorily over the human life of Christ, to overlook his existence as man and consider only his existence as God. But it is as *man* that the Son is the mediator of grace; he is mediator in his humanity, according to the ways of humanity. His human mediation of grace therefore pre-supposes his corporeality, ". . . la face de l'âme qui est tournée vers les autres âmes." (Jean Guitton.) Redemption turns its face towards us in Christ's glorified bodiliness. Thus in the risen Christ the mystery of saving worship truly remains an active offer of grace for us. For the glorious body of Christ gives his soul the outward openness he as man must have if he is really to exercise influence upon us.

So even from considerations of what man is, the Greek patristic affirmation St. Thomas has taken over is seen clearly to be right; on the one hand "grace in us derives from Christ . . . only through the personal action of Christ himself," and on the other hand, "the whole of Christ's humanity, that is to say both body and soul, exercises an influence on men."

3. The Necessity for Earthly Sacraments so that the Encounter between the Glorified Christ and Men on Earth Might Take Place in Terms of Mutual Human Availability

On Christ's side, the possibility of a human encounter is positively established. Human encounter, however, calls for mutual availability. Now it is certainly true that because of his glorified corporeality the Christ of heaven can, full of grace, reach us and influence us whoever or wherever we may be. But we, earthly men, cannot encounter him in the living body (*in propria carne*) because his glorification has made him invisible to us. From this it follows that if Christ did not make his heavenly bodiliness visible in some way in our earthly sphere, his redemption would after all no longer be for us; redemption would no longer turn its face towards us. Then the human mediation of Christ would be meaningless. Once he had completed the work of redemption, there would no longer be any reason for the existence of Christ's humanity. The logical consequence would be the position taken by Julian of Halicarnassus, that once the work of redemption had been completed the incarnation ceased to exist.

But on the other hand it follows from the dogma of the perpetuity of the incarnation, and of Christ's human mediation of grace, that if Christ does not show himself to us in his own flesh, then he can make himself visibly present to and for us earthbound men only by taking up earthly non-glorified realities into his glorified saving activity. This earthly element replaces for us the invisibility of his bodily life in heaven. This is precisely what the sacraments are: the face of redemption turned visibly towards us, so that in them we are truly able to encounter the living Christ. The heavenly saving activity, invisible to us, becomes visible in the sacraments.

We do not propose to study the historical revelation of the sacraments here. Taking it for granted, and seeking an understanding of the inner significance of this reality of saving history, we must hold that the sacraments are intrinsically required, since the mediation of grace by the *man* Jesus is a permanent reality. From the moment that, by his ascension, the "primordial sacrament" leaves the world, the economy of the "separated sacraments" becomes operative in consequence of the incarnation and as its prolongation. From Scripture we learn that while none of the twelve Apostles who enjoyed immediate contact with the "primordial sacrament" himself was baptized, St. Paul, the "thirteenth Apostle," who had not encountered the earthly Christ in faith, was in fact baptized. Sacramentality thus bridges the gap and solves the disproportion between the Christ of heaven and unglorified humanity, and makes possible a reciprocal human encounter of Christ and men even after the ascension, though in a special manner. A permanent sacramentality is thus an intrinsic requirement of the Christian religion.

From this account of the sacraments as the earthly prolongation of Christ's glorified bodiliness, it follows immediately that the Church's sacraments are not things but encounters of men on earth with the glorified man Jesus by way of a visible form. On the plane of history they are the visible and tangible embodiment of the heavenly saving action of Christ. They are this saving action itself in its availability to us; a personal act of the Lord in earthly visibility and open availability.

Here the first and most fundamental definition of sacramentality is made evident. In an earthly embodiment which we· can see and touch, the heavenly Christ sacramentalizes both his continual intercession for us and his active gift of grace. Therefore the sacraments are the visible realization on earth of Christ's mystery of saving worship. "What was visible in Christ has now passed over into the sacraments of the Church."

The fact which we must now begin to analyse in detail is therefore this: Through the sacraments we are placed in living contact with the mystery of Christ the High Priest's saving worship. In them we encounter Christ in his mystery of Passover and Pentecost. The sacraments *are* this saving mystery in earthly guise. This visible manifestation is the visible Church. This will be the first point to analyse.

Karl Rahner

1904-

*Karl Rahner was born in Freiburg, Germany, and joined
the Jesuits in 1922. His probing theological style and his sympa-
thetic use of insights from modern philosophy brought him
under suspicion in earlier years, but the consistency and relevance
of his achievement guaranteed his vindication, which occurred
in the era of Vatican II. At that Council he was personal theologian to both Cardinal König of Vienna and Cardinal Döpfner
of Munich, and was twice called for private audiences with Pope
Paul VI.*

*One of Rahner's strengths has always been his dialectical
handling of the tradition. He views a dogma not as the end of
a conversation but as the beginning. Thus earlier definitions are
to be taken very seriously but not simply repeated in petrified
form. The Church has never claimed that any of the historical
formulations of faith are adequate, exhaustive expressions of
biblical truth. In fact, any given one is liable to distortion by
loss of historical context in being understood by later ages. This
holds for the Christology formulated at Chalcedon.*

*Rahner called attention to the fact that current views of
the formula of Chalcedon often contained an implicit if unconscious tendency toward Monophysitism through failure to do
justice to the New Testament portrayal of Jesus as Messiah. The
Incarnation thus becomes almost a "transient episode" in God's*

plan and the continuing significance of Christ's manhood tends to be overlooked.

Whenever he voices such a criticism of the tradition, Rahner never gives up until he has made a vigorous attempt at "retrieving" that tradition, reformulating it in a contemporary manner so that the shortcoming is avoided. Nowhere does he apply this penetrating approach more effectively than in the realm of Christology. The real significance of the Incarnation has not been grasped if one has not plumbed the depths of its metaphysical consequences. It has as much to do with the understanding of what it means to be human as of what it means to be divine.

Thus a Christian "anthropology" is inherent in a proper understanding of the mystery of Christ. And the radical meaning of being human is found in the paradox that self-fulfillment is only to be found in self-emptying. Man comes to be in the degree to which he gives himself away. In this sense human nature is potential for obedience. Thus when the Word of God "assumes" this nature, that potential comes to its highest development.

Rahner had already been working out these ideas in the 1940s and 1950s. The Incarnation became so central to his theology that all else was viewed in its light. It is "the unambiguous goal of creation as a whole." In Christ's human life all of us can see what our human lives really mean. This "anthropological turn" in Catholic theology is probably the most striking characteristic of the documents of Vatican II, so it is useful to see how it was being developed before that event. The essay that follows is a good example of the fruitful originality which marked the thought of Karl Rahner on the eve of Vatican II, i.e., right before it was to make its greatest impact on the Church of our era.

THEOLOGICAL INVESTIGATIONS

CHAPTER 8

CHRISTOLOGY WITHIN AN EVOLUTIONARY VIEW OF THE WORLD

T he subject to be discussed here is: 'Christology within an evolutionary view of the world'. This discussion will therefore be concerned with showing how one statement can be or is fitted into a complex of other statements; it will not be concerned with each of these statements themselves. This makes it clear right away that the problem posed here is neither the exposition of Christian and Catholic Christology itself nor the exposition of what is described—even though vaguely—as the evolutionary view of the world. It is here rather a question of the possibility of correlating these two views. For our present purposes, we will simply presuppose that there is such a thing as an evolutionary view of the world, even though this is neither self-evident objectively nor unobjectionable from a methodological point of view. Having boldly presupposed this, we will inquire as to whether Christology fits into such a view, and not vice versa, although the converse would also be a possible question—and indeed in itself the better and more radical one. Once more: we are not going to attempt to give an exposition of Christology itself and to unfold it theologically, nor will we try to prove that Jesus of Nazareth laid claim to what we subsequently explain in theological language as metaphysical sonship of God, Incarnation and Hypostatic Union, or that this claim of his can be made comprehensible as a legitimate (i.e. believable) claim. All this is presupposed here or will be treated from a different point of view. Furthermore, when we speak of the 'inclusion' of a doctrine in a 'view of the world'—of Christology fitted or fitting into the evolutionary view of the world—we do not mean by this that the Christian doctrine of the Incarnation can be deduced as a necessary consequence and as a demanded extension of the evolutionary view of the world (this would be an extreme which we do no envisage)—nor do we mean by it that the doctrine of the Incarnation does not directly contradict, either simply in an objective sense or in a logical sense, any certain knowledge and scientific conclusion contained in this view of the world (which would be the other extreme, which it would be easy to prove but which would not be particularly significant and so is not sufficient for us).

If we did mean the former, then we would be making an attempt at constructing a theological rationalism—an attempt to transform faith, revelation and dogma into philosophy—which, of course, is not what is intended here. If, on the other hand, we were to aim simply at the other extreme, then we would be discussing something which is not really a problem at all and so would be achieving too little. For even if the doctrine of the Incarnation of the divine Logos is seen as a doctrine not directly denied by the present-day evolutionary view of the world—or is seen as a doctrine not invalidated by propositions contradicting it on purely logical grounds—it would still be experienced as something foreign in the mind of man. For a man disposed to think in terms of the evolutionary view of the world would in this case experience the doctrine of the Incarnation as something quite unrelated to his other thoughts and feelings; if such a man were or is nevertheless a Christian for some other reasons, he would then be forced to think along two completely unrelated lines of thought. Hence—while not attempting to make the Christian doctrine of the Incarnation a necessary and inner moment of the present-day view of the world, of its way of thinking and the present-day feeling of life—our task lies precisely in not only removing formal logical contradictions (or better: in showing that no such contradictions exist, particularly not where they seem to appear) but in bringing out clearly the inner affinity of these two doctrines— a sort of similarity of style—and in explaining the possibility of their being mutually related. Of course, in a short lecture like this, there cannot be any question of considering the *general* problem of a certain sameness of human perceptions in one period or in one individual—which is a problem concerning the possibility of a kind of common *style* of thinking or of one thought-form which gives a common pattern to many perceptions of quite different material content—although, of course, there would be many obscurities and important points to be considered even in this general problem. For the rest, what exactly we do and do not intend to do should become clearer as we actually proceed in our attempt to answer our question.

Given a certain previous understanding of the problem posed, however, the difficulty, laboriousness and breadth of this problem will also appear quite clearly. Everything with which the Society of St Paul concerns itself seems to enter into this question: all the questions concerning the reconciliation of the Christian teaching and interpretation of existence with the present-day way of living, thinking and feeling, are necessarily concentrated in our problem; all the objective and historical difficulties brought to mind by the phrase 'Christianity and the contemporary spirit' enter also into our question. For our question concerns the most central and most mysterious assertion of Christianity but an assertion which at the same time refers to a reality said to belong precisely to that dimension with which the man of today is most familiar on the scientific, existential and affective plane, i.e. the dimension of the material world and of tangible history. In short, our question concerns an assertion of God's presence (i.e. God as he is meant in theology) in precisely *that* dimension where man feels himself at home and in which alone he feels himself competent, viz. in the world and not in heaven. This makes it again quite obvious that it cannot be our job here to speak of the most general questions and difficulties connected with the reconciliation of the Christian religion and modern thought (no matter how fundamental these questions may be). It is quite obvious that we must confine ourselves to dealing with the special questions posed by our subject, even though we are quite aware of the fact that modern man's sense of bewilderment and astonishment when faced with the doctrine of the Incarnation is perhaps due in great part to his feeling of strangeness in the face of metaphysical and religious statements in general. But enough of introduction.

We must, however, add a few preliminary remarks about the plan of our reflections. We will start with the present-day evolutionary view of the world, presupposing rather than describing it. We will ask first of all, therefore, about the connection made in this view between matter and spirit—in other words, about its view of the unity of the world, of natural history and the history of man. All this will of course be treated only very briefly, touching only on those connections which— if we may put it this way—are 'common to all Christian thought' and 'general theology'. To put it in another way: we will try to avoid those theorems with which you are familiar from your study of Teilhard de Chardin. If we arrive at some of the same conclusions as he does, then that is all to the good. Yet we do not feel ourselves either dependent on him or obligated to him. We want to confine ourselves to those things which any theologian could say if he brings his theological reflection to bear on the questions posed by the modern evolutionary view of the world. This means, of course, that we must put up with a certain abstractness which will perhaps disappoint the natural scientist a little. For it would be quite understandable if the latter expected more exact details than we will actually give, about a certain homogeneity between matter and spirit. He would probably expect us to give details based on those findings of natural science or their evaluation to which he is accustomed. If (like Teilhard) we were to do this, however, our reflections would not only have to lay claim to such scientific knowledge— which we poor theologians can after all gather only very much at second hand—but we would also have to contend with all the drawbacks which are inevitably connected with such evaluations of the results of truly scientific inquiries, i.e. with evaluations which are not entirely undisputed. We have quite enough difficulties of our own, however, arising out of the philosophy and theology of these questions.

Following on this, we must then pass on to a second consideration and try to see man as the being in whom the basic tendency of matter to find itself in the spirit by self-transcendence arrives at the point where it definitely breaks through; thus in this way we may be in a position to regard man's being itself, from this view-point within the basic and

Karl Rahner

total conception of the world. It is precisely this being of man, seen from *this* view-point, which—both by its highest, free and complete self-transcendence into God, made possible quite gratuitously by God, and by God's communication of himself—'awaits' its own consummation and that of the world in what in Christian terms we call 'grace' and 'glory'.

The first step and definitive beginning, and the absolute guarantee that this ultimate and basically unsurpassable self-transcendence will succeed and indeed has already begun, is to be found in what we call the Hypostatic Union. At a first approximation, this must not be seen so much as something which distinguishes Jesus Our Lord from us, but rather as something which must happen once, and once only, at the point where the world begins to enter into its final phase in which it is to realize its final concentration, its final climax and its radical nearness to the absolute mystery called God. Seen from this viewpoint, the Incarnation appears as the necessary and permanent beginning of the divinization of the world as a whole. In so far as this unsurpassable nearness by complete openness takes place precisely in relation to that absolute mystery which is and remains God—and in so far as this final phase of the history of the world has indeed already begun but is not yet consummated—the course of this phase and its end-result remain shrouded in mystery. Hence the clarity and finality of Christian truth consist in man's unflinching surrender to the Mystery: it is not clarity in the sense of a clear view over a certain partial element of the world and of man. These then, in preview, are the steps in our considerations which we want to embark on together as far as strength of mind and heart—and time—will allow. If these steps are fairly successful, then—it seems to me—we will have covered what was intended to be our subject here. The extent of our success will depend, of course, on how far the immensity of our subject, its unaccustomed nature, our lack of practice in this kind of subject and the ridiculously short time of one hour will permit us to succeed.

THE CATHOLIC TRADITION: The Saviour

I

The Christian professes in his Faith that all things—heaven and earth, the material and the spiritual world—are the creation of one and the same God. This does not simply mean that everything *in* its variety stems from *one* cause, which—since infinite and omnipotent—can create the most varied things. It means also that this variety shows an inner similarity and community: that the contents of this variety must not be simply regarded as essentially different or even contradictory but rather that this variety and difference be seen to form a unity in origin, self-realization and determination, in short: *one* world. It follows from this that it would be quite wrong and unchristian to conceive matter and spirit as realities simply existing side by side in the actual order of things while being really quite unrelated to each other, the spirit in its human form having—unfortunately—to utilize the material world as a kind of exterior stage. A Christian theology and philosophy deems it self-evident that spirit and matter have more things in common (to put it this way) than things dividing them.

This 'community' shows itself first of all—and at its clearest—in the unity of man himself. According to Christian teaching, man is not an unnatural or merely temporary composite of spirit and matter but is a unity which is logically and objectively prior to the diversity of his distinguishable elements, so that the properties of these elements are intelligible only when the elements are understood precisely *as* elements of the *one* man into which this originally one being of man necessarily spreads and unfolds itself. This helps us to understand that, ultimately, we know what matter and spirit are only by starting from the one man and hence from his one self-realization, and that we must therefore conceive of them from the outset as mutually related elements. To this corresponds also the Christian doctrine which tells us that the consummation of the finite spirit which is man must be thought of only in terms of the one (however 'unimaginable') consummation of his *whole* reality and that of the cosmos; yet the materiality of man and of the cosmos—however impossible we may find it to form any positive image of a perfect state of materiality, and however

290

little this is required for being a true Christian—must not be simply eliminated from this consummation as if it were a merely temporary element.

Natural science, taken by itself as merely one element of man's one and complete knowledge, i.e. ultimately the knowledge of himself in his basic orientation to the unutterable Mystery, knows a lot 'about' matter, i.e. it defines ever more exact relationships of a 'functional' kind between the various phenomena of nature. Since, however, natural science does its work in methodical abstraction from man himself, while knowing a great deal *about* matter it cannot know matter *itself*, even though this knowledge about the functional and temporal relationships of its isolated object does in the end lead it back again to man himself in an *a-posteriori* manner. This is really quite obvious: the field, the whole as such, can*not* be determined by the same means as those used for the determination of its parts. Only in relation to man is it possible to say what matter is—and not vice versa, what spirit is in relation to matter. We have said in relation to *'man'* and not in relation to *'spirit'*. The latter would be something quite different—it would again simply be that platonism which is likewise contained in materialism. For materialism, like platonic spiritualism, believes that it has discovered a jumping-off point for its understanding of the whole and its parts: but this is done quite independently of the understanding of man as the one totality in which alone these two elements of spirit and matter can be experienced in their real nature. Starting from the original self-experience of the one man, however, it can be said that spirit is the one man in so far as he becomes conscious of himself in an absolute consciousness of being-given-to-himself. This man does by the very fact that he is always already referred to the absoluteness of reality as such and to its one root (called God), and by the fact that this 'return to himself' and his 'being referred to the absolute totality of all possible reality and its root' mutually determine each other. This 'being referred to', however, is not like a possession of the known which has an emptying effect by its very power of penetration. It should be characterized rather as the process of being lifted out of oneself and being drawn into the infinite mystery. This process of being 'abducted from oneself' is therefore such that it can be genuinely undergone only in loving acceptance of this mystery and within the unpredictable designs God has for us—in that freedom which is necessarily given together with this transcendence over oneself and everything individual. To the extent in which man is *matter,* he grasps himself and the environment necessarily belonging to him in so far as the act of this return to himself—in the experience of his orientation to a mystery which must be accepted lovingly—always and primarily takes place only in an encounter with the individual, with what shows itself spontaneously and with the concrete which cannot be disposed of but is given unavoidably (though only to a limited extent). As matter, man experiences himself and the world he directly encounters precisely in so far as he is a fact, someone who is added to, someone who is pre-defined for himself and who as such is someone not yet fully penetrated; and precisely in so far as, in the midst of knowledge (understood as self-possession), there stands what is alien and each individual, something foreign and something unaccountable to himself. Matter is the condition of possibility for the objectively 'other' which the world and man are in their own eyes. Matter is the condition of what we experience directly as space and time (precisely when we cannot objectify this for ourselves); it is the condition of that otherness which estranges man from himself, which forms the requirement for the possibility of a direct intercommunication with other spiritual existents in space and time—i.e. in history. Matter is the basis for the pre-required existence of the 'other' considered as the material of freedom.

This condition of mutual relatedness between spirit and matter is not simply a static condition, but has itself a history. Man, considered as a spirit becoming conscious of himself, experiences his pre-established nature in otherness; he experiences his self-estrangement as something having temporal duration and as belonging to natural history; he comes to himself as someone who has already existed in time both in himself and in his surroundings (which also belong to him and his constitution). And conversely, this temporal materiality understood as the pre-history of man considered as reflex freedom must be understood as being orientated to the history of the human spirit. This last point should be expressed a little more exactly. Without separating them from each other, we have tried to understand spirit and matter as two correlated elements of the one man, elements which are inseparable from each other and yet are not reducible to each other. This irreducible pluralism of elements in the one man can also be stated in such a way as to express a difference of nature between spirit and matter. To make this distinction is of paramount importance and significance, for only in this way do one's eyes remain open to all the dimensions of the one man in all their immense and indeed infinite extent. But, as we have already pointed out, this difference of nature must not be misunderstood to mean that these two elements are opposed in nature or absolutely different in nature or indifferent to each other. Starting from ths inner interrelation between these two factors and concentrating on the *temporal* duration of this relationship between these two factors, it may be said without scruple that matter develops out of its inner being in the direction of the spirit. But we must not leave the question there—we must go on to make this statement a little clearer still and defend this way of speaking by making it intelligible. First of all, if there is any 'becoming' at all (and this is not merely a fact of experience but a basic axiom of theology itself, since man's freedom, responsibility and perfecting by his own responsible activity would otherwise have no real meaning at all), then 'becoming' in its true form cannot be conceived simply as a 'becoming *other*' in which a reality becomes different but does not become more. True 'becoming' must be conceived as something 'becoming *more*', as the coming into being of more reality, as an effective attainment of a greater fullness of being. This 'more' must not be imagined, however, as something simply added to what was there before, but, on the one hand, must be something really effected by what was there before and, on the other hand, must be the inner increase of being proper to the previously existing reality. This means, however, that if it is really to be taken seriously, 'becoming' must be understood as a real self-transcendence, a surpassing of self or active filling up of the empty. This notion of active self-transcendence—self-transcendence by which an existing and acting being actively approaches to the higher perfection still lacking to it—must not, however, turn non-being into the very ground of being and turn emptiness as such into the source of fullness—in other words, we must not violate the metaphysical principle of causality. Consequently (and I am merely summarizing very briefly all the extensive considerations which would be necessary here) this self-transcendence cannot be thought of in any other way than as an event which takes place by the power of the absolute fullness of being. On the one hand, this absolute fullness of being must be thought of as something so *interior* to the finite being moving towards its fulfilment that the finite being is empowered by it to achieve a really *active self*-transcendence and does not merely receive this new reality passively as something effected by God. On the other hand, this power of self-transcendence must at the same time be thought of as so distinct from finite, acting being that it is *not* permissible to conceive it as a constitutive principle of the *essence* of this finite being achieving itself. For otherwise, if the absoluteness of being—which gives efficacy to a being and empowers it to be effective—were to constitute the nature of the finite acting being, then this being would no longer be capable of any real becoming in time and history, since it would already possess the absolute fullness of being as something absolutely proper to it. These reflections cannot be developed further here; above all, it cannot be explained here how the experience of spiritual transcendence, understood as the movement of the evolving spirit, directly shows this dialectic as something experienced. In other words, it is impossible to explain here how being is both absolutely the most interior and yet the most foreign factor of this movement and how, in this dialectic of its relationship to the finite evolving spirit, it can support the whole of this movement and yet allow it to be the movement of this spirit itself. We must content ourselves with stating the thesis that the notion of an *active self-transcendence* (in which the 'self' and the 'transcendence' are to be taken equally seriously) is a necessary notion in our thought if the phenomenon of becoming—which is possible, since it exists—is to be saved. Let us simply remark in this connection that this notion of self-transcendence includes also transcendence into what is substantially new, i.e. the leap

to a higher *nature*. To exclude the latter would mean emptying
the notion of self-transcendence of its content; it would mean
that one could no longer evaluate certain phenomena with an
untroubled mind, e.g. such notions as the procreation of a
new human being by the parents in what appears at first sight
to be a merely biological event. An essential self-transcendence,
however, is no more an intrinsic contradiction than (simple)
self-transcendence, as soon as one allows it to occur in the
dynamism of the power of the absolute being which is within
the creature and yet is not proper to its nature—in other words,
in what in theological language is called God's conservation of
the creature and his concurrence with its activity, in the inner
and permanent need of all finite reality to be held in being
and in operation, in the being of becoming, in the being of self-
becoming—in short, in the self-transcendence which belongs to
the nature of every finite being. Given, however, that this
notion is a metaphysically legitimate one, and that the world
is one and thus has one history, and that in this one but not
always already all-comprehensive world everything is not
always already present from the very beginning—then there is
no necessary reason for disputing the fact that matter has
evolved in the direction of life and of man in that self-transcendence whose notional content we have just now been trying
to bring out. This is, of course, a question of an *essential* self-
transcendence, for we do not mean to deny or obscure in any
way the fact that matter, life, consciousness and spirit are not
the same thing. Quite the contrary. But precisely this difference,
this essential difference, does not exclude development, if there
is becoming and if becoming does or can mean a really active
self-transcendence and if self-transcendence does or can mean at
least *also* a self-transcendence of nature. And what is grasped
in this way, as logically possible by an *a-priori* reflection, is also
confirmed as real by better and more comprehensively observed
facts. It is not merely a question here of an inner solidarity of
spirit and matter. We must also take into consideration the
known history of the cosmos as it has been investigated and
described by the modern natural sciences: this history is seen
more and more as one homogeneous history of matter, life and
man. This one history does not exclude differences of nature

but on the contrary includes them in its concept, since history is precisely not the permanence of the same but rather the becoming of something entirely new and not merely of something other. These differences of nature also do not exclude the fact of there being one history, since history itself results precisely from an essential self-transcendence in which what was previously, surpasses itself in order to dissolve and conserve itself in very truth in the new which it itself has effected.

In so far as the self-transcending always remains present in the particular goal of its self-transcendence, and in so far as the higher order always embraces the lower as contained in it, it is clear that the lower always precedes the actual event of self-transcendence and prepares the way for it by the development of its own reality and order; it is clear that the lower always moves slowly towards the boundary line in its history which it then crosses in its actual self-transcendence—that boundary line which is only seen to have been clearly crossed from the vantage point of a clearer development of the new condition, without it being possible however to give an absolutely clear definition of this line itself. Of course, these are all very abstract and vague statements. Naturally, it would in itself be desirable to show more concretely what common traits are to be found in the evolution of material, living and spiritual beings—to show (more exactly) how the merely material is a prelude in its own dimensions to the higher dimension of life, and how the latter in its dimension is a prelude to the spirit in its ever greater advance towards the border line to be crossed by self-transcendence. Certainly, if we really postulate a unified history of all reality, it would be necessary to indicate which permanent formal structures of this total history pertain in common to the basic constitution of matter, life and spirit, and how even the highest (even though it is *essentially* new) can still be understood as a change of something previously existing.

But all this would lead the theologian and philosopher too far afield from his own sphere and would necessitate his developing these basic structures of the one history by the more *a-posteriori* method proper to the natural sciences and with the aid of concepts such as are developed by Teilhard, for instance. Obviously this cannot be the task of the theologian—

and particularly not in the present context. It should be noted here, however, that the theologian not only can admit (even in the case of all material reality) an analogous notion of self-possession—which finds its fullest natural expression in con-sciousness—but also as a good thomistic philosopher he really *ought* to admit it. For what he as a thomist calls the 'form' in every being is for him also essentially the 'Idea'; and that reality which we call the 'unconscious' in the ordinary and—in its place—quite correct sense, is from the metaphysical point of view the kind of being which possesses only its own 'Idea'; it is something which, being caught up in itself, has only itself and its own 'Idea' and hence—is not conscious. Seen in this way, it becomes understandable even from the thomistic point of view that a really higher, more complex organization can appear also as a step towards consciousness, and finally towards self-consciousness, even though *self*-con-sciousness at least does include a real essential self-transcendence of the material as opposed to its previous condition.

If man is thus the self-transcendence of living matter, then the history of Nature and spirit forms an inner, graded unity in which natural history towards man, continues in him as *his* history, is conserved and surpassed in him and hence reaches its proper goal with and in the history of the human spirit. In so far as this history of Nature is dissolved in man into freedom, this natural history reaches its goal in the history of the free spirit. In so far as the history of man always still includes the natural history of living matter, it is always still supported—even in the midst of its freedom—by the structures and necessities of this material world. Hence, in so far as man is not *only* the spiritual *observer* of nature—since he is a part of it and must precisely continue its history too—his history is not only a history of culture (in the sense of an ideological history situated above natural history) but is also an active alteration of this material world itself. Thus, man and nature can reach their one common goal only by activity which is spiritual and by spirituality which is activity. It is true, of course, that precisely because this goal corresponds to the transcendence of man into the absolute reality of God who is the infinite mystery—and because it consists in the finite fullness of God—this goal itself remains hidden and unattainable for the natural powers of man. It can be reached only by accepting the fact of its being hidden and withdrawn. In so far as this history of the cosmos is the history of the free spirit, this history—like that of man—is posed in freedom as guilt and trial. In so far as this history of freedom, however, always remains based on the pre-determined structures of the living world, and in so far as (as the Christian professes) the freedom-history of the spirit is enveloped by the grace of God which perseveres victoriously unto the good, the Christian knows that this history of the cosmos as a whole will find its real consummation despite, in and through the freedom of man, and that its finality as a whole will also be its consummation.

II

Before we can even think of connecting these initial assessments and basic conceptions with Christology, we must first try to state more exactly what stage the world has reached in man.

First of all, it must be stated that—despite the wonderful results and perspectives of his science—even the modern natural scientist still remains to a large extent confined within the limits of a pre-scientific as well as pre-philosophic and pre-theological outlook. For very often he still maintains even today that it is a peculiarly characteristic part of the spirit of the natural sciences to regard man as only a weak, fortuitous being exposed to a Nature quite indifferent to it and passing its existence in this world as a kind of day-fly until it is swallowed up again by a 'blind' Nature which had produced it quite by accident in one of her careless moods. This contradicts not only metaphysics and Christian thought but also natural science itself. If man exists, if he is the 'product' of Nature, if he does not come onto the scene just at any time at all but at the end of a development which, at least partially, only he can steer by going out to meet this his producer and by himself objectifying and transforming it—then Nature does become conscious of itself in *him,* then Nature is planned for him, since 'chance' is a word without any real meaning for the natural scientist who concludes from the result to a movement orientated towards it. If things are not regarded in this way, then there is right away no sense in seeing the history of the cosmos and that of man as *one* history. One would sooner or later fall back into a platonic dualism. For a spirit who is thus regarded as a chance stranger on earth, will not for long let himself be despised and reproached as being unimportant and powerless. If the spirit is not regarded as the goal of Nature—if it is not seen that Nature found herself in him, in spite of all the physical powerlessness of the individual man—then the spirit will after a while be regarded more and more as merely the opponent of Nature who exists quite apart from it.

The characteristic which becomes reality in man, which reaches finite reality in him and into which matter transcends itself, is first of all the fact of being present to oneself and of being referred to the absolute totality of reality and to its first ground as such. There then flows from this the possibility of a real objectification of individual experience and of the individual object, which thus becomes capable of being separated from any immediate reference to man in his vital sphere. If this is seen to be the end of the history of the cosmos, then it can be said absolutely that the established world finds itself in man, and that in man it makes itself its own object and is no longer referred to its ground merely as presupposed behind it but rather as an imposed task before it. This assertion is not invalidated by the objection that such concentrations of the spatio-temporal dispersion of the world into itself and within its foundation are present in man only in very formal, almost empty beginnings, and that this could be conceived to be present in nonhuman spiritual persons (monads) which would be much better suited to accomplishing this, without being—like man—subjects of the totality and self-presence of the world in such a way that they have to be at the same time also a *part*-factor of this world. Such beings may exist. The Christian is even sure that they do exist, and calls them angels. But precisely this concentrating, synthesizing—even though still very much incipient—self-consciousness of the totality of the cosmos in the individual man is something which can occur many times over (and each time in an absolutely unique manner), particularly if it springs from a part-factor considered as a spatio-temporal individual magnitude of the cosmos. Hence one cannot say (especially when one bears in mind the uniqueness of each act of freedom) that this cosmic self-consciousness need not be given in man or can be given only once. It occurs each time, in its own unique way, in each individual man. The one material cosmos is, as it were, the *one* body of the *multifarious* self-presence of this self-same cosmos and of its orientation to its absolute and infinite foundation. Even though this cosmic bodily presence of the innumerable personal self-consciousnesses in which the cosmos can become conscious of itself begins to appear (like man's own bodily presence in the narrower sense) only very tentatively in the self-consciousness and freedom of the individual human being, it is nevertheless present in every man as something which is intended to be and can become actual. For in his corporeality, every man is an element of the cosmos which cannot really be delimited and cut off from it, and in this corporeality he communicates with the whole cosmos in *such* a way that through this corporeality of man taken as the other element of belonging to the spirit, the cosmos really presses forward to this self-presence in the spirit. This self-presence of the cosmos in the spirit of the individual man, which is still in the process of becoming and in its very initial stage, has its still-continuing history; this history is still taking place in the internal and external history both of the individual and of humanity as a whole, in the act of thought and in the self-present external act, both individually and collectively. We are certainly again and again under the impression that nothing final will ever come of this unnecessarily long and laborious process by which the cosmos finds itself in man. For this process seems always to dissipate itself again, and instead a kind of hidden contrariness against self-consciousness—a kind of will to the unconscious—seems always to assert itself again. But once we presuppose that evolution proceeds in the final analysis in a one-way direction and ordination (and that anything else makes the notion of evolution quite unthinkable from the outset since something which simply wants to return again to the beginning and has no other tendency at all, would not have left this beginning in the first place), then this process by which the cosmos gradually becomes conscious of itself in man—in the

individual totality and freedom which each individual realizes—
must also have a final result. The result seems to disappear and
dissipate itself, it seems to fall back into the misty beginnings
of the cosmos and of its dispersion, only because we who exist
at this *present* determined moment in space and time are quite
incapable of experiencing the final coming to itself of such a
monadic unity of the world and the uniqueness of the fully
grasped totality of the cosmos at our particular point in space
and time. It must however exist. In Christian language we
usually call it the immortality of the soul; it must, however, be
clearly seen here that this immortality, if it is properly understood, is precisely a (formal, and of itself empty) finality and
consummation of this very process by which the cosmos finds
itself, and hence must not be confused with the escape of a
spiritual soul—an alien in this cosmos—from the totality of that
world which is always also material (and is so precisely in the
service of the spirit) and has always had and still has also a
material history.

　According to Christian teaching, this self-transcendence of
the cosmos in man towards its own totality and foundation,
which has itself a history, has really reached its final consummation only when the cosmos in the spiritual creature, its goal
and its height, is not merely something set apart from its
foundation—something created—but something which receives
the ultimate self-communication of its ultimate ground itself, in
that moment when this direct self-communication of God is
given to the spiritual creature in what we—looking at the historical pattern of this self-communication—call grace and glory
(in its consummation). God does not merely create something
other than himself—he also gives himself to this other. The
world receives God, the Infinite and the ineffable mystery, to
such an extent that he himself becomes its innermost life. The
concentrated, always unique self-possession of the cosmos in
each individual spiritual person, and in his transcendence
towards the absolute ground of his reality, takes place when this
absolute ground itself becomes directly interior to that which is
grounded by it. The end is the absolute beginning. This beginning is not infinite emptiness or nothingness, but the fullness
which alone explains the divided and that which begins, which

alone can support a becoming and which alone can give to that which begins the real power of movement towards something more developed and at the same time more intimate. But by the very fact that this movement of the development of the cosmos is thus carried along both from the outset and in all its phases by the urge towards ever greater fullness and intimacy and towards an ever closer and more conscious relationship to its ground, the message which says that there will be an absolutely direct contact with this infinite cause, is already given in this movement—not indeed as something which must necessarily be recognized from this movement in all its phases, but at least as something which can certainly be more and more approximately envisaged as the absolute goal of this development. If the history of the cosmos is always basically a spiritual history —the desire to become conscious of itself and of its cause—then the direct relationship to God in his self-communication to his spiritual creature, and in it to the cosmos in general as the goal which corresponds to the meaning of this development, is basically an indisputable fact, provided that this development is allowed to any degree at all to reach its own absolute goal and is not merely moved by it as something unattainable. We, as single and physically conditioned individuals, experience only the uttermost beginning of this movement towards this infinite goal. Yet we are after all beings who, even in that consciousness with which we engage in our physico-biological fight for existence and for our earthly dignity, live and act (in distinction to the brutes) out of a formal anticipation of the whole. We are those even who in the experience of grace experience the event of the promise of the absolute nearness of the all-founding mystery (even though this experience is an unobjectified one). And this fact gives us the right to that courage of faith in the fulfilment of the coming history of the cosmos and of each individual cosmic consciousness, which consists in the direct experience of God as he communicates himself in a most real and unveiled manner. Such a statement also implies naturally and most radically in the very nature of things the preservation of the ineffable mystery which reigns over our existence. For if God himself, the inexpressible infinity of mystery, is and becomes the reality of our perfection—and if the world understands itself in its most proper truth only when it commits itself radically to this infinite mystery—then this message does not merely say this or that, sayings which stand as *one* content of expression *among* others, and fall under a common co-ordinated system of concepts. Rather, it states that before and behind every individual thing, which has to be incorporated into an over-all order and in view of which the sciences engage in their search, there always stands and is already presupposed the infinite mystery—and it states that in this abyss, the origin and the end are the beatifying end. Man may feel irritated by a seemingly excessive demand and may declare himself to be uninterested in this abyss of the beginning and the end—he may try to take refuge in the comprehensible clarity of science, regarding this as the only sphere of his existence suited to his powers . . . yet the question of the Infinite is one which envelops man and is one which alone answers itself. Even if he were capable of it on the surface of his objective consciousness, man may not and cannot leave this question unsolved in the all-supporting and all-nourishing depths of the really spiritual person. For this question exists: there is nothing which could answer it from outside but rather it is a question which answers itself when accepted in love. It is a question which moves man; only when he concerns himself with this movement which belongs to the world and to the spirit, does he become really conscious of himself, of God and of his goal in which the beginning is given directly.

III

Only in the light of all we have seen can we now determine the place of Christology in this evolutionary world-picture.

We presuppose, therefore, that the goal of the world consists in God's communicating himself to it. We presuppose that the whole dynamism which God has instituted in the very heart of the world's becoming by self-transcendence (and yet not as that which constitutes its nature) is really always meant already as the beginning and first step towards this self-communication and its acceptance by the world. In exactly what way are we then to conceive this self-communication of God to the spiritual creature in general and to all those subjects in which the cosmos becomes conscious of itself, of its condition and of its basic cause? To understand this, it must first of all be pointed out that these spiritual subjectivities of the cosmos signify freedom. We can only state this baldly here and must abstain from going into the transcendental reasons for it. Once we presuppose this, however, we presuppose also that this history of the self-consciousness of the cosmos is always necessarily also a history of the inter-communication of these spiritual subjects. For the fact that the cosmos becomes conscious of itself in the spiritual subjects must mean above all and necessarily that these subjects—in which the whole is present to itself each time after the manner proper to that subject—become more closely associated with each other, as otherwise the 'becoming present to itself' would separate and not unite. God's self-communication is, therefore, communication of freedom and inter-communication between the many cosmic subjectivities. Hence this self-communication necessarily turns in the direction of a free history of the human race, and can only happen in *free* acceptance by these free subjects and in a *common* history. God's communication of himself does not suddenly become uncosmic—directed merely to an isolated, separate subjectivity— but is given to the human race and is historical. This event of self-communication must therefore be thought of as an event which takes place historically in a specifically spatio-temporal manner and which then turns to everyone and calls upon their freedom. In other words, this self-communication must have a permanent beginning and must find in this a permanent guar-antee of its reality so that it can rightly demand a free decision for the acceptance of this divine self-communication. (In this connection it should be mentioned briefly that this free accep-tance or refusal on the part of individual free beings does not really determine the actual event of self-communication but, more exactly, only determines the attitude adopted by the spiritual creature towards it; of course, normally only that is called self-communication which is accepted freely and hence beatifies, i.e. only the successful, accepted self-communication of God.)

From this there follows first of all the explanation of the notion of Saviour. We give the title of Saviour simply to that historical person who, coming in space and time, signifies that beginning of God's absolute communication of himself which inaugurates this self-communication for all men as something happening irrevocably and which shows this to be happening. This notion does not imply that God's self-communication to the world in its spiritual subjectivity begins *in time* only with this person. This does not need to be the case at all; it can quite easily be conceived as beginning before the actual coming of the Saviour, indeed as co-existent with the whole spiritual history of humanity and of the world—as was actually the case according to Christian teaching. The historical person whom we call Saviour is that subjectivity in whom this process of God's absolute self-communication to the spiritual world is *irrevocably* present as a whole; through him this self-communication can be clearly recognized as something irrevocable, and in him it reaches its climax, in so far as this climax must be thought of as a moment in the total history of the human race and in so far as this climax is not simply identified with the totality of the spiritual world subject to God's communication of himself (which is a different, though absolutely legitimate notion of the climax of the divine self-communication). For, in so far as this self-communication must be conceived as free on the part of God and of the history of the human race which must accept it, it is quite legitimate to conceive of an event by which this self-communication and acceptance attains an irrevocable and irreversible character in history—an event in which the history of this self-communication realizes its proper nature and in which it breaks through—without it thereby becoming necessary that this history of God's self-communication to the human race has already simply found its end and conclusion both in its extension and in regard to the spatio-temporal plurality of the history of humanity. It must be noted in this connection that this moment in which the irreversible character of this historical self-communication of God becomes manifest refers equally to the communication itself and to its acceptance. Both these factors are included in the notion of the Saviour. In so far as a historical movement already lives in virtue of its end even in its beginnings—since the dynamism of its own being desires its end, carries its goal in itself as that towards which it is striving and really unveils itself in its own proper being only in this goal—it is absolutely legitimate, and indeed necessary, to think of the whole movement of God's communication of himself to the human race (even when it takes place during the time *before* the event which makes it irrevocable in the Saviour) as something based on this event—in other words, as something based on the Saviour. The whole movement of this history lives only for the moment of arrival at its goal and climax—it lives only for its entry into the event which makes it irreversible—in short, it lives for the one whom we call Saviour. This Saviour, who represents the climax of this self-communication, must therefore be at the same time God's absolute pledge by self-communication to the spiritual creature as a whole *and* the acceptance of this self-communication by this Saviour; only then is there an utterly irrevocable self-communication on both sides, and only thus is it present in the world in a historically communicative manner.

Seen in this light, it now becomes possible to understand what is really meant by the doctrine of the Hypostatic Union and of the Incarnation of the divine Logos and how, following quite naturally from what has been said, it fits into an evolutionist view of the world. In the first place, the Saviour is himself a historical moment in God's saving action exercised on the world. He is a moment of the history of God's communication of himself to the world—in the sense that he is a part of this history of the cosmos itself. He must not be merely God acting on the world but must be a part of the cosmos itself in its very climax. This is in fact stated in the Christian dogma: Jesus is true man; he is truly a part of the earth, truly a moment in the biological evolution of this world, a moment of human natural history, for he is born of woman; he is a man who in his spiritual, human and finite subjectivity is just like us, a receiver of that self-communication of God by grace which we affirm of all men—and hence of the cosmos—as the climax of development in which the world comes absolutely into its own presence and into the direct presence of God. Jesus is the one who—by what we call his obedience, his prayer and the freely accepted destiny of his death—has achieved also the acceptance of his divinely given grace and direct presence to God which he possesses as man. All this is Catholic Dogma. If one is not to fall into a false belief or heresy, one must not think of the God-man as if God or his Logos had put on a kind of livery for the purpose of his saving treatment of man, or as if he had disguised himself, as it were, and had given himself merely an external appearance to enable him to show himself in the world. No, Jesus is truly man. He has absolutely everything which belongs to the nature of man; he has (also) a finite subjective nature in which the world becomes present to itself and which has a radical directness to God which, like ours, rests on that self-communication by God in grace and glory which we too possess. It must also be underlined in this connection that the statement of God's *Incarnation*—of his becoming *material*—is the most basic statement of Christology. This is not self-evident. This was not at all in keeping with the 'tendencies of the day' and the spirit of the age in which the dogma of the Incarnation was defined. If a God—who, as spiritual transcendence, is conceived as simply and absolutely superior to the material world—draws near to the world in order to save it, then he must be conceived as a God who, as a spirit, draws carefully nearer to the spirit of the world from outside, meets the *spirit* and finally, if at all, also takes effect in this way—psychothera-peutically as it were—for the salvation of the material world. And this was in fact the view adopted by the most dangerous heresy against which primitive Christianity had to fight, i.e. the view of Gnosticism. Christianity, however, teaches differently. According to Christian teaching, God takes hold of the world in the Incarnation and in the fact of the Logos becoming part of the material world—or better—precisely in that one point in which matter becomes present to itself and the spirit has its own being in the objectification of the material: in short, in the unity of a human nature. In Jesus, the Logos bears the matter just as much as the soul, and this matter is a part of the reality and the history of the cosmos. Theology even stresses the fact that in that phase of the human existence of Jesus during which, on account of his death, there existed a different relationship between his 'soul' and his 'body' than during the period of the biological life familiar to us, the relationship of the Logos to his body did not become any looser on account of this greater distance between body and soul. The divine Logos himself both really creates and accepts this corporeality—which is a part of the world— *as his* own reality; he brings it into existence as something other than himself in such a way, therefore, that this very materiality expresses *him,* the Logos himself, and lets him be present in his world. His taking hold of this part of the one material-spiritual world-reality may quite legitimately be thought of as the climax of that dynamism in which the Word of God who supports everything, supports the self-transcendence of the world as a whole. For we are quite entitled to conceive what we call creation as a part-moment in that process of God's coming-into-the-world by which God actually, even though freely, gives expression to himself in his Word become part of the world and of matter; we are perfectly entitled to think of the creation and of the Incarnation, not as two disparate, adjacent acts of God *'ad extram'* which in the actual world are due to two quite separate original acts of God, but as two moments and phases in the real world of the unique, even though internally differentiated, process of God's self-renunciation and self-expression into what is other than himself. For such a conception can certainly appeal to a most ancient Christian tradition of 'Christocentricity' as found in the history of Christian theology, and it does not deny in any way that God *could* have created a world without an Incarnation, i.e. that he could have denied the final climax of grace and Incarnation to the self-transcendence of the material in the spirit and towards God by His own dynamism inherent in the world (without thereby becoming constitutive of its being). For every such essential self-surpassing always stands in a relationship of grace—the unexpected and the gratuitous—to its lower stage, even though it is the 'goal' of this movement. But we have run ahead of the actual course of our reflections. At this stage we are merely concerned with understanding that the Saviour, whom we comprehend as the climax of the history of the cosmos, is indeed the climax of this history itself (but of course within that climax of history itself which allows the whole world of the spirit to transcend into God) and that the Christian dogma of the Incarnation tells us exactly this: Jesus is truly man with everything this implies, i.e. with man's finiteness, his being-in-the-world, his materiality and his participation in the history of this cosmos which leads him through the narrow gates of death.

That is one side of the question. Now we must look also at the other side. We have already said that the very event of salvation must take place in the world and in its history in such a way that God's self-communication to the spiritual creature becomes something definitive and irrevocable and becomes present in such a way that this self-communication of God to spiritual creation is seen to be given in the light of a unique, individual history. If we presuppose this, however, as the 'normal' consummation of the history of the cosmos and of the spirit, without implying that this development must *necessarily* go this far or has already done so, then we must say that this limit-notion of the Saviour implies that notion of the hypostatic unity of God and man which constitutes the real content of the Christian dogma of the Incarnation.

This is perhaps the point where we reach the real crux of the problem which runs through the whole of our reflections. And so we must not rush on but must exercise a little patience. We want first of all to clarify a little more what exactly we are *asking* now. It seems to me that we should have no particular difficulty in representing the history of the world and of the spirit to ourselves as the history of a self-transcendence into the life of God—a self-transcendence which, in this its final and highest phase, is identical with an absolute self-communication of God expressing the same process but now looked at from God's side. This final and absolute self-transcendence of the spirit into God must, however, be conceived as something which happens in all *spiritual* subjects. In the nature of things, one could of course think that a real self-transcendence does not take in every 'specimen' of the original state but only in a certain few, just as in the biological evolution there survive, side by side with the new and higher forms, certain specimens of the lower forms from which the higher are derived. But in man's case this is not rationally conceivable, since man is 'by nature' and by his very being the possibility of transcendence become conscious of itself—the self-conscious reference to the absolute and the knowledge about the infinite possibility. If

309

the accomplishment of this final self-transcendence is granted generally (i.e. to other similar spiritual subjects), then it can hardly be refused to such beings in individual cases. But be that as it may, the Christian revelation tells us that all men are offered this self-transcendence as a real possibility of their individual existence, one to which they can close themselves only by guilt. Hence, in accordance with the characteristic of the spiritual being, the end taken as the perfection of the spirit and of the world must be regarded as something intended for *all* spiritual subjects. And in so far as Christianity understands grace and glory as the direct self-communication of God, it also professes this insurpassable consummation to belong to *all* men (and angels). How then does the doctrine of the Hypostatic Union of a determined *single* human nature with God's Logos fit into this basic conception? Is this to be conceived merely as a *proper,* still higher stage of an essentially newer and higher kind of divine self-communication to the creature, which this time is given only in one single 'case'? Or is it possible to conceive that, even though this Hypostatic Union is given only once in its essential characteristics, it is nevertheless precisely the way in which the divinization of the spiritual creature is and *must* be carried out if it is to happen at all? In other words, is the Hypostatic Union a higher stage in which the gift of grace given to the spiritual creature is surpassed (even though it is also 'conserved') or is it a peculiar moment in this process of the granting of grace which cannot really be conceived without this Hypostatic Union taking place on account of it?

We hope that the significance of this question for our subject as a whole is clear. For if the Incarnation is to be regarded as an absolutely proper and new rung in the hierarchy of world-realities which quite simply surpasses all the world-realities given so far or to be given in the future yet without being itself necessary for these lower stages themselves, i.e. without being the condition and possibility of the general granting of grace to the spiritual creature, then this could mean one of two things. Under this presupposition, either the Incarnation could still be seen as the climax surpassing all the other world-realities arranged in ascending layers, so that it could be positively fitted into an evolutionary world-view—or both thoughts must be abandoned, i.e. it could no longer be thought that the Incarnation of the Logos is the climax of the development of the world, towards which the whole world is orientated even though it remains free in grace—and it could also no longer be thought that the Incarnation fits into an evolutionary picture of the world. But it is almost impossible or even absolutely impossible to see how one could understand the Incarnation as a higher or even the highest stage in the reality or development of the world in *such* a way that it also appears as the goal and end of this world-reality, without the aid of the theory that the Incarnation is itself already an intrinsic element and condition of the general gift of grace by which God gives himself to the spiritual creature. The Incarnation would, of course, always appear as the highest stage in this world-reality because it is the hypostatic unity of God and a world-reality. But this does not yet make it intelligible as the goal and end, as the climax which can indeed be envisaged from below but always only as something unreachable. This seems possible only by presupposing that the Incarnation itself is to be made intelligible *in* its uniqueness and *in* the degree of reality given by it (in and not despite this uniqueness) as an intrinsic and necessary element in the process of God's giving himself in grace to the world as a whole and not only as an actually utilized means for this process (this no Christian can deny) which could quite easily have happened in some other way, a way in which it would not be shared in itself by the Incarnation as such.

The theologian who puts this question in this way can first of all take note of the fact that the Hypostatic Union takes effect interiorly *for* the human nature of the Logos precisely in what, and really only in what, the same theology prescribes for *all* men as their goal and consummation, viz. the direct vision of God enjoyed by Christ's created human soul. This same theology emphasizes the fact that the Incarnation occurred 'for the sake of our salvation', that it does not give any real increase in reality and life to the divine nature of the Logos, and that the prerogatives which accrued interiorly to the human reality of Jesus on account of the Hypostatic Union are of the same essential kind as those intended by grace also for other spiritual subjects. This fact alone should make us careful in answering the question posed. Theology has already tried to clarify this problem for itself by asking the in itself, of course, unreal question as to what, for instance, would have to be preferred if one had to choose: the Hypostatic Union without the direct vision of God or this vision of God—and decides for the second alternative. It can be clearly seen from this also how difficult it is to determine more exactly the relationship between the kind of consummation which the Christian faith professes to be common to all men and the unique consummation of human possibility (in the sense of *potentia obedientialis*) which we profess by the doctrine of the Hypostatic Union. And yet such a more exact definition of this relationship is demanded by the question we have posed ourselves, viz. whether we can, must or may think of what we call the Incarnation of the Logos as the manner in which the divinization of the spiritual creature in general is realized, so that we implicitly envisage this Hypostatic Union at the same time as we see the history of the cosmos and of the spirit arriving at the point at which are found both the absolute self-transcendence of the spirit into God and the absolute self-communication of God to all spiritual subjects by grace and glory. Hence the thesis towards which we are working purports to show that, even though the Hypostatic Union is in its proper nature a unique event and—when seen in itself— is certainly the highest conceivable event, it is nevertheless an intrinsic factor of the whole process of the bestowal of grace on the spiritual creature in general. Why is this so? We have already pointed out that, if this total event of the divinizing sanctification of humanity attains its consummation, it must be a concrete, tangible phenomenon in history (in other words, it must not suddenly become a-cosmic) and hence must be an event in such a way as to spread out spatio-temporally from one point (in other words, it must not destroy the unity of mankind and men's essential community and intercommunication but must on the contrary come into existence within these very factors); it must be an irrevocable reality in which God's self-communication proves itself not merely as a temporary offer, but as an absolute offer accepted by man; it must (in accordance with the nature of the spirit) become conscious of itself. Whenever God—by his absolute self-communication—

brings about man's self-transcendence into God, in such a way that both these factors form the irrevocable promise made to all men which has already reached its consummation in this man, there we have a hypostatic union. When we think of 'hypostatic union', we must not simply remain attached to the imagined model of any sort of 'unity' or connection. To grasp the proper nature of this particular unity, it is also not enough simply to say that, on account of this unity, the human reality must also be attributed in all truth to the divine subject of the Logos. For this is precisely the question:—*why* is this possible, and *how* are we to conceive this unity which justifies such a statement of the 'communication of idioms'? This 'assumption' and 'unification' has the nature of a self-communication; there is 'assumption' so that God's reality may be communicated to what is assumed, viz. the human nature (and in the first place the human nature of Christ). But this very communication which is aimed at by this 'assumption' is *the* communication by what we call grace and glory—and the latter are intended for all. It must not be objected that *this* (latter) communication is possible even without a hypostatic union, since it does in fact occur without it in our own case. For in us this communication is possible and effected precisely by this union and acceptance as it occurs in the Hypostatic Union. And, theologically speaking at least, there is nothing against the assumption that grace and hypostatic union can only be thought of together and that, as a unity, they signify one and the same *free* decision of God to institute the supernatural order of salvation. In Christ, God's self-communicating takes place basically for all men, and there is 'hypostatic union' precisely in so far as this *unsurpassable* self-communication of God 'is there' irrevocably in a historically tangible and self-conscious manner. Once more we ask: why? Apart from the case of the Beatific Vision (and perhaps even this is no different in this respect from other cases, but we cannot deal with this here), every self-manifestation of God takes place through some finite reality—through a word, an event, etc., which belongs to the finite realm of creatures. As long as this finite mediation of the divine self-manifestation, however, is not in the strictest sense a divine reality itself, it is basically transitory and surpassable (since it is finite) and is not in this finiteness simply the reality of God itself; and thus can be surpassed by God himself simply by positing a new finite reality. Hence, if the reality in which God's absolute self-communication is pledged and accepted for the whole of humanity and thus becomes 'present' for us (i.e. Christ's reality) is to be really the final and unsurpassable divine self-communication, then it must be said that it is not only posited by God but is God himself. The pledge itself cannot be anything else than a human reality which has been absolutely sanctified by grace. For a mere word would not be the actual event of self-communication but would merely tell us about it: in other words, it would not be in any sense (since the event itself in its openness, and not a word *about* it, is the primary proclamation of itself) the *actual* and really primary communication addressed to us about this self-communication made to us. If this is so, and if this pledge must be truly and absolutely God himself, then it must be a human reality which belongs absolutely to God—in other words, exactly what we call 'Hypostatic Union'. Hence, if we may put it this way, the Hypostatic Union does not differ from our grace by what is pledged in it, for this is grace in both cases (even in the case of Jesus). But it differs from our grace by the fact that Jesus is our pledge, and we ourselves are not the pledge but the recipients of God's pledge to us. But the unity of the pledge, and the inseparability of this pledge from the one who pledges (indeed, pledges *himself to us!*) must be conceived in accordance with the peculiar nature of the pledge. If the real pledge made to us is precisely the very human reality itself which has been given grace and in which and through which God pledges himself to us in his grace, then the unity of the one who pledges and the pledge cannot be considered as a merely 'moral' one—as for instance the unity between a human 'word' (or something similar which is merely a sign) and God— but must be conceived as an *irrevocable* unity between this human reality and God making a separation between the proclamation and the giver of this proclamation impossible— which, in other words, makes of the really humanly proclaimed and the pledge given to us, a reality of God himself. And this is precisely what is meant by hypostatic union. It means this and, properly speaking, nothing else: in the human reality of Jesus,

God's absolute saving purpose (the absolute event of God's self-communication to us) is simply, absolutely and irrevocably present; in it is present both the declaration made to us and its acceptance—something effected by God himself, a reality of God himself, unmixed and yet inseparable and hence irrevocable. This declaration, however, is the pledge of grace to us.

It is of course impossible here to pursue this initial consideration any further and to unfold the whole of Christology from this initial insight: an insight which would give us a much better understanding also of the rest of Christology. The time at our disposal is far too short for this. But such a study would show us that the genuine and properly understand doctrine of the Hypostatic Union has nothing in common with mythology. It would become clear that the monophysite interpretation of Christology adopted unconsciously and implicitly—and for that very reason all the more effectively—by many Christians, is really a misunderstanding.

IV

In conclusion, let us merely add a few remarks which will help us, at least to some extent, to round off our subject.

Up till now we have simply tried to fit Christology into the framework of an evolutionary world-view of a cosmos which evolves towards that spirit who attains absolute self-transcendence and perfection through and in an absolute self-communication given by God in grace and glory. Hence we have not so far spoken yet of guilt and redemption, i.e. liberation from sin. And yet the perspective of redemption and remission of sin is the perspective which would show us the Incarnation of the Logos in its clearest light. Does this mean that we have after all deviated in some unlawful way from the traditional Christology? We must at least make a few brief remarks concerning this question. It should be stated, first of all, that there is quite a long established school of thought among Catholic theologians (usually called the 'Scotist school') which has always stressed that the first and most basic motive for the Incarnation was not the blotting-out of sin but that the Incarnation was already the goal of the divine freedom even apart from any divine fore-knowledge of freely incurred guilt. This

School holds therefore that—seen as the free climax of God's self-expression and self-effacement into the otherness of the creature—the Incarnation is the most original act of God anticipating the will to create and (presupposing sin) to redeem, by including them, as it were, as two of its moments. In the light of this conception—which has never been objected to by the Church's *magisterium*—it is therefore impossible to say that the view of the Incarnation proposed by us could arouse some real misgivings on the part of the *magisterium*. In the Catholic Church it is freely permitted to see the Incarnation first of all, in God's primary intention, as the summit and height of the divine plan of creation, and not primarily and in the first place as the act of a mere restoration of a divine world-order destroyed by the sins of mankind, an order which God had conceived in itself without any Incarnation. It would be heretical, of course, to deny that the reality and the actual event of the Logos becoming a creature signify also the victory over sin. But this proposition itself does not determine its own 'place-value' (to put it this way) and it can be shown, as we will indicate in a moment, that the proposition concerning redemption from sin can be deduced quite freely, and without forcing things at all, from our own systematic starting-point. Secondly, the unity of the history of the spirit and of matter—of the one corporeal and spiritual cosmos—which was our starting point, need not and must not be misunderstood to mean that freedom, guilt and the possibility of ultimate perdition by final, self-willed self-closure to the meaning of the world and of its history have no place in this unity. It need not and must not be misunderstood to mean that in such a conception of the world guilt could be nothing more than a kind of unavoidable difficulty which is all part of the development and is included dialectically from the outset as one of the factors of this process. It is also well-known that Teilhard has been reproached with rendering sin harmless in this way—a reproach which H. de Lubac has surely invalidated most lucidly in his most recent book about Teilhard. If such an evolutionary world-view is properly understood, there is no real need to reproach it with this. The cosmos evolves towards the spirit, transcendence and freedom, it evolves in a really essential self-transcendence towards the spirit, the person and freedom. In that moment in which spirit and freedom have been attained in the cosmos, the history of the cosmos receives its structures and its interpretation from the spirit and from freedom and not from matter, in so far as the latter is still in a pre-spiritual way the otherness of the spirit as such. (And this is then true also of the whole cosmos, including its material part, a fact which a purely idealist world-view is completely incapable of explaining; and so by this very fact it reveals its insufficiency for the requirements of Christian theology.) But wherever there is freedom in and before the reality of the cosmos as a whole, and in a transcendence towards God, there can also be a guilt and freedom which closes itself against God: there can also be sin and the possibility of perdition. Whether, and to what extent, this possibility and its actualization are once more conquered by the greater freedom of God in his grace, is a different question again. In any case, it may not be said that freedom and a genuine guilt which can no longer be blotted out by man can have no place in such a conception of the world. Once we have presupposed and emphasized this, it is possible to understand, precisely on the basis of our conception, that in a history which, through the free grace of God has its goal in an absolute and irrevocable self-communication of God to the spiritual creature—in a self-communication which is finally established through its goal and climax, i.e. through the Incarnation—the redeeming power which overcomes sin is necessarily found precisely in this climax of the Incarnation and in the realization of this divine-human reality. The world and its history are from the outset based on the absolute will of God to communicate himself radically to the world. In this self-communication and in its climax (i.e. in the Incarnation), the world becomes the history of God himself. And so if and in so far as it is found in the world, sin is from the outset embraced by the will to forgive and the offer of divine self-communication becomes necessary. For, since on account of Christ this offer is not conditioned by sin, it becomes necessarily an offer of forgiveness and of victory over guilt; indeed, sin is permitted merely because, being finite human guilt, God knew it to remain always imprisoned within his absolute will regarding the world and his

offer of himself. This possibility of forgiveness does not orig-
inate from man—from 'Adam' as such or from the human stage
of history as such—but comes from that power of God's self-
communication on which, on the one hand, depends the development of the whole history of the cosmos and which, on the
other hand, becomes historically tangible from the outset in its
own identity and which, by establishing its own goal, becomes
manifest in the existence and existential realization of Christ.
And this is the meaning of the proposition which states that we
have been redeemed by Christ from our sins. This already becomes clear by the fact that this very decision of God, to give
existence to Christ and his saving work, is the basis of this
saving work and is not dependent on it; properly speaking, it is
not Christ's action which causes God's will to forgiveness, but
vice versa, and this redemption in Christ (one might also say:
in view of Christ) was already effective from the beginning of
humanity. Added to this is the fact that according to Catholic
teaching the 'redemption' and destruction of sin must not be
understood as a merely moral or legal transaction, or as a mere
acquittal from guilt, or as a mere nonreckoning of guilt. It is
the communication of divine grace and takes place in the
ontological reality of God's self-communication. It is, therefore, in any case the continuation and accomplishment of that
existential process which consisted from the very beginning in
the supernatural pardoning and divinization of humanity. If it
is supposed that this original pardoning of humanity's sin
existed and continued to exist not merely as a demand but as
an effective force because, and in so far as, it was from the very
beginning orientated towards the Incarnation and God's self-
communication to the whole human race (and not because it
had begun in 'Adam'), then we have formed the idea of the
Christian redemption in such a way that it follows of itself
from a Christological evolutionary conception of the world.
For in this way the original pardoning became of itself also the
victory over sin—the obstacle to this self-communication—as
soon as this obstacle appeared by man's free choice during the
history of the carrying out of this self-communication.

We do not mean to give the impression that we have
sounded all the depths and breadth of a harmatology and

soteriology by these brief pointers. All we have intended to indicate by our remarks is how redemption incorporates itself into the developed ground-scheme of a Christological evolutionary world-view.

We must touch here on a further question. We have, one might say, projected the idea of a possible Incarnation from the formal scheme of a world-evolution which reaches its climax in God's communcation of himself. Naturally, the historical nature of human and also metaphysical knowledge permits us in actual fact to formulate such a formal scheme with such clarity only because we already know about the fact of the Incarnation, all of which is possible only *post Christum natum.* This is not however really very surprising. Even a metaphysical reflection always involves 'bringing in' an experience already had. The transcendental scheme of man as a free being, for instance, is transcendental in an *a-priori* way and yet is in fact dependent in its accomplishment on an actual experience of freedom. But there is one thing which cannot be accomplished even in this way, viz. the proof that this transcendental scheme of a possible Incarnation has in fact been actualized precisely in Jesus of Nazareth—in him and only in him. The *idea* of the God-man and the acknowledgement of Jesus and of no one else as the one, unique and real God-man are two quite different perceptions. Only this second perception, which is one of faith, makes one a Christian. In other words, one is a Christian only once one has grasped the uniquely concrete fact of this particular man, and once it has been grasped as God's absolute expression of himself and as God's pledge of himself to you and me. The fact that the salvation of man does not depend merely on the idea but also on the contingent, concrete facts of real history—that belongs to Christianity. But this again shows the significance of all our considerations. Within our briefly outlined ground-scheme in which the spirit is not something alien in the material world but is the factor by which this bodily reality itself becomes present to itself, all that has really to be made clear is that only a concrete bodily reality—and not a universal idea—can really save and be eternally valid—and that Christianity cannot really be an 'Idealism' if it is properly understood. The act of grasping the concrete reality of this determined man and seeing that it is the reality of the saving God-man is other and more than the *a-priori* projection of the idea of a God-man conceived as the basic ground of a divinized humanity as a whole and as the basic ground in which the world reaches God himself. But it is not longer the task of our present reflections to show *how* by his historical experience and his faith man comes to the knowledge of faith that in the very person of Jesus of Nazareth the history of the world has reached—not indeed its full and absolute perfection—but its unsurpassable final phase of perfection. All we can do here is to draw attention to this further question.

A correctly understood incorporation of Christology into an evolutionary world-view must also stop to think about the *point in time* in this one, complete world-history at which the Incarnation took place. Even the theological reflection of the early ages of the Church already found difficulty in answering this question. On the one hand, it regarded the coming of Christ as the end, and as the arrival of the last ages of world-history, as the last hour pointing directly to the end of all history and to an early return of Christ—in short, it saw the coming of Christ as the beginning of the end. On the other hand, the Incarnation and Christ's victory appeared to this reflection as the beginning of a new epoch, as the foundation of a Church which is to expand only slowly in an unforeseeably long history, and as the beginning of a leavening process within the very matter of world-history, a raw material which only this divinization of the world—which seems to begin in Christ—can change from an unformed material into the form God really intends it to have. Under both these aspects, however, the field of vision of early Christianity was very limited with regard to both the past and future temporal extent of the history it had to interpret in its theology of history. And in both cases this was due to the very limited spatio-temporal horizon of its own historical existence. Today we believe that we know a history of humanity which stretches several hundred times further back into the past than had been imagined in the old days, and we get the impression that, after a very long and up till now almost stagnant starting period, humanity has a history before it, a history whose future in this world has only just begun. Hence, whereas previously one had the impression that God had entered the world through the Incarnation of his Word in the evening of world-history, we now get the impression that (in terms of large periods) he came approximately at the moment when the history of man's active self-possession and of his knowing and active self-steering of history was just beginning. Someone recently estimated the total number of human beings who have lived on this earth up until now to be in the vicinity of seventy-seven milliards; this would mean, therefore, that in perhaps a thousand years from now (which is but a tiny fraction of the total time man has lived on this earth) more people will have lived *after* Christ than before him, and this proportion would then increase ever more rapidly so that Christ would recede further and further towards the beginning of humanity. The really important theological factors in this question may perhaps be expressed briefly as follows:

(a) It is certainly true that Christ is the beginning of the end (it being quite immaterial in this respect as to how long the history of the human race will last and as to what results it will still produce). This is true in so far as in Christ there has basically and irrevocably arrived the event of humanity's radical self-transcendence into God, and in so far as—understood as promise and task of humanity—this event cannot in the very nature of things be surpassed any longer by any further and higher self-transcendence of history. To this extent is the *telos* of all previous ages present in Christ (I Cor 10.11), and in a way which is unsurpassable.

(b) On the other hand, nothing in this properly eschatological interpretation of the saving period of the New Testament which began definitely and finally with Christ prevents us from seeing this Incarnation also as the start of other, even intramundane ages of humanity, at the very beginning of this epoch. This means that—beginning with Christ and including also the modern age and the future planetary age, with its higher social organization, an age in which man will gain ever greater control over nature and regulate it more and more, instead of just serving it—the history of the West can be regarded as one which in certain not unessential aspects, and viewed from within the world and history without falling into a Communistic utopianism, is only beginning to be that epoch towards which the past life of humanity has been striving and in which humanity is discovering itself actively and not only contemplatively, really and not merely aesthetically—thereby also permitting the world to discover itself.

It is absolutely legitimate to regard this new period as one whose ultimate reason is to be found in the faith of Christianity. For only the demythologization and secularization of the world which not only actually takes place but is willed and carried out by Christianity has turned the world into a material which man himself can manipulate technologically: and only through the Christian message concerning the final self-transcendence of the spirit by grace into an absolute God who is totally distinct from the created world, has cosmocentricity been turned into an anthropocentricity. Viewed in this light, it is perfectly meaningful and understandable that the Incarnation stands at the beginning of this first really all-human period.

This leads us immediately to our final consideration. Christology both constricts and frees all intramundane ideological and utopian views of the future, in so far as the dogma of the Incarnation of the Logos does not contain any definite mention about the future course of intramundane history, in so far as it declines to accept any kind of chiliastic view, and in so far as it has already gone beyond the whole history of the world and its future (without wishing to imply that it has declared it to be futile or indifferent) no matter how man may shape it by his efforts in this world. For in the very nature of things, the being directly present to the absolute and infinite mystery of God has necessarily already surpassed any particular form of intramundane achievement of man, including the human achievements of the future, however great they may be expected to be. Christology frees these views, since it does not wish to enter into competition with, or become a substitute for, such intramundane planning of the future, but leaves the latter to do its own work with regard to determining the duration and content, the planning and the incalculable challenge of the particular matters of man's future. It liberates it because this doctrine of the Incarnation does not deny, but includes the fact that man can realize his transcendental future, his attainment of God in himself, only by means of the material of this world and its history, i.e. also by exposing himself to, and either holding his own or failing in, this intramundane future with both the happiness and death necessarily attendant on it. To this extent, the promise of a supra-historical consummation in the absoluteness of God himself—a promise given together with Christology—does not diminish man's task in this world but provides it with its ultimate dignity, urgency and danger. Because man cannot effect his salvation apart from his worldly task but only through it, the latter attains its highest dignity, honour, danger-point and ultimate significance by this very fact. Through this task man also accepts the salvation which is God himself in his absoluteness and immediacy; time and space are the space of time in which the true eternity matures as their fruit and permanence. At the same time, however, Christology also binds all intramundane categorical projects and ideologies concerning the future. These are never salvation itself but are always only the material which man uses to exercise his openness in order to accept salvation from God's hand, since this salvation is God himself whom man does not create but always finds already there in the ground and abyss of his existence. Thus Christology sobers down and subdues man's own plan of action for the future. The future which man creates by his own action is never the only factor justifying man as he really is. For man is always already justified by God through the decree by which God in his holy, incomprehensible and unspeakable infinity pledges himself to man so that every action of man, right down to the last, consists in the acceptance of God's action on him. But in the long run, this sobered and subdued intramundane will for the future is the more fruitful for the future. In this way, man is not tempted to cruelly sacrifice the present for the future; he does not need to become brutal so as to take eternal peace by brute force; he does not need to let everyone be submerged in a sterile equality when he does not wish anyone to feel himself worse off than anyone else. If Christ is the decisive existential factor of man's life, then man will experience the unrest caused by the infinite extent of a divine future whose greatness overshadows every age and temporal deed; then is there peace, since the real, ultimate and infinite salvation is then already known and accepted as something present and as the gift given to man's action of faith, and does not require to be taken forcibly by the desperate and at the same time ridiculous over-exertion of man for the future; then is the dignity of the individual protected, since then he does not find the sole justification for his existence in using it up for the benefit of individuals of a future still to come, but also remains safe as an individual of eternal worth—safe in God and in his love; then is the community also justified and established with absolute validity in the face of this individual and his eternal dignity, for one cannot find the salvation of Christ unless one loves one's brothers and sisters—Christ's brothers and sisters; then is despair redeemed, for every fall into the abyss of the unspeakable and incomprehensible in spirit and life means falling into the hands of the one whom the Son addressed as his Father, when in death he commended his soul into his hands.

Aloys Grillmeier
1910-

Aloys Grillmeier was born in Peschbrunn in Bavaria. He became a Jesuit and studied theology at Valkenburg, Frankfurt, and at the Gregorian University in Rome. In 1942 he received his doctorate in theology from the University of Freiburg. He began teaching theology in 1945, and since 1950 has taught in Frankfurt as Professor of Theology and the History of Dogma. He was a peritus at Vatican II.

The full title of Grillmeier's book is Christ in Christian Tradition From the Apostolic Age to Chalcedon (451). *Its "first draft" was an extensive article prepared by him for inclusion in a Festschrift marking the 1500th anniversary of the Council of Chalcedon in 1951. He revised and expanded that article in 1959 and again in 1963, from which the English translation was made by Rev. J. S. Bowden of Nottingham University.*

Ever since the 19th century it has been especially the growth of biblical and patristic studies that has spurred Catholic theologians to attempt new syntheses. Speculative theology, stemming from the Middle Ages, never had more than limited access to the kind of historical information presented here by Grillmeier. It would be scandalous if studies such as this did not have a considerable impact on our understanding of Christ.

Grillmeier has organized an impressive array of early Christian thinkers and tried to isolate the chief developments represented in their writings. The first part is called "The Birth of Christology" and extends from the New Testament material to the contributions of Origen early in the third century. Part Two presents "The First Theological Interpretations of the Person of Christ," and covers the period from Origen to the Council of Ephesus (431); this is sub-divided into two sections, one on the "Logos-Sarx" Christology and the other on the "Logos-Anthropos" Christology, the two chief frameworks of interpretation to appear in this period. Then Part Three completes the story from Ephesus down to Chalcedon (451).

There is clearly no way in which a work like Grillmeier's can be appreciated properly by excerpting or summarizing. The history, as he unravels it, has a real sense of drama about it, and the long-dead questions of earlier generations of Christians suddenly find new life as he recreates their contexts. All that can be attempted in the following selection is to give a taste for the richness of his approach. We present first his summary of the data from the Synoptic Gospels, then from the Fourth Gospel, the "Biblical Starting-Points," as he calls them. Then we skip to the end of his story, nearly four centuries later, for his final evaluation of "Chalcedon and the History of Theology."

It is easy for the novice to lose patience with the plodding analysis of the veteran historian. Cries of relevance are readily raised and calls for pastoral orientation. Yet it is clear that the quality of Christian faith depends greatly on the integrity of its roots. All manner of enthusiasts have found it simple to shout the name of Jesus and pretend they had a grasp of His significance. It is in the face of such superficiality, which cheapens the Christian message, that the stolid research of a man like Grillmeier proves its worth. In putting the labors of early Christian theologians into perspective and clarifying the issues that gripped them, he has put a challenge before contemporary Christians to make comparable efforts at understanding the meaning of Christ.

CHRIST IN CHRISTIAN TRADITION

CHAPTER ONE

BIBLICAL STARTING-POINTS FOR PATRISTIC CHRISTOLOGY

I. The Present Situation

The nineteenth century used all its energy to work out a purely historical picture of Jesus by means of techniques of historical investigation. In this investigation, the dogma of the incarnation was not to be accepted as a basic presupposition: the life of Jesus was to be treated as a purely human life which developed in a human way. The attempt came to nothing. Thereupon there followed a return to the theological treatment of the New Testament statements about Christ. Martin Kähler stood at the beginning of the new movement; he brought to German Protestant theology the recognition,

> that the Christian faith is related to Jesus of Nazareth as he was preached in the apostolic proclamation as the crucified and the risen one. The message of the apostles is the proclamation of a *kerygma* for which they have been commissioned by the appearance of the risen one. . . . The reminiscences of the Jesus of history were preserved, shaped and interpreted within the framework of the proclamation of the risen one and this interpretation is the right and legitimate one for the Christian faith.

The pendulum has now swung in the opposite direction: whereas the slogan used to be 'the pure Jesus of history', it is now 'the pure Christ of faith'. To this effect, Bultmann pursues Kähler's views to their conclusion. As one of the founders of 'dialectical theology' he breaks with an isolated liberal scholarship, though he incorporates its results extensively in his programme of 'demythologization'. The picture of Christ offered by Bible and church, which represents Christ as *Kyrios* and *Theos*, is declared to be a myth the roots of which lie partly in Hellenism, partly in Jewish apocalyptic. It is impossible, he argues, for modern man with his unmythological view of the world to accept the Chalcedonian Definition as a final result. While the 'Christ myth' of the New Testament is not, of course, to be excluded, as it was in the elimination-work carried on by the Liberals, it should be utilized for a Christian self-understanding by means of 'existential interpretation'. This existential interpretation is to be independent of any objective and affirmative statement about Christ and the acceptance of it in faith, such as, say, Paul demands in I Cor. 15. It is to be pure self-understanding before God in Christ, the crucified one, and therefore pure faith which is not directed towards a content believed objectively. As a result, the problem of the 'Jesus of history' is bracketed off from 'theology', and the latter is made dependent on itself.

To illustrate this theological position, occupied by a part of German Protestant scholarship, the words of one of its best representatives may be quoted, Hans Conzelmann writes:

> We (i.e. the representatives of this radical *kerygma* theology are accustomed to begin our thinking with the *gap* which lies between Jesus of history and the community, marked by his death along with the Easter experiences, and with the difference between Jesus' preaching of the Kingdom of God and the *kerygma* that has *him* as its subject, between Jesus the proclaimer and the proclaimed Christ. Yet self-evident as this viewpoint may seem to us, we must be clear that outside central Europe it convinces only a few. The majority of English theologians either do not react to form criticism at all, or they acknowledge it merely as a formal classification of literary types and contest that it leads to historical or systematic judgements. They thus reserve for themselves the possibility of drawing a continuous line from Jesus' understanding of himself to the faith of the community. Easter is in no way ignored, but the content of the Easter faith, and with it the basic christological terms and titles, is traced back to Jesus' own teaching. The theology of the community appears as the working out of the lega-

cy of the Risen Christ on the basis of his appearance....
To the representatives of this position the form-critical
reconstruction seems to be a rationalist abstraction,
foreign both to history and to reality, and from a
practical point of view a reduction of Christianity to
a general religious consciousness, a formal dialectic of
existence.

But Conzelmann himself has to recognize that:

> The advantage of this solution is that an estab-
> lished community is in itself historically more probable
> than the assertion of a dicontinuity which is hardly
> able to explain the formation of the categories of the
> faith of the community. Furthermore, it can make
> plausible the transformation that the christological
> concepts (Servant, Messiah, Son of Man) have under-
> gone between their Jewish (biblical and apocalyptic)
> origin and their Christian usage: they received their
> present concrete meaning in Jesus' interpretation of
> himself. The way from here to the formation of the
> gospels also becomes clear: the material deriving from
> Jesus received its shaping in the teaching work of the
> community; the proof from scripture, for example,
> may have been a formative factor. And as Jesus used
> to work on the same basis, a substantial agreement is
> assured.

So today—and in a part of German Protestant theology too—
a synthesis is being sought between the extremes (pure Jesus of
history—pure Christ of faith); the Jesus of history is taken as a
presupposition of the Christ of faith. There is a recognition that
the primitive community itself already achieved this conjunction.
It identified the humiliated Jesus of Nazareth with the exalted
Kyrios. With this twofold recognition it was in a position to with-
stand the error of docetism on the one hand and the denial of
the transcendence of the *Kyrios* on the other. Indeed, it was just
this tension, this war waged on two fronts by the New Testament authors, that demanded clarity of expression in talking
about Jesus and hence depth in theological interpretation. They
knew that the earthly, crucified Jesus was to be seen only in the

light of Easter day. But it was also realized 'that the event of Easter cannot be adequately comprehended if it is looked at apart from the earthly Jesus'. It follows from this that for the understanding of the primitive church 'the life of Jesus was constitutive for faith, because the earthly and the exalted Lord are identical'. Recent scholarship also understands the special position of the Fourth Gospel from this tension. Its special character lies in the fact that 'it portrays the story of the exalted Lord as one and the same with that of the earthly Lord. . . . It is precisely the Fourth Gospel, originating in the age of the anti-docetic conflicts, which neither can nor will renounce the truth that revelation takes place on earth and in the flesh.' According to Käsemann there is a consequence for us as well: 'We also cannot do away with the identity between the exalted and the earthly Lord without falling into docetism and depriving ourselves of the possibility of drawing a line between the Easter faith of the community and myth.'

This problem of the 'Jesus of history' and the 'Christ of faith' has been posed, both terminologically and methodologically, in a more exact and fruitful way in recent discussion. From the results achieved we can draw a few conclusions for our interpretation of patristic christology as well.

First of all, the concept of 'the historical Jesus' has itself been clarified, after its somewhat vague usage proved to have unfortunate consequences for New Testament theology. The following definition has recently been suggested and has found acceptance: the phrase 'historical Jesus' refers to 'Jesus, in so far as he can be made the object of critical historical research'. This formulation brings into consideration, along with the question of historical content, the historical consciousness of the modern researcher, as well as the recently developed array of tools and methods at his disposal. G. Ebeling once put it this way: ' "Historical Jesus" is therefore really an abbreviation for Jesus as he comes to be known by strictly historical methods, in contrast to any alteration and touching up to which he has been subjected in the traditional Jesus picture.' To speak of the 'historical Jesus', then, is not only to refer to a thoroughly undogmatic wandering preacher of Galilee—to the Jesus characterized historically in this concrete way—but also to a certain way of considering him, from our side. F. Hahn has recently recommended a more detailed range of expression: (1) if one is discussing problems in the history of biblical traditions, he suggests a distinction between the 'pre-Easter Jesus' and the 'post-Easter community'; (2) if one is referring to the specifically christological interest of primitive Christian preaching, it would be better to speak of 'the earthly Jesus' and 'Jesus, the risen Lord'. Along these lines, the earliest community was interested in the 'earthly Jesus' to varying degrees which were articulated more or less clearly, but not in the 'historical Jesus' in the sense of modern criticism. So Hahn urges that we follow the suggestion of R. Slenczka and choose a way of speaking which shows that by 'historical Jesus' we always mean our own modern range of questions as well. Thus we shall avoid speaking of the 'historical Jesus' when we simply mean the earthly Jesus of primitive Christian preaching, and at the same time we can make it clear that we are interested in the very same Jesus of the time before Easter, if in a different way. So we shall bring to expression both the sameness of our point of view and its difference from that of the first Christians, in that we are concerned with the same 'object', but are using a mode of 'observation' which depends on modern presuppositions.

The method which exegetes have worked out for specifying the relation between the 'pre-Easter, earthly Jesus', and the 'post-Easter community' (in discussing the traditions behind the biblical text) and the 'earthly Jesus' and 'Jesus, the risen Lord' (in investigating the content of the early Christian preaching) can be important, too, *mutatis mutandis*, for the post-apostolic patristic age and for our interpretation of it. This is surely true of the three terms which F. Hahn has coined to characterize the transition from the pre-Easter Jesus to post-Easter reflection: (1) *selection* in the tradition about Jesus; (2) the *forming* and *re-forming* of this tradition within the New Testament; and (3) *reinterpretation*. The whole process is one of transformation, within which we must expect—in accordance with the first term—both the loss and the elaboration of traditional material. After Easter, in fact, we can even observe a 'narrowing of focus', in that a kerygmatic tradition comes to be developed—largely independent of the individual traditions of the story of Jesus which already existed—which refers almost exclusively to his death and resurrection, and to his being sent, or being made man. The church deliberately concentrates on certain main lines in Jesus' preaching, and on events and controversies in his life which have lasting relevance.

Let us apply this to the patristic period. Alongside the reception of the total picture of Christ there takes place (1) a *selection* or special highlighting of certain features of this picture. We can observe this (a) in the use of scripture. However much the whole of Scripture continued to be read, theological polemics, precisely in trinitarian and christological discussion, restricted themselves to a certain number of important or disputed scriptural texts. We shall present most of this selection of texts in the course of this book. (b) Beginning with the question of the function and meaning of Jesus for us and our salvation, christology undoubtedly concentrates its efforts more and more on the narrower question of his nature: on whether he is true God, whether he is true man, whether he is one and the same in true Godhead and true manhood. In its original context, however, this question of Jesus' nature was precisely the question of his soteriological function and meaning. (c) The process of selection also includes the different 'christologies', which come more and more to be distinguished as 'orthodox' or 'heretical'. A great deal seems to lie unused alongside the path of tradition. Some have even seen in its progress decided traces of a power-struggle, in which the stronger party, not necessarily the truth, has usually carried the day. Still, in forming judgements on this process we ought not to fasten our attention upon individual names, such as those of the early Christian monarchians and adoptionists, Theodotus of Byzantium or Noetus of Smyrna, or later those of Paul of Samosata, Photinus of Sirmium or even Nestorius. Just such a series of names as this shows that the theological concern they represent does in fact keep reappearing in the church, if always on a new level of reflection. Their concern did indeed penetrate more or less unnoticed into the history of the Christian interpretation of Christ, even though their names remained a source of horror. It can be shown that the opposed extremes of christological heresy have, in the end, decisively influenced what came to be, in the tension between them, the church's middle road. Chalcedon was to preserve the authentic kernel of what both Monophysitism and Nestorian-ism wanted to say, and hand it on to the future.

The second century after Christ is especially instructive on this process of selection. The truly endless stream of popular anonymous and pseudonymous literature seemed to be aiming at one thing: reversing the 'selection' given by the New Testa-ment. The life of the pre-Easter Jesus was filled out again with all sorts of purported information about words and deeds and events. The most notable feature in all of this was that the infla-tion of information could not call forth a deeper faith than the New Testament had already done, even through the sayings of Jesus in the Gospel of Thomas. On the contrary, in many ways these writings distracted the reader with trivialities. The 'selective' New Testament stands far above the inflated picture of Jesus given in the apocrypha. Of course, the interpretation of the events of Jesus' death given by the *descensus*-theology should not be included in this 'inflationary' christology; it belongs already to reflection on the post-Easter Jesus.

(2) The patristic period continues the process of *transforma-tion* which F. Hahn assumes for the time of the New Testament. This process, which leads first of all from lived experience to the preached gospel, the *kerygma,* then leads further from *kerygma* to dogma, without implying any opposition between them. Dog-ma is, after all, nothing other than a more reflective *kerygma,* clarified by theology and borne by a deepened consciousness of the reality of the church. We can see here, if we are properly cautious, a kind of analogy: just as the post-Easter *kerygma* always orientates itself by the earthly pre-Easter Jesus and in-corporates him—selectively, forming and interpreting what it takes—so patristic christology always remains dependent on the *kerygma* and on the earliest Christian experience, which remains present, in its own peculiar way, in the liturgy and the sacraments. Arius is as much a witness of this as is Nicaea, the Chalcedonian controversy as much as the Nicaean. One of our aims here will be to keep directing attention to this kerygmatic foundation.

(3) As the *kerygma* was handed on, a *new interpretation* of the tradition which had gone before, as well as of the New Testa-ment itself, took place necessarily at every step. As the Septuagint

and the New Testament themselves had done, the church assimilated language and concepts from the world around—language which was of increasing philosophical intensity, but not such that the theological nature of the interpretation would be lost in the process. Even so, the danger that theology might be overgrown by philosophy became acute from time to time, as Arius himself and the second generation of Arians show. Doubtless, too, there was a disadvantage in the fact that precisely christology and the trinitarian interpretation of Christian monotheism tended to end in formulas whose biblical and kerygmatic origin was no longer apparent. Still, as we hope to show, this emphasis on isolated formulas *in re trinitaria et christologica* is more the product of scholastic selection and abstraction than the real centre of the church's thinking in the patristic period.

Just as New Testament exegesis must face the problem of accurately specifying the relationship between the pre-Easter Jesus and the Christ preached by the early Christian community, so patristic studies and all theology have the task of specifying with the same accuracy the relationship between the New Testament *kerygma* and theology, and of keeping the tension between them always in mind. Nicaea and Chalcedon did not see their formulations as a distortion of the *kerygma*, but as its defence and its confirmation. The content of the *kerygma*, however, was always the person of Christ and his uniqueness. The theological struggles of the patristic period are nothing else than an expansion of this central question; this gives them their continuity. For from the gospel of Jesus Christ as Son of God, and of his subsequent history (as pneuma, *en pneumati*), grew the question of Christian monotheism (of the one God as Father, Son and Holy Spirit). And this expanded theological horizon remained contained within yet another: the question of the peculiar nature of the salvation God has given us in Christ and in the Holy Spirit. Soteriology remained the actual driving force behind theological inquiry, even—as we shall see especially in the period from the third to the fifth century—behind reflection on the identity of Christ and the Holy Spirit.

It will not be possible, nor even necessary, always to demonstrate this connection between soteriology and the theology of the Trinity in the same way at every phase of their development. Nevertheless, we must never lose sight of it. If even the New Testament has managed to concentrate its attention on the person of Christ, it must be legitimate to go on making the question of his person the focal point of our investigation. But just as the Christ of the New Testament can only be understood in his relationship to the Father who sends him and to the Spirit, so he can never be discussed, even for the period that follows, wholly apart from them.

As a starting-point, then, for the history of the christological *kerygma* in the patristic period, we must sketch the basic christological features of the most important groups of documents in the New Testament. With this as our goal, we can omit an investigation of the relationship of the earthly, pre-Easter Jesus to the Lord of Easter—and leave that task to the exegetes.

2. New Testament Outlines

(a) The christology of the primitive community

The earliest christology must be sought in the primitive Jewish-Christian community. It derived from the resurrection of Jesus, which was understood as his appointment to heavenly power. In his resurrection, Jesus was made 'both Lord and Christ' (Acts. 2. 33-36). In other words, Jesus is now 'Messiah' in the full sense of the Jewish expectation. He is the redeemer king who rules in the name of God (cf. Matt. 28. 18). The use of the language of Ps. 2. 7 in Acts 13. 33 to say that he is the 'adopted Son of God' is not necessarily an indication of strict adoptionism.

> On the contrary, only the career of Jesus, which, while always messianic, leads through humiliation to exaltation, is here approximated to Jewish thought. The ignominious death of the Messiah, inconceivable to Jewish sentiment, is the necessary prelude to his saving dominion which offers even to blinded Israel one more opportunity for repentance and the forgiveness of sins (cf. Acts 3. 18ff.; 5. 31). Neither the baptism of Jesus nor his resurrection is the basis for an "adoptionist' christology in the later sense.

The career of Jesus is regarded as a revelation of the divine work of salvation. Two stages or periods, however, were seen in it—one earthly, in the flesh, and one heavenly, in the spirit (Rom. 1. 3f.; I Pet. 3. 18; I Tim. 3. 16a). Whenever Jesus is described according to his earthly descent as Son of David, his transcendence is also being emphasized at the same time, in contrast to his ancestor (cf. Mark 12. 35ff.; Acts. 4. 25 ff.). This title is in any case important for Matthew (1. 1; 9. 27; 12. 23; 15. 22; 20. 30f.; 21. 9, 15) and for Luke (1. 32, 69; 2. 4, 11). Even the Apocalypse still knows it (3. 7; 5. 5; 22. 16). Jesus is the fulfilment of the Messiahship promised in David.

As well as this title 'Son of David', the earliest christology also knows another, 'Servant' (Matt. 12. 18 = Isa. 42. 1; Acts 3. 13, 26; 4. 27, 30). A reference to the servant songs may justifiably be assumed here. The designation of Jesus as 'prophet' was only short-lived; it had a reference to Deut. 18. 15, 18 and served to explain Jesus' mission to Jewish audiences (Acts 3. 22; 7. 37; John 6. 14; 7. 40). And even if the Fathers are right later in emphasizing that the transcendence of Christ is something more than a heightened prophetical office, this title nevertheless embraces his mission as revealer of the Father and teacher of men. In any case, it has a high soteriological significance. Finally, the relation of the exalted Lord to the church and to the world is further expressed through the idea of the *parousia*. It is of great importance in the Christian picture of history, even though at first, in the apostolic preaching, it stands in the background. For of course the exaltation of the crucified one had first to be proclaimed (cf. Acts 3. 20f). But a strong belief in the *parousia* (Matt. 24. 3) was alive in the primitive community, and found its liturgical expression in the Aramaic cry of longing *Marana-tha* (I Cor. 16. 22; Rev. 22. 20; I Cor. 11. 26). It is at the same time evidence of worship offered to Jesus as 'Lord'.

* * * * *

(c) The 'Word made flesh'

The climax in the New Testament development of christological thought is reached in John. His prologue to the Fourth Gospel is the most penetrating description of the career of Jesus Christ that has been written. It was not without reason that the christological formula of John 1. 14 could increasingly become the most influential New Testament text in the history of dogma.

The Johannine christology has a dynamism all of its own. Christ appears as the definitive Word of God to man, as the unique and absolute *revealer,* transcending all prophets. As αὐτόπτης he and he alone can bring authentic tidings from the heavenly world (John 1. 18; 3. 11, 32ff.; 7. 16; 8. 26, 28, etc.). He is not only lawgiver, as Moses, but also giver of grace and truth. In him God is present: 'He who sees me sees the Father also' (14. 9). His revelation therefore has as its theme not only the Father, but also the person and mission of Christ. 'He himself' belongs to the content of his message. This is expressed in the many 'I' sayings, in which he describes himself in particular as 'Light' and 'The Life of the World' (8. 12; 9. 5; 11. 25; 14. 6; cf. 1. 4), but most strongly in the absolute ἐγώ εἰμι (8. 24, 28, 58; 13. 19). This last is a theophany formula. The wonders (*'signa'*) also play their part in Jesus' revelation of himself (2. 11; 11. 4). But this activity of revelation is directed completely towards the *salvation* of men, for it brings life. Whoever believes on the Son of Man (9. 35) or the Son (μονογενής, υἱός) as the eschatological ambassador of God has (eternal) life (3. 15, 36; 5. 24, etc.) For this Son is the true God (οὗτός ἐστιν ἀληθινὸς θεός, I John 5. 20).

In John, Christ's activity of revelation and redemption is represented as a dramatic descent and ascent. The course traversed by Christ begins in the heavenly world (1. 1ff.) and leads to the earthly world (1. 11, 14), to the cross (19. 17ff.). The return then follows in the re-ascent of the risen one into his earlier glory (3. 13, 31; 6. 62; 13. 1; 14. 28; 16. 28; 17. 5). Thither Christ also leads those who become his own from 'this world' and who therefore can participate in the world of life and light. For he is to all 'the Way' (14. 6), the sole access to the life to come ('the door', 10. 7, 9). The way in which John marks the turning points on the course of redemption, the 'becoming flesh' (1. 14) and the 'being exalted' (= 'being glorified', cf. 3. 14; 8. 28; 12. 23, 32; 13. 31f.; 17. 1f.) is of extraordinary significance for future theology. It is principally the incarnation of the Logos which occupies the centre of theological reflection. What is the reason for this? It is surely the tension which is present in the Johannine formula 'Logos-sarx'. Let us attempt to measure its force.

1. *Logos*: Christ is here for the first time in Christian literature described by a name which is to be repeated countless
times. First of all, let us try to paraphrase its content from John
himself. The first element which underlies the Johannine Logos
concept is the idea of 'revelation' and the 'revealer'. Christ is the
Word of God, already existing before the world, and spoken into
the world. The office of 'revealer' is so closely bound up with the
person of Jesus that Christ himself becomes the embodiment of
revelation. Not only his words, but the very fact of his coming
and of his being are in themselves a divine self-revelation. In Rev.
19. 11-16, the office of the divine ambassador is described in the
imagery of the rider on a white horse. His name, ὁ Λόγος τοῦ θεοῦ,
is quite explicit. It is his task to bring to man the 'Word' of God.
This he can do because he is this Word. In John, 'Logos' is primarily the spoken word in contrast to the Logos as reason (*ratio*).
This also forms the basis for the close relationship between Logos and revelation. A further description of the intrinsic and
essential relationship between the person of Christ and his office
occurs in I John 1. 1-3, though it is a disputed point whether
'Logos' here is to be understood of the *person* of Jesus Christ or
of his *teaching*. Both are certainly included. Christ is the personal
'Word of Life' which comes from eternity and is sent to men.
These are themes from the prologue.

Essential as the idea of the revealer is for the Logos concept,
it does not exhaust it. The associated expressions θεός and
μονογενής serve to deepen and clarify the concept decisively. The
content of the teaching and the authority have their particular
source in the conjunction of the activity of the revealer and the
status of the Son of God (1. 18; P 66 and P 75 now show that
μονογενής θεός in this verse is almost certain, so at the beginning
and at the end of John (cf. 20. 29) we have a declaration of
Christ's divinity). True, the two concepts Logos and Son are not
to be equated formally. But in fact λόγος, θεός, μονογενής at the
least imply one and the same subject who is to be understood as
pre-existent, beyond time and beyond the world. The Logos is
God in God, mediator of creation and bringer of revelation—and
this in the full sense by virtue of his appearance in the flesh. He
'is' the Word of God in the flesh.

The sources of a theology of this kind have often been sought all too far from the material revealed in the Old and New Testaments—scholars have been misled in particular by the Logos concept. Yet the obvious course would seem to be to begin from the spiritual home of a disciple of John the Baptist and Christ, such as John is, i.e. from the Old Testament. The Old Testament 'Theology of the Word' gives us a first point of contact. This theme of the Word of God recurs constantly. It contains not only the idea of the revelation of God but also the conception of the Word as power and wisdom, which are made manifest in the cosmic workings of God. But it is impossible to derive the Johannine Logos conception from the Old Testament 'Theology of Word' alone. The idea of cosmic power and revelation is still insufficiently developed, and, above all, the notion of the 'Word' as personal is missing.

The Old Testament *Wisdom teaching* takes us considerably further. The Wisdom of the Old Testament and the Logos of John have many features in common. Both exist from the beginning (Prov. 8. 22; Ecclus. 24; John 1. 1; cf. Gen. 1. 1) and dwell with God (Ecclus. 24. 4. LXX; Prov. 8. 23-25, 30). Common to both is their work in the world, though this is emphasized more strongly in Proverbs and Ecclesiasticus than, for example, in John 1. 3, 10. Wisdom and Logos come to men (Ecclus. 24. 7-22 LXX; Prov. 8. 31) and 'tabernacle' with them (Ecclus. 24. 8 LXX— John 1. 14). So strong is the similarity between the Johannine prologue and Prov. 8 and Ecclus. 24 that one can speak of a literary dependence. But in that case, why did John not retain the name 'Wisdom'? His choice of the name Logos may have been influenced by the rabbinic identification of Wisdom and Torah. Moreover, the feminine form 'Sophia', and her place in Gnostic speculations, would be no recommendation in the Greek cultural sphere.

A further influence on the evangelist John will have been the New Testament formulas and ideas which had already taken shape before him. In Paul, moreover, the Old Testament confronts him once again. True, I Cor. 1. 24 (Christ as the 'Power of God' and the 'Wisdom of God') may be not so much a christological expression as a definition of Christ's part in the economy of salvation, and in this way may refer more to the work than to the person of Christ. But Col. 1. 15; 2 Cor. 4. 4 and Heb. 1. 3, which speak of 'effulgence' and 'image', certainly refer to Wisd. 7. 26 and contain an expression of Christ's essential being. The cosmological status of Wisdom in Prov. 8. 22-31 and Wisd. 7. 22-28 may have had an influence on Col. 1. 15ff. But the Pauline expression themselves, such as the formula of 'equality with God' (ἴσα εἶναι θεῷ) and 'form of God' (μορφὴ θεοῦ) or even Heb. 3 (ἀπαύγασμα τῆς δόξης καὶ χαρακτὴρ τῆς ὑποστάσεως αὐτοῦ) already point in the direction of the Johannine concepts and terminology and stand on the same theological plane as John does.

Finally, however, if the apostle chooses a particular word and a particular concept which is borrowed from Greek philosophy, there must be some connection between the two. Do John and his Logos concept, then, already point in a direction in which the history of the dogma of the incarnation is to lead us again and again—to Alexandria? The Epistle to the Hebrews indicates that there is already some connection between the New Testament and Alexandrian theology and exegesis. Alexandrian influence on John goes hand in hand with the place given to Old Testament Wisdom teaching in his theology. According to Irenaeus, the Fourth Gospel is directly opposed to Cerinthus, a Jew from Alexandria, who comes to Ephesus to preach his gnosis there, a gnosis in which Hellenistic theosophy plays a predominate role. There can be no doubt that we have in John a witness of the encounter between Christianity and the spirit of Hellenism at this early date, and it would be most remarkable if no trace of this manifested itself in his gospel, not only in a positive way by the recognition that Christianity and Hellenism were connected, but also in a negative way by repudiating the baleful influence of the latter.

It can certainly be assumed that the prologue to the gospel is directed primarily, if not exclusively, towards the Greeks. It stands apart, like a Greek facade to the Jewish-Christian building that is behind—the gospel. It was the Logos concept that moulded this facade. The analogy should not be pressed, for the facade too is essentially of the Old Testament, and Christian, even though Hellenistic influence is unmistakable. This Logos concept

340

is certainly more than a mere frontage, put up on the outside; it is intrinsically bound up with the gospel. But at the same time it represents a real acceptance of ideas from the Greeks, even though the content assigned to them by John gives back to the Greeks infinitely more than they were able to bring to him. The Greek view of the Logos is in itself by no means sufficient explanation of the Johannine concept. While Heraclitus and the Stoics make the Logos the principle governing the cosmos, they allow that it is immanent. The Logos of the prologue, on the other hand, is at the same time both personal and transcendent. Nor, despite the great similarity of many of his formulas, is Philo sufficient to explain the heights reached by John. Granted the Philonic Logos is already a being distinct from God, with divine properties and a function embracing the creation of the world and God's relationship with men; in the two writers the relationship between God and the Logos is completely different, and, most of all, in Philo the idea of incarnation is missing.

2. *The Logos in the flesh.* John now says of the divine Logos that 'He was made flesh and dwelt among men'. The personal presence of the revealer is a presence in the flesh. The Word of God has appeared *visibly* (I John 1. 1ff.). The Logos of God *is* man. The peculiarly Johannine contribution lies in the sharpness of the *antithesis* and the depth of the *synthesis* of Logos and sarx.

In no book of the New Testament is the christological opposition of pre-existent being and fleshly nature so sharply drawn out as in John. Divine though the Logos may be in his abode with God, beyond the sense, beyond time and beyond the world, his presence in true fleshly nature is none the less absolutely real. The apostle 'in his tripartite introduction in I John 1. 1, 2, 3 can never be satisfied in stressing over and over again that he who has appeared ($\grave{\epsilon}\,\phi\alpha\nu\epsilon\rho\acute{\omega}\theta\eta$) has done so in the concreteness of time and space'. A statement on the incarnation in these terms must have made an unimaginable contrast to the background of the Hellenistic Logos concept in its different forms. The expression 'sarx', 'flesh', would, it is true, emphasize the visibility and genuineness of the divine and immortal Logos, but in so doing would point to the mortality of his human nature. A Greek could certainly think of no greater opposition than that of 'Logos' to 'sarx', especially if the idea of suffering and death was associated with it. For this reason, the Christian proclamation saw ever-repeated attempts of a docetic kind to deny the reality of Christ's flesh or to loosen the unity of Logos and sarx. These two factors were those which Irenaeus stressed against Cerinthus. It is precisely to meet such attacks that the apostle chooses the strong expression the 'flesh' of the Logos, by which he surely understands a complete human nature. He deliberately mentions what is most visible in man to demonstrate that the coming of Christ, the God-Logos, was visible.

It is hardly a fault of John's that such an emphasis could turn into heresy again and again. We will, however, see how it was that this pointed antithesis gave occasions for far-reaching misrepresentations of the nature of Christ, just as it inspired the theology of the church to its deepest expressions. In view of the later misrepresentations it is important to point out how John represents his Christ as a real man, with body and soul, and therefore capable of spiritual feeling and inner emotion. The apostle who has an unparalleled vision of the Logos in Jesus always sees him as having a human psychology (11. 33; 12. 27; 13. 27). The Logos concept has not been able to obliterate the true picture of Christ's humanity. The reality of his life stands too clearly in view. The Greek thought-world will experience the same idea as a temptation and will largely succumb to it.

This attempt to obtain a general view of New Testament christology has—as far as possible—taken the present state of exegesis as its starting point. The transition from the apostolic age to the post-apostolic and patristic period confronts us with other conditions. The study of the use and understanding of scripture would be of the greatest significance for the whole of patristic christology. Up to now, however, there have been very few studies of the subject, and these differ both in method and in results. The mere position of the gospel of John in the church and among the Gnostics during the second century throws particular light on the spiritual state of the early church.

CHAPTER TWO

CHALCEDON AND THE HISTORY OF THEOLOGY

Though the dogma and dogmatic formula of Chalcedon represent no real innovation in the Christian tradition, the Fourth General Council, along with Nicaea, is the ancient synod which did the most to spur on theological reflection. Terms like *homoousios, hypostasis, physis* and *prosopon* found their way into dogmatic formulas not with an exact technical meaning, but with a content which had hardly been determined prescientifically, or even by popular science. This content was sufficient for the Fathers to express their dogmatic truth, in this case, that there is only one person in Christ despite the unimpaired duality of the natures. What they wanted to say was not unskilfully expressed by the frequently repeated 'one and the same'. So Chalcedon did not need to give an exact metaphysical analysis of the concepts of *prosopon* and *hypostasis*. Nor did it need to adopt a particular philosophical system in which such concepts could acquire a special significance. This is true for the sphere of dogma proper. But in so far as the concepts employed in the expression of this dogma also had a more exact philosophical content, it was at the same time possible to make a speculative theological analysis of the dogmatic expressions, in which, of course, the character of analogy in the use of the concepts was to be noted.

But what possibilities were there for such a speculative analysis at the time of Chalcedon? We have already seen that they were very few. The only significant attempt at giving a theory of the incarnation had been made by Nestorius on the basis of the Stoic-Cappadocian analysis of *physis (ousia)* and *hypostasis*. Our investigation has shown that one particular concept played a special part in this theory which was also used by Chalcedon, the concept of *proprietas, ἰδιότης*. The *hypostasis*, the *prosopon*, comes into being by the addition of the *ἰδιότης* to the *ousia*. Is it possible to arrive at a tolerable speculative interpretation of the Chalcedonian Definition with these Stoic-Cappadocian presuppositions? To this question we must give a negative answer. If we have as a basis the Cappadocian conception of *hypostasis* the result is, in fact, a contradiction between the expressions *magisque salva proprietate utriusque naturae* and *et in unam personam atque subsistentiam concurrente*. On one hand it is said that each nature keeps that which makes it a *hypostasis,* and yet at the same time it is said that there is only one *hypostasis* or *prosopon.* It follows from this that the Chalcedonian Definition already points into the future. For its speculative understanding it requires a different metaphysical idea of *hypostasis* and *prosopon* from that recognized hitherto. It also follows that while Nestorius might well have accepted the dogmatic formula of Chalcedon, he could not have vindicated it in a speculative analysis. He need not be faulted for this; Chalcedon provided new motives for christological reflection too, and, in addition impulses for the working out of the concept of person and its differentiation from the concept of nature. The stimulus provided did in fact have some effect, and after careful work first produced some results in the course of the sixth century. All possibilities have not been exhausted even today.

The position of the Chalcedonian Definition in the history of theology is determined not merely by the concepts which it contains but also by its basic christological framework, i.e. by the particular way in which it gives a theological interpretation of the person of Jesus Christ. The character of the Chalcedonian framework may best be defined in the light of its contrast with the antithesis of the chief formula of Cyril of Alexandria, 'The one nature of the Word made flesh'. It is a characteristic of this formula to define Christ from the *physis* of the Logos. The Logos is mentioned first. This *physis* is not symmetrically opposed to the *physis* of the manhood. Instead, we hear of a historical event which has happened to the *physis* of the Godhead of the Logos, namely that it has taken flesh. This is really John 1. 14, ὁ λόγος σάρξ ἐγένετο, with a closer interpretation of the subject and a stress on his unity. In Cyril's interpretation, the complete human nature of Christ is meant to be expressed by the one word σεσαρκωμέη (ου).

In contrast to this, the Chalcedonian Definition looks symmetrical and undynamic because of the juxtaposition of the divine and the human natures. Even if the two natures are said to '*concurrere*', there is no thought of capturing the act of incarnation in an historical perspective. But whereas the *mia physis* formula can only express a 'katagogic' christology, the Chalcedonian form is also capable of providing a basis for an 'anagogic' christology. In other words, it is possible to advance from the human reality of Jesus into the depths of the divine person. At the same time, Chalcedon leaves no doubt that the one Logos is the subject of both the human and the divine predicates. We can trace quite clearly in the Chalcedonian Definition the wish of the Fathers to take the Nicene framework as their starting point: *ante saecula quidem de Patre genitum secundum deitatem, in novissimis autem diebus eundem propter nos et propter salutem nostram ex Maria Virgine Dei genetrice secundum humanitatem.* . . . In the view of Chalcedon, Christ is not just a *'homo deifer'* or a human subject, *habens deitatem*, but the God-Logos, *habens humanitatem*, or rather, *habens et deitatem et humanitatem.* The person of Christ does not first come into being from the concurrence of Godhead and manhood or of the two natures, but is already present in the person of the pre-existent Logos. Thus the Chalcedonian picture of Christ, too, is drawn in the light of the Logos. But now the features of Christ's manhood are depicted with unmistakable clearness, even though only in outline. It will be the task of later developments both in preaching and theology to let the 'fullness of Christ' shine out even through the sober language of Chalcedon. It is no coincidence that in Monergistic and Monothelitic disputes recourse will be had to Chalcedon in particular, to think further into the completeness of the human nature of Christ and its capacity for action. All future discussion on the will, knowledge and consciousness of Christ belong in the end in that area of christological problems which was marked out by Chalcedon.

Theological reflection about Christ was given special impetus by the Fourth Council and above all by the contrast of ἀσυγχύτως-ἀδιαιρέτως, or by the four characteristics of the hypostatic union in Christ, regarded with such distrust by Harnack: ἀσυγχύτως, ἀτρέπτως, ἀδιαιρέτως, ἀχωρίστως. 'Without confusion' and 'without separation' represent the two extreme poles of christological tension. These concepts (along with the other two) had already found a firm footing before the Council of Chalcedon. But now they are given a new emphasis, indeed to

345

some extent they are put in a new order. For now the 'without confusion', directed againt Eutyches, is put in the first place, which at Ephesus had been occupied by 'without separation'. Both are given the same weight, though in the history of christology now one and now the other had to come further into the foreground. Unity of person and distinction of natures may be thought through right to the limit, to the establishment of a theological law which acquires the weight of an equation: 'Union as far as distinction.' Maximus Confessor had already put it like this: 'For there is evidently a union of things in so far as their physical distinction is preserved.' The christological unity contains its own tension.

If the person of Christ is the highest mode of conjunction between God and man, God and the world, the Chalcedonian 'without confusion' and 'without separation' show the right mean between monism and dualism, the two extremes between which the history of christology also swings. The Chalcedonian unity of person in the distinction of the natures provides the dogmatic basis for the preservation of the divine transcendence, which must always be a feature of the Christian concept of God. But it also shows the possibility of a complete immanence of God in our history, an immanence on which the biblical doctrine of the economy of salvation rests. The Chalcedonian Definition may seem to have a static-ontic ring, but it is not meant to do away with the salvation-historical aspect of biblical christology, for which, in fact, it provides a foundation and deeper insights.

Raymond Edward Brown
1928-

Raymond Brown was born in New York City and received his academic degrees from Catholic University, St. Mary's Seminary, Johns Hopkins University, and the Pontifical Biblical Commission in Rome. He joined the Sulpicians in 1951, was ordained in 1953, and taught Scripture at St. Mary's Seminary in Baltimore from 1959 to 1971. Since then he has been teaching at Union Theological Seminary in Manhattan.

Brown is clearly one of the most gifted Scripture scholars of our day. His achievements have been recognized internationally with the conferral of honorary doctorates by the Universities of Edinburgh, Scotland (1972), of Uppsala, Sweden (1974), and of Louvain, Belgium (1976), all before he was 50 years old. His two-volume commentary on The Gospel according to John (vol. I–1966; vol. II–1970) in the Anchor Bible series won the National Catholic Book award as well as a Christopher award, and is generally regarded as the finest, most complete treatment of the Fourth Gospel in the English language. Together with Joseph Fitzmyer and Roland Murphy, he edited the Jerome Biblical Commentary, (1967), the work that signaled the arrival of American Catholic Biblical scholarship at full maturity. Bernhard Anderson of Princeton Theological described it as "a landmark in the history of biblical interpretation."

Brown has continued his phenomenal productivity. In 1977 he dedicated The Birth of the Messiah *to the three European universities that had honored him. A commentary on the Infancy-Narratives of Matthew and Luke, it demonstrates beyond all reasonable dispute the extraordinary fruit to be derived from modern Biblical studies when responsibly done.*

The article that is presented here first appeared in Theological Studies *in 1965. It later came out as the first half of his book called* Jesus God and Man *(1967). The chief reason for including it here is to emphasize and illustrate why and how Biblical studies have had such a profound impact on Catholic theology. A Christology that failed to take account of the impressive contribution of Biblical studies in our day would be simply irresponsible.*

"Does the New Testament Call Jesus God?" The very fact that the question could be raised is as important as the nuanced answer given to it. It meant that the "proof-text" approach that had become all too common in many theological manuals had to give way, that the implicit fundamentalism that characterized so much of the earlier use of the Bible by theologians could no longer be tolerated. For those living in the overlap, trained in one era and finding the transition to a new age difficult, painful, and demanding, Brown's work had both encouraging and discouraging aspects. It augured well for a new generation provided with the proper tools, but it was disheartening to those whose theological training lacked the henceforth prerequisite Biblical roots. But, in view of the results, there was clearly no real choice involved; the only justifiable direction to take was the path that promised fuller enrichment of the theological tradition by more ample incorporation of the Bible.

JESUS, GOD AND MAN

CHAPTER ONE

DOES THE NEW TESTAMENT CALL JESUS GOD?

his chapter has a very limited goal; perhaps we can
best make this clear by stating what the chapter does
not intend to discuss. First, this chapter will not raise
the question of whether Jesus was God. This question was
settled for the Church at Nicaea, where it was clearly confessed
that the Son was God and not a creature; he was "true God of
true God." The recognition that such a belief is still the hall-
mark of the true Christian is found in the Amsterdam Confession
of the World Council of Churches, which stated that the World
Council is composed of "Churches which acknowledge Jesus
Christ as God and Savior." Yet, if we take for granted that
Jesus was God as confessed at Nicaea, there still remains the
question, to what extent and in what manner of understanding
and statement this truth is contained in the New Testament.
A development from the Scriptures to Nicaea, at least in formulation and thought patterns is recognized by all. Indeed, the
council fathers at Nicaea were troubled over the fact that they
could not answer the Arians in purely biblical categories. As
contemporary scholars have so well shown, by the time of Nicaea
there had been a definite progression from a functional approach
to Jesus to an ontological approach. And so, it is perfectly
legitimate to push the question about the divinity of Jesus back
before Nicaea and to ask about the attitude of the New Testament toward the problem.

However—and this is our second delimitation—the New
Testament attitude toward the divinity of Jesus is much broader
than the scope of this chapter. To treat such a question, one
would have to discuss all the important Christological titles, e.g.,
Messiah, Son of God, Lord, Savior, etc., much in the manner of
full-scale works by V. Taylor, O. Cullmann, F. Hahn, R. H.

Fuller, and others. Such titles are an index of the way in which the early Church confessed its understanding of what Jesus meant for men. Even more important, one would have to analyze the descriptions of Jesus' actions and miracles; his attitudes toward the Temple, the Sabbath, and judgment; his self-assurance in his proclamations and teaching; his sinlessness; etc. If Jesus presented himself as one in whose life God was active, he did so not primarily by the use of titles or by clear statements about what he was, but rather by the impact of his person and his life on those who followed him. Thus, the material that would have to be treated in discussing the divinity of Jesus in the New Testament is very broad in range.

It is to only one small area of this material that we confine this chapter, namely, the New Testament use of the term "God" (*theos*) for Jesus. Naturally, if the New Testament does use the term "God" in referring to Jesus, this is an important element in the larger question of the New Testament attitude toward the divinity of Jesus. But were we to discover that the New Testament never calls Jesus God, this would not necessarily mean that the New Testament authors did not think of Jesus as divine. There is much truth to Athanasius' contention that the Nicene definition that Jesus was God and not a creature "collects the sense of Scripture," and thus, as we may deduce, is not dependent on any one statement of Scripture.

The limited nature of the topic we are treating does not diminish its importance, especially in ecumenical relations. In Protestant-Catholic dialogue a preference on the part of some Protestants for avoiding the phraseology "Jesus is God" is quite evident. The above-mentioned confession of the World Council of Churches provoked considerable criticism precisely because it stated that Jesus Christ was God. Some Catholics may suspect that neo-Arianism lies behind such criticism, and yet often it came from Christians who wholeheartedly accepted the truth implied in the phraseology. The uneasiness about calling Jesus God arises on several counts.

First, it has been argued that the statement "Jesus is God" is not a biblical formulation. It is to this problem that our chapter will be directly addressed. At the outset we may call attention to articles by such distinguished scholars as R. Bultmann and V. Taylor, who conclude that the New Testament exercises great restraint in describing Jesus as God and who do not favor the designation. Other treatments by Oscar Cullmann and A. W. Wainwright seem to be slightly more positive in their evaluation of the evidence.

Second, it has been contended that this formula does not do justice to the fullness of Christ. Taylor says: "To describe Christ as God is to neglect the sense in which He is both less and more, man as well as God within the glory and limitations of His incarnation." This fear that an exclusive emphasis on the divinity of Christ may lead to a failure to appreciate his humanity is quite realistic. Many believers unconsciously drift into a semidocetic understanding of Jesus which would exclude from his life such human factors as trial, fear, ignorance, and hesitation. However, the answer to this difficulty lies more in the direction of emphasizing the humanity of Jesus, rather than in questioning the validity of the formula "Jesus is God." Another aspect of the fear that this formula is open to a Sabellian interpretation that would reduce the Son to an aspect of God the Father. This danger seems less real in our times than the danger of semidocetism. If anything, the tendency in our times is to emphasize the Son at the expense of the Father and of the Holy Spirit.

Third, it has been contended that this formula objectivizes Jesus. Bultmann says: "The formula 'Christ is God' is false in every sense in which God is understood as an entity which can be objectivized, whether it is understood in an Arian or Nicene, an Orthodox or a Liberal sense. It is correct, if 'God' is understood as the event of God's acting." He would avoid the danger by referring to Christ not as "God" but as "the Word of God." We may well wish to disengage ourselves from any exaggerated stress on the functional, for we maintain that it is meaningful and necessary to ask what Christ is in himself and not only what he is as far as we are concerned or for me personally. Yet Bultmann's remarks do point up the danger of neglecting the soteriological implications of the formula, rather than in its rejection. Nicaea certainly did not ignore the soteriological aspect, for in the one breath it described Jesus as "true God of true God . . .

who for us men and our salvation . . . became man, suffered and rose."

Thus, it seems that the last two objections are centered primarily on the objectionable meaning that one can give to the formula "Jesus is God" and can be answered in terms of a corrective emphasis. We shall concentrate on the first objection and the scriptural justification for the formula. We shall discuss the important relevant texts under three headings: (I) texts that seem to imply that the title "God" was not used for Jesus; (II) texts where, by reason of textual variants or syntax, the use of "God" for Jesus is dubious; (III) texts where Jesus is clearly called God. We shall then evaluate the information that these texts give us about the frequency, antiquity, and origin of the use of "God" for Jesus.

I. TEXTS THAT SEEM TO IMPLY THAT THE TITLE "GOD" WAS NOT USED FOR JESUS

It seems best to begin with negative evidence which is often somewhat neglected in Catholic treatments of the subject. It is quite obvious that in the New Testament the term "God" is applied with overwhelming frequency to God the Father, i.e., to the God revealed in the Old Testament to whom Jesus prayed. The attitude toward Jesus in the early sermons of Acts is that Jesus was a man attested by God (2:22) and that God preached to Israel through Jesus (10:36). Throughout most of the New Testament there tends to be a distinction between God (= the Father) and Jesus. We may illustrate this by several texts.

1) Mk 10:18. In response to the man who addresses him as "good teacher," Jesus says: "Why do you call me good? No one is good but God alone." The crucial phrase (*ei me heis ho theos*) may also be translated: ". . . but the one God." Lk 18:19 agrees with Mark but omits the article before *theos*. Mt 19:17 seems to reflect embarrassment at the thrust of the Marcan saying, for it reads: "Why do you ask me about what is good?" V. Taylor lists a number of interpretations of this Marcan verse. A frequent patristic interpretation is that Jesus is trying to lead the man to a perception of his divinity, i.e., that Jesus is showing the man what he is really (and correctly) implying when he addresses Jesus as good. One cannot but feel that such an exegesis is

352

motivated by an apologetic concern for protecting the doctrine of the divinity of Jesus. Other interpreters stress that Jesus is trying to direct attention away from himself to his Father. This is undoubtedly true, but it should not disguise the fact that this text strongly distinguishes between Jesus and God, and that a description which Jesus rejects is applicable to God. From this text one would never suspect that the evangelist thought of Jesus as God.

2) Mk 15:34; Mt 27:46. As Jesus hangs on the cross, he cries out: "My God, my God, why have you forsaken me?" If either evangelist was accustomed to think or speak of Jesus as God, it is indeed strange that he would report a saying where Jesus is portrayed as addressing another as "my God." Of course, this argument is weakened by the fact that Jesus is citing Ps 22:1 and thus is using a conventional form of address. However, no such explanation is possible for the similar use of "my God" in Jn 20:17: "I am ascending to my Father and your Father, to my God and your God."

3) Eph 1:17: "The God of our Lord Jesus Christ, the Father of glory." (See also 2 Cor 1:3, 1 Pt 1:3.) in Eph 1:3 we hear of the "God and Father of our Lord Jesus Christ," but the abruptness of 1:17 makes an even stronger impression. Just as in the preceding Gospel examples wherein Jesus speaks of "my God," these examples from the Epistles make it difficult to think that the author designated Jesus as God.

4) There are several passages that by means of immediate juxtaposition seem to distinguish between the one God and Jesus Christ. We give a sampling:

> Jn 17:3: "Eternal life consists in this: that they know you, the only true God [ton monon alethinon theon], and the one whom you sent, Jesus Christ."
> 1Cor 8:6: "For us there is one God, the Father, from whom are all things and for whom we exist, and one Lord, Jesus Christ, through whom are all things and through whom we exist."
> Eph 4:4-6 distinguishes between ". . . one Spirit . . . one Lord . . . one God and Father of us all." In 1 Cor 12:4-6 a similar distinction is made: ". . . the same Spirit . . . the same Lord . . . the same God"; see also

2 Cor 13:14. Formulae distinguishing between the one God and Jesus Christ continued even after the New Testament period.

1 Tim 2:5: "For there is one God, and there is one mediator between God and men, the man Christ Jesus."

Such passages closely associate Jesus the Lord and God the Father (and sometimes the Spirit as well); therefore, they are useful in discussing the New Testament attitude toward the divinity of Jesus and the New Testament roots of the later doctrine of the Trinity. However, for our purposes they show that while Jesus was associated with God and was called the Lord or the mediator, there was a strong tendency to reserve the title "God" to the Father who is the one true God.

5) Tangentially related to our discussion are a number of texts which seem to state that Jesus is less than God or the Father. A full-scale exegesis of these texts would be germane to a paper discussing the divinity of Jesus in the New Testament; it is not germane to our study here, for they do not directly involve the use of the title "God." Nevertheless, it is well at least to list them:

Jn 14:28: "The Father is greater than I." This is the third Johannine text we have mentioned in this section. It is important to note that there are Johannine passages that do not favor the application of the term "God" to Jesus. This will serve as a balance to the emphasis below that the fourth Gospel supplies us with clear examples of such an application.

Mk 13:32: "Of that day or that hour no one knows, not even the angels in heaven, nor the Son, but only the Father."

Phil 2:5-10: "Christ Jesus, who, though he was in the form (morphe) of God, did not count being equal with God a thing to be clung to, but emptied himself, taking the form of a servant. .... Therefore God has highly exalted him and bestowed on him the name which is above every name . . . that every tongue should confess that Jesus is Lord, to the glory of God the Father."

1 Cor 15:24 speaks of the triumphant Christ of the
Second Coming, who is to deliver the kingdom to
God the Father. In 15:28 Paul continues: "Then the
Son himself will also be subjected to Him who put
all things under him, that God may be everything to
everyone." Some have suggested that Paul is speaking
of the Son in his role as head of the Church, but in
any case "God" is reserved as the title for Him to
whom the Son is subjected.

II. TEXTS WHERE THE USE OF "GOD" FOR JESUS IS DUBIOUS

The doubts about these texts arise on two scores, namely,
the presence of textual variants and problems of syntax.

A. Passages with textual variants

1) Gal 2:20: "It is no longer I who live, but Christ
who lives in me; and the life I now live in the flesh I
live in faith, faith in the Son of God who loved me
and gave himself for me."

The crucial words are *en pistei zo te tou huiou tou theou.*
Some important witnesses ((P, B, D, G) read *tou theou kai
Christou* instead of *tou huiou tou theou.* There are two ways to
translate this variant: "faith in God and in Christ who loved me
and gave himself for me," or "faith in the God and Christ, etc."
Only in the second interpretation of this variant is "God" used
as a title for Jesus. In general, critical editions of the Greek
New Testament prefer the reading "Son of God" to the variant;
but, in part, this is probably because the editors consider
"Son of God" to be the less developed reading from a theological
viewpoint and thus more original. The phrase *tou theou kai
Christou* is never found elsewhere in the Pauline writings, and so
is suspect. Thus, this text should not be counted among those
passages which call Jesus God.

2) Acts 20:28: "The Holy Spirit has made you over-
seers to feed the church of God which he obtained
with his own blood."

The crucial words are *ten ekklesian tou theou hen periepoiesato
dia tou haimatos tou idiou.* There are two problems: one con-

cerns the variant reading; the other concerns grammatical understanding.

In this instance "the church of God" is the best attested reading, with support in B, S, and the Vulgate. However, there is another reading, "the church of the Lord," which is supported by A, D, and some minor versions. This second reading removes the possibility that Jesus is called God and is thus the less difficult reading—a fact which makes it suspect. However, an argument has been advanced for the second reading on the grounds that "the church of the Lord" is a much more unusual expression than "the church of God," and therefore some scribe may have tried to make the text conform to the usual expression, "the church of God." Yet the weight of the arguments favors "the church of God" as more original. One very plausible reason why some scribes may have changed "God" to "Lord" is that a reading which has God shedding blood seems to smack of Patripassianism.

If we accept "the church of God," then it is possible that the text is referring to Jesus as God, for the modifying clause "which he obtained with his own blood" would more appropriately be spoken of Jesus than of the Father. However, there is another possibility: perhaps *theos* refers to the Father and *idios* refers to the Son; thus, "the church of God (the Father) which He obtained with the blood of His own (Son)." Such a grammatical expert as Moulton favors this, and Hort once suggested that the Greek noun for Son may have been lost at the end of the verse. A recent and exhaustive Catholic treatment of this discourse in Acts translates the verse in the way just proposed. And so, even if we read "the church of God," we are by no means certain that this verse calls Jesus God.

> 3) Jn 1:18: "No one has ever seen God; it is God the only Son, ever at the Father's side, who has revealed Him."

The textual witnesses do not agree on the italicized words; there are three major possibilities:

a) [*ho*] *monogenes theos*, "God the only Son" or, as some would translate, "the only-begotten God." This is supported by the evidence of the best Greek manuscripts, by the Syriac, by Irenaeus, Clement of Alexandria, and Origen. The fact that both of the recently discovered Bodmer papyri from *ca.* A.D. 200 have this reading gives it great weight. Some exegetes suspect that the reading is too highly developed theologically, but we shall see that elsewhere in John Jesus is clearly called God. Once cannot maintain that this reading was introduced into copies of John as part of the anti-Arian polemic, for the Arians did not balk at giving such a title to Jesus. Perhaps the only real objection to the reading is the strangeness of the affirmation that God reveals God and that only God has seen God.

b) *monogenes huios,* literally "the Son, the only one." This reading is supported by some early versions (Latin, Curetonian Syriac), by a good number of later Greek manuscripts, including A, by Athanasius, Chrysostom, and many of the Latin Fathers. In three of the other four uses of *monogenes* in the Johannine writings, it is combined with *huios,* and so the appearance of this combination here may be the reflection of a scribal tendency to conform.

c) *monogenes,* "the only Son." This reading has the poorest attestation; it is found in Tatian, Origen (once), Epiphanius, and Cyril of Alexandria. Some scholars, e.g., Boismard, have favored it as the original reading, of which the above two readings would represent an expansion and clarification. However, the complete lack of attestation in the Greek copies of the Gospel makes it suspect. When one is dealing with patristic citations of the Gospel, one is never certain when, for the sake of brevity, the Fathers are citing only the essential words of a passage.

In our personal opinion, since the discovery of the Bodmer papyri, there is very good reason for accepting the first reading above as original—the reading which calls Jesus God.

B. Passages where obscurity arises from syntax

1) Col 2:2: ". . . that they may attain to all the riches
of the fullness of understanding, unto the knowledge
of the mystery of God, Christ, in whom are hidden
all the treasures of wisdom and knowledge."

Several interpretations of the italicized phrase (*tou theou Christou*) are possible:

a) "Christ" is in apposition to "God," or at least dependent on "God": "the knowledge of the mystery of the God Christ." This interpretation calls Jesus God. There is no article before "Christ," and so the two nouns may be united. However, in the New Testament there is no other instance of the formula "the God Christ."

b) The genitive "Christ" qualifies "God": "the knowledge of the mystery of the God of Christ." Grammatically this offers no difficulty, and we saw above that Eph 1:17 speaks of "the God of our Lord Jesus Christ"; see also Col 1:3.

c) "Christ" is the content of the mystery: "the knowledge of the mystery of God which is Christ." This is actually the reading in D: *tou theou ho estin Christos*—a reading which reflects an early interpretation. Yet, the reading in D points up the grammatical difficulty behind this interpretation. If Paul had meant to say "the mystery which is Christ," then he would normally have used the Greek that is in Codex D, and not the *tou theou Christou* which seems to be the original reading of the passage. The grammatical difficulty is not insuperable, however, and an understanding of Paul's concept of "the mystery" would incline us to accept this interpretation.

Be this as it may, the interpretations (b) and (c) are clearly preferable to (a), and therefore this text is not a good one to use in our discussion.

2) 2 Th 1:12: "So that the name of our Lord Jesus may be glorified in you, and you in him, according to the grace of our God and (the) Lord Jesus Christ."

The crucial Greek words are *kata ten charin tou theou hemon kai kyriou Iesou Christou.* There are two possible interpretations of the genitives: (a) "the grace of our God-and-Lord Jesus Christ"; (b) "the grace of our God and of the Lord Jesus Christ."

The first interpretation, which gives Jesus the title of "God," is favored by the absence in the Greek of an article before "Lord," giving the impression that the two genitives are bound together and governed by the one article which precedes "God." Yet, perhaps "Lord Jesus Christ" was so common a phrase that it would automatically be thought of as a separate entity and could be used without the article. The second inter-

358

pretation is favored by the fact that *hemon* separates the two titles; but, as we shall see below in discussing 2 Pt 1:1, this is not a decisive argument. The most impressive argument for the second interpretation is that *ho theos hemon,* "our God," occurs four times in 1-2 Thessalonians as a title for God the Father; and on this analogy, in the passage at hand "our God" should be distinguished from "(the) Lord Jesus Christ." Most commentators accept this distinction, and the latest and most comprehensive Catholic commentary says that it must be accepted. Therefore, this text cannot be offered as an example of the use of the title "God" for Jesus.

3) Tit 2:13: ". . . awaiting our blessed hope and the appearance of the glory of (the) great God and our Savior Jesus Christ."

The crucial Greek words are *epiphaneian tes doxes tou megalou theou kai soteros hemon Iesou Christou.* Three interpretations are possible:

a) "the glory of the great god and of our Savior Jesus Christ." This interpretation, which clearly separates "the great God" and "our Savior Jesus Christ," is not really favored by the Greek, which binds together *theou kai soteros.* Once again it may be argued that the absence of an article before *soteros* is not too important, because "our Savior Jesus Christ" was so common a credal formula that it would automatically be thought of as a separate entity. However, the argument is less convincing here than it was above in the instance of 2 Th 1:12 where *hemon* broke up *theou . . . kai kyriou.* Moreover, the separation proposed in this interpretation of Tit 2:13 means that the author is speaking of a twofold glorious appearance, one of God and the other of the Savior Jesus Christ. There is no real evidence in the New Testament for such a double epiphany.

b) "the glory of our great God-and-Savior, which (glory) is Jesus Christ." This interpretation binds together "God" and Savior" but applies the compound title to the Father. Jesus Christ is taken to represent the personification of the glory of God the Father, and grammatically *Iesou Christou* is treated as a genitive in apposition with the genitive *doxes.* The objection to this interpretation is the same as we faced in dealing with interpretation (c) of Col 2:2, namely, that we would expect in the Greek an explanatory "which is." Otherwise, there is no real objection to the application of the title "Savior" to the Father, for other passages in Titus (1:3; 2:10; 3:4) speak of "God our Savior" (as contrasted with 1:4 and 3:6, which speak of "Jesus Christ our Savior"). Nor can one object to the idea that Jesus is the glory of the Father, for other New Testament passages identify Jesus as the bearer of divine glory.

c) "the glory of our great God-and-Savior Jesus Christ." Here the compound title "God-and-Savior" is given to Jesus Christ. This is the most obvious meaning of the Greek. It implies that the passage is speaking only of one glorious epiphany, namely, of Jesus Christ; and this is in harmony with other references to the epiphany of Jesus Christ in the Pastoral Epistles (1 Tim 6:14-15; 2 Tim 4:1). That "Savior" is applied to Jesus Christ rather than to God the Father is suggested by the next verse in Titus (2:14), which speaks of the redemption wrought by Jesus. Some would rule out this interpretation which gives Jesus the title of "God" because elsewhere in the Pastorals (1 Tim 2:5; see above) a clear distinction is made between the one God (= the Father) and the man Jesus Christ. However, as we have noted, in the fourth Gospel there are passages which call Jesus God along with passages which distinguish between Jesus and the one true God.

It is very difficult to come to a definite decision. Careful scholars like Ezra Abbot and Jaochim Jeremias have decided against interpretation (c). Yet Cullmann thinks that it is probable that Jesus is called God here, and the most complete Catholic commentary on the Pastorals argues strongly for this interpretation. Personally, we are inclined to recognize interpretation (c) as the probable meaning of the passage. It is unfortunate that no certainty can be reached here, for it seems that the passage is the one which shaped the confession of the World Council of Churches in "Jesus Christ as God and Savior."

> 4) 1 Jn 5:20: "And we know that the Son of God has come and has given us understanding to know Him who is true; and we are in Him who is true, in His Son Jesus Christ. This is the true God and eternal life."

In the first sentence of this passage it is quite obvious that "He who is true" (*ho alethinos*) is God the Father; indeed, some textual witnesses clarify the first "Him who is true" by adding "God," a combination that would be translated ". . . understanding to know the true God" (cf. Jn 17:3, cited above). This first sentence tells us that the Son has come and enabled men to know the Father, and the Christian abides in Father and Son.

The real problem concerns the opening of the second sentence in the passage: *houtos estin ho alethinos theos.* To whom does the "this " (*houtos*) refer? C. H. Dodd suggests that "this" is a general reference to the teaching of the Epistle. More often, however, it is seen as a reference to either "Jesus Christ" or to "Him who is true" in the preceding sentence. Grammar favors a reference to the nearest antecedent, and this would be "Jesus Christ." In this case Jesus Christ is called true God. Yet, since God the Father was referred to twice in the preceding sentence as *ho alethinos,* one might suspect that the statement *houtos estin ho alethinos theos* is really a reference to Him. Certainly in Jn 17:3 *ho monos alethinos theos* refers to God the Father and not to Jesus Christ.

Can we learn something from the second predicate in the sentence, i.e., "eternal life"? Twice in the fourth Gospel Jesus is called "the life" (11:25; 14:6), while the Father is never so called. Yet Jn 6:57 speaks of "the living Father" and makes it clear that the Father is the source of the Son's life. Thus it seems probable that in Johannine terminology either the Father or the Son could be designated as "life," even as they are both designated as "light" (1 Jn 1:5; Jn 8:12; note that it is the Epistle that calls the Father light, while the Gospel calls Jesus light). It may be, however, that the predicate "eternal life" does favor making Jesus Christ the subject of the sentence we are discussing, for only eight verses before (5:12) the author of the Epistle stated: "He who has the Son has life."

R. Schnackenburg, who has given us the best commentary on 1 John, argues strongly from the logic of the context and the flow of the argument that "This is the true God" refers to Jesus Christ. The first sentence in 5:20 ends on the note that we Christians dwell in God the Father ("Him who is true") inasmuch as we dwell in His Son Jesus Christ. Why? Because Jesus is the true God and eternal life. Schnackenburg argues that the second sentence of 5:20 has meaning only if it refers to Jesus; it would be tautological if it referred to God the Father. His reasoning is persuasive, and thus there is a certain probability that 1 Jn 5:20 calls Jesus God—a usage not unusual in Johannine literature.

> 5) Rom 9:5: "Of their race [i.e., the Israelites] is the Christ according to the flesh God who is over all blessed forever."

The crucial Greek words are *ho Christos to kata sarka ho on epi panton theos eulogetos eis tous aionas*. The problem may be phrased in terms of various possible punctuations:

a) A full stop may be put after *sarka* ("flesh") as in Codex Ephraemi. The following words then become a separate sentence: "He who is God over all be [is] blessed forever"; or "He who is over all is God blessed forever." With either reading we have an independent doxology which seemingly refers to God the Father. Why Paul should stop here and introduce a doxology to the Father is not clear; for 9:1-5 concerns Christ, and one would expect praise of Christ, not of the Father. Moreover, the word order in the Greek offers considerable difficulty for this interpretation. In independent doxologies *eulogetos* ("blessed") as a predicate nominative normally comes first in the sentence; here it is the sixth word in the sentence. The presence of the participle *on* is also awkward for this interpretation, for in either of the above readings it is superfluous. The construction *ho on* is normal only if there is an antecedent in the previous clause.

b) A full stop may be put after *panton* ("all"), with a comma after *sarka*. Thus one obtains the reading: ". . . the Christ according to the flesh, who is over all. God be [is] blessed forever." This interpretation avoids the difficulty just mentioned about the presence of the participle *on*. In the independent doxology, however, *eulogetos* still does not have the normal first position in the sentence (it is now second) and the lack of contextual justification for suddenly introducing a doxology to the Father remains a difficulty. On the whole, however, this interpretation seems preferable to (a).

c) A full stop may be put at the end, after *aionas* ("forever"), a comma after *sarka*. In this punctuation all the words after *sarka* are a relative clause modifying "Christ." Thus,

". . . the Christ according to the flesh, who is over all, God blessed forever." This interpretation would mean that Paul calls Jesus God. From a grammatical viewpoint this is clearly the best reading. Also, the contextual sequence is excellent; for, having spoken of Jesus' descent according to the flesh, Paul now emphasizes his position as God. The only real objection to this is that nowhere else does Paul speak of Jesus as God.

This passage is a famous crux, and we cannot hope to reach a decision that will be accepted by all. Distinguished scholars are aligned on both sides. Among those who think that Rom 9:5 applies the title "God" to Jesus are Sanday and Headlam, G. Findlay, Boylan, Nygren, Lagrange, and O. Michel. Among those who think that the reference is to the Father are H. Meyer, Dodd, Bultmann, J. Knox, Barrett, and Taylor. Personally, we are inclined to accept the grammatical evidence in favor of interpretation (c), but at most one may claim a certain probability that this passage refers to Jesus as God.

> 6) 2 Pt 1:1: "To those who have obtained a faith of equal standing with ours in the righteousness of our God and Savior Jesus Christ."

The crucial Greek words are *en dikaiosyne tou theou hemon kai soteros Iesou Christou*. The grammatical problem is the same as we saw in 2 Th 1:12, where we favored the interpretation "the grace of our God and of the Lord Jesus Christ," a reading that distinguished between God (the Father) and Jesus Christ. If one were to follow the analogy, one would translate here "the righteousness of our God and of the Savior Jesus Christ." However, 2 Peter offers a parallel construction which enables us to decide that the author very probably intended both titles, "God" and "Savior," to be applied to Jesus Christ. In 2 Pt 1:11 we hear of "the eternal kingdom of our Lord-and-Savior Jesus Christ" (*basileian tou kyriou hemon kai soteros Iesou Christou*). Here there can be no reasonable doubt that "Lord" and "Savior" constitute a compound title for Jesus, and it seems logical to interpret 1:1 on the analogy of 1:11. This passage could almost be classified in the next section of our article under texts which clearly call Jesus God.

In the second main section, we have considered nine texts where the use of "God" for Jesus is dubious. In the first subsection (passages with textual variants) we rejected Gal 2:20 and Acts 20:28 as too uncertain, but recognized Jn 1:18 as a very probable instance where Jesus is called God. In the second subsection (passages where obscurity arises from syntax) we rejected Col 2:2 and 2 Th 1:12, but recognized in Tit 2:13; 1 Jn 5:20; Rom 9:5; and 2 Pt 1:1 instances in which in ascending order there is increasing probability that Jesus is called God. Thus, five of the nine instances must be taken seriously in our discussion. A methodological note is in order here. Often these five examples are rejected by scholars, despite the grammatical arguments in their favor, on the grounds that the use of "God" for Jesus is rare in the New Testament and therefore always to be considered improbable. However, is not the rarity of the usage to some extent dependent on the rejection of these examples? If these five instances are joined to the three we shall cite in the next section, then the usage is not so rare.

III. TEXTS WHERE JESUS IS CLEARLY CALLED GOD

There are a number of passages in the New Testament which imply that Jesus is divine, but we shall confine our attention to three passages that explicitly use *theos* of Jesus.

1) Heb 1:8-9: The author says that God has spoken of Jesus His Son the words of Ps 45:6-7:

"Your throne, O God, is forever and ever . . . and the righteous scepter is the scepter of your [his] kingdom.

You have loved justice and hated iniquity; therefore, O God, your God has anointed you with the oil of gladness. . . ."

The psalm is cited according to the Septuagint. The first question we must ask is whether *ho theos* in v. 8 is a nominative or a vocative. A few scholars, including Westcott, have taken it as a nominative and have suggested the interpretation: "God is your throne for ever and ever." This is most unlikely. In the preceding verse of the psalm in the Septuagint we read: "Your weapons, O Mighty One, are sharpened"; the law of parallelism would indicate that the next verse should read: "Your throne, O God, is for ever and ever." Moreover, the parallelism from the very next line in the psalm, cited in v. 8 ("and the righteous scepter is . . ."), suggests that "throne" and not "God" is the subject of the line under consideration. There can be little doubt, then, that the reading of v. 8 which we have proposed is the correct one. Cullmann assures us that "Hebrews unequivocally applies the title 'God' to Jesus," and we believe that this is a true estimate of the evidence of v. 8.

V. Taylor admits that in v. 8 the expression "O God" is a vocative spoken of Jesus, but he says that the author of Hebrews was merely citing the psalm and using its terminology without any deliberate intention of suggesting that Jesus is God. It is true that the main point of citing the psalm was to contrast the Son with the angels and to show that the Son enjoys eternal domination, while the angels are but servants. Therefore, in the citation no major point was being made of the fact that the Son can be addressed as God. Yet we cannot presume that the author did not notice that his citation had this effect. We can say, at least, that the author saw nothing wrong in this address, and we can call upon the similar situation in Heb 1:10, where the application to the Son of Ps 102:25-27 has the effect of addressing Jesus as Lord. Of course, we have no way of knowing what the "O God" of the psalm meant to the author of Hebrews when he applied it to Jesus. Ps 45 is a royal psalm; and on the analogy of the "Mighty God" of Is 9:6, "God" may have been looked on simply as a royal title and hence applicable to Jesus as the Davidic Messiah.

2) Jn 1:1: "In the beginning was the Word;
    and the Word was in God's presence,
    and the Word was God."

The crucial Greek words of the second and third lines are *kai ho logos en pros ton theon kai theos en ho logos.* The debate about the third line centers on the fact that *theos* is used without an article. Clearly, in the second line *ho theos* refers to God the Father, but in predicating *theos* without the article *ho* of the Word in the third line is the author trying to suggest that the Word is somewhat less than the Father (see Jn 14:28)?

Some explain the usage with the simple grammatical rule that predicate nouns generally lack the article. However, while *theos* is most probably the predicate, such a rule does not necessarily hold for a statement of identity (e.g., the "I am . . ."

formulae in Jn 11:25 and 14:6 are followed by predicate nouns which have an article).

To preserve the nuance of the anarthrous *theos,* some (e.g., Moffatt) would translate: "The Word was divine." But this is too weak. After all, there is in Greek an adjective for "divine" (*theios*) which the author did not choose to use. The *New English Bible* paraphrases the line: "What God was, the Word was." This is certainly better than "divine," but loses the terseness of the Prologue's style. Perhaps the best explanation of why the author of the Prologue chose to use *theos* without the article to refer to the Word is that he desired to keep the word distinct from the Father (*ho theos*).

Several factors suggest that we should not attach too much theological importance to the lack of the article. This first verse of the Prologue forms an inclusion with the last line of the Prologue, and there (1:18; see above) we hear of "God the only Son" ([*ho*] *monogenes theos*). Moreover, as the beginning of the Gospel, the first verse of the Prologue also forms an inclusion with the (original) end of the Gospel, where in 20:28 Thomas calls Jesus "My Lord and my God." Neither of the passages involved in these inclusions would suggest that in Johannine thought Jesus was *theos* but less than *ho theos.* To a certain extent, calling Jesus God represents for the fourth Gospel a positive answer to the charges made against Jesus that he was arrogantly making himself God (Jn 10:33; 5:18). The Roman author Pliny the Younger describes the Christians of Asia Minor as singing hymns to Christ as to a God. The Prologue, a hymn of the Johannine community at Ephesus, fits this description, as do the similar Pauline hymns in Philippians and Colossians.

It may be well to re-emphasize what we stated at the beginning of this article, namely, that the Prologue's hymnic confession "The Word was God" does not have the same ideological content found in Nicaea's confession that the Son was "true God of true God." A different problematic and a long philosophical development separate the two.

3) Jn 20:28: On the Sunday evening one week after Easter Jesus appears to Thomas and the other dis-

ciples, and Thomas confesses him as "My Lord and my God."

This is the clearest example in the New Testament of the use of "God" for Jesus, for the contention of Theodore of Mopsuestia that Thomas was uttering an exclamation of thanks to the Father finds few proponents today. Here Jesus is addressed as God (*ho theos mou*), with the articular nominative serving as a vocative. The scene is designed to serve as a climax to the Gospel: as the resurrected Jesus stands before the disciples, one of their number at last gives expression to an adequate faith in Jesus. He does this by applying to Jesus the Greek equivalent of two terms applied to the God of the Old Testament. The best example of the Old Testament usage is in Ps 35:23, where the psalmist cries out: "My God and my Lord." It may well be that the Christian use of such a confessional formula was catalyzed by Domitian's claim to the title *dominus et deus noster.*

IV. EVALUATION OF THE EVIDENCE

The question that forms the title of this chapter must be answered in the affirmative. In three clear instances and in five instances that have a certain probability Jesus is called God in the New Testament. The use of *theos* of Jesus which is attested in the early second century was a continuation of a usage which had begun in New Testament times. Really, there is no reason to be surprised at this. "Jesus is Lord" was evidently a popular confessional formula in New Testament times, and in this formula Christians gave Jesus the title *kyrios* which was the standard Septuagint translation for YHWH. If Jesus could be given this title, why could he not be called *theos,* which the Septuagint often used to translate *'elohim*? The two Hebrew Terms had become relatively interchangeable, and indeed YHWH was the more sacred term.

This does not mean that we can take a naive view about the development that took place in the New Testament usage of "God" for Jesus (nor, for that matter, in the gradual development in the understanding of Jesus' divinity). The eight instances with which we are concerned are found in these New Testament writings: Romans, Hebrews, Titus, John, 1 John, and 2 Peter. Let us see what this means in terms of chronology.

Jesus is never called God in the Synoptic Gospels, and a passage like Mk 10:18 would seem to preclude the possibility that Jesus used the title of himself. Even the fourth Gospel never portrays Jesus as saying specifically that he is God. The sermons which Acts attributes to the beginning of the Christian mission do not speak of Jesus as God. Thus, there is no reason to think that Jesus was called God in the earliest layers of New Testament tradition. This negative conclusion is substantiated by the fact that Paul does not use the title in any epistle written before 58. The first likely occurrence of the usage of "God" for Jesus is in Rom 9:5; if we could be certain of the grammar of this passage, we could thus date the usage to the late 50's.

Chronologically, Heb 1:8-9 and Tit 2:13 would be the next examples, although the uncertainty of the date of composition of these epistles creates a problem. Hebrews cannot be dated much before the fall of Jerusalem, and many would place it even later. The date of Titus depends on the acceptance or rejection of the Pauline authorship of the Pastorals—scholarly views range from the middle 60's to the end of the century. The Johannine writings offer us the most frequent examples of the use of the title (three in John; one in 1 John), and these writings are generally dated in the 90's. The common opinion of recent exegetes, Catholics included, is that 2 Peter is one of the latest New Testament works.

If we date New Testament times from 30 to 100, quite clearly the use of "God" for Jesus belongs to the second half of the period and becomes frequent only toward the end of the period. This judgment is confirmed by the evidence of the earliest extrabiblical Christian works. At the beginning of the second century Ignatius freely speaks of Jesus as God. In *Ephesians* 18, 2 he says: "Our God, Jesus the Christ, was conceived by Mary"; in 19, 3 he says: "God was manifest as man." In *Smyrnaeans* 1, 1 Ignatius begins by giving glory to "Jesus Christ, the God who has thus given you wisdom." We have already cited Pliny's testimony at the turn of the century that the Christians of Asia Minor sang hymns to Christ as to a God. by mid-second century, the so-called *2 Clement* (1, 1) can state: "Brethren, we must think of Jesus Christ as of God."

The geographical spread of the usage is also worth noting. If Rom 9:5 is accepted, then Paul, writing from Greece, betrays no hesitation about the acceptability of the usage to his Roman audience. (Yet Mark, traditionally accepted as the Gospel of Rome, written in the 60's, does not hesitate to report a saying of Jesus in which he refuses to be called God: see Mk 10:18 above.) If Titus is accepted as a genuinely Pauline epistle, it was probably written from Macedonia to Titus in Crete. The place of the composition of Hebrews is not known: Alexandria is a prominent candidate, and either Palestine or Rome is thought to be the destination. The Johannine works are associated with Ephesus in Asia Minor. Ignatius, from Antioch, seems free to use "God" of Jesus when writing both to Asia Minor and to Rome. Pliny's statement reflects the Christian practice in Bithynia in Asia Minor. Thus, the usage seems to be attested in the great Christian centers of the New Testament world, and there is no evidence to support a claim that in the late first century the custom of calling Jesus God was confined to a small area or faction within the Christian world.

Is this usage a Hellenistic contribution to the theological vocabulary of Christianity? Since we have no evidence that Jesus was called God in the Jerusalem or Palestinian communities of the first two decades of Christianity, the prima-facie evidence might suggest Hellenistic origins. This is supported by the fact that in two New Testament passages "God" is intimately joined to "Savior" as a title for Jesus (Tit 2:13; 2 Pt 1:1), and "Savior" is to some extent a Hellenistic title. However, there is other evidence to suggest that the usage had its roots in the Old Testament; and so, if the usage is non-Palestinian, it may have arisen among converts from Diaspora Judaism. As we saw, Heb 1:8-9 is a citation of Ps 45. The confession of Thomas in Jn 20:28 echoes an Old Testament formula (although, as we pointed out, one cannot exclude the possibility of an anti-Domitian apologetic). The background for Jn 1:1 is the opening of Genesis, and the concept of the Word reflects Old Testament themes of the creative word of God and personified Wisdom. Perhaps the best we can do from the state of the evidence is to leave open the question of the background of the custom of calling Jesus God.

The slow development of the usage of the title "God" for Jesus requires explanation. Not only is there the factor that Jesus is not called God in the earlier strata of New Testament material, but also there are passages cited in the first series of texts above, that by implication reserve the title "God" for the Father. Moreover, even in the New Testament works that speak of Jesus as God, there are also passages that seem to militate against such a usage—a study of these texts will show that this is true of the Pastorals and the Johannine literature. The most plausible explanation is that in the earliest stage of Christianity the Old Testament heritage dominated the use of the title "God"; hence "God" was a title too narrow to be applied to Jesus. It referred strictly to the Father of Jesus, to the God to whom he prayed. Gradually (in the 50's and 60's?), in the development of Christian thought "God" was understood to be a broader term. It was seen that God had revealed so much of Himself in Jesus that "God" had to be able to include both Father and Son. The late Pauline works seem to fall precisely in this stage of development. If Rom 9:5 calls Jesus God, it is an isolated instance within the larger corpus of the main Pauline works, which think of Jesus as Lord and of the Father as God. By the time of the Pastorals, however, Jesus is well known as God-and-Savior. The Johannine works come from the final years of the century, when the usage is common. Yet some of the material that has gone into the fourth Gospel is traditional material about Jesus which has been handed down from a much earlier period. Therefore, there are passages in John (14:28; 17:3; 20:17) that reflect an earlier mentality. We can only sketch the broad lines of such a development, but we can be reasonably confident that these lines are true.

We can, perhaps, go further and suggest the ambiance of this development. We think that the usage of calling Jesus God was a liturgical usage and had its origin in the worship and prayers of the Christian community. A priori, this is not unlikely. Bultmann has long maintained that the title "Lord" was given to Jesus in the Hellenistic communities as they recognized him as the deity present in the act of worship. Without committing ourselves to this theory and its implications, we do recognize the liturgical setting of some instances of the confession of Jesus as Lord, and therefore we might anticipate a similar setting for the confession of Jesus as God.

Of the eight instances of the latter confession, the majority are clearly to be situated in a background of worship and liturgy. Four are doxologies (Tit 2:13; 1 Jn 5:20; Rom 9:5; 2 Pt 1:1), and it is well accepted that many of the doxologies in the epistolary literature of the New Testament echo doxologies known and used by the respective communities in their public prayer. Heb 1:8-9 cites a psalm that was applied to Jesus, and we know the custom of singing psalms in Christian celebrations (1 Cor 14:26; Eph 5:19). Certainly this would include Old Testament psalms that were thought to be particularly adaptable to Jesus. Thus, it is not too adventurous of Wainwright to suggest that the author of Hebrews was calling on psalms that his readers sang in their liturgy and was reminding them of how these psalms voiced the glory of Jesus. The Prologue of John, which twice calls Jesus God, was originally a hymn, and we have already recalled Pliny's dictum about the Christians singing hymns to Christ as to a God.

Perhaps, at first glance, Jn 20:28 seems an exception to the rule, for the confession of Thomas is given a historical rather than a liturgical setting. Yet even here the scene is carefully placed on a Sunday, when the disciples of Jesus are gathered together. Moreover, it is a very plausible suggestion that the words in which Thomas confesses Jesus, "My Lord and my God," represent a confessional formula known in the Church of the evangelist's time. In this case it is not unlikely that the confession is a baptismal or liturgical formula along the lines of "Jesus is Lord."

This theory of the liturgical origins of the usage of the title "God" for Jesus in New Testament times has some very important implications concerning the meaning of this title, and, indeed, goes a long way toward answering some of the objections against calling Jesus God, such as those mentioned at the beginning of the article. For instance, it was objected that calling Jesus God neglects the limits of the incarnation. But this objection is not applicable to the New Testament usage, for there the title "God" is. not directly given to the Jesus of the ministry. In the Johannine writings it is the pre-existent Word

371

(1:1) or the Son in the Father's presence (1:18) or the resurrected Jesus (20:28) who is hailed as God. The doxologies confess as God the triumphant Jesus; Heb 1:8-9 is directed to Jesus whose throne is forever. Thus, in the New Testament there is no obvious conflict between the passages that call Jesus God and the passages that seem to picture the incarnate Jesus as less than God or the Father. The problem of how during his lifetime Jesus could be both God and man is presented in the New Testament, not by the use of the title "God," but by some of the later strata of Gospel material which bring Jesus' divinity to the fore even before the resurrection. Ignatius of Antioch does use the title "God" of Jesus during his human career. This may be the inevitable (and true) development of the New Testament usage of calling the preincarnational and the resurrected Jesus God; but from the evidence we have, it is a post-New Testament development.

The liturgical ambiance of the New Testament usage of "God" for Jesus also answers the objection that this title is too much of an essential definition, which objectifies Jesus and is untrue to the soteriological interest of the New Testament. As far as we can see, no one of the instances we have discussed attempts to define Jesus essentially. The acclamation of Jesus as God is a response of prayer and worship to the God who has revealed Himself to men in Jesus. Jn 1:18 speaks of God the only Son who has revealed the Father: Jn 1:1 tells us that God's Word is God. The confession of Jesus as God is a recognition by believing subjects of the sovereignty and lordship of divine rule in, through, and by Jesus: thus, Thomas' "My Lord and my God" (Jn 20:28), and Romans' (9:5) "God who is over all," and Hebrews' (1:8) "Your throne, O God, is for ever and ever." How could the confession of Jesus as God be more soteriological than when Jesus is called "our God-and-Savior" (2 Pt 1:1; Tit 2:13)? If there is validity in Bultmann's concern that belief in Jesus must have reference for men, then he can have no objection to what 1 Jn 5:20 says of Jesus Christ: "This is the true God and eternal life."

Thus, even though we have seen that there is a solid biblical precedent for calling Jesus God, we must be cautious to evaluate this usage in terms of the New Testament ambiance.

Raymond Edward Brown

Our firm adherence to the later theological and ontological developments in the meaning of the formula "Jesus is God" must not cause us to overvalue or undervalue the New Testament confession.

Gabriel Moran
1935-

Gabriel Moran was born in Manchester, New Hampshire. After joining the Christian Brothers, he taught from 1958 to 1961 in Providence, Rhode Island, then from 1962 to 1965 in Washington, D.C. In 1965 he received his Ph.D. from the Catholic University of America and joined the faculty of Manhattan College in the Bronx. In 1970 he was named professor of religion at New York Theological Seminary. Since 1972 he has been secretary of The Alternative, an adult education program based in New York City.

Various movements in European thought have made their impact felt in the theology of our century. The shortcomings resulting from certain earlier trends provoked the formulation of new syntheses that tried to restore priorities and put the accent on central rather than peripheral issues in Catholic thinking. Such developments as personalism, existentialism, and phenomenology would have to be considered in any complete account. These trends, however, found only limited resonance in any American Catholic writers until the eve of Vatican II. Thus when the work of Gabriel Moran began to appear in the 1960s, there were predictably mixed reactions. He was obviously articulate and had something to say, but his language and message were disturbingly different from the "manual-theology" that still prevailed.

In his Theology of Revelation *Moran demonstrated how a personalist approach could avoid much of the sterility that threatened the tradition when it was reduced to static catechism forms. The book consisting of ten chapters, is concerned chiefly with other issues than those of traditional Christology which we have been tracing. But in the process of elaborating a more dynamic understanding of "revelation," he has to deal with the central and indispensable role of Christ who is the Revelation of God. So, we have selected this section of Moran's work, chapter 3, "Christ as Revelatory Communion," for inclusion here. It represents a different kind of theological writing as well as thinking, a style that many welcomed with enthusiasm because it struck so many chords that harmonized with the spirit of renewal generated by the Council.*

It would be inaccurate to allude to the influence of personalism on Moran's thought without also acknowledging his serious attention to the Christological tradition. He puts constant stress on the need to push yet further in the direction of a more fully elaborated theology of Christ's consciousness, the very direction that has been the focus of the best theologians of the century, as we have seen in Guardini, Adam, Lonergan, Schillebeeckx, and Rahner. This coalescence of conviction is one of the promising signs of our time.

This is a good example of the way in which various issues come to the fore in different periods as a tradition develops. As perspectives change, deficiencies in earlier formulations are sensed and requirements for contemporary relevance are realized. These are some of the dynamics that keep theology alive and make it the expression of a meaningful tradition. And, as Avery Dulles said in his review of this book in Commonweal, *"Moran has unquestionably put the accent where it should and must be placed in the light of Vatican II—namely on the salvific encounter which takes place here and now between the believer and the God who graciously calls men into His friendship."*

THEOLOGY OF REVELATION

CHAPTER III

CHRIST AS REVELATORY COMMUNION

A t the third session of Vatican II, in a speech based upon many years of missionary experience, Archbishop (now Cardinal) Paul Zoungrana of the Upper Volta besought the bishops of the Council: "Say to the world that Jesus Christ is the revelation of God so that the figure of Christ may shine forth over the earth." Like many other pastoral pleas at the Council, the remark reflected a significant change in theological emphasis.

In striking contrast to the treatises *De Revelatione* that we mentioned earlier, the person of Jesus Christ has assumed a dominant role in discussions on revelation. Of course, Catholic theology always did give Christ a central place in the deliverance of revelation to mankind; but the statement now almost commonplace in theological writing is that Jesus Christ did not just bring the revelation but that he *is* the revelation. One can hardly deny that there had earlier been a failure to manifest a true Christocentrism in analyses of revelation, a failure which was puzzling if not scandalous to many Protestant brethren. Fortunately, the centrality of the person of Christ in the revelational redemptive process has now been insisted upon by the second Vatican Council in such a way that it would be difficult for Catholic theology to neglect it.

The simple repetition, however, of the phrase "Christ is the revelation" does not guarantee that a truly Christological understanding of revelation has been or will be attained. While it has been common in recent years to say that Christ is the revelation, there are few attempts to explain how the use of the word "revelation" in this sense is related to the other uses of the word in Catholic theology. One would suspect that the identification of revelation with Christ is usually not taken in literalness. It is assumed to be a beautiful metaphor indicating that not only the words of Christ taught us about God, but that his activities and attitudes did also. It would be thought, however, that strictly speaking revelation cannot be a person since revelation is truth that God makes known to man.

There is great need to examine what we do mean when we speak of Christ as the revelation. In particular we must, as the *Constitution* indicates, relate to this the revelational—redemptive history of which we have spoken earlier. We cannot be content to say that Christ is simply the last and greatest event of an historical chain. In this chapter I wish rather to assert: 1) that God's revelation not only reaches a high point in Christ but is recapitulated in him; 2) that the participating subject who first receives the Christ-revelation is not the apostolic community but Christ himself; 3) that the fullness of revelation reached at the resurrection cannot perdure in books or institutions but only in the consciousness of the glorified Lord.

God Totally Revealing

We have seen earlier that although God made use of many instruments in the revelational process it was always God who was being revealed. He was present among the people of the Old Testament giving himself to them in a communion of knowledge and love. For a truly personal communion with man, God had to be God for man in a human way. Since his desire was to manifest a tri-personal life and to reveal to man his share in that life, only a person, only God living a human life, could adequately reveal this. Revelation from the beginning was concerned not so much with problems, facts, or events, but an inner personal life; finally, it was in the flesh of a human nature that the unsuspected and unsurpassable revealing took place.

The Incarnation is not merely a brute fact out of the past. It is the opening of a human history which established a unique way of revelation. This is the true and primary *source of revelation:* God revealing in Christ. Jesus Christ is the gospel that springs up from within the inner life of the triune God. God's speaking to man had always been threatened with becoming an abstract, conceptual word emptied of its meaning. With Jesus Christ, the irreducible, concrete, fleshly word was spoken which expressed all that God wished to say or could say to the world. "The secret of God becomes the secret of man, because this man is God. . . . The light is given, the light is united to men, and this union is not a philosophical system or an inspired book, but is Someone living, the man Jesus Christ." From that moment onward, the expression "word of God" could have only one strict and primary meaning: the personal Word. Every other use of the expression is valid only insofar as it shares in or throws light upon the person of the Word.

That the Old Testament was the revelatory-redemptive preparation for Christ is a Christian belief reaffirmed by the Council. If such a preparation were something more than an external instruction, then we must conceive of Israel as the process and the partial realization of that body which issued from the Virgin Mary. By successive acts of freeing Israel from her selfish ways, God was preparing mankind for a definitive act of love which would free man from the bondage of flesh. The community itself could not be the bearer of the final revelation, but the community could help to form the one who, flesh of our flesh, could bear for his brothers the final gift of God's personal existence. If this one man were taken up into God's life, it would not help but have an effect upon the entire social body. The diffuse revelational acts of God in the Old Testament were thus contracted into the personal history which stands at the pinnacle of God's dealing with Israel. By Jesus' complete receptivity to the self-bestowing love of God, all that had haltingly and successively been made present in the history of Israel was recapitulated and focused in one life span.

It should hardly be surprising, therefore, that Christ was understood through the images and events of the Old Testament while at the same time he reciprocally threw light upon the ancient books. In reading the Old Testament Christ discovered the elements of his own biography and, conversely, it was in his own person that the separate strands of Old Testament development fused. Christ abolished neither Law, nor Sabbath, nor Temple; he brought them together and brought them to completion by becoming them. In the prophetic tradition and in the wisdom literature Christ (and later the Church) found the imagery and vocabulary to describe his person and his mission. It was not so much in isolated texts of the Old Testament that Christ was to be found, but in the whole flowing movement and development of man's relation to God.

It would also follow from what we have said previously that if Christ sums up the history of God's speaking to Israel, he also in some way contains the universal history of God's dealing with man. The Old Testament conceives of the redemptive covenant with Israel as paradigmatic, so that the creation of the universe and universal history are directed toward redemption and contained within the covenant. In viewing cosmic history in this way, 2 Isaiah represents the peak of Old Testament development; it is from that peak that Christ begins. Whatever the ontological consequences that might be drawn from this teaching, the scripture leaves little doubt that the whole of history moved toward its assumption in Christ. All of the words which God had spoken, beginning with the word of creation, are included in the Word who is personally God. What is chronologically first must be understood in the light of the later, full revelation.

Jesus Christ is God, the eternal subsistent Word; his words are the words of God. Nevertheless, God is still revealed in Christ through the veil of human flesh. Even when it is the Son of God in question, truth for man is always a veiling and an unveiling. Through bodily symbols man reveals himself to another, but it is at the same time the body which veils and makes impossible the total unveiling or disposition of the person. When we say, therefore, that Christ is the fullness of revelation we do not mean that God became clearly known to all who looked upon Christ. To most he is a puzzle, to some he is a scandal, to all he is incomprehensible. Even to Christ's most faithful followers God is revealed only partially and temporally and always through human symbols.

God revealed himself in Jesus Christ, but this personal existence incarnated itself in successive gestures and actions, and in human speech which attempts to incarnate thought. His being shone forth through his words as testimony to what he is. His credibility rested not upon the evidence of his ideas but upon the manifestation of his person. His teaching could not be separated from his person, and although later generations may find it impossible to write a biography of Jesus, his teachings preserved by the Church do give insight into his person.

In addition to his teaching which was revelatory of God, every action, appearance, and gesture of Christ was infinitely rich in meaning. Beyond the logic of his doctrine it was his manner of meeting people, the way he spoke, and his acts of merciful love which revealed the power of God. The miracles which play such a significant part in the scriptural accounts have this function in the revelatory process. They were not given primarily as proofs to convince unbelievers, nor as external testimonies to his teaching. Just as prophecy is the effect of revelation upon history, so miracles are the effect upon man's world of God's revealing presence. "Miracles happen spontaneously because the Kingdom is in the midst of men." Instead of external criteria for judging the word spoken, the miracles are part of the speaking process. Through Christ's miracles there is spoken to the world the power and the love of God and the conflict of good with evil in the world.

There is another point of crucial importance that cannot be neglected when one speaks of God revealing himself in Christ. The revelation of Christ is at one and the same time the revelation of the Trinity. Scripture does not merely say that God appeared, but that "the Father appeared to men in the Son; in fact, that is everything; the whole content of revelation is contained in that, and that is Christ." The role of the Logos-revealer seems at first glance to be an ambiguous one. On the one hand, he seems to be the one revealed, the one who is in possession of the truth. On the other hand, he seems more often to point beyond himself as faithful witness to the Father.

To set up an opposition here between a Christocentric and theocentric concept of revelation would be superficial and misleading. The Son is revealed but it is precisely in relation to the Father (and to the Spirit). Whoever sees him sees the Father (Jn. 14:9). The Son is the revelation of the Father and the person within the Trinity who expresses the truth. He is not only "one of the divine persons any of whom could become man if he wanted to, but *the* person in whom God communicates himself hypostatically to the world; the Incarnation mirrors the unique

personal character of the second divine person, the Word."
Others had spoken about God but the Eternal Logos was the witness who had seen him. No one else knew God in the full biblical
sense of knowing. The Son gives this knowledge to whom he
wishes (Mt. 11:27) not by explaining the Father, but simply by
speaking and acting. Christ in his person reveals the way that
men are to take to God; he is the way, the truth, and the life. In
revealing himself as the way and the gracious act of God, Christ
simultaneously makes known himself, the Father, and the plan
of salvation.

Christ as the Recipient of Revelation

That God was in Christ revealing himself to men and that
Jesus Christ is God's Word to the world is an affirmation repeatedly made in recent Catholic writing. That the man Jesus was
the recipient of God's revelation and fulfilled the vocation of the
man of faith is a statement equally important yet seldom made
in Catholic theological writing. It is perhaps one of the unfortunate legacies of the nineteenth and early twentieth centuries
(though the problem is much older than that) that orthodox
writing tends implicitly to devaluate the humanness of Jesus
Christ.

Every Catholic who has had a minimum of religious instruction knows that Christ is truly man and therefore has a human
nature. But in our real, existential thinking or in prayer, writes
Karl Rahner, we (theologians as well as simple faithful) tend to
put the humanity of Christ on God's side not man's. As a result
of this, the gospel record of the life of Christ is taken not as the
story of a human life but as a piece of play-acting in which nothing really happens and in which the personal reactions are little
more than pretension. "Such a piece of play-acting would be
unworthy," writes Daniélou, "Christ pretended nothing. He did
not pretend to be a man; he really *was* a man." In many theological considerations (for example, of grace, redemption, or
sacraments) there has developed a better understanding of the
place of Christ's humanity. In the most basic area of revelation,
however, there remains (despite appearances and assertions to
the contrary) an almost complete void.

This matter of Christ as the recipient or human participant in revelation is of no small importance. It is in fact the key to the personal, social, and historical character of Christian revelation. If our previous analysis is correct, that is, if revelation is found in the intercommunion of God and man, then one must look for the highest expression of his covenant bond and dialogue *in* the Lord Jesus. He is man receiving as well as God bestowing; the very meaning of the Incarnation is this intercourse of divine and human. The highest union of God and man is not that between Christ and his apostles; the one perfect union is in the Word which comes from the Father and is united to the humanity of Christ.

Jesus did not present himself as God speaking truths to be written down and learned by men. He did present himself as the one who lived in prayerful communion with the Father and one who invited men to join with him in this communion of knowledge and love. "The whole religious life of Christ was dominated and directed by this personal relation to God, his Father: God revealed and communicated himself interiorly as *his* Father; Christ lived in an ineffable, personal communion, in a permanent 'I-Thou' dialogue with God *his* Father."

As Christ recapitulated the wonderful works of *God,* so too he recapitulated man in all his levels of uniqueness and universality. He is the summation of all that was best in the religious life of mankind. He is the supreme case of the "man who orders his life, his whole existence, upon the real and living word that dominates everything in him, to the point at which he is ultimately 'taken up' into the Word, and bears witness to it with his life and blood." Christ is the first of men whose own existence throws light on all of human existence as it is constituted by a nature that is open upward and perfected in freedom by its nearness to God.

One of the most pressing needs of contemporary theology is to work out a theology of Christ's consciousness and psychological development as a complement to the theology expressed in the Chalcedonic categories. Though the topic may seem esoteric and unnecessary for the ordinary Christian, it is a fact nonetheless that if theology fails to provide the concrete data,

Christian piety fills in the abstract categories with unexamined and to a large extent erroneous detail. The exegete's task is to trace the development in Christ's life as it is recorded in the historical accounts. The theologian for his part can provide a framework for this study, Catholic theology insisting that a phenomenology of consciousness cannot be entirely separated from a metaphysical structure.

The concrete and detailed study of Christ's knowledge is yet to be written; even the basic principles of that development go beyond what can be covered here. I would insist, however, upon the centrality of this question, upon the truly human character of Christ's knowledge, and upon consciousness as springing up from within human life as a point of receptivity. In the unique consciousness of this unique individual there takes place fully and definitively the encounter of God and man in redemptive revelation. "A new knowledge finds its way into mankind, a knowledge that comes from God himself to man, and springs up in the deepest center of mankind, in the heart of this man who is the heart of the whole race—God gives this knowledge, and it is formed in the God-man, it is human and at the same time divine. It is what we call revelation.

Attempts to speak of the revelation coming to its fullness in the human understanding of Christ are hampered by a superficial understanding of what it means "to know." In a common-sense view of knowing, one either knows a fact or does not know it; the knower possesses a thing called knowledge by looking at a world of objects and seeing it as it is. It does not take much philosophical probing to reveal how inadequate this conception of knowledge is. Modern philosophy has emphasized the difference between knowing an object and knowing a person. Even more fundamental is the difference between the knowledge of another and the knowledge of oneself. Whatever explanations are given for man's self knowledge it is certain that man does not view himself as one among many objects, in the universe. Man knows and affirms himself at least implicitly in the affirmation of every individual being. Knowing oneself is not simply the possessing of a fact; it is the taking hold of one's identity in a way which may vary from a simple, global awareness to a detailed, reflexive understanding.

Gabriel Moran

A knower is simply a being capable of reflecting back upon itself and its relation to others. To know is to be aware of and to possess one's self presence. A being with such perfection and power, one that has to some degree emerged from the conditions of the material being dispersed in space and time, we call spiritual. If knowing is simply the perfection of being it does not necessarily imply a split between knower and known; in a being of pure actuality, knowing and being would be identical. For man, the finite and material being, knowing is always mediated by what is other than himself. Although there is a basic presence to self which inclines man toward knowing, he is born without any actual knowledge. The conjunction of the capacity or thirst for knowledge with bodily presence to the world brings him into conscious reflexive presence to himself and others.

Concerning Christ's knowledge, theologians have long wrestled with several problems, particularly: 1) the question of the beatific vision; 2) the possibility of ignorance, development, and experiential knowledge—all three of which are closely related and all three apparently excluded by the beatific vision; 3) the presence of infused knowledge.

Catholic teaching has strongly defended the thesis that Christ always had a consciousness of his divine sonship. The question which has divided theologians has been the manner in which Christ had this "vision." Too often, however, it has been assumed that Christ possessed the facts of who he was and there was nothing more to learn, that he had a vision of God which excluded any real growth in knowledge. The word "vision" here is partly responsible for this misunderstanding since it seems to assume an object presented from the outside and looked at. Christ would not have gained a knowledge of God by objective data being presented to him. Such a conception springs from the reduction of knowledge to a looking out upon the world of objective fact. Christ's human nature was immediately present to the Word through the hypostatic union. Since this union is an act of a spiritual being at its highest point, the reality of this union cannot be entirely unconscious. Christ was present to God because he was present to himself. The basic self-identity and self-presence that is the *a priori* of objective and conceptual knowledge implies that Christ knew himself in every act of objective knowing. Thus

God was attained in the human understanding of Christ as the first reality known and as always known insofar as a knower knows himself at least implicitly in his knowledge of any other thing.

If this is the way in which Christ's consciousness attained to the knowledge of God, it is possible for him to have been ignorant of objective facts. He stood in need of the knowledge which comes through temporal and bodily existence in the world with other men. The peculiar mark of human knowledge is that despite a drive toward the plentitude of being, man's specific, actual knowledge is gained only through and in bodily experience. Christ's presence to the Logos did not provide any objective, communicable knowledge. He had to experience the world to acquire his explicit knowledge of factual situations.

There should, therefore, be no great problem in attributing ignorance and thereby real human development in Christ. The history of his self-expression was not only the history of his psychological adaptation to his surroundings, but a human growth in understanding and knowledge. There were certainly limits to Christ's knowledge; the question is the way in which the limitation is to be conceived. It would not help to imagine a large body of numerable facts, some of which Christ had and some of which he did not have. Rather, within the perspective indicated above, Christ's knowledge is a presence to himself which is at once a consciousness of God and a global awareness of all that is related to God. Such a relation in knowledge not only does not exclude a development of knowledge, but demands as its necessary complement the emergence of conceptual and communicable knowlege.

Contemporary theology's insistence upon the limitations of Christ's knowledge is not intended to denigrate his greatness as man. Christ possessed human knowledge to an extraordinary degree, but it was *human* knowledge, that is partial, temporal, and experiential. Whereas medieval theology thought that it was fitting to attribute all gifts and all knowledge to Christ's humanity, we realize today that it is more fitting and more accurate to see Christ living his human life as the recapitulation of man's revelational history, like to us in all things save sin. Whereas medieval theology made no distinction between an immediate knowledge of God and the "beatific vision," contemporary theology attributes to Christ a direct knowledge of God that is not necessarily beatifying while he is on earth.

The so-called "infused knowledge" traditionally asserted of Christ's consciousness cannot be deduced from his divine sonship. Some theologians assert that this knowledge is required by Christ's redemptive mission. The gospels show Christ with an extraordinary prophetic or messianic knowledge that perhaps requires some special illumination in addition to his knowledge by experience. This knowledge would not have to be conceived of as a pouring of concepts into his consciousness, but rather as the providing of an impetus to a special insight into the knowledge implicit in him by reason of who he was. The extent and nature of any infused knowledge remains an open question exegetically and theologically, but the question is at any rate not central to the main concern of this chapter.

The revelation of God to mankind was thus formed in the conscious human experience of Jesus Christ, sustained by his love. His awareness of God was embedded in the patterns appropriate to each stage of his life so that there was continuous growth. He advanced in wisdom and age and favor before both God and man. Having gone out from the Father in the likeness of sinful flesh, he experienced the pain and suffering of his return journey. Son though he was, he learned obedience by the things he suffered. Suffering worked upon, drawing out the deepest resources of his heroism. Day by day he was able to gather more clearly the details of his coming passion. He did not attempt to escape from the human situation, but wished to experience and ratify it in its completeness. He came in fulfillness of the lineage of great Old Testament prophets with an attitude similar to theirs but rising above them. "What the Jews should always have done," writes Guardini, "but actually did so seldom, i.e., ascend by faith above immediate, tangible nature to the realm of the mind and the spirit so as to become what God desired them to be, had finally become accomplished in Christ."

To say that Christ lived by vision but that his followers live by faith is true, but it can also be misleading. If we conceive of faith as the patient acceptance of what God wills over what man desires, Jesus' fundamental human attitude was the same as that of the true servant of Yahweh and the faithful Christian. The Christian's life of faith means an imitation and a following of him on the road of obedience. Though Catholic theology denies that Christ had the theological virtue of faith, he is nevertheless the archetype and ideal of faith. His knowledge was measured by his mission; his "hour" was untouchable both by his enemies and by himself. He lived in the sheer, naked, unqualified acceptance of what came from the Father.

Fullness of Revelation: The Glorified Christ

The story of the gospel moves inexorably towards its climax. The double theme of Son revealing the Father and Father glorifying the Son finds its perfect fusion at "the hour" to which his life pointed. It was at that hour that God's love for man encountered the total responsiveness of man's love; at that hour the revelation-redemption was accomplished.

Throughout his life Christ had taught, healed, comforted, preached, but all of these symbols were inadequate to express what he was. Like other men, Christ knew more than he could say; he was more than he could consciously grasp. His self-expression through word and action awaited the most perfect expression of the cross. "All that was incommunicable in the divine communication expresses itself in the arms outstretched, the body emptied of blood and the heart pierced by the centurion's lance (Jn. 19:34). The word of love was given over fully to man. The revelation by word was consummated and sealed by revelation in action."

The final action of his life was the event which recapitulated his history just as his life recapitulated the whole revelational history. In that one act there was concentrated the supreme revelation of God's self-gift to the world. God gave him up to death to reveal the face of his glory. Death, which had been the sign of sin in the world (Rom. 5:12), became the expression of divine love and the revelation of divine grace.

In addition to being the final revelation of God's love, the cross is the final revelation of the power of evil in man, of man's emptiness, and of man's need for redemption. With Christ's death sin was revealed in all of its horror. Sinful man is frightened of love, he is frightened of freedom, and most of all he is frightened of God. The one time in our history, therefore that the divine appeared in all of his love and freedom, could have only one result. Sinful flesh could not endure it and so the Christ had to suffer and die (Lk. 24:26). To be Son of God in a sinful race was a terrifying thing.

If the cross represented the supreme revelatory action on God's part, it must also have been the supreme act of participating receptivity on the part of man. There is no revelation unless there is a human consciousness taking part in it receptively and answering to God. Clearly, it was not the apostles who were here the recipients; it was the one who as main participant in the action on Calvary offered his life for his brothers. With cries of agony in the Garden and on the cross (Lk. 22:42-44; Mk. 15:34), Christ passed through a kind of dark night of the soul to the final reception of revelation. Having entered the struggle in behalf of the true destiny of mankind, having perceived what was necessary to set man free, he was obedient to the will of his Father, obedient to the death of the cross. He ascended the cross as man's answer to God, but not without suffering, fear, and the desire to let the chalice pass. "We are astounded, we are shocked at this weakness and longing; it would have been more heroic, we feel, to accept unmoved this death which was to save the world. But this astonishment is born of a lack of understanding. We forget that the drama of mankind in search of salvation was first played out in Christ, and that he himself was the first to be raised by the Father."

Revelation reached its fullness, therefore, only at *the* hour when Christ burst through the gates of death by handing over the Spirit (Jn. 19:30). At that moment the redemption of the world was accomplished in his flesh, and revelation as the cognitive expression of redemption was brought to perfection in the consciousness of Christ: he beheld the glory that was his. Though in a sense Christ had already possessed all, there was yet genuine novelty in his exaltation in glory: "When the hour comes and the Father gives it to him as supreme gift of his love, the Son will not say to the Father that he has always known this hour, that it holds nothing new for him, brings only what has been familiar, what he has already savored through and through in thought, already handled and thumbed over in his mind."

389

In this high point of revelation, therefore, death was but one aspect of the total act. What was from our side death was from the Father's side resurrection. Opening himself completely to God, Christ was transformed by the inrushing Spirit. The reception of Christ into glory is the never to be surpassed event in the revelational process. The resurrection was not only an event of the past; it was the beginning of a new life and the beginning of the total revelation in the risen Christ. Fixed in the act of redeeming us, he continues to offer his life for his brethren, and he continues to receive the revealing and redeeming love of the Father for all mankind.

When viewed in this perspective the time of the "forty days" takes on a much greater significance. "The mode of time revealed during the forty days remains the foundation for every other mode of his presence in time, in the Church, and in the world." A new mode of existence and a new mode of time were contracted into the first born from the dead and shone forth during the paschal time. Christ was now able to bring to light the meaning of words and deeds that his disciples could not previously understand. He had instructed them before his resurrection, but now he had to make them recall these things in the light of the Spirit. The resurrection was for the apostles not so much a proof of his divinity as the light of understanding which was cast upon all the facts of his life. The forty days was a time for instruction but not all was spoken in word, for there is a communication deeper than words can convey. There is noticeable in the post-resurrectional scenes a striking emphasis on eating and drinking, seeing and touching.

In the psyche of the risen Lord revelation was received (or taken part in receptively) in fullness not only for himself but for all his brothers. At the end of the forty days and then the pentecostal experience, the apostles had received the revelational communion of God's love. They did not receive it, however, in the same way and to the same extent as Christ did (and does). If God's revelation is not to fall off from its high point, it must remain in the one consciousness where it is totally accomplished. The risen and glorified Lord is the one place where revelation continues to happen in fullness.

The Church of time is a Church *en route* toward reunion with Christ in the vision of the blessed. But even while in time the Church is not cut off from the consciousness. Christ remain present to his Church as mediator of her revelation and redemption. "He 'goes before' first as a pillar of fire and then as a presence which moved from Jerusalem to Samaria to the ends of the earth. He is always ahead of the Church, beckoning it to get up to date, never behind it waiting to be refurbished."

Many books say that Christ revealed God during his historical life; some books say that he will reveal God in heaven; but few books say that he is *now revealing* God. This is most unfortunate. At the resurrection Christ was constituted Son of God for us; at that time he *began* his revelatory-redemptive activity in fullness. The Church must take seriously her continuing life in world history so as to understand what God is asking of her at each moment. There is no question of adding objective truths to the deposit of faith, nor is there question of going beyond Christ. What is of utmost importance is that the revelational process first accomplished in Christ should now be participated in by all Christians through a continuing revelational process.

It is a remarkable fact that whereas Catholic writing on grace and redemption leaves no doubt that the process of sanctification goes on in our world (without detriment to the once for all and final character of the redemption on Calvary), there is a great hesitancy to affirm a continuing revelational process in our world. This second, however, is just as necessary and just as important as the first. Unless both are affirmed and both joined in the risen Lord, there is bound to be a splintering of Catholic faith and theology into separate compartments of truths. What Jungmann has shown to be the disastrous effects of separating grace from the risen Christ is at least as true of the separation of revelation from the same risen Lord. A faith that is personal, social, and historical cannot spring from the acts of God in the Old Testament, nor the accounts of the historical Christ; rather, "this faith is the result of the *actual,* present, self-revelation of the heavenly Christ *through* his Spirit in the Church."

With the passage of this person through history and the contraction of time within his glorified person, the norm of history was revealed to be not an abstract law but a person. He is the norm of our concrete history, both that of the individual and that of the race; he is the one "concrete-universal." The truth, the law, the good were revealed not as external criteria for judging the person, but as realized in the person. This is the way in which Christ is the final standard of human entelechy. Man's whole bodily self is to be lifted up to God in the light and power of that one bodily existence lifted above and drawing all things.

David Tracy
1939-

David Tracy was born in Yonkers, New York, and studied in Rome, receiving his doctorate in theology from the Gregorian University in 1969. From 1967 to 1969 he was on the faculty of the Catholic University of America, and since 1969 has been teaching at the Divinity School of the University of Chicago. In 1970 he emerged as a talented interpreter of the contemporary scene with his impressive book on The Achievement of Bernard Lonergan. *He had done his doctoral dissertation on the development of Lonergan's thought on theological method up to 1965, and thus was in a unique position to draw attention to the significance of the Canadian Jesuit under whom he had studied in Rome.*

In 1975 he published Blessed Rage for Order: The New Pluralism in Theology, *the work that is excerpted here. It has generally been greeted as one of the most noteworthy contributions to theology in recent years. Building on the work of Lonergan, Tracy nonetheless demonstrates his own creativity in organizing and analyzing an impressive array of philosophical, biblical, and theological positions. Rather than viewing contemporary pluralism in the negative terms that so many do, he argues that this diversity can be made comprehensible and evaluated as well by delineating the models within which each thinker operates. After illustrating the four models that have dominated the recent past (the orthodox, the liberal, the neo-orthodox, and the radical), he then tries to formulate a new model, one that is still in the making, a "revisionist" model. Then in the second part of the book he applies this model to three principal areas of contemporary debate: the meanings of religion, theism, and Christology.*

The selection that follows is thus chapter nine of his ten-chapter book. It is not easy reading, since it builds upon the extensive groundwork that Tracy lays in the first part. The justification for including it here is that our collection may thereby close on a note of challenge. Once one embraces a model that brings the theologian out of his ivory tower, there is no way in which stale formulae of the past can simply be repeated. One of the principal insights which Bernard Lonergan has instilled in the new generation of Catholic theologians is that "theology is a function not only of revelation and faith but also of culture, so that cultural change entails theological change. For over a century theologians have gradually been adapting their thought to the shift from the classicist culture, dominant up to the French revolution, to the empirical and historical mindedness that constitutes its modern successor." (Lonergan, in the foreword to Tracy's first book).

Despite all the new demands which the revisionist model places on the modern theologian, because of the complexity of modern culture, the potential for enrichment of the tradition is obvious, as exemplified, for instance, in Tracy's contrast of "exclusivist" and "inclusivist" Christologies. Much has yet to be done if the meaning of Jesus as Savior is to be fully elaborated for today, and in that process the work of David Tracy is certainly among the most serious and promising on the current scene.

BLESSED RAGE FOR ORDER

CHAPTER 9

THE RE-PRESENTATIVE OF LIMIT-LANGUAGE OF CHRISTOLOGY

Introduction: The Question of Christology

The analysis of the metaphysical character of Christian theism concluded with an expression of the need to find symbolic religious language to re-present the truth of religious theism in a manner consonant with our actual situation. For Christians such language does not need invention, but rediscovery and reappropriation. Since the New Testament period to the present, Westerners generally, and Christians specifically, turn to the story of Jesus as the illuminating symbol for their religious understanding of existence. From the earliest language of the New Testament, the preaching, teaching, and deeds of Jesus of Nazareth himself, through the moment when the preacher becomes that which is preached, a continuous series of interpretations of this singular story by theologians, painters, musicians, writers, teachers, ethicians, and even politicans, have dominated the religious consciousness of the West.

Before deciding that this story has lost its power to disclose our present situation, to evoke those limit-experiences and that limit-image of a living and loving God which can transform and reorient our lives, one should see whether this historical symbol can be experienced anew. My own conviction, which this chapter shall try to document, is that hearing that story—or perhaps better, "over-hearing" it anew—still allows for those singular moments of a redescription of life's possibilities and a transformative reorientation of life's actualities which Christians have suggested by such traditional phrases as redemption and salvation.

By all means, let us hear with fresh minds those other stories —of the Buddha, of Mohammed, of Krishna—which we have too long and too ignorantly kept at a psychic distance. But to hear again the story of Jesus the Christ we owe at least to the memories of our earliest—our childhood—selves who once heard it freshly. More importantly, we owe it to the authentic religious possibilities inherent in our own lives to see what mode-of-being-in-the-world this "supreme fiction," this re-presentative fact, might yet allow.

I shall employ the same criteria as those spelled out in Part I: just how, phenomenologically, can we understand the existential meaningfulness of this central Christian symbol for our common experience; just how, metaphysically, can we understand the nature of and the means of validation for the specific cognitive claims of christology. The strategy of the present chapter can be described as a kind of "detour" through a discussion of the nature of "facts" and "fictions" to that question of existential meaningfulness. A detour seems demanded if the character of christology, at once factual and fictional, is to find contemporary clarification. In the Christian story of Jesus as the Christ we find ourselves presented with a story—a fiction—which needs reinterpretation, and with a claim to fact which needs clarification and perhaps restatement. That christological fact, for example, is not really a metaphysical reality in traditional Christian self-understanding. A proper understanding of God is an understanding of a metaphysical reality. For the concept of God, when conceived coherently, is either necessary or impossible. The reality of God, for the Christian, is a reality which either necessarily touches all our experience or necessarily does not exist. Yet the christological reality—the reality of God's self-manifestation in Jesus as the Christ—is not a metaphysical reality but a fact. There was and is no strict necessity for that action. Yet, for the Christian tradition, God did act in Jesus Christ. That action is represented in the limit-language of the New Testament by and about Jesus as the Christ. Before one can understand that action and that story, however, one must first ask whether any matters of fact—as distinct from metaphysical realities—can be described as appropriate disclosures of more than a particular cultural situation, as meaningful to our common human experience. On logical grounds alone, a matter-of-fact claim cannot be validated metaphysically in the manner of the theistic claim itself. Yet a factual claim can be validated as intrinsic to the life we all actually—as a matter of fact—lead.

David Tracy

What facts, then, do we need to investigate? At least three suggest themselves: first, the fact of our common human need for story, fiction, and symbol; second, the fact of "evil" in the human situation; third, the fact that facts are not exhaustively defined in terms of actualizations of possibilities, but also include re-presentations of possibilities. If we can clarify the kinds of facts relevant to our factual situation and thereby meaningful to our common experience, then we shall be prepared to investigate some more specific meanings involved in the Christian proclamation of Jesus as the Christ.

Before our detour through the nature of facts and fictions begins, a presuppositon of this entire discussion may well need some brief explanation. We presuppose as fact what history and common sense alike testify: that any specific religious tradition starts with some moment or occasion of special religious insight. This moment, if authentically religious, will be experienced as a limit-experience and will be expressed in a limit-language representative of that insight and that experience. If the language and the experience bear universal implications, if they are not purely at the mercy of psychological or sociological forces which adequately explain their meaning without remainder, then we may describe this religious tradition as a universal, a major religion. Such a designation of universality implies two characteristics: the religion arises from a special historical occasion of religious insight, but the special religious experience and language are sufficiently evocative of our common experience to bear the claim of universal meaningfulness. As that claim is clarified—for example, through the *Logos* tradition of Christianity—the full import of the special occasion is itself felt with more and more existential force. The special occasion of the preaching and person of Jesus of Nazareth seems clearly to meet these criteria; as the Christian religion develops in and beyond the New Testament itself, one finds that this process of universalization is radicalized to the point where he who preached the Kingdom becomes the focus of the preaching!

This strange history—an intensification process which includes at one and the same time a universalization of religious meaning and a radicalization of the special occasion itself—allows one to see something of the peculiar complexity of the Christian

397

religion. As that complexity has been traditionally interpreted, one finds the insistence that all Christian self-understanding—of God, humanity, and cosmos—is irrevocably christocentric. As that complexity has been more coherently "unpacked" through the history of christological reflection, one finds the concept "christocentrism" accepted as constitutive of the Christian religion in two radically different ways. In a first and still widely influential form, christocentrism means that only and solely God's "special revelation" in Jesus Christ is meaningful for a proper human self-understanding. This form of christocentrism, more accurately labelled "exclusivist" christology, may be found in most forms of Christian fundamentalism or in such sophisticated theological forms as the christology of Karl Barth. Any exclusivist christocentrism, however, is unavailable to anyone who agrees with the basic purposes and criteria of a revisionist theology. The revisionist position holds that christocentrism is not the exclusive property of fundamentalists and Barthians. Rather, it insists that not only does our common experience deny such claims to exclusivity but so do the Christian scriptures! For there, as this chapter shall attempt to show, one finds a claim for Jesus Christ that does place an understanding of his role and person at the center of Christian self-understanding; that does believe that such understanding of Jesus Christ is universal in its applicability to the human situation; but does not find any exclusivist understanding of that reality to be meaningful. For this second christocentric position, probably best described as an "inclusivist" christology, the disclosure manifested by the Christian proclamation of Jesus Christ is genuinely disclosive of all reality, is meaningful for our common existence, is central for a human understanding of the limit-possibilities of human existence. What that special occasion ("special" or "categorical" revelation) manifests is the disclosure that only God present to all humanity at every time and place ("original" or "transcendental" revelation) is present explicitly, actually, decisively, as my God in my response to this Jesus as the Christ.

This tradition of an inclusivist christology, present implicitly in historical Catholic Christianity's fidelity to the theological motif of the "universal salvific will of God" and in liberal Protestant Christianity's reformulations of christocentrism, is the basic christological position which informs any interpretation. Yet a contemporary interpretation, committed to a revisionist model for theological reflection, cannot remain content simply to announce its position in terms of God's universal salvific will. Rather one must try to show how and why this christological understanding, once reinterpreted in more explicitly contemporary terms, can be faithful to both the central meanings of our common experience and the central meanings of the New Testament texts. To the first step of that larger task we now turn by means of our detour through facts and fictions.

The Fact of the Need for Fiction

A variety of disciplines cite sufficient evidence to suggest that a near consensus has emerged on the human need for more than conceptual analysis for understanding human existence. More positively, human beings need story, symbol, image, myth, and fiction to disclose to their imaginations some genuinely new possibilities for existence; possibilities which conceptual analysis, committed as it is to understanding present actualities, cannot adequately provide. This section shall briefly describe certain of such evidence on our need for fiction and suggest certain formulations which may allow us to describe the meaning and the intention of this crucial human fact.

A kind of evidence has already been investigated in the earlier discussion of the meaning of religious language. In summary terms, one of the major conclusions of the third stage of analytic philosophy's investigation of the uses (meaning) of religious language was its firm insistence upon the legitimately non-cognitive uses (evocative, aesthetic, attitudinal, performative, etc.) which religious language fills. Such language, as R. B. Braithwaite's distinguished analysis shows, ordinarily involves the use of some "story" or "parable" by means of which the attitude of the speaker can be more deeply internalized. More specificially, the very notion of "fiction" may provide the first key to the present question. Fictions do not operate to help us escape reality, but to redescribe our human reality in such disclosive terms that we return to the "everyday" reoriented to life's real—if forgotten or sometimes never even imagined—possibilities. The greatest works of fiction—even of that genre called "realism"—do not simply describe our lives as a merely journalistic or merely photographic account might. Rather by redescribing the authentic possibilities of human existence—through such structural strategies as plot, narrative, comic and tragic genres—fictions open our minds, our imaginations, and our hearts to newly authentic and clearly transformative possible modes-of-being-in-the-world.

Such fictions, precisely by means of this process of redescription, can and often do reorient our lives into possibilities which, left to ourselves, we would more than likely never imagine, much less attempt. The artist who can capture some moment in our common history and redescribe it through the traditional or novel structural genres of fiction does not merely capture that "moment." He often reorients it. In such ways do artists function, as Ezra Pound reminds us, as the "antennae of the race." Ernest Hemingway, for example, does not attempt a careful analytical account of ethical possibility in the manner of a Kant or an Aristotle. Yet Hemingway's creative ability to redescribe our experience through believable and transformative fictions allows us to understand and to feel what "grace under pressure" might mean as a real possibility. Probably more than we know, all of us are indebted to those artists who have captured moments in our common history and redescribed those moments in their full possibilities for authentic and inauthentic life. We often find ourselves more deeply transformed and more radically reoriented by such "supreme fictions" than by the most careful analytical discussions of the distinction between "is" and "ought." To capture how it feels to live a certain way, to provide by that distanciation process we call genre both a proper imaginative entry into and a psychic distance from the "world" of the novel, film, or poem frees us to experience that possibility in all its experiential reality. When those possibilities degenerate into a reader's mere literalization of them—desperate attempts to act out the life of a Hemingway character, a Bogart toughness, a Monroe vulnerability—then we may also recognize the pathetic consequences of taking symbols literally and not seriously. Yet when that possibility is allowed to function as a fiction—a redescription of what reality is and might be—we find that the consequence often includes a reorientation of our own most basic moods, feelings, reactions and actions, our very way of living in this world.

We have, in fact, learned too much about the primordial and all-pervasive impact of such orientating conscious and unconscious moods to dismiss either fiction or mood itself as mere escape in the manner of our Victorian forefathers. Every generation in human history has needed fiction. Our own is one which ordinarily admits this explicitly. As Whitehead and Heidegger alike testify, our very fidelity to the need for careful conceptual analysis need not deter us from recognizing this fact of our need for fiction. We need to analyze not merely descriptions of the everyday reality which is, but also those redescriptions of the everyday disclosed in the great symbols, images, stories, myths, and fictions of our culture. In this sense, we all recognize the existential correctness of Paul Ricoeur's oft-cited dictum: "The symbol gives rise to [critical] thought; yet thought is informed by and returns to the symbol." There is, to my knowledge at least, no strict metaphysical way to "prove" or demonstrate this need for fiction and story. Yet there seems no need for such proof. The modern form of Pascal's wager may well have become the risk of entering imaginatively into those fictional worlds. We do so best by trying to appropriate the possibilities of those worlds of the imagination critically through literary, social-scientific, psychological, philosophical, and even theological analysis. At the conclusion of such critical appropriation, restored perhaps by the liberating experience of a second "naiveté," we find ourselves returning once again to the symbols themselves, to re-examine their transformative possibility anew.

This need for and this possibility of fictions remain, it seems, an uncommonly common matter of fact of our shared experience. If one demands a metaphysical necessity here, he will demand in vain. Yet few of us remain deeply troubled by this dilemma, for, even philosophically, the "risk," the "wager" of finding meaning in symbol, image, myth, story, fiction makes sense. Besides the metaphysical conditions of the possibilities of our common experience—besides, that is, such metaphysical realities as time and space and, yes, God—there remain those contingent facts of our actual lived time as we may experience them redescribed through the genius of a Proust; of space as we can experience it represented through the ever-changing vision of a Picasso; and even of God now experienced *as my God* as in the gospel proclamation that this Jesus is the Christ.

We find, as a matter of fact, that we need and want the disclosive power of symbols, images, myths, stories, and fictions to transform our common human experience into possibilities that remain deeply human because, somehow, those possibilities are more authentic than the everyday reality of our lives. To use a formulation reminiscent of Plato and Aristotle, we may then find that conceptual analysis alone will not suffice for character-forming action. Rather, individually and societally, we need stories, fictions, and symbols to allow our own and our society's character to discover appropriate heuristic models.

We find as well that common honesty demands that we bring to bear upon the reality-claims of even our most cherished stories the most penetrating tools of critical analysis presently available. In that familiar theological word, we need to demythologize in order to eliminate the literalizing temptations in our appropriation of myths which can at best becloud, at worst completely distort, the ways-of-being-in-the-world disclosed in the myths. We need to develop whatever scientific analyses are available—sociological, psychological, political, philosophical—to allow those stories to become critically purified of all that is not essential to their disclosure of an authentically human mode-of-being. Yet even at the end of our most rigorous critical endeavours, we all seem to find either that a second naiveté has been restored to us to allow the symbols, now purified of literalizing accretions, to speak again; or that our criticism has legitimately rendered these particular symbols, myths, fictions, no longer meaningful for the struggle to achieve authenticity. The latter case is evident in the powerful and new Christian theological myth developed in Thomas J. J. Altizer's post-death-of-God *Descent into Hell*, or in the histories of some of our best contemporary critics of the Christian story such as Freud, Nietzsche, or Marx. As in these instances, we eventually discover that the myth-breaker must either create new and more adequate myths (as Nietzsche attempted) or suffer the fate of finding his own story become a myth for his successors (as happened to

Marx and Freud alike). Both the hermeneutics of suspicion and the hermeneutics of recollection seem to end, however differently, in the same place: in a rediscovery of the need for some symbol, some myth, some fiction.

The criteria for judging the explicitly religious uses of symbolic, mythical, and fictional language remain the same as those employed throughout this work. Two exemplary formulations of this question may serve to suggest the general lines which a search for the meaningfulness of such language may presently take. One formulation we have already seen: for character-forming action we need metaphors, images, symbols, stories, parables, myths. This formulation, in fact, may lend itself to a ready adaption of the psychological and sociological analyses of the important role of symbol for individual and societal action. Admittedly, the formulation does not lend itself to the more easily formulated criteria for judgment of Aristotle's *Metaphysics*. But the tradition of Aristotelian ethical *phronesis*, a tradition continued in such diverse forms as Pascal's *esprit de finesse*, Newman's "illative sense," Bernard Lonergan's "judgments of value," reformulates the only criteria we have or need for judging the adequacy of character-forming symbols. Only Aristotle's "just man" can adequately distinguish the stories of true justice from injustice. Only Lonergan's self-transcending human being can be trusted to weigh the relative real strengths and real weaknesses of competing character-forming myths. Highly "subjective" criteria, to be sure. But criteria which somehow—as a matter of fact—suffice.

A second exemplary and perhaps more contemporary formulation will be tested at greater length in the following chapter. For the moment, perhaps the reader will be patient with its somewhat peremptory entry and its all too brief exemplification. The second formulation is as follows: for an adequate *praxis* we need both rigorous theory and appropriate symbolization. This second formulation is obviously dependent upon the Hegelian-Marxist insistence that true *praxis* is only achieved by a union of correct theory and authentic practice. It develops that insistence on a single point, in the manner suggested by the revisionist Marxism of Ernst Bloch: besides theory and practice, true *praxis* also needs appropriate personal and societal symbols. The symbols of eschatological "liberation" as distinct from the liberal symbols of "development" may be taken as an example. Those former symbols have been rearticulated by contemporary Christian theologians of *praxis* as symbols designed by the creative imagination in order to allow both a negation of present oppressive practice, and an articulation of the possibilities for transforming that practice in accordance with certain creatively imagined (either Utopian or eschatological) possibilities for human beings.

A central question for these other non-cognitive uses of religious language becomes, of course, just how can we validate them? The present answer, in keeping with the revisionist model, is clear: first, one can and should determine the cognitive claims in the religious language and judge those claims in accordance with the general criteria of metaphysics. Second, one should continue to develop those criteria for existential meaningfulness which can be labelled (as they are by Paul Ricoeur in *Symbolism of Evil*) criteria of "existential verification." In sum, we should try to judge the relative adequacy of the various candidate systems of religious symbols in accordance with a contemporary understanding of the criteria of adequacy for "character" formation (principally ethical, aesthetic, and psychological criteria) and for *praxis* (principally ethical, political, and critical sociological criteria). The attempts to formulate what I call "criteria of relative adequacy," is, I admit, notoriously difficult. Yet one may be encouraged by such studies as those of Paul Tillich (esp. on the "demonic" and the "kairos") and of Paul Ricoeur (esp. his comparison of the adequacy of various mythic systems—e.g., the Orphic or Adamic—to deal with the problems of evil). In such studies as these we find, however tentatively formulated, a way by means of which an "existential verification" of the relative existential adequacy of the non-cognitive uses of religious symbolic language may in fact occur. What surely can occur is the simple insight which this section has attempted to document: *as a matter of fact,* our common experience testifies to the need for such fictions, myths, images, stories and symbols. As a matter of fact, we dismiss the seriousness of such fictions at the presumably unwelcome price of impoverishing our own humanity. A clear grasp of that fact is the first step needed to allow one to be willing to listen once again to the Christian story of Jesus

Christ. Another fact also needs articulation if that story is to be heard properly. That fact, too—the "fact" of evil—is not a metaphysical necessity. But that evil is a fact of our common situation seems to most of us, at the very least, highly probable.

The Fact of Evil

The philosophical distinction between a metaphysical necessity and a matter of fact is also applicable to the discussion of evil. That humanity possesses both freedom and nature can be shown to be necessary characteristics of the human being: as, for example, Paul Ricoeur's *Freedom and Nature*, argues. That human beings are also fallible, that we can commit error, is a direct consequence of the human reality as constituted by both freedom and nature. But that we in fact commit not merely error but evil cannot be a necessary characteristic of our being. If, in fact we are constituted by a metaphysical necessity to commit evil, then our freedom becomes a mere charade and our existential and reflective faith in either a good, loving God or in the very worthwhileness of existence becomes a lie.

Yet the fact of evil seems too obvious a reality for any adult to allow its lack of metaphysical necessity to dim explicit awareness of its presence. That evil is a necessary constituent of our being, we may know we cannot state without contradicting the metaphysical necessity of our own freedom or the metaphysical and Christian theological belief in the loving actions of a good God. But that physical and moral evil is our actual condition; that such evil is an omnipresent *fact*, whose inevitability we realize—in this century surely—on both individual and societal terms, is a reality which only the most unhappy and self-destructively among us feels free to deny.

The Christian theological tradition, I believe, has consistently attempted to be faithful to this insight into the inevitability but not metaphysical necessity of evil, or, in explicitly religious terms, of sin. For example, underneath the subtleties of the medieval scholastic discussion of "original sin" lies the same basic insight: we cannot logically say that each human being *must* sin with metaphysical necessity save at the unwelcome logical and the theological price of destroying the reality of individual freedom. And yet, the tradition argued, each human being is responsible for the fact that eventually, indeed inevitably, he or she does personally sin. To resolve this dilemma, discussions of the constitution of human freedom emerged in the medieval period. Does every free act demand explicit consent? Are not our habitual actions free and yet not necessarily explicitly consented to in each instance? To summarize a long and subtle discussion, the medievals claimed that there is something like a statistical necessity to personal sin (an inevitability, but not a metaphysical necessity). That inevitability allows one to understand how each human being, first trapped in a social situation where evil is clearly present, then unable to continue the constant reflection needed to ward off the habitual inclination to evil ("original sin"), eventually cannot but sin (*non posse non peccare*), yet does so freely and responsibly. The point of this medieval digression is not to defend either the traditional Christian understanding of "original sin" or the traditional scholastic understanding of habits and freedom. Rather the point is to indicate that the mainline Christian theological tradition has historically puzzled over the problem that evil—or, for the Christian, sin—is not a metaphysical necessity but is an inevitable matter of fact.

A powerfully disclosive, an existential description of the reality of sin and evil remains, in my judgment, one of the permanent achievements of the recent philosophical and theological past. On the occasion of the profound crisis of Western liberal culture (the horrors of two World Wars, the extermination of millions, the demonic outbursts of Fascist and Stalinist terror), both existentialist philosophy and neo-orthodox theology retrieved the classical Christian image of man as alienated, estranged, fallen, sinful. That classical Christian picture of humanity's radical possibilities for good and evil was and is antithetical to both the classical Greek philosophical view of humanity's inherent knowledge and goodness conquering error, and even to the classical Greek dramatists' profound view of humanity's tragic situation. The Christian image of humanity's actual state also proved to be, as the neo-orthodox noted, antithetical to the soon fatuous optimism of the modern liberal's belief in inevitable progress. As progress faded into apocalypse, the liberal had finally to face the fact that not all human beings—perhaps not even he himself—were reasonable and well-intentioned. As suggested symbolically

by the still pathetic figure of Prime Minister Chamberlain returning from Munich, umbrella and hope still in hand, liberalism—by
its stark refusal to face the fact of evil—could no longer understand, much less control, such demonic outbursts of the human
spirit as Nazism.

In American culture, the pioneering work of Reinhold
Niebuhr assured the success of this post-liberal insistence on fac-
ing the fact of evil when attempting to transform the human
situation. As Niebuhr's enduring work *The Nature and Destiny
of Man* argues, this fact is present everywhere, to all cultures, to
all individuals. The contemporary task is not to deny our true
situation through a liberalism—Christian or otherwise—which
cannot admit one of the most glaring facts of our fate. Rather,
if one admits the reality of evil, then he may investigate critically
and comparatively those symbol-systems which promise a transformation of that fact on an individual societal, and a historical
scale. One need not continue to bless those Cold-War, "realistic"
politics which Niebuhr's work sometimes aided in order to see
the essential correctness of his vision and the realistic description
he portrayed of our actual destiny. In a similar fashion, one need
not commit oneself to the kind of seeming political naiveté
which several of Jean-Paul Sartre's political judgments suggest in
order to see that his frozen vision of man's limited, indeed nau-
seous, condition does disclose a truth unfamiliar to his idealist
philosophical predecessors. In American culture, where the terrors of the sixties, especially the twin evils of a now open racism
and that war upon the Vietnamese people and their culture
which was not a "mistake" but was and is an evil, we hear almost
daily that the surely too long prolonged American "innocence"
is finally dead. And yet neither the finally fatuous optimism of
"consciousness III," nor the cries for "law and order," for "nor-
malcy," perhaps even for "innocence," from men whose moral
sensitivities can include Watergate as a merely "over-zealous"
mistake and Cambodia as a needed exercise in military expertise,
promise that our own culture is yet willing to face the fact of
evil, starting with its own.

One of the permanent achievements of the neo-orthodox
theologians was their willingness both to face that fact and to
attempt to find authentic Christian possibilities for its transfor-

mation. Their main accomplishment was the development of a powerfully disclosive, an existentially meaningful anthropology. If revisionist theology is to succeed materially, I believe, it should incorporate that neo-orthodox anthropological vision into its own twin vision of a common faith in the worthwhileness of existence which sustains us even beyond good and evil and a reflective belief in a credible, a suffering and loving Christian God. A first step in that direction can be taken when, singly and as a society, we admit to the reality of that central fact of our own experience which we name evil or, in explicitly religious limit-language, sin. A second step can be taken when we follow that admission with a second one: that for character-forming action we need to study any symbols of transformation which both face and promise authentically to transform that situation. In the manner initiated by Paul Ricoeur's and Reinhold Niebuhr's comparative analyses of the existential adequacy of various symbol-systems for transforming personal and historical evil, the fundamental theologian needs to take the risk that a critical investigation of all such symbols, stories, images, myths, and fictions may yet disclose a means of authentic human transformation. As a single step in that direction, the contemporary fundamental theologian might look anew at the story of Jesus the Christ and attempt to articulate some of its transformative existential possibilities. Before that task is attempted, one final discussion of "fact" remains: how facts themselves are constituted.

Fact and Possibilities: Actualizations and Representations

The most obvious and legitimate logical alternative to a fact is a "mere" possibility. When we speak of facts, we mean that which actually is; the given; the "situation"; not a possible world but the actual one. Yet this familiar and necessary contrast between facts and possibilities includes an important ambiguity. Actually there are two ways by which possibilities may become facts.

The first and more familiar way is one which the Greek tradition of philosophy has so clarified that only that way ordinarily seems "factual" to us. The Greek insight can be succinctly formulated: a fact is an actualization of a possibility. I project all sorts of possibilities for myself. Those few possibilities which

I manage to actualize in my own life constitute the concrete facts (the actuality) about myself that, presently, I really am. With such facts, as actualizations-of-possibility, we are all familiar.

The second kind of fact, however, is less familiar to most of us, at least on a reflective level. Besides the actualization of a human possibility in human action, there remains the alternative of representing a certain possibility in disclosive symbolical language and action. The category "re-presentation" was employed in the earlier discussion on religious language but now needs analytical clarification of its status as fact. On one level, one may recall that religious language is basically re-presentative as making present anew, through symbolical expression, a human reality (for example, our basic trust in the worthwhileness of existence) which somehow had become threatened or forgotten. On a second level, fiction, by redescribing our everyday experience, represents a certain imaginative possible modes-of-being-in-the-world that can become actualized by us. Indeed, all the primordial symbols of our culture are not *mere possibilities*. They are facts: facts, to be sure, not as the actualization of a possibility but facts as ritual, as fictional, as symbolic representations of a real possibility. All genuine re-presentations are not to be assigned to the category "mere possibility" but to the category "fact."

The presence of this insight into the factual status of symbolical representations can also be found in several Christian traditions, in certain contemporary theories of interpretation, and in our everyday cultural lives. What does the Christian tradition mean by "sacrament" but a *fact,* not a mere possibility? A Christian sacrament is traditionally believed to be a fact as the re-presentation of a real possibility which God has made present to humanity in Christ Jesus. At least since the time of Augustine's struggle against the Donatists, the major Christian traditions have not believed that the fact (or, for some traditions, the validity) of the sacramental rite depends upon the personal actualization by the minister of the possibility ritually re-presented. In principle, the minister, even while partaking in the ritual re-presentation, can live contrary to the religious possibility there re-presented without affecting the fact of an authentic sacramental re-presentation. To be sure, the minister's own personal actualization of that possibility is eminently desirable. But the fact of the sacramental re-presentation itself does not depend upon it.

For the hermeneutical theory outlined in chapter four, moreover, the meaning of a text does not depend upon the author's own intention, much less his own actualization of the possibility which his text represents. The question of whether Ernest Hemingway was himself a "Hemingway character" (whether, for example, he actualized "grace under pressure" in his own life) is an interesting biographical question, but not a major one for understanding Hemingway's fiction. That latter fictional fact represents a certain possibility for human existence by means of the process of redescription present in the various literary genres of fiction. In that representative sense, these possibilities are no longer mere possibilities but representative facts of our common experience. They remain so whether or not Hemingway himself—or any other person—personally actualized them. When we speak of fictional characters as "larger than life," more faithful to the meaning of our experience than everyday experience itself, we recognize that we do not find mere possibilities in the great symbolic representations of our culture. We find re-presentative facts, symbols, rituals which disclose to us possibilities that we might wish to actualize.

In our everyday cultural lives, we may also recognize this distinction between fact as actualization and fact as representation. For most of us certain historical personages begin to take on "symbolic dimensions." He or she begins to become representative of a certain human possibility for a particular cultural period. In recent history, for example, the slain Kennedy brothers and Martin Luther King, both before and especially after their deaths, began to take on this symbolic dimension for many in American culture. Dr. King was not simply a human being who actualized certain possibilities. He became a symbol, a cultural fact representative of a certain possible mode-of-being-in-this-world. That he himself actualized that possibility seems entirely likely. But that is not the fact of central cultural importance. Rather, as the culture experienced his preaching, his actions, his teaching, the culture's own memory-image of Martin Luther King became itself a cultural fact, a symbol, a representation of a particular authentic possibility. It appears evident that we ordinarily do not find the human reality we actually live exhausted by the more usual alternatives: either "facts-as-actualizations-of-possibility" or "mere possibilities." Rather we also find, most clearly in symbols as distinct from sins, certain undeniable realities which are neither "mere possibilities" nor "personal actualizations of possibilities." These realities, these great representative images, symbols, rituals, stories, and myths of our cultural history, are not mere possibilities. They are the representative facts of a particular culture. Just this distinction between two kinds of "facts" can become of real theological significance when we ask ourselves the initial christological question: what kinds of factual claims are present in the Christian confession that Jesus is the Christ?

The following section will be one interpretative attempt to respond to that crucial Christian theological question. For the present, it may be sufficient to remind ourselves that the title "the Christ" or "the Messiah" is the title of an office. In other words, messiahship, like ministry in general, may be said to refer to that office which represents a certain possibility (here God's action for Israel and through Israel for humankind). It does not refer explicitly to the actualization of that possibility by the one who holds the office. In more familiar christological terms, the very question of the "Messianic self-consciousness" of Jesus is not really a primary question of fact for an adequate christology to answer. What is primary is the meaning and truth of the claim that this Jesus is in fact the Christ; that the representational reality present in the office of Messiah may be found in the words, deeds, and destiny of Jesus of Nazareth.

The primary question of christology, therefore, does not take the form of attempting to establish the psychological state (the actualization of the possibility) of Jesus as the Child. Rather the primary question becomes the different but still factual one of understanding the inclusive claim to meaning and truth represented in the affirmation that this Jesus is the Christ; that in the proclamation through word and sacrament of the singular history of Jesus of Nazareth as the Christ the truth of human existence is re-presented with factual finality. Exactly what meanings that deeper re-presentation may include, the next section shall attempt to delineate. At present, however, it may now be possible to clarify why the two more usual modern articulations of the factual status of the Christian claim for Jesus the Christ are not, in fact, exhaustive options for contemporary christology.

The first of such routes, present in modern christology from Friedrich Schleiermacher and Albrecht Ritschl through Karl Rahner and Paul Tillich, effectively proposes a modern (sometimes metaphysical) psychologizing of the ontological high christology of Chalcedon and the Joannine *Logos* tradition. However, impressive these modern philosophical christological reconstructions may be (employing as they do with real originality that "turn to the subject" characteristic of modern metaphysics), they still seem to rest on a central assumption which the present alternative position challenges. That assumption holds that only an actualization of a possibility secures the status of fact for christological meaning. Hence the familiar modern theological route of analyzing Jesus the Christ's own actualization of the possibility he represented as the Christ and, more importantly, re-presented as God's self-manifestation, by means of a philosophical investigation of the "consciousness" of Jesus—whether as the primal religious, the Messianic, or the divine consciousness—becomes a primary form of modern christological reconstruction.

Indeed that same assumption is operative in the other major modern route to the question of an adequate christology. In this second alternative, as expressed in the work of the New Hermeneutic and theologically articulated in the positions of Gerhard Ebeling and Ernst Fuchs, the scriptural sources are studied with more sophisticated hermeneutical methods and with greater interest in the earliest christologies of the New Testament. The latter claim holds insofar as the practitioners of the New Hermeneutic argue their case not from the high christologies of the Joannine literature nor of Chalcedon but from the earliest christologies, implicit and explicit, in the synoptic accounts of Jesus' own preaching, teaching, and destiny. Moreover, the heremeneutical sophistication of this position seems clear since the New Hermeneutic combines the high standards of traditional historical

David Tracy

scholarship with a Heideggerian understanding of the primary relationship of language and existence.

Granted these solid gains, the new quest for the historical Jesus, so central for the proponents of the New Hermeneutic, still results in a psychologizing of the christological tradition. One ends the quest somehow assured that now one may understand the "faith" or "self-understanding" of Jesus himself. Thereby one is also assured a new, a more historically "factual" route to an adequate contemporary christology. Yet even aside from the implicit and, it would seem, insuperable difficulties of claiming a historical reconstruction of the psychological state of any historical figure (especially one about whom we really know so little), a more basic question remains: does the factual status of the Christian affirmation of Jesus as the Christ really need this historical-psychological reconstruction? Admittedly something like the New Hermeneutic (or its alternative, a philosophical-psychological reconstruction of Jesus' consciousness) would be needed if the only kind of "fact" was an actualization of a possibility.

But if representations are also facts, we do not really need to understand Jesus' own consciousness of his actions and teaching in order to formulate a christology grounded in fact. Rather we need to know what his words, his deeds, and his destiny, as expressions of his office of messiahship, authentically re-present as real human possibilities for genuine relationship to God. In a word, we need to know the existential meaning and truths represented for our present human experience by the christological affirmations. The need to study that christological affirmation seems especially pertinent to anyone who agrees with the earlier description of our present matter of fact condition. If we recognize both the fact of the presence of evil and the fact of the need for symbolic expressions in our lives, we may also recongize the desirability of studying the christological affirmation in terms of its symbolic, its re-presentative factual character in order to seek out its possibly transformative meanings. If that task can be successfully executed, then the positive existential meanings of christology (including those existential meanings delineated by both forms of modern christology described above) can be

413

rearticulated. That new articulation will be new, at least insofar as it will free the discussion from the insuperable difficulties present in any attempt to reconstruct Jesus' own actualization of those possibilities by either historical or modern philosophical methods. An initial rearticulation in that line will be the primary aim of the final section of this chapter.

Christological Language as Re-Presentative Limit-Language

The prior sections of this chapter attempted to set a context for a study of some of the existential meanings in the early christological affirmations: those meanings present in the representative language of the New Testament on the words, deeds and destiny of Jesus of Nazareth as the Christ. With that purpose in mind, this section will summarize some of the results of the historical reconstruction of the words and deeds of and about Jesus of Nazareth and delineate the primary existential meanings re-presented by those earliest christological affirmations. On that basis, this section will also summarize just how this interpretation of the re-presentative character of christological language seems both faithful to our common experience and to the primary Christian scriptural meanings.

In the earlier discussion of chapter six we advanced the claim that a principal fruit of the application of sophisticated methods of historical inquiry to the scriptures was the reconstruction of the parabolic, proverbial, and proclamatory words of Jesus. When one recalls the work of Joachim Jeremias on the parables of Jesus, for example, he recalls a singular achievement of careful historical inquiry: the reconstruction of the present New Testament parabolic texts into the parables *of Jesus*. That historical reconstruction, moreover, is not limited to the *words* of Jesus: in fact, the historical study of Jesus' words (especially the parables) remains the central clue to his deeds and his destiny. As the work familiar to New Testament scholarship in such paradigmatic studies as Günther Bornkamm's *Jesus of Nazareth* and Norman Perrin's *Rediscovering the Teaching of Jesus* exemplify, that latter process seems secure in its main outlines: Jesus' teaching—as expressed in parable, proverb, and proclamatory saying alike—(is dominated by the powerful motif of the sovereignty or reign (the Kingdom) of God which brings and demands a new righteousness.

414

David Tracy

By means of the various gospel processes of intensification brought to bear upon the several literary genres employed, this eschatological "Kingdom" language can be legitimately described as a limit-language disclosing certain limit-experiences of fundamental faith, hope, and agapic love. That this limit-language of Jesus' central teaching receives a parallel representation in the historically reconstructed deeds of Jesus also seems a fair conclusion to be drawn from the dominant consensus of contemporary New Testament scholarship. There, one finds, amidst a myriad of disagreement upon details, a clear main outline of the deeds and destiny of the historical Jesus: his ministry in Galilee, his baptism (probably a baptism of repentance) by John the Baptist; his amazing conduct of open, unself-righteous, forgiving identification with the despised of his society (publicans, prostitutes, the sick and weak, the "outcasts" of his time), and his equally liberating conduct of righteous denunciation of the established powers. The deeds of Jesus, in their turn, seem clearly re-presentative of the central eschatological teaching proclaimed in the parables. As the reign of God and his promise of a new righteousness for humanity, a new, a faithful, an agapic mode-of-being-in-the-world is proclaimed with existential urgency in the limit-language of Jesus' teaching, so that reign and that new and liberating agapic righteousness—that limit-experience—seems re-presented in the actual deeds of the historical Jesus.

The existential re-presentative power of the words and the deeds of the historical Jesus are summarized in that central representation of his life and his destiny, his paradigmatic role as the crucified one. The passion narratives, when historically reconstructed as the original core of all four gospels, allow scripture scholars to affirm that this man, whose words and deeds attest to a new possibility for human existence, met the dishonorable and obscene fate of crucifixion. Not in vain have Christians signalized this fact of Jesus' disgraced destiny as the central symbol, the all-important representation of the central existential meaning of Jesus as the Christ. Indeed, once that destiny is understood not *in vacuo* but in the context of the representative words and deeds of the historical Jesus, a mutual illumination of meaning is disclosed. The strangeness of the power of God as the power of love proclaimed in the teaching is decisively repre-

415

sented in the Christian symbol of the cross; God's very power seems weakness to the self-righteous, the secure, the established ones. In a directly parallel fashion, the strangeness of Jesus' liberating freedom in his conduct, his representation of a new and agapic possibility for existence, finds appropriate paradigmatic representation in a destiny where his self-sacrificing love seems destroyed by the stupidity and sin of the unloving, the self-righteous, the self-secure.

The fact that the central representative symbol of the cross is always joined to the symbol of the resurrection is the final existential clue to the central meaning of Jesus' words, deeds, and destiny. For the resurrection as a representative symbol both recapitulates, reinforces, and intensifies the profound religious meaning of this representative figure, this Christ, this Jesus. Whatever the historical occasion of the resurrection-belief so central to the New Testament may be, the basic existential meaning of that belief remains the same: the representative words, deeds, and teachings of this representative figure, this Jesus as the Christ, can in fact be trusted. He is *the* re-presentation, *the* Word, *the* Deed, *the* very Destiny of God himself. The God disclosed in the words, deeds, and destiny of Jesus the Christ is the only God there is—a loving, righteous Father who promises the power of this new righteousness, this new possibility of self-sacrificing love to those who will hear and abide by The Word spoken in the words, deeds, and destiny of Jesus the Christ. In that limit-sense, the witness re-presented in those words, those deeds and that very destiny is true. Its truth can still be heard by any human being (whether, in contemporary times, with the aid of historical reconstruction or, in prior ages, with the aid of mythological categories) who "has ears to hear" that re-presentative Word which illuminates what an authentically human existence under the sovereignty of a living God may be. And yet this claim for the existential significance of those re-presentative words, deeds, and destiny does not depend upon a historical claim to have unraveled the consciousness or faith of Jesus himself. That latter study, in fact, is not needed; when attempted it seems to lead at best to historical claims with a low degree of probability. What *is* needed is precisely what the contemporary historical reconstruction of those words, deeds, and destiny of the historical Jesus provides: those historically reconstructed facts as providing the text for the proclamation of the signal re-presentative fact of God's true limit-representation of divine love in this representative, this Messiah, this Christ, this Jesus of Nazareth.

In keeping with the hermeneutical method employed throughout this work, one may formulate the principal meaning referred to by the historically reconstructed re-presentative words, deeds, and destiny of Jesus the Christ as follows: the principal referent disclosed by this limit-language is the disclosure of a certain limit-mode-of-being-in-the-world; the disclosure of a new, an agapic, a self-sacrificing righteousness willing to risk living at that limit where one seems in the presence of the righteous, loving, gracious God re-presented in Jesus the Christ. The confession of either the significance for my life of the representative words, deeds, and destiny of the historical Jesus, or the confession of this Jesus Christ as my Lord is not an invitation to live in the presence of the Christian god over against other "gods." On the contrary, the summons proclaimed in that confession is an invitation to risk living a life-at-the-limits: a committed, a righteous and agapic life in the presence of the only God there is, here manifested as the "Father" of the Lord Jesus Christ.

From the point of view of the present hermeneutical theory, one may approach this Christian limit-mode-of-being-in-the-world as simply a *possible* one; one which one can at least imagine as a genuine human possibility. Yet once anyone judges that this possibility is one which appropriately and truly re-presents the fundamental actualities of his or her life—that common faith in the worthwhileness of existence, that fundamental trust whose reflective clarification is a metaphysical affirmation of God's loving reality—one may find here not merely a project for the imagination, but a project which re-presents in and with truth *the* truth of our lives. In the confession of Jesus as the Christ, in the further confession of Jesus Christ as Lord, Christians find a true, a limit-re-presentation of their lives as lives whose basic faith is grounded in the action of a loving God. They find that they can have faith and trust and love in the belief that even the power of sin can be transformed by the limit-forgiveness, the grace, of a loving God. What Christians find re-presented in the affirmation of Jesus Christ as Lord is no timeless truth of metaphysics.

Rather they find there the factual, symbolic re-presentation of the fundamental existential truth of existence: each Christian can—and in the affirmation of Jesus Christ commits himself to try to—live a life that dares to tread not merely beyond the bounds of the limits-to the everyday, but to sense something of the gracious character of the limit-of the whole of reality. Nor does this manifestation cease with Jesus for the Christian tradition. Rather that very same re-presentation continues to happen through the re-presentative words and sacraments of the community named the Christian church. The church has as its central particular task the need to re-present in word and ritual that definitive limit-re-presentation of the life of God-with-humanity which Christians affirm when they proclaim that Jesus Christ is Lord.

The heart of Christian self-understanding, therefore, remains radically christocentric. This is the case insofar as, for Christians, the symbolic fact of Jesus the Christ provides a re-presentative summary of their deepest understanding of themselves as religious, as before a gracious God, and as in a community which re-presents that possibility in word and sacrament. That christological language discloses those worlds of meaning with a decisiveness whose urgency was felt by the hearers of the historical Jesus, by the believers of the early church's proclamation of this Jesus as the Christ, by the Christian tradition's preaching of this Jesus Christ as Lord. To endorse christocentrism, however, is not really for Christians to speak of some new God racially different from the only God who lives. To speak of the truth of the proclamation of Jesus the Christ renders more factual, more re-presentative, more human one's basic faith in the God who always and everywhere is manifested.

That basic and universal faith in a loving God is not fundamentally arrived at as a conclusion from a phenomenological and transcendental analysis of common existence. Indeed, a fuller existential faith is clearly witnessed to in the Christian scriptures themselves: when Paul, for example, in Romans 1:18 ff proclaims that all are "without excuse" who refuse to witness to this God. There Paul seems to be testifying to neither the presence of some personal "natural theology" nor some temporary lapse from his constant christocentric theme. Rather he can be interpreted as proclaiming that our limit-situation as human beings discloses our basic limit-faith in the gracious God who is manifested in Jesus the Christ. If that interpretation holds, then there is scriptural encouragement for the Catholic tradition's insistence upon the possibility of a reflective account of that universal experience (in that restricted sense, a "natural theology"). At the same time, the central Reformation insistence (crystallized in the image of humanity as *"simul iustus, simul peccator"*) seems equally faithful to the fuller complexity of Paul's vision. Precisely because of human failures—through error, through inattention, through self-righteousness and the false security of a mere adherence to some "natural" or "traditional" law, through destructive innocence, through forgetfulness and distraction, in a word, through that limit-reality Christians call sin—most Christians too rarely and too fleetingly allow the limit-reality of the presence of the God of Jesus Christ become the real orientation of their way of living in the world.

The fact of the matter of fact limit-situation and the fact of the need for symbolic expression may unite to allow Christians to hear again the stark re-presentative words and to see anew the strange disclosive power of the Christian limit-symbol, the cross-resurrection of Jesus the Christ. Then that symbolic and transformative re-presentation of the meaning of life may strike them anew with its full disclosive power. Then one may recognize that this symbol's existential meaningfulness is not to be found by justifying miracles and prophecies, nor by historically validating some interpretation or other of the resurrection-belief, nor by developing a metaphysics which can spell out the "timeless truths" of this symbol's meanings, nor by formulating new laws and new beliefs to surround the symbol and becloud its existential meaning and power. Rather, when the full disclosive force of that symbol is existentially seen, one may realize that here any human being is asked to decide with an urgency for which that limit-language we call eschatological is an appropriate expression: to decide to risk living a life-at-the-limits, a faithful, hopeful, loving life, which the Christian gospel proclaims as both a true understanding of the actual human situation in its reality and its possibility and an ever-to-be renewed decision.

What is re-presented in the Christian proclamation of Jesus Christ as Lord is not, I believe, the exclusivist insistence that only and solely here may human beings find the meaning of their lives before a loving God. What is re-presented in this faith for Christians is the basic faith and the only God whom all humanity experiences. So appropriate does that christological limit-representation seem—both in the words, deeds, and destiny of Jesus of Nazareth, and in the proclamation and celebration of this Jesus Christ as Lord by the Christian community—that, for Christians, that Word has all the power of a complete and true manifestation of the fundamental meaning of authentic human existence. As thus appropriate to the universal human situation, as thus disclosive of the struggle for an authentic humanity, christology does bear an inclusivist character. For Christians, christological language suffices because it fulfills certain factual understandings of human and divine reality: the fact that our lives are, in reality, meaningful; that we really do live in the presence of a loving God; that the final word about our lives is gracious and the final power is love.